Applying Enterprise JavaBeans™

The Java™ Series

Lisa Friendly, Series Editor
Tim Lindholm, Technical Editor
Ken Arnold, Technical Editor of The Jini™ Technology Series
Jim Inscore, Technical Editor of The Java™ Series, Enterprise Edition

---

Ken Arnold and James Gosling, David Holmes
The Java™ Programming Language, Third Edition

Greg Bollella, James Gosling, Ben Brosgol, Peter Dibble,
Steve Furr, David Hardin, Mark Turnbull
The Real-Time Specification for Java™

Mary Campione, Kathy Walrath, Alison Huml
The Java™ Tutorial, Third Edition:
A Short Course on the Basics

Mary Campione, Kathy Walrath, Alison Huml,
Tutorial Team
The Java™ Tutorial Continued: The Rest of the JDK™

Patrick Chan
The Java™ Developers Almanac 2000

Patrick Chan, Rosanna Lee
The Java™ Class Libraries, Second Edition, Volume 2:
java.applet, java.awt, java.beans

Patrick Chan, Rosanna Lee
The Java™ Class Libraries Poster, Fifth Edition, Covering
the Java 2™ Platform, Standard Edition, v1.3

Patrick Chan, Rosanna Lee, Doug Kramer
The Java™ Class Libraries, Second Edition, Volume 1:
java.io, java.lang, java.math, java.net, java.text, java.util

Patrick Chan, Rosanna Lee, Doug Kramer,
The Java™ Class Libraries, Second Edition, Volume 1:
Supplement for the Java™ 2 Platform,
Standard Edition, v1.2

Zhiqun Chen
Java Card™ Technology for Smart Cards:
Architecture and Programmer's Guide

Li Gong
Inside Java™ 2 Platform Security:
Architecture, API Design, and Implementation

James Gosling, Bill Joy, Guy Steele, Gilad Bracha
The Java™ Language Specification, Second Edition

Jonni Kanerva
The Java™ FAQ

Doug Lea
Concurrent Programming in Java™, Second Edition:
Design Principles and Patterns

Rosanna Lee, Scott Seligman
JNDI API Tutorial and Reference:
Building Directory-Enabled Java™ Applications

Sheng Liang
The Java™ Native Interface:
Programmer's Guide and Specification

Tim Lindholm and Frank Yellin
The Java™ Virtual Machine Specification, Second Edition

Vlada Matena and Beth Stearns
Applying Enterprise JavaBeans™: Component-Based
Development for the J2EE™Platform

Henry Sowizral, Kevin Rushforth, and Michael Deering
The Java 3D™ API Specification, Second Edition

Kathy Walrath, Mary Campione
The JFC Swing Tutorial: A Guide to Constructing GUIs

Seth White, Maydene Fisher, Rick Cattell,
Graham Hamilton, and Mark Hapner
JDBC™ API Tutorial and Reference, Second Edition:
Universal Data Access for the Java™ 2 Platform

Steve Wilson, Jeff Kesselman
Java™ Platform Performance: Strategies and Tactics

The Jini™ Technology Series

Jim Waldo/Jini™ Technology Team
The Jini™ Specifications, Second Edition,
edited by Ken Arnold

Eric Freeman, Susanne Hupfer, Ken Arnold
JavaSpaces™ Principles, Patterns, and Practice

The Java™ Series, Enterprise Edition

Patrick Chan, Rosanna Lee
The Java™ Class Libraries Poster, Enterprise Edition,
version 1.2

Nicholas Kassem, Enterprise Team
Designing Enterprise Applications with the Java™ 2
Platform, Enterprise Edition

Bill Shannon, Mark Hapner, Vlada Matena, James
Davidson, Eduardo Pelegri-Llopart, Larry Cable,
Enterprise Team
Java™ 2 Platform, Enterprise Edition:
Platform and Component Specifications

http://www.javaseries.com

Applying Enterprise JavaBeans™

Component-Based Development for the J2EE™ Platform

Vlada Matena
Beth Stearns

ADDISON-WESLEY

Boston • San Francisco • New York • Toronto • Montreal
London • Munich • Paris • Madrid
Capetown • Sydney • Tokyo • Singapore • Mexico City

The publisher offers discounts on this book when ordered in quantity for special sales. For more information, please contact:

Pearson Education Corporate Sales Division
One Lake Street
Upper Saddle River, NJ 07458
(800) 382-3419
corpsales@pearsontechgroup.com

Visit us on the Web at www.awl.com/cseng/

Library of Congress Control Number: 00-132776

Text printed on recycled and acid-free paper.

ISBN 0201702673

2 3 4 5 6 7   MA   04 03 02 01

2nd Printing   March 2001

To my family.
—Vlada Matena

To John, Charles, and Woodrow.
And especially, to Tonton.
—Beth Stearns

Contents

Foreword

NOT since the 1880s have we had such rapid, sustained growth, innovation, and intellectual achievement as we had in the latter part of the 1990s. New forms of commerce and communications are being created, new companies dominate the industrial landscape, dispelling geographic boundaries and challenging governmental and other regulatory agencies to rise up to the change. At the heart of all this change is the World Wide Web and the technologies, such as Java™, that enable corporations to take advantage of this paradigm shift.

It was not too many years ago that the World Wide Web was a small network used largely by scientists to share documents. Today, it has evolved to a large network of networks, connecting millions of users to millions of computers worldwide. It is used not just for sharing documents now; it is perhaps the largest repository of up-to-date information. It is used to run business operations and to handle financial transactions. It has created a burgeoning new marketplace for financial and commercial transactions. The Internet offers a nonproprietary way to link large numbers of different computers together.

The new world economy has resulted in corporations being acquired or merging with others at a rapid rate; most of them have global reach. Their workforce is becoming increasingly mobile, largely because hand-held devices are affordable and available, providing the ability to access corporate information resources securely, as needed, to get the job done. Not just employees, but customers and suppliers too must be able to connect to corporate networks to obtain the service they need, when they need it. The ability of corporate information technology (IT) departments to provide a reliable, bulletproof solution that seamlessly transcends the boundaries between disparate data centers, between enterprise information systems built on different proprietary platforms, is what will distinguish the winners from the losers. The big question facing all corporate information technologists is, What is the new application architecture for this new-age commerce?

Since its launch in 1995, the Java programming language, along with Java platform technologies, has been taking an increasingly important role in this IT evolution. The Java programming language started as a way of writing portable client applications (applets) that ran on Web browsers to provide dynamic content. It was then used to write stand-alone client applications, using JDBC™ as a means of connecting to the corporate database servers. Servlet technology enabled the creation of server-side applications. The combination of applet/servlet technologies enabled the development of client/server applications capable of serving dynamic content and handling secure transactions in a significantly more scalable, reliable manner than was possible through the use of CGI (cgi-bin scripts) interface technology.

Web browsers running applets, the client side of this architecture, are low cost and pervasive. They come with a built-in security model that prevents the introduction of viruses. Applets are discarded after use and can be trusted if digitally signed by a trusted source. Deployment of these client/server systems is simple and convenient. Applets and servlets can be hosted on a Java programming language–compliant Web server and are simply pointed to by a uniform resource locator, or URL. A large number of new Java middleware vendors emerged, giving rise to a market for Java programming language Application Servers.

Even with this new paradigm of client/server applications, significant challenges remain for corporate information technologists as well as vendors of application platforms. HTTP (Hypertext Transfer Protocol) is a conversational protocol and is not well suited for use in high-performance client/server applications. Corporations faced with the requirement to automate new business processes rapidly, typically need to leverage and extend valuable information assets locked in their pre-Internet era enterprise application systems. An important distinguishing attribute of these older systems is that they have been carefully tuned and made robust over a period of several years to provide security, performance, scalability, and transactional capabilities reliably. Besides, corporations have, over a long period of time, carefully built trusted relationships with their existing vendors, such that they have a mutual, vested interest in each other's success. Displacing these older systems was not viable; leveraging proven enterprise infrastructures was essential.

The promise of programmer productivity resulting from the use of object oriented technologies, of rapid time to market, and cost-effective deployment of new client/server applications, and of seamless integration across different vendor systems based on the common UNIX interfaces was still largely unrealized. Each Java programming language Application Server supported its own proprietary component model, integrated with enterprise information systems in its own proprietary manner. Yet the Java programming language had proved itself as significantly enhancing programmer productivity. Widespread industry support of the

JavaBeans™ technology established the feasibility of a component model for the Java programming language, although the focus was on components for graphical user interfaces. A clear need for a standard for developing business logic components was emerging.

One of the primary tenets of the Java platform is application portability: "Write Once, Run Anywhere."™ This is made possible because vendors have integrated the Java Virtual Machine (JVM), which provides a common runtime environment for applications, on to their operating systems. However, distributed infrastructure services—such as database, transaction processing, session management, and messaging services—are often separate from the underlying operating systems. A typical corporation may use many different products and configurations from multiple vendors to implement their infrastructure services. Integrating these disparate systems was often the responsibility of the corporate IT department. It was very expensive because it required specialized, scarce programmer skills, and was very difficult to complete on time. The challenge of providing a seamless service-driven network of applications to employees, customers, suppliers, and partners had to be enabled by vendors, not corporate information technologists. Corporations should only focus their energies on creating business logic to support their emerging business processes.

The Internet has added a new dimension to the concept of scalability. Internet applications are likely to have to support hundreds of thousands, perhaps millions, of concurrent users connected to the service-driven network by client devices of varying capabilities, not all of which are capable of supporting a full-featured browser. Whether connected by a cell phone, a Palm device, a laptop, or a permanently connected desktop computer, users need access to enterprise information services, with the appropriate user interface. Corporations should be able to develop the most compelling user interaction suitable for each device, and should rapidly adapt applications to support newer devices as they are deployed.

In late 1997, a few of us—Java programming language enthusiasts from Sun Microsystems, BEA, IBM, Oracle, and Sybase—began articulating a vision for enterprise computing based on Java language technologies; a vision that was compelling because of its focus on business benefits and a persuasive strategy for execution. Our goal was to create a Java platform standard to which enterprise system vendors could implement compliant products while providing room for differentiation; that corporate information technologists could readily benefit from the advantages of portable component technology, focusing on supporting their business process requirements rather than solving distributed infrastructure product integration problems; and that independent software vendors would find attractive to participate in a flourishing component industry.

We worked energetically in forging a strong partner alliance, mobilizing independent software vendors, enterprise software vendors, application system providers, and major computer systems vendors. The result of this industry collaboration was a set of technologies that together comprise the Java 2 Platform, Enterprise Edition (J2EE™).

J2EE includes support for the primary application programming interfaces (APIs).

> **Enterprise JavaBeans (EJB),** which is a server component model that provides portability across application servers, and implements complex system logic such as transactions, security, and so forth, on behalf of the application components.

> **JavaServer Pages™ (JSP) and servlets,** which provide support for dynamic HTML generation and session management for browser clients

The other APIs in J2EE enable Java applications to access enterprise infrastructure services through a set of standard programming interfaces. The APIs include the following.

> **JDBC** for uniform access to relational databases such as Oracle, Sybase, Informix, and DB2

> **Java Transaction Service (JTS)** for accessing distributed transaction service, based on CORBA's Object Transaction Service (OTS)

> **Java Transaction API (JTA)** for providing transaction demarcation within an application

> **Java Message Service (JMS)** for accessing various asynchronous, reliable messaging systems including reliable queues and publish-and-subscribe services

> **Java Naming and Directory Interface (JNDI)** to provide access to various naming and directory services including DNS, LDAP, and CORBA naming service

> **Remote Method Invocation (RMI) over Internet Inter-ORB Protocol (IIOP)** for providing remote method invocation over the CORBA IIOP protocol

EJB was released at JavaOne in 1998, along with the announcement of the Java Platform for the Enterprise (JPE), which has since been renamed J2EE. Within moments of its release, at least 15 vendors announced support for the technology within their products, including providers of relational database systems, message-oriented middleware systems, application servers, tools, and integrated development environments. Industry support has continued unabated since then, and in fact has accelerated, with many more products available to support EJB, and quite a few EJB applications deployed in production, solving business critical requirements. An industry focused on creating and marketing reusable EJB-based business components is taking off. At long last the architecture, technologies, and products appear to be on hand to assist corporate information technologists in achieving their goals of fast time to market of applications to support new business requirements using off-the-shelf, portable, business logic components while continuing to leverage their existing investments in enterprise information systems.

In this book, Vlada Matena, the Chief Architect of EJB, and Beth Stearns do a fabulous job of explaining the motivations, goals, and functionality of EJB. They make it easy for the reader, whether an IT manager or an application developer, to understand the technology, the finer points of the API, and proper usage of the API via easy-to-read text, annotated appropriately by a substantial programming example.

It was my pleasure to have been associated with Vlada, Beth, and the other stellar contributors to the EJB technology, too numerous to mention here. It was my privilege to write this foreword. Enjoy!

Mala Chandra
Vice President, Engineering
Firedrop, Incorporated
(Formerly Sr. Director, Enterprise Java, Sun Microsystems, Inc.)
California, May 29, 2000

Preface

THIS book provides in-depth coverage of the Enterprise JavaBeans™ (EJB) architecture. It describes how to distribute enterprise applications using the EJB component architecture.

Readers of this book should be familiar with the Java™ programming language and should have had some exposure to enterprise beans and the EJB architecture. Although we briefly cover the basics of the EJB architecture, this book is not meant to be a tutorial for those just getting started with enterprise beans. Instead, the book provides in-depth coverage of the EJB architecture for information technology (IT) personnel implementing applications in-house and for independent software vendors (ISVs) developing generic applications for sale to enterprises.

The EJB architecture defines a component model for enterprise applications. It describes

- How to design an application as a set of components

- How the components interact with each other

- How the components interact with their EJB container

The EJB architecture defines these interactions as contracts, which enable applications to use components from different sources. Because EJB components must adhere to these contracts, an application can consist of software components from multiple vendors.

The EJB 1.1 specification defines the architecture contracts mainly from the point of view of the container vendor. In contrast, this book presents the EJB architecture from the point of view of the application developer—that is, the person who develops EJB applications.

A detailed description of the development of two enterprise applications forms the backbone of the book. Although the example applications are relatively simple, they illustrate many of the typical problems encountered in enterprise application development. We use these examples to show how the EJB architecture helps developers solve these problems.

The first example is a benefits enrollment application developed in-house by an IT department. This application works well for explaining how a session bean works and for illustrating how developers use session beans.

The second example takes the benefits application from the first example, which was developed in-house, and turns it into an application developed by an ISV. An ISV has different design goals from that of an in-house IT department. The ISV must design the application so that it can be easily deployed in many different customers' operational environments. Because each customer has a unique operational environment, the ISV must address a number of challenges. In addition, an ISV typically needs to design the application so that it can be extended by a customer or integrator. We illustrate how the entity bean architecture helps ISVs to overcome these challenges.

These two annotated examples illustrate many of the techniques for applying the EJB architecture to specific problems in enterprise application development. In addition to the two application examples, we describe the individual features of the EJB architecture and discuss when and how they should be used in applications.

Although the typical application developer does not need to know how the EJB container works, we illustrate some of the inner workings of the EJB container. We do this mainly to give the reader an appreciation of how much work the container performs on behalf of the application.

Conventions Used in This Book

The following are the conventions used in this book.

Graphics

Many of the graphics in this book depict Unified Modeling Language (UML) diagrams. The conventions used in these diagrams follow the UML standard. Briefly, Figure 1 illustrates the arrows and connectors used in standard UML diagrams.

Typographic Conventions

Table 1 describes the typographic conventions used in this book.

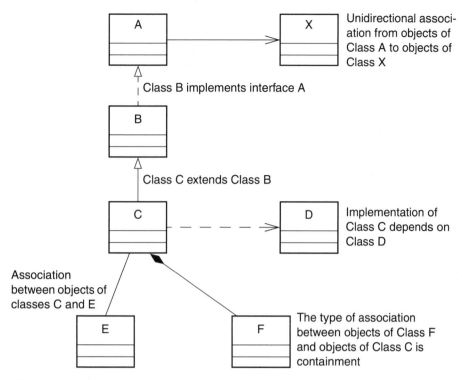

Figure 1 UML Symbols

Table 1 Typographic Conventions

Typeface or Symbol	Meaning	Example
AaBbCc123	The names of commands, files, and directories; interface, class, method, variable, and deployment descriptor element names; programming language keywords	Edit the file AccountBean.java. Uses an AccountHome object. Invokes the method ejbCreate.
AaBcCc123	Book titles, new words or terms, or words to be emphasized.	Read Chapter 2 in *EJB 1.1 Specification*. This is a *stateless session bean*. You *must* be careful when using this option.

Other Sources of Information

You should refer to other publications related to the Java 2 platform, Enterprise Edition application architecture (J2EE™). The following books are of particular interest to those developing other application components besides enterprise beans.

- *Java™ 2 Platform, Enterprise Edition Specification, Version 1.2* copyright 1999, Sun Microsystems, Inc. Available at `http://java.sun.com/j2ee/docs.html`.

- *Java™ 2 Platform, Enterprise Edition, Connector Specification*, copyright 2000, Sun Microsystems, Inc.

- *Java™ 2 Platform, Enterprise Edition, Platform and Component Specification*, Shannon, Hapner, Matena, Davidson, Pelegri-Llopart, Cable, Enterprise Team, copyright 2000, Sun Microsystems, Inc.

- *Enterprise JavaBeans™ 1.1 Specification, Final Release,* copyright 1999, 2000, Sun Microsystems, Inc.

- *Enterprise JavaBeans™ 2.0 Specification, Public Draft,* copyright 2000, Sun Microsystems, Inc.

- *Developing Enterprise Applications with the Java™ 2 Platform, Enterprise Edition, Version 1.0,* Kassem, Enterprise Team, copyright 2000, Sun Microsystems, Inc.

- *RMI over IIOP 1.0.1 Specification,* copyright 1999, Sun Microsystems, Inc. Available at `http://java.sun.com/products/rmi-iiop`.

Note about the Example Applications

It is important to note that the example application in Chapter 4, Working with Session Beans, and the entity bean application in Chapter 7, Entity Bean Application Example, are written *without* the use of an interactive development environment (IDE). Normally, enterprise developers use a commercial IDE when developing EJB applications. An IDE generates much of the JDBC and other database access code—code that is often tedious to write by hand. However, we wanted our examples to illustrate how the EJB architecture works and, had we used an IDE, the code generated by the IDE would obscure the discussion of the EJB architecture. Therefore, we chose to write all the code manually. Keep this in mind and realize that developing with the EJB architecture is easier than some of our code samples may indicate because in practice a lot of the code is generated automatically by the IDE.

Because our goal is to illustrate the use of the EJB architecture, we wanted to keep the code relatively simple. As a result, we don't always show what some developers would consider to be the best coding practices for enterprise applications. By including code to show such practices, we would have obscured the EJB discussion. For the sake of simplicity of the code examples, we sometimes do not handle properly all exceptions thrown by the code.

Contents of the Book

The book begins by describing the advantages of the EJB architecture. Chapter 1, Advantages of the Enterprise JavaBeans™ Architecture, discusses the different enterprise application architectures and how they have evolved, especially with the growth of the Web. It describes the current state-of-the-art EJB and J2EE architectures, and how they are well suited to meet today's enterprise computing needs.

Chapter 2, Enterprise JavaBeans Architecture Overview, provides a concise overview of the EJB architecture. For someone not so familiar with the EJB architecture, this chapter is a good starting point because it defines the EJB terminology and the structure of enterprise beans. It defines and describes EJB applications, and such basic concepts as business entities and business processes. It provides an overview of the different enterprise bean types, the parts that comprise an enterprise bean, and how to use enterprise beans to model business logic of enterprise applications.

The development of an EJB application can be thought of in terms of the tasks that need to be performed. To that end, Chapter 3, Enterprise JavaBeans Roles, delineates the roles and tasks involved during the application development process.

Once the stage has been set and the introductory material explained, the book focuses on session beans and entity beans. Two chapters focus on session beans and two chapters focus on entity beans. Chapter 4, Working with Session Beans, focuses on typical programming styles for applications using session beans. This chapter is of interest to bean developers implementing session beans and to application programmers developing session bean clients. For bean developers, the chapter describes how best to implement the methods of a session bean. For application programmers developing session bean clients, it shows how to use the session bean home and remote interfaces properly. An extensive benefits enrollment application example illustrates the key points about session beans.

Chapter 5, Session Bean in Its Container, describes the support and services that an EJB container provides for a session bean. Containers typically provide services to session beans when they are deployed and customized for a particular operational environment, and at runtime, when a client application invokes the session bean. Although the container services are hidden from the bean developer and the client programmer, these services go a long way in simplifying bean and application development. This chapter describes much of what goes on behind the scenes.

After completing its discussion of session beans, the book shifts its focus to entity beans. Entity beans differ significantly from session beans. Chapter 6, Understanding Entity Beans, combines a presentation of the basic concepts regarding programming with entity beans, from both the client and bean developer points of view, along with a discussion of the services that the container provides to entity beans. This chapter is analogous to Chapter 5 for session beans. The chapter also provides a detailed description of strategies for managing entity object state. Chapter 7, Entity Bean Application Example, takes the benefits enrollment application example used for session beans and shows how to write the same application using entity beans. The example illustrates many of the techniques for working with entity beans. It also illustrates how entity beans can be used by ISVs to make their application reusable across many customers' operational environments.

Virtually all applications using enterprise beans rely on transactions. Chapter 8, Understanding Transactions, describes the EJB architecture approach to transaction demarcation. It covers the essential aspects of transactions necessary for application developers.

Security is another area of critical importance to enterprise applications. The EJB architecture provides declarative support for security management. Chapter 9, Managing Security, describes the EJB security environment, particularly from the point of view of the application developer.

Last, the book includes an appendix that contains the API reference, a second appendix that contains code samples of supporting classes, and a glossary of terms. The reference section contains all the interfaces defined by the EJB architecture as well as the methods within each interface.

Acknowledgments

WE would like to thank the following individuals who, on short notice, took the time to review the early draft of the book and who provided us with invaluable feedback: Mark Hapner, Bill Shannon, Rahul Sharma, Rick Cattell, George Copeland (IBM), Susan Cheung (Oracle), Liane Acker (Encore Development), Jim Frentress (nPassage, Inc.), Moshe Sambol (GTE), and John Stearns.

Likewise, we want to thank the following individuals for reviewing the final draft of the book and for providing feedback: Liane Acker (Encore Development), Ken Nordby (IBM), Jorgen Thelin (Orbware), Marc Fleury (Telkel), Jim Healy, and Jim Frentress (nPassage, Inc.).

We especially want to thank Walter Jenny and Rahul Sharma. Walter's programming brought the entity bean example application to life at the JavaOne show this past June. Rahul not only reviewed both drafts of the book, he also developed the PayrollBean to use the Connector specification to access a mainframe application.

We also want to acknowledge the following people who helped us accomplish all the tasks necessary to publish this book: Jeff Jackson, for enthusiastically encouraging us to do this book; Lisa Friendly and Jim Inscore, for assisting us with publication details; and Mike Hendrickson, Julie DiNicola, Sarah Weaver, and Julie Steele, among others at Addison-Wesley, who had the flexibility to adapt their schedules to ours.

CHAPTER 1

Advantages of the Enterprise JavaBeans™ Architecture

ENTERPRISE JavaBeans (EJB) is a state-of-the-art architecture for developing, deploying, and managing reliable enterprise applications in production environments. This chapter illustrates the benefits of using the EJB architecture for enterprise applications.

This chapter discusses the evolution of enterprise application architectures. It is inevitable that such architectures must evolve because the underlying computer support and delivery systems have changed enormously, and they will continue to change in the future. With the growth of the Web and the Internet, more and more enterprise applications are now Web-based, including both intranet and extranet applications. The Java™ 2 platform, Enterprise Edition (J2EE™), and EJB architectures together provide superior support for Web-based enterprise applications.

There are many benefits to using the EJB architecture. This chapter describes the advantages of the EJB architecture and its benefits to both application developers and customers.

1.1   From a Two-Tier to a J2EE Architecture

Enterprise application architectures have undergone an extensive evolution. The first generation of enterprise applications was centralized mainframe applications. In the late 1980s and early 1990s, most new enterprise applications followed a two-tier architecture approach (also known as the *client/server architecture*). Later, the enterprise architecture evolved to a three-tier, then to a Web-based architecture. The current evolutionary state is now represented by the J2EE application architecture.

This section discusses the evolution of enterprise application architectures, starting with the two-tier architecture. We chose not to describe how the architectures evolved from the centralized mainframe architecture to the two-tier architecture, in part because this has little relevance to the material in this book.

1.1.1   Two-Tier Application Architecture

With a two-tier application, a business system is structured as a collection of operating system-level application processes that execute on the client machine. Typically, this would be a PC in a corporation. Each such application implements one or several business processes, plus the GUI presentation logic for the interactions between the business processes and the user. (A business process is an encapsulation of a user's interactions with some enterprise information.) The application running on the client PC communicates over the network with a database server storing the corporate databases. The database server stores the corporate data, and the client application typically accesses the data via Structured Query Language (SQL) statements (Figure 1.1).

The two-tier architecture worked well for most applications before the existence of the Web. Its main advantage is that it is easy to develop two-tier applications, particularly because the presentation logic and business logic reside in the same process, and the developer does not have to deal with the complexity of a distributed application.

However, its disadvantages outweigh its advantages. The main disadvantage of the two-tier architecture is that it does not separate business logic from presentation logic. Programmers cannot cleanly separate business logic from presentation logic in two-tier architecture applications. This results in a number of problems: easily compromised database integrity, difficult to administer, difficult to maintain, exposure to security violations, limited scalability, restricted client architecture requirements, and limitation to one presentation type.

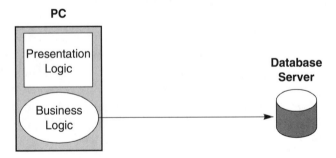

Figure 1.1   Two-Tier Application Architecture

- **It is easy to compromise database integrity.** Because each client program embeds the business logic, an error or bug in the client program can easily compromise the integrity of the corporate database.

- **It is difficult to administer in a large enterprise.** In this architecture, the application is deployed on the client machines, and the information technology (IT) department of the corporation must maintain the application. If a business process changes, the IT department must replace all copies of the old version of the application with a new version of the application. This is a difficult task in a corporation with tens of thousands of PCs, especially when many of them may be "unmanaged" laptop machines.

- **It is difficult to maintain the code.** The two-tier architecture does not support modular programming, which makes it difficult to maintain application code. Maintenance difficulty increases exponentially for larger organizations because they typically use more programmers to code and maintain applications.

- **It exposes the applications to security violations.** A skillful programmer may "hack" the application installed on the PC to alter the business process that the application implements.

- **Its scalability is limited; it is difficult to scale to a high number of users.** Each running application typically needs a connection to the corporate database. Because the number of open connections is typically limited by the database product, it may not be possible for all users to run the application at the same time.

- **It requires a homogeneous client architecture.** Before the advent of the Java language, the two-tier architecture typically required the client machines to be homogeneous. For example, it typically required all client machines to be PCs running the same type of operating system.

- **It ties the application to one particular presentation type.** Because the same application implements not only the business processes but also the presentation, it may not be possible to reuse the implementation of the business process with a different presentation type, such as a browser or intelligent cell phone.

Although the corporation could live with the limitations of the two-tier architecture before the Web, the onset and growth of the Web changed all the rules. These limitations essentially make it completely incompatible with the Web. This is chiefly because Web clients inherently lack intelligence, and because there are a massive number of such clients. As a result, application developers and their customers have been seeking alternative application architectures.

1.1.2   Traditional Three-Tier Application Architecture

The traditional three-tier architecture overcomes some of the limitations of the two-tier architecture. The three-tier architecture splits the presentation logic from the business logic. It places the business logic on a server; only the presentation logic is deployed on the client PCs (Figure 1.2).

The three-tier architecture brings about a number of improvements. The middle-tier server improves scalability by reusing expensive resources, such as database connections, across multiple clients. Improved scalability results in improved performance. This architecture also improves security and application management. The three-tier architecture has been used in most enterprise resource planning (ERP) systems and in the systems specialized for high-volume transaction processing (CICS, Tuxedo, and others).

Although the three-tier architecture eliminates some of the flaws of the two-tier architecture, it too has certain disadvantages—complexity, lack of application portability, vendor incompatibility, limited adoption, and Web incompatibility.

- **Complexity**—Developing a three-tier application is more complex than developing a two-tier application. For example, the programmer must deal with distribution, multithreading, security, and so forth. Distributed applications introduce substantial system-level programming complexities with which the developer must deal. Also, distributed applications require the customer IT department to compensate for the lack of application deployment and administration support. In an attempt to reduce the complexity of distributed applications, vendors resorted to using application frameworks such as transaction processing (TP) monitors. ERP vendors used the concept of an application server. The intention of the application frameworks was to free the application program-

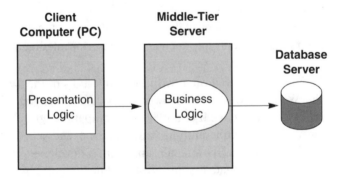

Figure 1.2   Three-tier Application Architecture

mer from having to deal with these complexities. Today, *application server* is the most frequently used term for a distributed application framework.

- **Lack of application portability**—Because each vendor of an application framework for the three-tier platform uses different application program interfaces (APIs) in its framework, it is not possible for independent software vendors (ISVs) to write applications that are deployable on application servers provided by other vendors.

- **Vendor incompatibility**—It is difficult to integrate applications from different vendors because each vendor uses a different set of protocols, and there is no standard interoperability among protocols.

- **Limited adoption**—ISVs have no incentive to write applications for multiple competing frameworks that are not widely adopted. Although tools exist to support distributed applications, these tools work only on the frameworks for which they were developed. Many tools do not work across most frameworks. As a result, there is limited support for a consistent set of tools. Likewise, programmers' knowledge of tools and frameworks is also limited.

- **Incompatibility with the Web**—The traditional three-tier architecture does not work directly with the Web. The three-tier architecture uses a proprietary protocol for the communication between the client and the application running on the server, and this proprietary protocol does not work with the Web. Although many application framework vendors have added support for Web clients as a front end to their existing products, the resultant architecture still suffers from the other drawbacks listed here.

1.1.3 Early Web-Based Application Architecture

The introduction and growth of the Web changed everything. Because neither the two-tier nor the traditional three-tier architecture supports the development of Web applications, early Web application developers had to devise another approach. They used various plug-in extensions to Web servers. These extensions invoke programs on the server that dynamically construct HTML documents from the information stored in corporate databases. Likewise, the Web server extensions also enter information submitted in HTML forms into the corporate database.

An example of such an extension is cgi-bin scripts. (CGI is an acronym for Common Gateway Interface, an interface for developing HTML pages and Web applications. CGI applications are commonly referred to as *cgi-bin scripts*.) Although cgi-bin scripts and similar mechanisms allowed a corporate developer to build simple Web applications, the cgi-bin approach does not scale to more complex enterprise applications for the following reasons.

- Cgi-bin scripts do not provide well-structured encapsulation of the underlying business process or of a business entity.

- Cgi-bin scripts are hard to develop, maintain, and manage. High-level application development tools do not provide good support for the development of cgi-bin scripts.

- Cgi-bin scripts intertwine the implementation of business processes with the implementation of the presentation logic. When it is necessary to change one part of the implementation (such as a business process), there is a risk of inadvertently changing the other part.

- Cgi-bin script implementation does not foster the maintenance of the integrity of business rules. The implementation of an enterprise's business rules is scattered across the cgi-bin scripts deployed on numerous Web servers in the enterprise. Because of this, it is difficult for the enterprise to maintain the integrity of its business rules.

1.1.4   J2EE Application Architecture

J2EE is a standard architecture specifically oriented to the development and deployment of enterprise Web-oriented applications using the Java programming language. ISVs and enterprises can use the J2EE architecture both for the development and deployment of intranet applications, thus effectively replacing the two-tier and three-tier models, and for the development of Internet applications, effectively replacing the cgi-bin-based approach. Figure 1.3 illustrates the J2EE application programming model for Web-based applications.

J2EE also provides support for two-tier and three-tier applications. Figure 1.4 illustrates the support for two-tier applications. (Note that Application-Client Container refers to the Java 2, Standard Edition [J2SE] programming environment.)

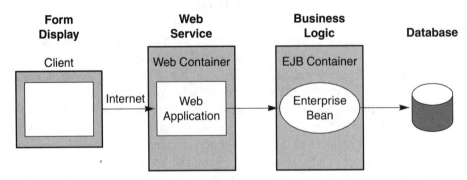

Figure 1.3   J2EE Application Programming Model for Web-Based Applications

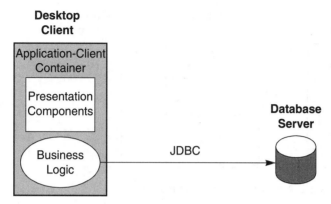

Figure 1.4   J2EE Application Programming Model for
Two-Tier Applications

Figure 1.5 illustrates the support for three-tier applications.

The J2EE platform also provides supports for Java applets, which are small programs loaded from the Web container to the browser (Figure 1.6).

The J2EE platform consists of four programming environments, called *containers*.

1. **The EJB container**—Provides the environment for the development, deployment, and runtime management of enterprise beans. Enterprise beans are components that implement the business processes and entities.

2. **The Web container**—Provides the environment for the development, deployment, and runtime management of servlets and JavaServer Pages™ (JSP). The servlets and JSP are grouped into deployable units called *Web*

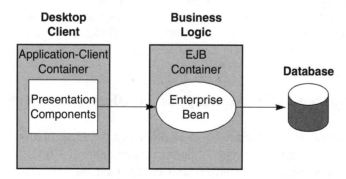

Figure 1.5   J2EE Application Programming Model for
Three-Tier Applications

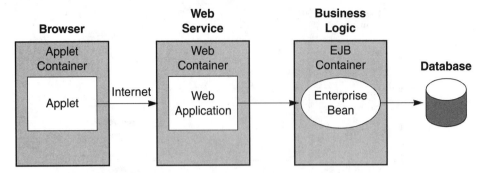

Figure 1.6   J2EE Application Programming Model for Web-Based Applets

applications. A Web application implements the presentation logic of an enterprise application.

3. **The Application-Client container**—Provides the environment for executing J2EE application clients. This environment is essentially J2SE.

4. **The Applet container**—Provides the environment for executing Java applets. This environment is typically embedded in a Web browser.

In this book we focus mainly on the development and deployment of enterprise beans, rather than the development of the other application parts. We only demonstrate fragments of the other parts (Web applications) to illustrate the interactions between enterprise beans and their clients. Refer to *Developing Enterprise Applications with the Java 2 Platform, Enterprise Edition* (Sun Microsystems, Inc., 2000) for a more complete description of how to develop these other parts of a J2EE application.

Note also that the J2EE platform embraces the Common Object Request Broker Architecture (CORBA). All J2EE containers include a CORBA-compliant Object Request Broker (ORB). The interoperability protocol between EJB containers from multiple vendors is based on CORBA standards, such as Remote Method Invocation over Internet Inter-ORB Protocol (RMI-IIOP) and the Object Transaction Service (OTS).

1.2   Advantages of the Enterprise JavaBeans Architecture

The EJB component architecture is the backbone of the J2EE platform. The core of a J2EE application is comprised of one or several enterprise beans that perform the application's business operations and encapsulate the business logic of an application. Other parts of the J2EE platform, such as the JSP, complement the

EJB architecture to provide functions such as presentation logic and client interaction control logic.

ISVs, integrators, and customers can develop and customize EJB applications. We now explain how EJB applications overcome the limitations of the two-tier, the three-tier, and the early Web application architectures, and enjoy additional advantages not found in these architectures.

As you read this section, keep in mind that the EJB architecture defines six major roles, which Chapter 3, Enterprise JavaBeans Roles discusses in detail. In brief, these roles are the following.

- Bean developer—Develops the enterprise bean component.

- Application assembler—Composes the enterprise bean component into larger, deployable units.

- Deployer—Deploys the application within a particular operational environment.

- System administrator—Configures and administers the enterprise computing and networking infrastructure.

- EJB container provider and EJB server provider—A vendor (or vendors) specializing in transaction and application management, and other low-level services.

The EJB architecture provides benefits to all these roles. We focus here on the benefits to application developers and customers.

1.2.1 Benefits to the Application Developer

The EJB architecture provides the following benefits to the application developer: simplicity, application portability, component reusability, ability to build complex applications, separation of business logic from presentation logic, deployment in many operating environments, distributed deployment, application interoperability, integration with non-Java systems, and educational resources and development tools.

- **Simplicity**—It is easier to develop an enterprise application with the EJB architecture than without. Because the EJB architecture helps the application developer access and utilize enterprise services with minimal effort and time, writing an enterprise bean is almost as simple as writing a Java class. The application developer does not have to be concerned with system-level issues, such as security, transactions, multithreading, security protocols, distributed programming, connection resource pooling, and so forth. As a result, the application developer can concentrate on the business logic for the domain-specific application.

- **Application portability**—An EJB application can be deployed on any J2EE-compliant server. This means that the application developer can sell the application to customers who use any J2EE-compliant server.

- **Component reusability**—An EJB application consists of enterprise bean components. Each enterprise bean is a reusable building block. There are two essential ways to reuse an enterprise bean.

  1. An enterprise bean not yet deployed can be reused at application development time by being included in several different applications. The bean can be customized for each application without requiring changes, or even access, to its source code.

  2. Other applications can reuse an enterprise bean that is already deployed in a customer's operational environment by making calls to its client-view interfaces. Multiple applications can make calls to the deployed bean.

  In addition, the business logic of enterprise beans can be reused through Java subclassing of the enterprise bean class.

- **Ability to build complex applications**—The EJB architecture simplifies building complex enterprise applications. These EJB applications are built by a team of developers and evolve over time. The component-based EJB architecture is well suited to the development and maintenance of complex enterprise applications. With its clear definition of roles and well-defined interfaces, the EJB architecture promotes and supports team-based development, and lessens the demands on individual developers.

- **Separation of business logic from presentation logic**—An enterprise bean typically encapsulates a business process or a business entity (an object representing enterprise business data), making it independent of the presentation logic. The business programmer need not worry about formatting the output; the programmer developing the Web page need only be concerned with the output data that will be passed to the Web page. In addition, this separation makes it possible to develop multiple presentation logic for the same business process, or to change the presentation logic of a business process without needing to modify the code that implements the business process.

- **Deployment in many operating environments**—The goal of an ISV is to sell an application to many customers. Because each customer has a unique operational environment, the application typically needs to be customized at deployment time to each operational environment, including different database schemas.

- The EJB architecture allows the bean developer to separate the common application business logic from the customization logic performed at deployment.

- The EJB architecture allows an entity bean to be bound to different database schemas. This persistence binding is done at deployment. The application developer can write code that is not limited to a single type of database management system (DBMS) or database schema.

- The EJB architecture facilitates the deployment of an application by establishing deployment standards, such as those for data source lookup, other application dependencies, security configuration, and so forth. The standards enable the use of deployment tools. The standards and tools remove much of the possibility of miscommunication between the developer and the deployer.

- **Distributed deployment**—The EJB architecture makes it possible for applications to be deployed in a distributed manner across multiple servers on a network. The bean developer does not have to be aware of the deployment topology when developing enterprise beans. He writes the same code whether the client of an enterprise bean is on the same machine or on a different machine.

- **Application interoperability**—The EJB architecture makes it easier to integrate applications from different vendors. The enterprise bean's client-view interface serves as a well-defined integration point between applications.

- **Integration with non-Java systems**—The related J2EE APIs, such as the Connector specification and the Java Message Service™ (JMS) specification, make it possible to integrate enterprise bean applications with various non-Java applications, such as ERP systems or mainframe applications, in a standard way.

- **Educational resources and development tools**—Because the EJB architecture is an industry-wide standard, the EJB application developer benefits from a growing body of educational resources on how to build EJB applications. More important, the powerful application development tools available from the leading tool vendors simplify the development and maintenance of EJB applications.

1.2.2   Benefits to Customers

A customer has a different perspective on the EJB architecture from the application developer. The EJB architecture provides the following benefits to the customer: choice of application server, facilitation of application management, integration with customer's existing applications and data, and application security.

- **Choice of the server**—Because the EJB architecture is an industrywide standard and is part of the J2EE platform, customer organizations have a wide choice of J2EE-compliant servers. Customers can select a product that meets their needs from the perspective of scalability, integration capabilities with other systems, security protocols, price, and so forth. Customers are not locked into a specific vendor's product. Should their needs change, they can easily redeploy an EJB application in a server from a different vendor.

- **Facilitation of application management**—Because the EJB architecture provides a standardized environment, server vendors have had the motivation to develop application management tools to enhance their products. As a result, there are sophisticated application management tools provided with the EJB container that allow the customer's IT department to perform such functions as starting and stopping the application, allocating system resources to the application, and monitoring security violations, among others.

- **Integration with a customer's existing applications and data**—The EJB architecture and the other related J2EE APIs simplify and standardize the integration of EJB applications with any non-Java applications and systems at the customer operational environment. For example, a customer does not have to change an existing database schema to fit an application. Instead, an EJB application can be made to fit the existing database schema when it is deployed.

- **Application security**—The EJB architecture shifts most of the responsibility for an application's security from the application developer to the server vendor, system administrator, and the deployer. The people performing these roles are more qualified than the application developer to secure the application. This leads to better security of the operational applications.

1.3   Conclusion

This chapter provided a high-level discussion of the different enterprise application architectures and described their advantages and disadvantages. It showed how these architectures have evolved to the EJB architecture and highlighted its unique benefits from the perspective of both the developer and the customer or client.

The chapter also introduced the terms *bean developer, deployer,* and *system administrator*—three of the six major roles defined by the EJB architecture. These roles are described further in Chapter 3, Enterprise JavaBeans Roles.

From here, we focus on the EJB architecture in greater detail.

CHAPTER 2

Enterprise JavaBeans Architecture Overview

THIS chapter provides an overview of the EJB architecture, the backbone of the J2EE platform. The EJB architecture specifies how to develop and deploy server-side application business logic components written in the Java programming language.

Enterprise beans serve as the building blocks of distributed enterprise applications. This chapter talks about the structure of enterprise beans—the enterprise bean class, the home interface, the remote interface, the deployment descriptor, and so forth. This chapter introduces the session and entity enterprise bean types and discusses how the two enterprise bean types model and implement different types of business logic—business entities and business processes. Finally, the chapter talks about the EJB container environment in which EJB applications run, and the services and functions provided by the container.

2.1 What Are Enterprise JavaBeans Applications?

Enterprise beans are components that are used as parts of distributed enterprise applications. Each enterprise bean encapsulates a part of the business logic of the application. An enterprise bean typically communicates with resource managers, such as database management systems, and other enterprise beans.

At the same time, different types of clients access enterprise beans. The clients of an enterprise bean can be other enterprise beans, Web applications, servlets, or application clients.

At runtime, an enterprise bean resides in an *EJB container*. An EJB container provides the deployment and runtime environment for enterprise beans, including services such as security, transaction, deployment, and concurrency and instance life cycle management. (Refer to Container Tools and Services on page 34 for a complete discussion of the EJB container and its services.) The process of installing an enterprise bean in an EJB container is called *enterprise bean deployment.*

An enterprise application can include a single enterprise bean or multiple enterprise beans. When an application includes multiple enterprise beans, the enterprise beans can be deployed either in a single container or in multiple containers located on the enterprise's network.

Figure 2.1 illustrates an enterprise application that includes six enterprise beans (marked EJB1 through EJB6), as well as components that are not enterprise beans. These other components include a Web application (WebApp1) comprised of several JavaServer Pages and an application client program (Client1). Figure 2.1 illustrates how an enterprise bean can function as a client of another enterprise bean. Each enterprise bean that invokes a method on another enterprise bean is considered a client of the second enterprise bean. For example, EJB2 is a client of EJB4 and EJB5, whereas EJB1 is a client of EJB2 (and EJB3).

An enterprise can deploy the enterprise beans of the application illustrated in Figure 2.2 in either a single EJB container or in multiple EJB containers. Figure 2.2 illustrates the deployment across three different EJB containers that reside on multiple machines on a network.

A client accesses an enterprise bean through the enterprise bean's *client-view API*. The client-view API is location transparent. This means that a client invokes an enterprise bean using the same API regardless of whether the client executes in the same Java Virtual Machine™ (JVM) as the enterprise bean or in a different JVM. If the client and the enterprise beans are in the same JVM, the container uses an optimized internal path to perform the invocation. If they are in different containers, the client communicates with the enterprise bean over the network to perform the invocation.

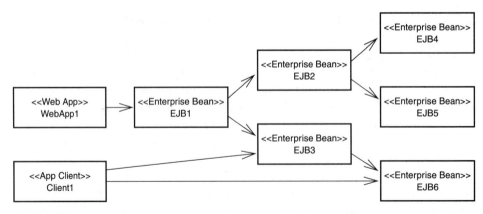

Figure 2.1   Enterprise Application with Multiple Enterprise Beans

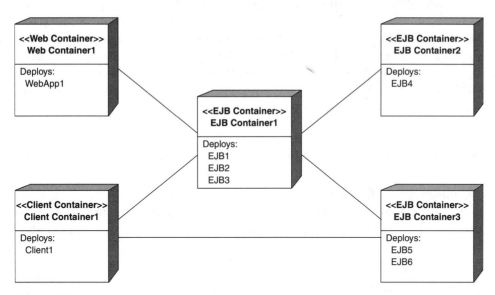

Figure 2.2   Deployment across Multiple EJB Containers

The client-view API is independent from the type of the client using the API. This means that a client that is itself an enterprise bean uses the same API to invoke another enterprise bean as, for example, a Web application and a stand-alone Java client program. (Refer to Structure of Enterprise Beans on page 23 for more information on the client-view API.)

The client-view API is uniform across all enterprise beans of the same type (that is, entity or session). Clients use all enterprise beans in a similar way. The uniformity of the enterprise bean's client-view API makes it possible to develop powerful tools that simplify the entire application development process. Developers use these tools for the following tasks.

- To assemble enterprise beans into multitier applications
- To construct enterprise bean clients, such as Web applications
- To integrate enterprise bean applications developed by multiple vendors

To succeed in the marketplace, all enterprise applications must quickly adapt to rapidly changing requirements, and at the same time enterprises need to evolve their business. It is essential that an application environment allow for this evolution, and the EJB architecture and the client-view API do allow for this. The organization of an application's business logic into components that communicate with each other via a well-defined client-view API enables application evolution to be accomplished with a minimum of overhead and disruption or downtime. If business rules change, an enterprise needs to upgrade only the enterprise bean that implements the changed business rules. If the upgraded enterprise bean preserves the original client-view API, or if it provides a backward-compatible client-view API, an enterprise does not need to change the rest of the application to accommodate the changed business rules.

2.2   Business Entities and Processes, and Enterprise Bean Types

As already noted, EJB applications organize the application's business rules into components. Each component typically represents a business entity or a business process. Some EJB components implement business entities whereas others implement business processes.

2.2.1   Business Entities

A *business entity* is a business object representing some information maintained by an enterprise. A business entity has state, or data values, and this state is kept persistently, typically in a database. Business processes can change the state of a business entity. However, the business entity and its state exist independently of the business processes that change the entity state.

For example, you may have a business entity such as Customer that represents your customer data and the business rules associated with the data. You might also have an Order entity that encapsulates customer order data with its associated business rules. Other examples of business entities are Account, Employee, and so forth. Each business entity maintains state about itself. For example, the Customer entity keeps the customer's shipping and billing address as part of its state. The business rules associated with a business entity constrain the values of the entity state. For example, a business rule may dictate that the ZIP code field in the customer billing address field must be a valid five- or nine-digit ZIP code. It is desirable to enforce this business rule when changes are attempted to the ZIP code field, irrespective of the business process that makes the changes to the ZIP code.

Often, there are relationships defined between business entities. For example, there is a one-to-many association relationship between the Customer entity and the Order entities. The business rules for the entities involved in a relationship include the maintenance of the relationship. The rules for the maintenance of relationships involve deciding under what conditions one entity becomes associated with another entity, what conditions may change that association, and how the deletion of one entity impacts associated entities. For example, the designer of an application needs to ask questions such as, Does an Order have to be associated with some Customer? If a Customer is deleted, should all Orders associated with the Customer be deleted as well?

2.2.2 Business Processes

A *business process* is a business object that typically encapsulates an interaction of a user with business entities. A business process typically updates or changes the state of the business entities. A business process may also have its own state. If a business process has its own state, the state exists only for the duration of the business process; when the business process completes, the state ceases to exist.

Although some business processes require that the state of a business process be implemented as persistent, the state of other business processes can be implemented as transient.

Persistent state is usually required when a business process has multiple steps, each possibly performed by different actors. A business process with multiple actors is called a *collaborative business process*. This need for multiple steps performed by multiple actors may occur, for example, when processing a loan application or an expense report.

Transient state is usually sufficient if one actor in one conversation can complete the business process. In this book, we refer to a business process with one actor as a *conversational business process*. A conversational business process means that one actor engages in a conversation with the system. (An actor can be a user or another program.) A good example of a conversational business process is an individual withdrawing money at an automated teller machine (ATM) or an employee enrolling into a company's benefits program.

Other examples of business processes are actions such as fulfilling an order, promoting an employee, scheduling a meeting among multiple participants, closing a bank account, processing a loan application, electing members to the board of directors, scheduling a payment via an on-line banking application, and so forth.

Note that most business-to-customer Web applications can be considered business processes. These processes are typically conversational business processes.

2.2.3 Implementation of Business Rules

Once the application architect has identified the business entities and the business processes, it is then time to formulate the business rules. The business rules are organized by the components that implement the business entities and processes.

The business rules that apply to the state of a business entity should be implemented in the component that represents the business entity. The idea is to keep rules that pertain to an entity's state independent from any business process that acts on the business entity. Certainly, the business rules should be independent from the component representing the business process. For example, the business rule that an account balance must not be allowed to become negative should be implemented in the component that represents the Account entity because this rule is independent from the business processes that cause the account balance to change.

Likewise, the business rules that apply to a specific business process should be implemented in the component that represents the business process. For example, the business rule that the dollar amount of an ATM withdrawal transaction must be a multiple of twenty dollars should be implemented in the component that implements the ATM withdrawal business process. It should not be implemented in the Account entity.

2.2.4   Enterprise Bean Types

In the EJB environment, the business entities and processes are implemented as enterprise beans. The EJB architecture defines two types of enterprise beans: *session beans* and *entity beans*. The syntax of the session bean and entity bean client-view API is almost identical. However, the two enterprise bean types have different life cycles, different persistence management, and provide different programming styles to their clients.

It is important to understand the life cycle and programming differences between a session bean and an entity bean to understand whether a business process or business entity should be implemented as a session bean or an entity bean. These differences principally pertain to object sharing, object state, transactions, and container failure and object recovery.

Regarding object sharing, only a single client can use a session bean. Multiple clients can share an entity object among themselves.

The container typically maintains a session bean's object state (note that stateless session beans do not have state) in main memory, even across transactions, although it may swap that state to secondary storage when it deactivates the session bean.

The object state of an entity bean is typically maintained in a database, although the container may cache the state in memory during a transaction or even across transactions. Other, possibly non-EJB-based, programs can access the state of an entity object that is externalized in the database. For example, a program can run a SQL query directly against the database storing the state of entity objects. In contrast, the state of a session object is accessible only to the session object itself and the container.

The state of an entity object typically changes from within a transaction. Because its state changes transactionally, the container can recover the state of an entity bean should the transaction fail. The container does not maintain the state of a session object transactionally. However, the bean developer may instruct the container to notify the session objects of the transaction boundaries and transaction outcome. These notifications allow the session bean developer to synchronize manually the session object's state with the transactions. For example, the session bean object that caches changed data in its instance variables may use the notification to write the cached data to a database before the transaction manager commits the transaction.

Session objects are not recoverable; that is, they are not guaranteed to survive a container failure and restart. If a client has held a reference to a session object, that reference becomes invalid after a container failure. (Some containers implement session beans as recoverable objects, but this is not an EJB specification requirement.) An entity object, on the other hand, survives a failure and restart of its container. If a client holds a reference to the entity object prior to the container failure, then the client can continue to use this reference after the container restarts.

Table 2.1 depicts the significant differences in the life cycles of a stateful session and entity bean. (Note that the Session Bean column pertains to stateful session beans.)

Table 2.1   Entity and Stateful Session Bean Life Cycle Differences

Functional Area	Session Bean	Entity Bean
Object state	Maintained by the container in main memory across transactions. Swapped to secondary storage when deactivated.	Maintained in database or other resource manager. Typically cached in memory in a transaction.
Object sharing	A session object can be used only by one client.	An entity object can be shared by multiple clients. A client may pass an object reference to another client.
State externalization	The container internally maintains the session object's state. The state is inaccessible to other programs.	The entity object's state is typically stored in a database. Other programs, such as a SQL query, can access the state in the database.
Transactions	The state of a session object can be synchronized with a transaction, but it is not recoverable.	The state of an entity object is typically changed transactionally and is recoverable.

(continued)

Table 2.1   Entity and Stateful Session Bean Life Cycle Differences *(Continued)*

Functional Area	Session Bean	Entity Bean
Failure recovery	A session object is not guaranteed to survive failure and restart of its container.[a] The references to session objects held by a client become invalid after the failure.	An entity object survives the failure and the restart of its container. A client can continue using the references to the entity objects after the container restarts.

[a.]Some containers may implement session objects as recoverable objects, but this is not required by the EJB specification.

2.2.5   Choosing Entity Beans or Session Beans

The architect of the application chooses how to map the business entities and processes on the enterprise beans. There are no prescriptive rules that dictate whether to use a session bean or an entity bean for a component—different designers may map business entities and processes to enterprise beans differently.

You can also combine the use of session beans and entity beans to accomplish a business task. For example, you may have a session bean represent an ATM withdrawal that invokes an entity bean to represent the account.

The following guidelines describe the recommended mapping of business entities and processes to entity and session beans. The guidelines reflect the differences in the life cycle of the session and entity objects.

- A bean developer typically implements a business entity as an entity bean or a dependent object of an entity bean.

- A bean developer typically implements a conversational business process as a session bean. For example, developers implement the logic of most Web application sessions as session beans.

- A bean developer typically implements as an entity bean a collaborative business process (a business process with multiple actors). The entity object's state represents the intermediate steps of a business process that consists of multiple steps. For example, an entity object's state may record the changing information (state) on a loan application as that loan application moves through the steps of the loan approval process. The object's state may record that the account representative entered the information on the loan application and that the loan officer reviewed the application, but that application approval is still waiting on a credit report.

- If it is necessary for any reason to save the intermediate state of a business process in a database, a bean developer implements the business process as an entity bean. Often, the saved state itself can be considered a business entity. For example, many e-commerce Web applications use the concept of a shopping cart. The shopping cart stores the items that the customer has selected but not yet checked out. The state of the shopping cart can be considered to be the state of the "customer shopping" business process. If it is desirable that the shopping process span extended time periods and multiple Web sessions, the bean developer should implement the shopping cart as an entity bean. In contrast, if the shopping process is limited to a single Web session, the bean developer can implement the shopping cart as a session bean.

2.2.6　When to Use Dependent Objects

The architect of the application also faces the issue of whether to model all business entities as entity beans, especially if the business entities are very fine-grained objects. One goal for entity bean design is to allow entity beans to function as well-defined integration points between applications developed not only by multiple parties but also possibly running on different nodes on a network. To meet this goal, an entity bean is a more heavyweight component than a simple Java class. Although containers can provide an optimized invocation path between entity objects installed in the same container, the overhead of method invocation on an entity object is always likely to be somewhat higher than the overhead of method invocation on a simple Java class.

To avoid the container overhead for business entities that are not directly exposed to other applications, the entities can be implemented as *dependent objects*. External clients access dependent objects only through some entity bean. The entity bean can access its dependent objects directly without the involvement of the container. For example, line items on a purchase order can be implemented as dependent objects of the Purchase Order entity bean. Similarly, a customer address can be implemented as a dependent object of the Customer entity bean.

2.3　Structure of Enterprise Beans

A main goal of the EJB architecture is to free the enterprise application developer from having to deal with the system-level aspects of an application. Once freed from system-level concerns, the bean developer can focus solely on the business aspects of an application.

The bean developer produces the application as a set of enterprise beans. Each enterprise bean consists of the following parts: the enterprise bean class, the enterprise bean client-view API, and the deployment descriptor.

- **The enterprise bean class**—The *enterprise bean class* is a Java class that implements the business methods and the enterprise bean object life cycle methods. The enterprise bean class may use other helper classes, or entire class libraries, to implement the business methods.

- **The enterprise bean client-view API**—The *client-view API* consists of the enterprise bean *home interface* and enterprise bean *remote interface*. The enterprise bean home interface defines the `create`, `remove`, and find methods that control the life cycle of the enterprise bean objects. The enterprise bean remote interface defines the business methods that a client can invoke on the individual enterprise bean objects. The methods in the remote interface, and the `create` and find methods in the home interface, reflect the needs of each particular bean, and thus they vary from bean to bean.

- **The deployment descriptor**—The *deployment descriptor* is an XML document that contains the declarative information about the enterprise bean. (XML is the eXtensible Markup Language, which is a markup language that lets you define tags to identify data and text in documents.) This information is intended for the enterprise bean consumer; that is, the application assembler and deployer. The deployment descriptor also contains the declaration of the enterprise bean's environment entries. These entries are used for customizing the enterprise bean to the operational environment.

The method names declared in the enterprise bean class correspond to the method names declared in the home and remote interfaces. There is a naming convention that correlates the method names in the enterprise bean class with the corresponding names in the home and remote interfaces. See Enterprise Bean Class on page 30 for more details on this naming convention.

There is also a recommended naming convention for the enterprise bean class, home interface, and remote interface, although you are not required to adhere to this convention.

- The enterprise bean class name is typically a descriptive name of the business entity or process with the word "Bean" appended.

- The home interface is the same business entity name with the word "Home" appended.

- The remote interface name is just the business entity name.

- The name of the enterprise bean as a whole is the same business entity name with "EJB" appended.

For example, if you have an Account business entity, you might name the enterprise bean class AccountBean. Following the convention, you would name its home interface AccountHome and the remote interface Account. You would refer to the entire enterprise bean as AccountEJB. Because the client works mostly with the remote interface, this convention provides the most natural name for the remote interface type.

Figure 2.3 illustrates the parts that comprise the AccountEJB entity bean.

The AccountHome interface is the enterprise bean home interface. It defines the `create`, find, and `remove` methods that control the life cycle of the Account objects. The client of an enterprise bean uses these home interface methods to create new Account objects, to find existing Account objects, and to remove existing Account objects.

The Account interface is the enterprise bean remote interface. It defines the business methods that the client of an enterprise bean can invoke on the individual Account objects.

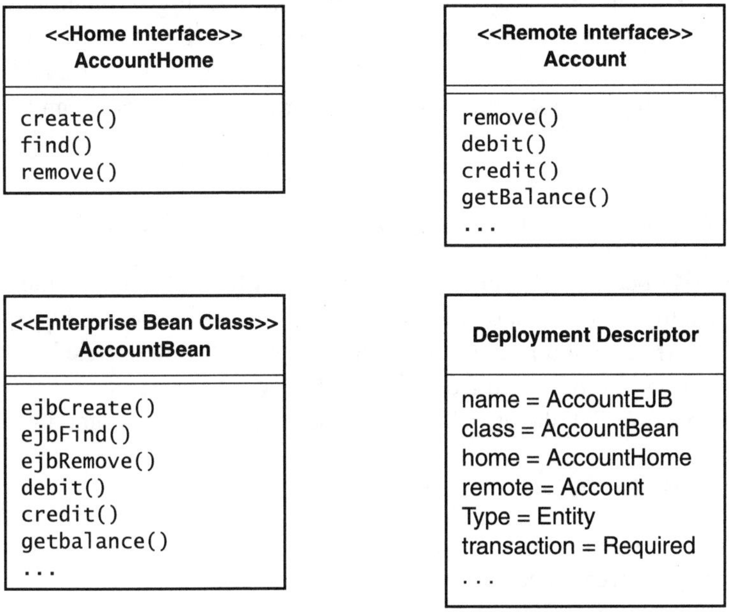

```
<<Home Interface>>
AccountHome

create()
find()
remove()
```

```
<<Remote Interface>>
Account

remove()
debit()
credit()
getBalance()
...
```

```
<<Enterprise Bean Class>>
AccountBean

ejbCreate()
ejbFind()
ejbRemove()
debit()
credit()
getbalance()
...
```

```
Deployment Descriptor

name = AccountEJB
class = AccountBean
home = AccountHome
remote = Account
Type = Entity
transaction = Required
...
```

Figure 2.3   Enterprise Bean Parts

The AccountBean class is the enterprise bean class. It defines the implementation of the life cycle methods defined in the home interface, and the implementation of the business methods defined in the remote interface. As noted previously, the bean developer follows a naming convention that ensures a match between the names of the methods of the home and remote interfaces, and the names of the methods of the enterprise bean class.

The deployment descriptor for the enterprise bean is an XML document. The deployment descriptor specifies the following.

- The enterprise bean name

- The names of the home and remote interfaces

- The name of the enterprise bean class

- The enterprise bean type

- Information that describes the services that the enterprise bean expects from its container, such as transactions

- The enterprise bean environment entries (the entries provide, for example, information about dependencies on other enterprise bean and resource managers)

Note that a single deployment descriptor can provide information about multiple enterprise beans. For enterprise beans that have been assembled into an application, the deployment descriptor also captures the application assembly information.

The following sections explain the enterprise bean structure and its parts in more detail.

2.3.1   Enterprise Bean Home Interface

The enterprise bean home interface controls the life cycle of the enterprise bean objects. It defines the methods that `create`, find, and `remove` enterprise bean objects. The `create` and find methods are defined in the enterprise bean class; the `remove` methods are inherited from the EJBHome interface.

Code Example 2.1 shows the code for the AccountHome home interface.

Code Example 2.1   AccountHome Interface

```
import java.rmi.RemoteException;
import javax.ejb.CreateException;
import javax.ejb.FinderException;
import java.util.Collection;
```

```
public interface AccountHome extends javax.ejb.EJBHome {
    // create methods
    Account create(String lastName, String firstName)
        throws RemoteException, CreateException, BadNameException;
    Account create(String lastName)
        throws RemoteException, CreateException;
    ...

    // find methods
    Account findByPrimaryKey(AccountKey primaryKey)
        throws RemoteException, FinderException;
    Collection findInActive(Date sinceWhen)
        throws RemoteException, FinderException, BadDateException;
    ...
}
```

The home interface may define multiple `create` and find methods. In the previous example, the AccountHome interface defines two `create` methods and two find methods. Although the bean developer must name all `create` methods "create," he can arbitrarily define the type and the number of arguments for the `create` methods. For example, one AccountHome `create` method takes two arguments—`lastName` and `firstName`. The other AccountHome `create` method takes only one argument—`lastName`. These arguments are all `String` types. Another developer could just as easily have defined a `create` method to take three arguments, with one argument a `String` type, another a `Date` type, and the third a `Double` type. Note that the home interface `create` methods all return the enterprise bean remote interface, which in our example is Account, and throw `javax.ejb.CreateException`.

The names of the find methods always begin with "find" followed by some descriptive word. The AccountHome interface defines two find methods—`findByPrimaryKey` and `findInActive`. Like the `create` methods, the bean developer arbitrarily defines the arguments for the find methods. The find methods return either the enterprise bean remote interface or a collection of such interfaces, and they throw `javax.ejb.FinderException`. For example, the `findInActive` method has one argument—`sinceWhen`—and it returns a `Collection` of Account remote interfaces. The `findByPrimaryKey` method has one argument—`primaryKey`—and it returns one Account remote interface.

Note that the bean developer may define the `create` and find methods to throw additional application-specific exceptions. In our example, one `create` method throws `BadNameException`, and the `findInActive` method throws `BadDateException`.

Keep in mind that not all enterprise beans have `create` and find methods. Session beans do not have find methods. Some entity beans may choose not to define a `create` method. See Chapter 6, Understanding Entity Beans for more information on these exceptional cases.

Notice, too, that the home interface is a valid remote interface for the Java RMI-IIOP. (RMI-IIOP is a version of RMI implemented to use the CORBA IIOP protocol. It provides interoperability with CORBA objects regardless of their implementation language if all remote interfaces are originally defined as RMI interfaces.) By valid for RMI-IIOP, we mean that the home interface methods throw the exception `java.rmi.RemoteException`, and that the arguments and return values for all home interface methods are legal types for RMI-IIOP.

Lastly, note that every enterprise bean home interface extends the `javax.ejb.EJBHome` interface. The EJBHome interface defines the methods supported by all enterprise bean home interfaces (Code Example 2.2).

Code Example 2.2   EJBHome Interface

```
import java.rmi.RemoteException;
public interface EJBHome extends java.rmi.Remote {
    void remove(Handle handle)
            throws RemoteException, RemoveException;
    void remove(Object primaryKey)
            throws RemoteException, RemoveException;
    EJBMetaData getEJBMetaData() throws RemoteException;
    HomeHandle getHomeHandle() throws RemoteException;
}
```

The EJBHome interface defines two `remove` methods. The first method removes an enterprise bean object identified by a handle. A handle is an object that provides a reference to an enterprise bean object and that can be stored in persistent storage. The second method removes an enterprise bean object identified by a primary key—this method pertains only to entity beans.

The method `getEJBMetaData` returns the metadata interface for the enterprise bean. Clients that use dynamic invocation (that is, clients written using a scripting language) use the EJBMetaData interface; its use is not discussed in this book. The `getHomeHandle` method is used to obtain a handle for the enterprise bean home object. See Use of Object Handles on page 117 in Chapter 4, Working with Session Beans, for more information on using session object handles.

2.3.2   Enterprise Bean Remote Interface

The enterprise bean remote interface defines the business methods that a client can invoke on the individual enterprise bean objects. Code Example 2.3 shows the Account remote interface.

Code Example 2.3   Account Interface

```
import java.rmi.RemoteException;
public interface Account extends javax.ejb.EJBObject {
    BigDecimal getBalance() throws RemoteException;
    void credit(BigDecimal amount) throws RemoteException;
    void debit(BigDecimal amount)
        throws RemoteException, InsufficientFundsException;
    ...
}
```

The bean developer defines the types of the method arguments, the return value type, and the exceptions thrown by the methods.

Like the home interface, the enterprise bean remote interface is a valid remote interface for RMI-IIOP. The bean developer must declare the remote interface methods to throw the exception java.rmi.RemoteException, along with the other exceptions that the methods throw. In addition, the arguments and return values for all remote interface methods must be legal types for RMI-IIOP.

Every enterprise bean remote interface extends the javax.ejb.EJBObject interface. This interface defines the methods supported by all enterprise bean remote interfaces. Code Example 2.4 shows the code for this interface.

Code Example 2.4   EJBObject Interface

```
import java.rmi.RemoteException;
public interface EJBObject extends java.rmi.Remote {
    public EJBHome getEJBHome() throws RemoteException;
    public Object getPrimaryKey() throws RemoteException;
    public void remove() throws RemoteException, RemoveException;
    public Handle getHandle() throws RemoteException;
    boolean isIdentical (EJBObject obj2) throws RemoteException;
}
```

The method getEJBHome allows the client to get the enterprise bean object's home interface. The getPrimaryKey method pertains only to entity bean remote interfaces. It enables a client to get the primary key of the entity object. The remove method deletes the enterprise bean object. The getHandle method returns a handle to the enterprise bean object, whereas the `isIdentical` method allows the client to determine whether two enterprise bean object references refer to the same enterprise bean object.

2.3.3   Enterprise Bean Class

The enterprise bean class provides both the implementation of the life cycle methods defined in the home interface and the implementation of the business methods defined in the remote interface. It also defines the implementation of the container callback methods defined in the `javax.ejb.SessionBean` and `javax.ejb.EntityBean` interfaces.

A client does not directly invoke methods on the enterprise bean class instances. The client invokes the methods of the home and remote interfaces. The implementation classes of these interfaces delegate to the enterprise bean class instances. Code Example 2.5 shows the AccountBean enterprise bean class.

Code Example 2.5 AccountBean Class

```
import java.rmi.RemoteException;
public class AccountBean implements javax.ejb.EntityBean {
    // life cycle methods from home interface
    public AccountKey ejbCreate(String lastName, String firstName)
        throws CreateException, BadNameException { ... };
    public AccountKey ejbCreate(String lastName)
        throws CreateException { ... }
    public void ejbPostCreate(String lastName, firstName)
        throws CreateException, BadNameException { ... };
    public void ejbPostCreate(String lastName)
        throws CreateException { ... }
    public AccountKey ejbFindByPrimaryKey(AccountKey primaryKey)
        throws FinderException { ... }
    public Collection ejbFindInActive(Date sinceWhen)
        throws FinderException, BadDateException { ... }

    // business methods from remote interface
    public BigDecimal getBalance() { ... }
    public void credit(BigDecimal amount) { ... }
    public void debit(BigDecimal amount)
        throws InsufficientFundsException { ... }
    ...
```

```
    // container callbacks from EntityBean interface
    public ejbRemove() throws RemoveException { ... }
    public void setEntityContext(EntityContext ec) { ... }
    public void unsetEntityContext(EntityContext ec) { ... }
    public void ejbActivate() { ... }
    public void ejbPassivate() { ... }
    public void ejbLoad() { ... }
    public void ejbStore() { ... }
}
```

The enterprise bean class begins by implementing the `ejbCreate`, `ejbPost-Create`, and `ejbFind` methods. These methods correspond to the `create` and find methods defined in the home interface. In the enterprise bean class, these method names are prefixed with "ejb." This naming convention prevents name collisions with the names of the business methods. Chapter 4, Working with Session Beans and Chapter 6, Understanding Entity Beans explain how the method arguments, return values, and exceptions of the `ejbCreate`, `ejbPostCreate`, and `ejbFind` methods correspond to the method arguments, return values, and exceptions for the `create` and find methods defined in the home interface.

Next, the enterprise bean class implements the business methods defined in the remote interface. The business methods implement the business rules for the business entity or process that the enterprise bean represents.

Lastly, the enterprise bean class implements certain container callback methods. An entity bean class implements the container callbacks defined in the `javax.ejb.EntityBean` interface. A session bean class implements the callbacks defined in the `javax.ejb.SessionBean` interface. The container invokes these callback methods as part of its life cycle management of an instance.

Note that the `javax.ejb.EntityBean` interface defines the `ejbRemove` method. The `ejbRemove` method corresponds to the `remove` methods defined in the enterprise bean home and remote interfaces.

Why do the parent interfaces define the signatures for the `remove` and `ejbRemove` methods, whereas the bean developer defines the `create`, `ejbCreate`, `ejbPostCreate`, find, and `ejbFind` methods? The reason for this asymmetry is that the signatures of the `remove` and `ejbRemove` methods are the same for all enterprise beans. However, the bean developer defines the signatures of the `create`, `ejbCreate`, `ejbPostCreate`, find, and `ejbFind` methods, and thus they can vary from one bean to another.

Note that the AccountBean class in our example does not implement, in the sense of the Java language, the Account interface. Although the EJB architecture allows the enterprise bean class to implement the enterprise bean's remote interface, it does not require the enterprise bean class to do this. If the enterprise bean class implements the remote interface, the bean developer must be careful not to pass `this` inadvertently as a method argument or result. Instead, the bean developer must call the `getEJBObject` method on the instance's `EntityContext` or `SessionContext` interface. The `getEJBObject` method returns an object reference to the associated enterprise bean object. (For more information, see Session Object Creation on page 95 in Chapter 4, Working with Session Beans.) This is illustrated in Code Example 2.6.

Code Example 2.6   Obtaining an Object Reference to an Associated Bean Object

```java
public class AccountBean implements javax.ejb.EntityBean, Account {
    ...
    public Account returnSelfWrong() {
        ...
        return this;  // THIS WOULD CAUSE A RUNTIME ERROR
    }

    public Account returnSelfCorrect() {
        ...
        return (Account)ctx.getEJBObject(); // CORRECT
    }
}
```

What could happen with the preceding code? If the AccountBean class implements the Account interface, as Code Example 2.6 illustrates, the programming error is detected at runtime, not at compile time. To put it another way, the application has a programming error that is only detected at runtime, not before.

If the AccountBean class does not implement the Account interface, the Java compiler detects the programming error when compiling the `returnSelfWrong` method. It is always better to catch errors at compile time rather than runtime. Therefore, it is recommended that the enterprise bean class not implement the remote interface.

The EJB architecture allows the enterprise bean class to implement the remote interface so that the EJB architecture can support higher level business object frameworks layered on top of itself. The use of such business object frameworks may lead to a situation in which the remote interface and enterprise bean class implement a common application-specific interface. Because of this, the EJB specification does not prohibit the enterprise bean to inherit the remote interface, or a superinterface of the remote interface.

2.3.4   Deployment Descriptor

The deployment descriptor is an XML document that contains the declarative information about one or more enterprise beans. The deployment descriptor ships with the enterprise beans in an ejb-jar file. An ejb-jar file is a Java archive (JAR) file that contains enterprise beans with their deployment descriptor.

The main role of the deployment descriptor is to define declaratively certain bean behavior rather than defining the behavior programmatically in the bean class. This allows the application assembler or deployer to change how the enterprise bean works, such as its transaction demarcation behavior or its database schema, without modifying the bean's code. The bean developer typically uses application development tools to produce the deployment descriptor. As noted previously, the deployment descriptor describes the following.

- The enterprise bean parts; it names the home and remote interfaces, and the enterprise bean class

- The services that the enterprise bean expects from its container; for example, it describes the transaction demarcation instructions for the enterprise bean methods

- The dependencies that the enterprise bean has on other enterprise beans and resource managers

The deployment descriptor is used by the application assembler and deployer. When an application assembler assembles multiple enterprise beans into an application, he uses tools to read the deployment descriptors of multiple enterprise beans. Using these tools, the application assembler adds information describing how to assemble the enterprise beans in an application. The application assembler may also describe in the deployment descriptor additional information intended for the deployer, such as the intended security model for the application.

Finally, the deployment tools process the deployment descriptor. For example, the deployment tools tell the deployer about the dependencies on other enterprise beans and resource managers. This serves as a prompt to the deployer to resolve the dependencies. Code Example 2.7 is a fragment of a deployment descriptor.

Code Example 2.7   Deployment Descriptor Fragment

```
...
<entity-bean>
    <ejb-name>AccountEJB</ejb-name>
    <home>com.wombat.AccountHome</home>
    <remote>com.wombat.Account</remote>
```

```
        <ejb-class>com.wombat.AccountBean</ejb-class>
        <persistence-type>Bean</persistence-type>
        <prim-key-class>com.wombat.AccountKey</prim-key-class>
        ...
    </entity-bean>
    ...
    <container-transaction>
        <method>
            <ejb-name>AccountEJB</ejb-name>
            <method-name>*</method-name>
        </method>
        <trans-attribute>Required</trans-attribute>
    </container-transaction>
    ...
```

The previous example shows only a portion of a typical deployment descriptor. It is not meant to be a complete list of all deployment descriptor elements. Rather, it is intended to give you an idea of the information contained in the descriptor. For example, the `ejb-name` element specifies the name that the bean developer gives to the enterprise bean. The `home` and `remote` elements specify the fully qualified names of the enterprise bean home and remote interfaces. The `ejb-class` element specifies the fully qualified name of the enterprise bean class. The `persistence-type` element specifies that the enterprise bean uses bean-managed persistence. The `prim-key-class` element specifies the Java class of the entity bean's primary key. (See Chapter 6, Understanding Entity Beans for more information on persistence management and entity bean primary keys.) The `container-transaction` element specifies that the container must invoke the enterprise bean methods in a transaction context.

The deployment descriptor is an XML file. It is usually produced by application development tools, although one could create a deployment descriptor by hand using a text editor. Note that the deployment descriptor is intended to be processed by application assembly and deployment tools, not by humans.

2.4   Container Tools and Services

Enterprise beans implement the business logic of an application. However, by themselves they are not a complete operational application. You must first deploy an enterprise bean in a container so that it becomes a part of a runnable application.

Deployment tools, provided by the container vendor (note that the commercial term for an EJB container is an *Application Server*), read the deployment descriptor for the enterprise beans and generate additional classes called *container artifacts*. The complete application consists of the enterprise beans, the generated container artifacts, and the container.

Recall that the container includes the implementation of the system-level services that are required by the application. The container artifacts enable the container to inject these system-level services into the application. In other words, the container uses the generated artifacts to interpose on the client calls to the enterprise beans so that the container can inject its services into the application.

2.4.1   Container Artifacts

Container artifacts are the additional classes generated by container tools at deployment. These classes are necessary to "bind" the enterprise beans with the container runtime. At a minimum, the container tools generate the classes that implement the enterprise bean home and remote interfaces. Because the goal of the EJB architecture is to allow clients to invoke the enterprise bean via the home and remote interfaces over the network, the objects that implement the enterprise bean remote and home interfaces cannot be simple Java objects. The home and remote objects are distributed objects that implement the communication between a remote client and the enterprise bean deployed in the container. The objects also communicate internally with the container at runtime to inject container services into the client method invocation path. Although the services provided by the container must meet the requirements of the EJB specification, container vendors still have a great deal of latitude in how they implement these services.

The current EJB specification does not prescribe the distributed object protocol used between the clients and the container. However, many container implementations, including the one in the J2EE reference implementation, use RMI-IIOP. When the container is based on RMI-IIOP, the container tools typically generate two RMI-IIOP object types (Figure 2.4). Each RMI-IIOP object type consists of multiple Java classes.

AccountRMI and AccountHomeRMI are RMI-IIOP object types. Their instances are distributed CORBA objects that implement the communication between the clients and the enterprise beans in the container. The AccountHomeRMI object type provides the implementation of the enterprise bean home interface, AccountHome. The AccountRMI object type provides the implementation of the enterprise bean remote interface, Account.

The instances of the AccountRMI object type are referred to as *enterprise bean objects*. The instances of the AccountHomeRMI object type are referred to as *enterprise bean home objects*. Most container implementations create only one instance of the enterprise bean home object type. This one instance is shared among all clients.

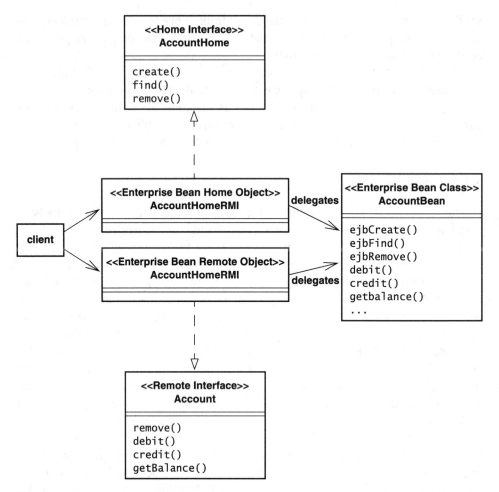

Figure 2.4   Container Artifacts

The client communicates with the enterprise bean objects—AccountRMI—and the enterprise bean home object—AccountHomeRMI. The client never communicates directly with the instances of the enterprise bean class. Because the container vendor defines the implementation of the AccountRMI and Account-HomeRMI objects, these objects have the capability to inject or add the container services when delegating the client-invoked methods to the enterprise bean instances.

Figure 2.5 illustrates the instances of the RMI-IIOP objects that exist at runtime in our AccountEJB example.

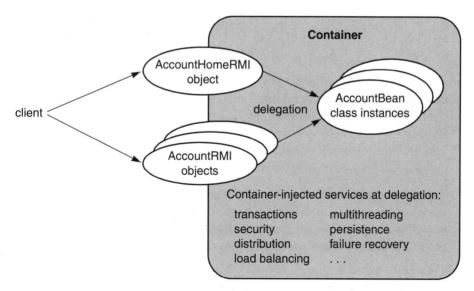

Figure 2.5   RMI-IIOP Objects at Runtime

2.4.2   Container Runtime Services

As we discussed in Container Artifacts, the EJB architecture uses a method-call interposition protocol to invoke the methods of the enterprise bean. Rather than invoking the methods of the enterprise bean directly, the client invokes them indirectly via the enterprise bean remote and home objects generated by the container tools. This method-call interposition allows the container to inject its services transparently to the enterprise bean and client application code. The deployer specifies the services that the container adds to a method call. The deployer bases this specification on the information in the enterprise bean's deployment descriptor.

The container provides the following services to enterprise beans deployed in the container: distributed object protocol, thread management and synchronization, process management, transactions, security, state management, resource pooling, data access, system administration support, failure recovery, high availability, and clustering.

- **Distributed object protocol**—The container implements the distributed object protocol used for communication between the enterprise beans and their clients. For example, if the container uses RMI-IIOP for the communication with clients, the container includes an ORB and RMI-IIOP runtime library. The container tools automatically generate the RMI-IIOP stubs and skeletons for the enterprise beans' home and remote interfaces at deployment. This service allows the bean developer to write only local Java code. The developer does not have to implement distributed programming.

- **Thread management and synchronization**—The container starts and stops threads as needed to serve multiple client requests. The container synchronizes the threads to avoid concurrent method invocations of an enterprise bean instance. This relieves the bean developer from having to implement complex multithreaded programming. Instead, the bean developer codes the business methods as if the enterprise bean instances were used only by one user.

- **Process management**—The container may use as many operating system processes as is optimal on the target server machine, and/or as set by the system administrator. Because the container handles system process usage, the bean developer does not have to learn how to manage operating system processes.

- **Transactions**—The container manages transactions according to the information in the deployment descriptor. Based on the deployment descriptor instructions, the container may

  - Wrap a method invocation in a transaction

  - Import a transaction from the client

  - Run the method without a transaction

  If a method executes in a transaction, the container propagates the transaction to resource managers and to other enterprise beans called by the enterprise bean.

  The container also performs the transaction commit protocol. Having the container handle transactions means the bean developer does not have to implement the complex management of transactions in a distributed system.

- **Security**—The container performs security checks before permitting a client to access an enterprise bean business method. The container checks whether a client is authorized to invoke a business method before it delegates a client call. This authorization service provided by the container means that security policies do not have to be hard-coded into the enterprise beans. The deployer and system administrator can set security policies to meet the needs of the enterprise using administration and deployment tools.

- **State management**—The container performs state management and optimizes resource usage. The container can deactivate an enterprise bean object when it needs to free resources. Later, the container activates the object when the object is invoked by a client. State management by the container means that the container can achieve scalability to a high number of users with minimal burden on the bean developer.

- **Resource pooling**—The container can efficiently reuse resources such as database connections to achieve better performance. As a result, the bean developer does not have to develop complex pooling logic as part of the application code.

- **Data access**—The container generates the data access logic for entity beans with container-managed persistence. This not only makes the development of the bean easier, but it also makes it possible to adapt an enterprise bean at deployment time to work with existing customer databases.

- **System administration support**—The container provides system administration tools to manage deployed applications. These tools enable the management of enterprise bean applications at runtime. This also relieves the bean developer from having to develop the administration support as part of the application. For example, the container may allow the system administrator to classify applications by priority and to set limits on the resources used by low-priority applications.

- **Failure recovery**—The container can provide automatic restart of a failed transaction or application. This means that the bean developer does not code failure recovery or restart logic into the application.

- **High availability**—Containers may provide sophisticated high-availability strategies to mask various server errors from the clients. It is important to note that the support for high availability is transparent to the bean developer. Thus, most well formed EJB applications can be made highly available simply by deploying them in a container that implements the support for high availability.

- **Clustering**—A high-end container may be distributed across multiple nodes of a clustered server. Clustering is transparent to the bean developer. This transparency enables all EJB applications to run on a clustered system.

Table 2.2 provides a summary of the services that the container provides to the enterprise beans at runtime.

Table 2.2   Container Runtime Services

Service	Description	Benefit
Distributed object protocol	The container implements the distributed object protocol used for communication between the enterprise beans and their clients.	The bean developer writes only local Java code and does not have to implement distributed programming.
Thread management and synchronization	The container starts and stops threads as they are needed to serve multiple client requests. The container synchronizes the threads to avoid concurrent method invocations of an enterprise bean instance.	The bean developer does not have to implement the complexity of multithreaded programs. The bean developer codes the business methods as if the enterprise bean was used by only one user.
Process management	The container may use as many operating system processes as is optimal on the target server machine and/or as set by the system administrator.	The bean developer does not have to learn how to manage operating system processes.
Transactions	Based on the information in the deployment descriptor, the container may wrap a method invocation in a transaction, import a transaction from the client, and propagate a transaction into resource managers and other enterprise beans used by the enterprise bean. The container also performs the transaction commit protocol.	The bean developer does not have to implement complex management of transactions in a distributed system.
Security	The container checks whether the client is authorized to invoke a business method before it delegates a client call.	Security policies do not have to be hard-coded into the enterprise beans. They can be set by the deployer and system administrator to meet the needs of the enterprise.

Table 2.2   Container Runtime Services *(Continued)*

Service	Description	Benefit
State management	The container can deactivate an enterprise bean object when it needs to free resources. Later, the container activates the object when the object is invoked by a client.	The container can achieve scalability to a high number of users with minimal effort by the bean developer.
Resource pooling	The container can efficiently reuse resources such database connections to achieve better performance.	The bean developer is not burdened with developing any complex pooling logic.
Data access	For entity beans with container-managed persistence, the container generates the data access logic.	An enterprise bean can be adapted at deployment to work with existing customer's databases.
System administration support	The container provides administration tools to manage deployed applications.	Enterprise bean applications are manageable at runtime. The bean developer does not have to develop the administration support as part of the application.
Failure recovery	The container can provide automatic restart of a failed transaction or application.	The bean developer does not code any failure recovery or restart logic into the application.
High availability	Containers may provide sophisticated high-availability strategies to mask various server errors to the client.	Because the support for high availability is transparent to the bean developer, any EJB application can be made highly available by deploying it in a container that supports high availability.
Clustering	A high-end container may be distributed across multiple nodes of a clustered server.	Because clustering is transparent to the bean developer, all EJB applications are enabled to run on a clustered system.

2.5 Conclusion

This chapter presented a detailed discussion of EJB applications and enterprise bean types. It defined business entities and processes, and showed how architects could implement business rules. It showed how the different enterprise bean types correlate with the business entities and business processes, and how enterprise beans implement the business logic of an application.

Enterprise beans also have a defined structure. This chapter described the three key parts that comprise an enterprise bean: the enterprise bean class, the client-view API, and the deployment descriptor. Using simple code examples, it was easy to understand the home and remote interfaces of the client-view API and a typical enterprise bean implementation class. Similarly, an example was used to demonstrate the key parts of the deployment descriptor, particularly the information that the deployment descriptor contains about each enterprise bean.

Beneath these enterprise beans and applications is the container. It is the container's services and tools that complete the operational environment. The chapter explained the runtime services provided by the container and summarized the benefits of these services.

Chapter 4, Working with Session Beans, brings this theoretical discussion to life using a real-world enterprise application example.

CHAPTER 3

Enterprise JavaBeans Roles

THE EJB architecture simplifies the development of complex business applications. To help understand how it accomplishes this simplification, the architecture views the development process in terms of the tasks that need to be performed. It divides the EJB application development and deployment processes into distinct roles, and gives each role a specific set of tasks. These roles address application development, infrastructure services, application assembly and integration, and deployment and administration issues.

We have grouped these tasks by functionality, identifying six major functional areas. Each functional area is responsible for a separate portion of the application development and deployment processes. To simplify things further, we can think of each functional area as a role. It is possible for an individual to perform one or more roles within an enterprise or EJB application development environment. However, it is highly unlikely that one person would perform all six roles. More often, one or more individuals together may be responsible for just one role.

This chapter describes the roles involved in the EJB application development and deployment processes. Given that there are six functional areas, there are six major roles defined by the EJB architecture.

- Bean developer

- Application assembler

- Deployer

- System administrator

- EJB server provider

- EJB container provider

In addition to the six major roles, this chapter also describes the tool vendor roles that frequently come into play in an EJB enterprise environment.

3.1 EJB Roles

The EJB architecture defines six distinct roles in the application development and deployment life cycle. A role may be fulfilled by a single individual or by an organization. The opposite may also occur, depending on the environment. It's possible that a single party may perform several EJB roles. For example, the EJB container provider and the EJB server provider are typically the same vendor. Or one programmer may perform the two EJB roles of enterprise bean developer and application assembler.

Usually, at least several distinct parties are responsible for these six roles, and these roles—or the functional areas that they represent—are interdependent. Because of this interdependency, the EJB architecture specifies a contract or set of requirements for each role. These requirements ensure that the product of one EJB role is compatible with the product of the other EJB roles.

How do typical enterprise software people fit in with the EJB architecture roles? That is, how do "traditional" information systems individuals and ISVs fit into EJB roles? In the EJB environment, a "traditional" application programmer becomes an enterprise bean developer and, possibly, an application assembler. A bean developer and an application assembler both are responsible for focusing on the business problem of their enterprise environment and for developing the business logic solutions. The EJB tasks defined for a bean developer and an assembler allow her to focus on the business problem and business logic.

The EJB container and server providers focus on the development of a scalable, secure, and manageable infrastructure used for the deployment of the applications created by the bean developers and application assemblers. In this book, the term *EJB container* often refers collectively to both the EJB container and the EJB server. The system administrator takes the container product from the EJB container provider and installs it in the enterprise's operational environment.

The deployer defines and sets the deployment policies for individual enterprise applications. He also integrates the applications with the existing operational environment.

Figure 3.1 illustrates how the six roles defined by the EJB architecture may interact when developing and deploying an EJB application in a typical enterprise environment. The following sections provide more information about these six EJB roles.

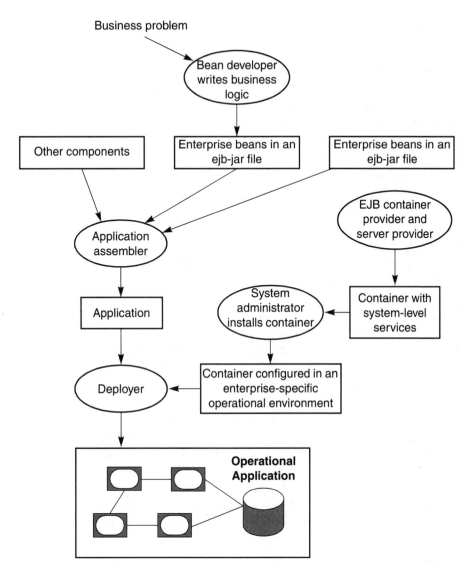

Figure 3.1   EJB Roles in an Enterprise Environment

3.1.1   Bean Developer

The bean developer is the programmer who writes and produces enterprise beans. The bean developer may be any of the following.

- Work for an ISV that produces enterprise beans components or applications that are comprised of enterprise beans
- Work within a corporate enterprise environment
- Be an application integrator

The bean developer starts with a perceived or existing business problem for which a solution is required. For example, an ISV may perceive a need for a generic application to view and modify employee benefits, or an enterprise may want to implement its own application for managing benefits. It is the bean developer who develops reusable enterprise beans that implement business processes or business entities and that provide a solution to the business problem.

Typically, a bean developer is an expert in the application domain. For example, the bean developer may be an expert in the financial or manufacturing industries. The bean developer implements the business processes and entities. Essentially, the bean developer is responsible for writing the enterprise beans that implement the business processes and entities. The business processes and entities are implemented in the Java language in the form of the enterprise bean classes.

The bean developer also defines the bean's remote and home interfaces and the bean's deployment descriptor. The deployment descriptor includes structural information about the enterprise bean, such as the name of the enterprise bean class. The deployment descriptor also declares all the enterprise bean's external dependencies, which are the names and types of the resource managers used by the enterprise bean. The bean developer outputs an ejb-jar file that contains one or more enterprise beans. An ejb-jar file is a JAR file that contains enterprise beans with their deployment descriptor.

Because the EJB container manages system-level tasks, the bean developer need not be concerned about the distribution, transaction, security, and other non-business-specific aspects of the application. This means that the bean developer is neither required to be an expert at system-level programming nor to program into the enterprise bean services such as transactions, concurrency, security, and remote distribution, among other system services. The bean developer relies on the EJB container to handle or provide these services.

A bean developer of multiple enterprise beans often performs the role of the application assembler by specifying how the enterprise beans are assembled; that is, how they should work together.

3.1.2 Application Assembler

The application assembler combines enterprise beans into larger, deployable application units. In a sense, the application assembler composes the application—the assembler identifies an application's required pieces and specifies how they fit together so that the application runs successfully.

Applications typically consist of numerous pieces and components. Often, an application requires multiple enterprise beans to carry out its business logic. In our example, one enterprise bean handles the logic for accessing employee data and another enterprise bean focuses on the logic for benefits information. The application often requires other nonenterprise bean pieces, in addition to the enterprise beans components. The application assembler must identify these pieces too, and combine them with the enterprise beans into the application.

Like the bean developer, the application assembler is also an application domain expert. However, the application assembler focuses on the enterprise bean's deployment descriptor and the enterprise bean's client-view contract. Although the application assembler must be familiar with the functionality provided by the remote and home interfaces of the enterprise beans, an intimate knowledge of the implementation of the enterprise beans is not needed.

The application assembler takes as input one or more ejb-jar files produced by the bean developer or developers. The application assembler adds the assembly instructions and outputs one or more ejb-jar files that contain the enterprise beans along with their application assembly instructions. For example, the application assembler may take an ejb-jar file that contains the session bean TransferEJB, and another ejb-jar file that contains the entity bean AccountEJB, and may produce a new ejb-jar file that contains both enterprise beans. The deployment descriptor of the new ejb-jar file includes the linkage between the TransferEJB bean and the AccountEJB bean.

When composing an application, the application assembler can also combine enterprise beans with other types of application components (such as Web applications). For more information on using other types of application components, refer to the J2EE publications listed in the Preface.

If you are familiar with the EJB specification, you may have noted that it describes the case in which the application assembly step occurs *before* the deployment of the enterprise beans. However, the application assembler can assemble the application *after* the deployment of all the enterprise beans or the deployment of some of the beans. The EJB architecture does not preclude the case of performing application assembly after the deployment of all or some of the enterprise beans.

3.1.3   Deployer

The deployer's job is to deploy enterprise beans in a specific operational environment that includes a specific EJB server and container. The deployer receives enterprise beans in one or more ejb-jar files produced by a bean developer or application assembler. The deployer, with his expert knowledge of the specific EJB container and operational environment, then customizes these beans for the target operational environment. Finally, he deploys these customized enterprise beans—or an entire assembled application that includes enterprise beans—in a specific EJB container, or in multiple containers on the enterprise network.

As part of the deployment process, the deployer must resolve all the external dependencies declared by the bean developer. For example, the deployer must ensure that all resource manager connection factories are present in the operational environment and must bind them to the resource manager connection factory references declared in the deployment descriptor. (A resource manager connection factory is an object that produces connections. For example, a JDBC DataSource object is a factory of JDBC Connection objects.) The deployer must also follow the application assembly instructions defined by the application assembler.

The deployer sets up the security environment for an application by mapping the security roles defined by the application assembler to the actual user groups and accounts that exist in the operational environment in which the enterprise beans are deployed.

To perform his deployment tasks, the deployer uses tools provided by the EJB container provider. The deployment process typically has two stages.

1. The deployer first generates the additional artifacts that enable the container to manage the enterprise beans at runtime. These artifacts are container specific.

2. The deployer performs the actual installation of the enterprise beans and the additional artifacts into the EJB container.

A qualified deployer may take on some tasks of the roles of the application assembler or bean developer by customizing the enterprise beans when deploying them. For example, a deployer may "subclass" the enterprise bean class and insert additional business rules into the subclass.

3.1.4   System Administrator

The system administrator configures and administers the enterprise computing and networking infrastructure. This infrastructure includes the EJB server and container.

The system administrator is also responsible for administering security at the enterprise. For example, the system administrator adds new user accounts, groups users into user groups, and manages the various mappings of security information necessary when the enterprise uses multiple systems. In large organizations, the system administrator may have multiple security-based roles. For example, there could be a security officer, separate from the system administrator, who oversees the mapping of users to roles.

The system administrator is also concerned with deployed applications. The administrator oversees the well-being of the deployed enterprise bean applications at runtime. This means that the administrator monitors the running application and takes appropriate actions in the event that the application behaves abnormally.

The EJB architecture does not define the requirements for system management and administration. The system administrator typically uses runtime monitoring and enterprise management tools provided by the EJB server and container providers to accomplish these tasks.

3.1.5   EJB Container Provider

The EJB container provider (container provider for short) provides

- The deployment tools necessary for the deployment of enterprise beans

- The runtime support for instances of the deployed enterprise beans

From the perspective of the enterprise beans, the container is a part of the target operational environment. The container runtime library provides the deployed enterprise beans with transaction and security management, network distribution of clients, scalable management of resources such as connections and threads, and other services generally required as part of a manageable server platform.

The container provider implements an EJB container that meets the functionality requirements set forth by the EJB specification. The container provider vendor may also implement the EJB server. The EJB specification does not dictate the interface between the server and the container, nor does it define how the provider is to devise the required functionality. As a result, the container provider vendor is free to split the implementation of the required functionality between the EJB container and server as needed. Typically, container providers market the EJB container and EJB server in a single product under the name application server.

For the most part, a container provider's expertise is system-level programming. The container provider focuses on the development of a scalable, secure, transaction-enabled container that is integrated with an EJB server. The container provider insulates the enterprise bean from the specifics of an underlying EJB server by providing the simple, standard EJB API between the enterprise bean and the container.

In addition to an API, the container provider provides various tools for system administration. These tools permit a system administrator to monitor and manage the container and its enterprise beans, particularly during runtime. There also may be tools for version control of installed enterprise bean components. For example, the container provider may provide tools to allow an administrator to upgrade enterprise bean classes without invalidating existing clients or losing the state of the existing enterprise bean objects.

The container provider also manages the persistence issues for its entity beans that use container-managed persistence. The container provider's tools generate code that moves data between the enterprise bean's container-managed fields and a database or an existing application. This code generation typically takes place at deployment time.

3.1.6   EJB Server Provider

The EJB server provider is a specialist in the area of distributed transaction management, distributed objects, and other lower level system-level services. A typical EJB server provider is an operating system vendor, middleware vendor, or database vendor.

The current EJB architecture assumes that the EJB server provider and the EJB container provider roles are the same vendor. Therefore, it does not define any interface requirements for the EJB server provider. The EJB specification draws the separation between the EJB container and the EJB server to illustrate that an EJB container can be developed on top of a preexisting transaction processing system (the latter would be referred to as the EJB server).

3.2   Tools

Tools are very important to the EJB application environment. The container provider or other third-party vendors may provide tools to support the EJB application development, assembly, integration, and deployment tasks. As in any environment, tools simplify everyone's job. The diversity of the EJB environment leaves room for a variety of tools, such as interactive development environment (IDE) tools, data access tools, Unified Modeling Language (UML) tools, Web page authoring tools, non-EJB application integration tools, deployment tools, and container and server management tools.

- **IDE tools**—An IDE tool supports the EJB architecture and simplifies enterprise bean development. An EJB-aware IDE frees the bean developer from learning the low-level details of the EJB specification. For example, a good IDE can generate template code for the enterprise bean class and its associated home and remote interfaces. Plus, an IDE can simplify the debugging process. An IDE can also provide an easy-to-use environment for application assembly.

- **Data access tools**—Most enterprise beans need to access data in databases. Good data access tools can greatly simplify the bean developer's efforts in programming database access. The most important are data access tools that implement the data access for entity bean container-managed persistence (see Container-Managed Persistence on page 168).

- **UML tools**—A UML modeling tool facilitates the high-level design of enterprise applications. It provides a graphical view of the business entities and processes, and their interactions. An EJB-aware modeling tool allows architects and bean developers to specify the mapping of a design model to a set of enterprise beans that implement the model, and it may generate the skeleton code for the enterprise beans.

- **Web page authoring tools**—Just about all recent enterprise applications have a Web component, which means that they display Web pages to their users. Web pages can be complex to design and develop, and these tools simplify this task. EJB-aware Web page authoring allows the components implementing the Web pages to invoke enterprise beans.

- **Non-EJB application integration tools**—Many enterprise bean applications will be added to environments that include preexisting enterprise information systems, such as ERP systems, mainframe applications, and so forth. It is essential that enterprises be able to integrate their existing systems with these newly developed enterprise bean applications. Although such integration can be a major task, it can be made easier with tools that address specific legacy systems. The next release of the J2EE platform will include the Connector specification, which simplifies and standardizes the task of integrating EJB and non-EJB applications.

- **Deployment tools**—The container vendors typically bundle deployment tools with their EJB products. Vendors other than the container provider may provide deployment tools. If so, then these tools are typically specific for a particular container. Deployment tools help with such tasks as processing the information in the XML deployment descriptor file and resolving the application's dependencies on the operational environment.

- **Container and server management tools**—These tools monitor the state of the EJB container within the system. They also monitor the state of deployed beans.

3.3 Conclusion

By now, you should have a good understanding of the major functional areas of the EJB architecture. This chapter introduced and explained the six major functional areas encompassed by the EJB architecture. To help understand these functional areas, we described them in terms of roles. These roles correlate with real-life enterprise positions—jobs that must be carried out to develop and implement an enterprise application. Subsequent chapters view the various parts of the EJB architecture from the perspective of these roles.

Keep the different roles in mind as you read these chapters. The chapters illustrating the session bean (Chapter 4) and entity bean (Chapter 7) example applications, in particular, discuss the different parts of these applications in terms of the roles that implement or are responsible for those parts. In some cases, these views may differ greatly from one another because each role sees different facets of an enterprise application according to its own functional responsibilities.

CHAPTER 4

Working with Session Beans

THIS chapter describes the typical programming style for applications using session beans. It focuses on the essential information necessary to use session beans in Web-based enterprise applications. The chapter describes a session bean from two points of view: the session bean developer who implements a session bean and the client application programmer who uses the session bean.

From the bean developer's point of view, there are sections that discuss how the developer should implement the session bean methods, including the business methods, `create` methods, and the `remove` method. These sections also describe how the bean developer defines the home and remote interfaces for a session bean.

From the client programmer's point of view, the chapter illustrates how the client creates and uses a session object. In particular, it shows how to use the session bean's home interface to create a session object, and how to use the remote interface to invoke business methods on the session object. (Session objects are explained later in Container Artifacts on page 138.)

The example application illustrated in this chapter uses only session beans. For simplicity, we assume that a single organization developed the application, and thus avoid dealing with the integration of application parts produced by multiple vendors. Chapter 7, Entity Bean Application Example, extends the example application to incorporate entity beans. It also illustrates how to use enterprise beans to integrate applications built by multiple organizations.

4.1   When to Use Session Beans

A session bean is a particular type of enterprise bean used to implement stateful communication between a client and a server. (Note that stateless session beans do not implement stateful communication between a client and a server. Refer to Section 4.2.1 for a discussion of the differences between stateless and stateful session beans.) A session object lasts for the duration of the client's session. This means that a session is defined as the time between the creation of the session bean and its removal. During that time, the session object stores the state information, or conversational state, for the client that creates and uses the session bean.

A session bean typically implements a business process that is performed from start to end by a single actor in a single session—the scope of which is referred to as a *conversation*. (For an in-depth discussion of conversational state, refer to Understanding Conversational State on page 58.) For example, session beans are suitable in the following two situations.

1. To implement the session logic of Web applications. One session bean or multiple session beans can usually implement the business process that drives the conversation with a user. For example, a session bean can implement the business process to enter a customer's shipping and billing information.

2. To implement the session logic of traditional (non-Web-based) three-tier applications. For example, a session bean can implement the business process performed by a teller at a bank when entering multiple checks on behalf of a customer.

These two cases are discussed in more detail in the following sections.

4.1.1   Using Session Beans in Web Applications

A session bean is well suited for the implementation of a business process that drives the conversation between a Web application and a user accessing the application through a browser. Figure 4.1 illustrates the segments of a Web application and shows the session bean's position within the business logic segment.

The user's browser exchanges information with the Web application in the HTML format using the HyperText Transfer Protocol (HTTP). The Web applica-

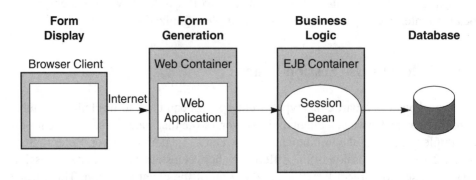

Figure 4.1   Session Beans in a Web Application

tion, which is a collection of JSP and servlets deployed in the Web container, processes the HTTP requests. The Web application is responsible for processing the requests sent by the user's browser and for generating the HTML pages that are sent back to the browser in reply. To accomplish this, the Web application invokes one or more session beans. These session beans process the data sent by the user and generate the data that is formatted (usually by the JSP or servlet) into the HTML page sent as the reply.

The Web application architecture (that is, the servlet and JSP specifications) define the concept of an HTTP session. An HTTP session spans multiple HTTP requests from the user; the Web application controls the start and end of an HTTP session. The Web container supports the HTTP session concept to allow the Web application to retain session-specific state across multiple requests from the same user.

Although it is possible to embed the implementation of a business process directly into the Web application, it is preferable to encapsulate the business process into a session bean. The encapsulation of the business process makes it possible to reuse the business process with a different presentation interface, such as a Palm Pilot™ or touch-tone phone interface. See Business Entities and Processes, and Enterprise Bean Types on page 18 in Chapter 2, Enterprise JavaBeans Architecture Overview, for more information about business processes.

4.1.2   Using Session Beans in Traditional Three-Tier Applications

The traditional three-tier application implements the presentation logic of the application as a Java client application that runs directly on the user's PC. The client application implements the GUI for the business process. Driven by the user's input, the client application interacts over the corporate network with the session bean that implements the business processes. Figure 4.2 illustrates how session beans fit within a three-tier application.

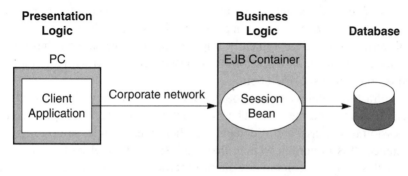

Figure 4.2   Session Beans in a Traditional Three-Tier Application

Session beans simplify the design and implementation of the three-tier application by shifting most of the complexities resulting from the distributed application design to the EJB container. Session beans often enable an existing two-tier application to be easily converted to a three-tier architecture. The session bean accomplishes this by allowing the designer to separate the code that implements the business process from the code that implements the GUI. The application designer packages the code that implements the business process as a session bean. The client application implementing the presentation logic can be implemented, for example, as a Swing application. (A Swing application uses the GUI components provided by J2SE.)

The remainder of this chapter illustrates how a session bean implements the business process of a Web application.

4.2   Understanding the State of a Session Object

Before we delve into the details of the example application, it is important to understand the state of a session object. The following sections explain how a session bean maintains its state. In particular, they explain the differences between stateful and stateless session beans. One section also describes the conversational state of a stateful session bean.

4.2.1   Stateful versus Stateless Session Beans

You can design a session bean to be either *stateful* or *stateless*. An instance of a stateful session bean class is associated with one client. The instance retains state on behalf of the client across multiple method invocations.

There is a one-to-one correspondence between session objects and the (stateful) instances of the session bean class. The EJB container always delegates the method invocations from a given client to the same stateful session bean instance. The instance variables of the stateful session bean class provide a convenient mechanism for the application developer to retain client-specific state on the server.

A stateful session bean typically implements a conversational business process. A stateful instance of a session bean class is associated with an object identity and is bound to a specific client.

In contrast, a stateless session object does not retain any client-specific state between client-invoked methods. The EJB container maintains a pool of instances of the session bean class, and it delegates a client method invocation to any available instance. It is important to note that the instance variables of a stateless session bean class may not contain any client-specific state when a method invocation completes. This is because the EJB container may reuse the instance of the stateless session bean class to service method invocations from a different client.

A stateless session bean typically implements a procedural service on top of a database or legacy application. The service is implemented as a collection of procedures that are bundled into a stateless session bean class. An instance of a stateless session bean class is not associated with any object identity and can be used by any client.

Our example (which we present in detail later in this chapter) uses a session bean, called EnrollmentEJB, to implement a conversational business process. It is implemented as a stateful session bean. The same example uses a different session bean, called PayrollEJB, to implement a procedural service on top of a database called PayrollDatabase. PayrollEJB is implemented as a stateless session bean.

Figures 4.3 and 4.4 illustrate the differences between a stateful and a stateless session bean. In Figure 4.3, the session objects obj1, obj2, and obj3 are distributed objects. Their object type, the EnrollmentRMI type, implements the Enrollment remote interface. The instances inst1, inst2, and inst3 are instances of the EnrollmentBean (stateful) session bean class. Each session object always delegates to the same instance of the EnrollmentBean bean class.

In Figure 4.4, by contrast, the session object obj is a distributed object. Its object type, the PayrollRMI type, implements the Payroll remote interface. The instances inst1 and inst2 are instances of the Payroll (stateless) session bean class, and the container keeps them in a pool. The object obj delegates to any available instance of the PayrollBean class. This is in contrast to the stateful session bean object in the previous example (Figure 4.3), which always delegates to the same instance.

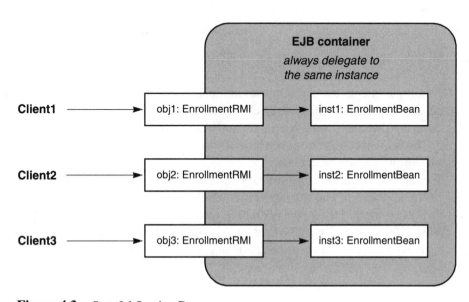

Figure 4.3   Stateful Session Bean

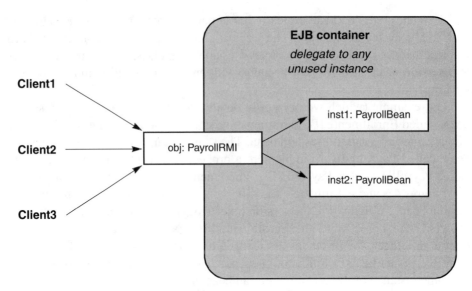

Figure 4.4   Stateless Session Bean

4.2.2   Understanding Conversational State

As noted earlier, a stateful session bean instance keeps the server-side state on behalf of a single client. The instance retains the state across multiple client-invoked methods. Keep in mind that the state consists of

- The instance variables defined in the session bean class

- All the objects reachable from the instance variables

If multiple clients use the same session bean, each client creates and uses its own session object. The session objects do *not* share state across multiple clients, thus ensuring that each client has its own private application-specific state on the server. The bean developer does not have to synchronize the access to the instance variables of the session bean class.

Because the session bean typically implements a conversation between the user of the application and the application itself, the state retained in the session object is often referred to as *conversational state*.

What information is usually kept in the conversational state? The conversational state typically consists of the following two types of information.

1. **Data read from databases**—The session object reads client-specific data from the database at the beginning of the business process (or the data is read for it by another session or entity object). The session object caches this data in its instance variables for the duration of the business process to avoid multiple database operations. Two examples of client-specific data in our sample application are the employee information and the current employee benefits information. The Enrollment bean reads the employee information (first name, last name, department, and so forth) and the current benefits information from the respective databases at the beginning of the business process, and caches both sets of information for the duration of the user conversation. The Enrollment bean uses the employee information in different steps of the business process. The Enrollment bean also reads the current benefits information to set the default selections for the multiple-choice options presented to the user.

2. **Information entered by the user**—The session object may keep information entered by the user in a previous step if a subsequent step of the business process requires that information. For example, the Enrollment bean retains the coverage option selected by the user in step 1 and the smoker status entered in step 2 because it must use this information in later steps to calculate the cost of the medical and dental insurance choices.

Why is it important for an application to retain the client-specific conversational state in the session bean instance variables? If the session object could not store a client's conversational state in its instance variables, then each client-invoked method on the session object would have to retrieve the state from the underlying database. Fetching data from the database can be expensive, especially if the database is located on a different network node than the application server, or if the data is such that it requires a complicated database query to retrieve it.

Retaining client-specific state across client-invoked methods is not unique to the session bean or the EJB architecture. For example, Web containers support the concept of *session state* in which a Web application is allowed to save client-specific state in the Web container. For example, the servlet API supports the `ServletContext.setAttribute(String name, Object value)` and `ServletContext.getAttribute(String name)` methods for saving and retrieving client-specific values.

However, using a session bean to implement a conversational business process offers distinct advantages over other approaches. A session bean has the following advantages.

- A single Java class—the session bean class—implements a session bean. The same Java class implements both the conversational state and the business methods that access the state. The application developer uses an intuitive paradigm—writing a Java class—to implement the business process. The instance variables of the Java class hold the conversational state, and the methods of the class are the business methods that can be called by the client.

- The business process is encapsulated in a well-formed session bean component. Both humans and application assembly tools can easily understand the client view of the session bean. Multiple applications can easily reuse the session bean.

- When implemented as a session bean, it is possible to customize the business process at application assembly or deployment using the enterprise bean environment mechanism. For example, an environment entry could be used to specify whether an Account bean converts local currency amounts to Euros or not.

- The bean developer does not have to be concerned with system-level issues such as thread management, scalability, transaction management, error recovery, security, and so on. The bean developer codes the session bean as a security-unaware, single-thread, single-user application. The container transparently adds these services at runtime to the session bean code.

The EnrollmentWeb Web application delegates the maintenance of the conversational state to the Enrollment session object. EnrollmentWeb creates this session object at the beginning of the user's conversation with the EnrollmentWeb application and stores its reference in the HTTP session state.

```
...
EnrollmentHome enrollmentHome = ...; // get home object from JNDI
Enrollment enrollment = enrollmentHome.create(emplNumber);
session.setAttribute("EnrollmentBean", enrollment);
...
```

EnrollmentWeb keeps the object reference of the Enrollment session object in its HTTP session state.

4.3   Overview of the Example Application

Our example application, called Benefits Enrollment, is an employee self-service Web application through which an employee manages his benefits enrollment selections. The application lets an employee enter, review, and change his selection of employer-provided benefits.

The Star Enterprise IT department developed the Benefits Enrollment application. The IT department relied on its knowledge of the human resources-related databases (payroll, employee, and benefits databases) and their schemas when developing the application.

4.3.1 User View of the Application

The employee invokes the application by pointing his browser at a specific uniform resource locator (URL). The application displays a sequence of HTML pages that contain the various benefits choices available to the employee. On each page, the employee can select from one of the displayed choices. After the employee selects a choice, the application displays the next page. After the employee makes all applicable selections, the application displays a summary of the employee's selections and prompts the employee to confirm his benefits selections. If the employee confirms the selections, the application updates the user's benefits record in the benefits database.

When the application displays choices to the user, it also indicates the most recent benefits selection, which it obtains from the user's benefits record. Before confirming his selections, the employee may use the browser's Back button to return to previous pages and change previous selections. The application updates the user's benefits record only if the user successfully completes all the pages and confirms his selections at the end of the page sequence. Otherwise, the application leaves unmodified his previous selections stored in the benefits database.

Figure 4.5 illustrates the sequence of pages displayed by the application. The figure does not show two pages: the initial login page and the final page that confirms that the user's changes have been accepted and that the changes become effective as of the next paycheck.

4.3.2 Main Parts of the Application

Figure 4.6 illustrates the main parts of the Benefits Enrollment application.

The EnrollmentEJB session bean implements the business rules of the benefits enrollment business process. The business process consists of a conversation between one user and the server. Therefore, we implement it as a stateful session bean.

The EnrollmentWeb Web application is a set of JSP that implements the presentation logic of the Benefits Enrollment application.

The Enrollment bean accesses a number of corporate databases. These databases include the EmployeeDatabase, PayrollDatabase, and BenefitsDatabase.

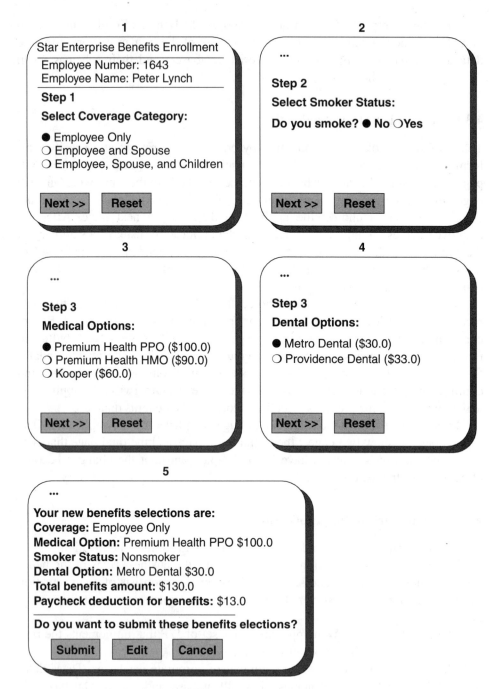

Figure 4.5   Benefits Enrollment HTML Page Sequence

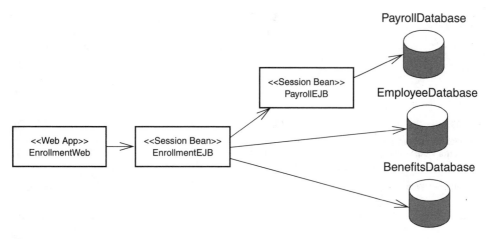

Figure 4.6   Parts of the Benefits Enrollment Application

- **EmployeeDatabase**—EmployeeDatabase contains information about employees, such as first name, last name, birth date, department, manager, and so on. EmployeeDatabase also maintains organizational information about the enterprise; specifically, how the enterprise is organized into various departments.

- **PayrollDatabase**—PayrollDatabase keeps payroll data for each employee, such as salary and various paycheck-related information. Employees are responsible for a portion of their benefit costs, which is handled by a payroll deduction. The payroll information includes the amount deducted from each employee's paycheck to cover the employee's portion of the premium paid by the company to the benefits providers.

- **BenefitsDatabase**—The BenefitsDatabase includes the information about available benefits and providers. It also contains the employee's current benefits selections.

Because of the sensitivity of the payroll information, the payroll department does not allow applications outside of the payroll system to access the PayrollDatabase directly. Applications, including the Benefits Enrollment application, must go through the PayrollEJB stateless session bean to access payroll information. The Payroll bean allows client applications to access only those parts of the payroll information to which they have been authorized by the payroll department.

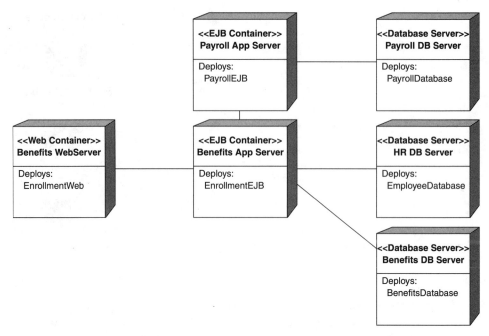

Figure 4.7   Deployment of the Benefits Enrollment Application

The application is deployed as a distributed application across multiple servers. Figure 4.7 illustrates the application deployment.

The EnrollmentWeb Web application is deployed in a Web container on a Web server maintained by the benefits department. The EnrollmentEJB enterprise bean is deployed in the application server owned by the benefits department. Note that the Web server and the application server can be two different servers, or they can be the same server providing an integrated environment for the deployment of both Web applications and enterprise beans.

The PayrollEJB enterprise bean is deployed on an application server owned by the payroll department. The three databases accessed by the benefits enrollment process may reside on three different database servers, as illustrated in our example deployment diagram in Figure 4.7.

4.3.3   The Benefits Enrollment Business Process

Figures 4.8 and 4.9 illustrate the interactions among the parts of the application that occur during the benefits enrollment business process. Notice how the interactions correspond to the sequence of pages shown in Figure 4.5 on page 62. (The numbers to the left of the interactions correspond to the page numbers in Figure 4.5, and also correspond to steps in the business process.) A step-by-step explanation of these interactions follows the diagrams.

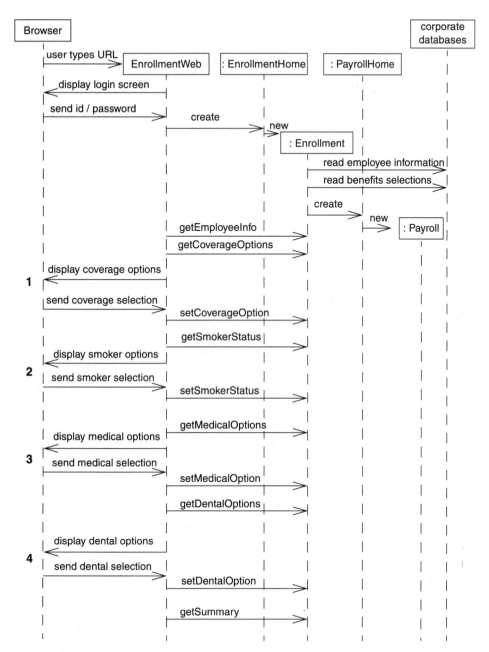

Figure 4.8 Benefits Enrollment Process Interactions, Part One

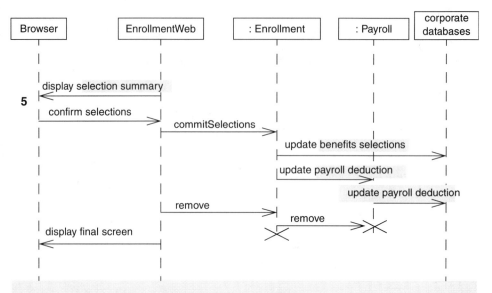

Figure 4.9   Benefits Enrollment Process Interactions, Part Two

- **Login Screen**—From a browser, the user starts by entering the URL of the EnrollmentWeb's starting JSP. Before invoking the EnrollmentWeb Web application, the Web container displays a login page to the user. The user logs in by entering his ID and password, and the Web container authenticates the user. Note that the authentication logic is implemented by the Web container, not by the EnrollmentWeb Web application. Once the Web container has authenticated the user, it invokes the EnrollmentWeb Web application. EnrollmentWeb invokes the `create` method on the EnrollmentHome interface, the home interface for the EnrollmentEJB enterprise bean, which creates a new Enrollment bean session object and a corresponding instance of the EnrollmentBean class. The EnrollmentBean instance sets up its initial state by reading the information from the corporate databases. The EnrollmentBean instance also creates a PayrollEJB object so that it can later update the payroll information. EnrollmentWeb invokes the Enrollment bean's `getEmployeeInfo` method, which uses the helper type `EmployeeInfo` to return the pertinent employee identification information. In a similar fashion, EnrollmentWeb next invokes the bean's `getCoverageOptions` method, which uses the helper type `Options` to return the available coverage options to EnrollmentWeb.

- **Step 1: Coverage Categories**—EnrollmentWeb displays the first HTML page of the benefits enrollment process. This page displays available coverage categories and asks the user to select his particular category. The employee makes his selection and presses the Next button to send his selection to EnrollmentWeb. EnrollmentWeb calls Enrollment bean's `setCoverageOption`, passing it the coverage category, so that the bean keeps the selected coverage category. EnrollmentWeb then invokes the bean's `getSmokerStatus` method, formats the returned data into an HTML page, and displays the next page to the user.

- **Step 2: Smoker Status**—The user indicates whether he smokes, presses the Next button to send his smoker status to EnrollmentWeb, which in turn invokes the `setSmokerStatus` method to store the status. Then, EnrollmentWeb invokes the bean's `getMedicalOptions` method, which uses the helper object `Options` to return the available medical insurance options to EnrollmentWeb. EnrollmentWeb formats the returned data into an HTML page for display to the user.

- **Step 3: Medical Options**—The user selects from the displayed list of medical options, presses the Next button to send his selection, and EnrollmentWeb calls the `setMedicalOption` bean method to store the selection. EnrollmentWeb next invokes the bean's `getDentalOptions` method, which returns to EnrollmentWeb a helper object `Options` with available dental options. EnrollmentWeb formats the returned data into an HTML page for display to the user.

- **Step 4: Dental Options**—The user selects one of the dental options and presses the Next button to send the selection to EnrollmentWeb. EnrollmentWeb calls the `setDentalOption` bean method, passing it the selected option, and stores the selection. EnrollmentWeb calls the bean's `getSummary` method, which returns all selections and their total costs in the `Summary` helper object. EnrollmentWeb formats the data into an HTML page and displays the selection summary page.

- **Step 5: Selection Summary and Confirmation**—When the user confirms his selections and sends the confirmation to EnrollmentWeb, it in turn calls the bean's `commitSelections` method, which updates the benefits record and the payroll deduction in the respective databases.

- **Acknowledgment Page** (not shown in Figure 4.5)—EnrollmentWeb sends an HTML page to the user's browser with a message acknowledging that the user's changes have been permanently recorded in the corporate databases. EnrollmentWeb also calls the `remove` method on the Enrollment object to end the enrollment business process. As part of processing the `remove` method, the Enrollment object invokes the `remove` method on the Payroll object.

4.4   EnrollmentEJB Stateful Session Bean in Detail

Let's now look at how the Benefits Enrollment example application uses the EnrollmentEJB stateful session bean. EnrollmentEJB illustrates the design of a typical stateful session bean. We start with a description of the EnrollmentEJB session bean implementation. Then we discuss how the client (that is, EnrollmentWeb in our example) uses the EnrollmentEJB's client-view interfaces.

4.4.1   EnrollmentEJB Session Bean Parts

Our example follows the recommended naming convention for an enterprise bean and its interfaces. Because this is a session bean implementing the enrollment business process, we name the session bean class EnrollmentBean. The remote interface for EnrollmentBean is Enrollment. The home interface is Enrollment-Home. We refer to the session bean as a whole using the name EnrollmentEJB.

Figure 4.10 illustrates the Java classes and interfaces that make up the EnrollmentEJB session bean. (Refer to Graphics on page xx for an explanation of the UML symbols used in this diagram.)

In addition to the remote and home interfaces and the session bean class, EnrollmentEJB uses a number of helper classes, which are illustrated in Figure 4.10.

The Options, Summary, EmployeeInfo, and EnrollmentException helper classes are visible to the client view because they are used by the Enrollment and EnrollmentHome interfaces. They are used to pass information between the client and the session bean. The EmployeeInfo helper class passes employee information, whereas the Options class passes a list of available benefits options to the client. The Summary helper class is used to pass a summary of the user's benefits selections, and the EnrollmentException class is the application-defined exception.

The DBQueryEmployee, DBInsertSelection, DBQuerySelection, and DBUpdateSelection classes are internal helper classes that implement data access operations. These classes follow the command bean design pattern explained in Data Access Command Beans on page 102.

The Employee and Selection classes are used internally by the EnrollmentBean class. They hold the information about employee and selection benefits in their conversational state.

The EnrollmentBean also uses one or more classes that implement the HealthPlan interface and encapsulate the plan-specific information, such as the calculation of the plan premium.

Subsequent sections describe these parts in greater detail.

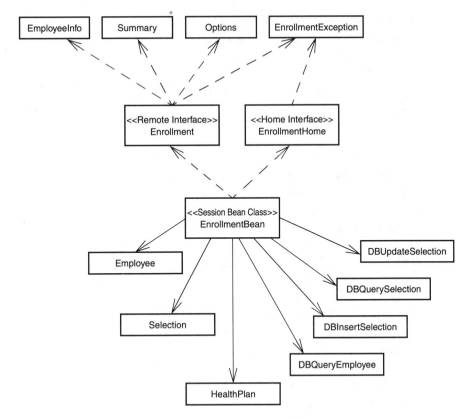

Figure 4.10 Main Parts of the EnrollmentEJB Session Bean

Session Bean Remote Interface

Every session bean has a remote interface that defines the business methods that a client may invoke on the individual session objects. The bean developer defines the remote interface, and the EJB container provides its implementation. The implementation delegates to the session bean class instances.

Code Example 4.1 shows the Enrollment remote interface for the Enrollment-Bean session bean.

Code Example 4.1 Enrollment Remote Interface

```
package com.star.benefits;

import javax.ejb.*;
import java.rmi.RemoteException;
```

```
public interface Enrollment extends EJBObject {
    EmployeeInfo getEmployeeInfo()
        throws RemoteException, EnrollmentException;
    Options getCoverageOptions()
        throws RemoteException, EnrollmentException;
    void setCoverageOption(int choice)
        throws RemoteException, EnrollmentException;
    Options getMedicalOptions()
        throws RemoteException, EnrollmentException;
    void setMedicalOption(int choice)
        throws RemoteException, EnrollmentException;
    Options getDentalOptions()
        throws RemoteException, EnrollmentException;
    void setDentalOption(int choice)
        throws RemoteException, EnrollmentException;
    boolean getSmokerStatus()
        throws RemoteException, EnrollmentException;
    void setSmokerStatus(boolean status)
        throws RemoteException, EnrollmentException;
    Summary getSummary()
        throws RemoteException, EnrollmentException;
    void commitSelections()
        throws RemoteException, EnrollmentException;
}
```

Note that our example Enrollment remote interface follows the EJB rules for all enterprise bean remote interfaces (see Enterprise Bean Remote Interface on page 29).

The remote interface methods can throw, in addition to the mandatory exception `java.rmi.RemoteException`, an arbitrary number of application-defined exceptions. We have declared the Enrollment remote interface methods to throw the application-defined exception `EnrollmentException`. The `EnrollmentException` exception defines the individual error codes thrown by the session bean to its clients.

Session Bean Home Interface

Every session bean has a home interface that allows the client to control the life cycle of the session objects. The bean developer defines the home interface, and the EJB container provides its implementation.

Code Example 4.2 shows the EnrollmentHome home interface for the Enroll-mentBean session bean.

Code Example 4.2   EnrollmentHome Home Interface

```
package com.star.benefits;

import javax.ejb.*;
import java.rmi.RemoteException;

public interface EnrollmentHome extends EJBHome {
    Enrollment create(int emplnum) throws RemoteException,
        CreateException, EnrollmentException;
}
```

The EnrollmentHome home interface follows the EJB rules for defining a session bean home interface (see Enterprise Bean Home Interface on page 26 for these rules).

Unlike the remote interface, the session bean's home interface cannot define arbitrary methods. It can only define `create` methods. Athough these `create` methods can have an arbitrary number of arguments and argument types, every `create` method must return the session bean's remote interface. Every session bean's home interface must define at least one `create` method.

The `throws` clause of every `create` method must define the `javax.ejb.CreateException` exception (in addition to `java.rmi.RemoteException`), and may define additional application-specific exceptions.

Remote and Home Interface Helper Classes

The client-view interfaces for the session bean use several helper Java classes to pass information between the client and the session bean.

Because the instances of the helper classes are passed through the remote and home interfaces, they follow the rules for RMI-IIOP. Specifically, they must be Java "serializable"; that is, they must implement the java.io.Serializable interface. Therefore, these helper classes are usually called *value classes*.

The Enrollment bean's client-view interfaces use four helper classes. The interfaces use the EmployeeInfo class to pass employee information, such as the employee's first name and last name. They use the Options class to pass a list of available options to the client. An Options object contains the description and cost of each option, and the currently selected option. The Summary class passes a summary of the user's selections, enabling the user to confirm the selections before they are committed to the corporate databases. The EnrollmentException class is an application-defined exception. The methods of EnrollmentBean throw this exception to the client to indicate various application-level errors, such as when invalid values are passed to the methods' input parameters.

Code Example 4.3 shows the definition of the four helper classes.

Code Example 4.3   Definition of Helper Classes

```java
package com.star.benefits;

public class EmployeeInfo implements java.io.Serializable {
    int employeeNumber;
    String firstName;
    String lastName;

    public EmployeeInfo() { }
    public EmployeeInfo(int emplnum, String fname, String lname) {
        employeeNumber = emplnum;
        firstName = fname;
        lastName = lname;
    }
    public int getEmployeeNumber() { return employeeNumber; }
    public String getFirstName() { return firstName; }
    public String getLastName() { return lastName; }
    public void setEmployeeNumber(int val) { employeeNumber = val; }
    public void setFirstName(String val) { firstName = val; }
    public void setLastName(String val) { lastName = val; }
}

package com.star.benefits;

public class Options implements java.io.Serializable {
    String[] optionDescription;
    double[] optionCost;
    int selectedOption;
    int size;

    public Options() {
        size = 0;
        selectedOption = -1;
    }
```

```java
    public Options(int size) {
        this.size = size;
        optionDescription = new String[size];
        optionCost = new double[size];
        selectedOption = -1;
    }

    public String getOptionDescription(int i) {
        return optionDescription[i];
    }
    public void setOptionDescription(int i, String val) {
        optionDescription[i] = val;
    }
    public String[] getOptionDescription() {
        return optionDescription;
    }
    public void setOptionDescription(String[] vals) {
        optionDescription = vals;
    }

    public double getOptionCost(int i) {
        return optionCost[i];
    }
    public void setOptionCost(int i, double val) {
        optionCost[i] = val;
    }
    public double[] getOptionCost() {
        return optionCost;
    }

    public int getSelectedOption() {
        return selectedOption;
    }
    public void setSelectedOption(int val) {
        selectedOption = val;
    }

    public int getSize() {
        return size;
    }
}
```

```java
package com.star.benefits;

public class Summary implements java.io.Serializable {
    String coverageOption;
    String medicalOption;
    String dentalOption;
    double medicalOptionCost;
    double dentalOptionCost;
    double totalCost;
    double payrollDeduction;
    boolean smokerStatus;

    public Summary() { }

    public String getCoverageDescription() {
        return coverageOption;
    }
    public void setCoverageDescription(String s) {
        coverageOption = s;
    }

    public String getMedicalDescription() {
        return medicalOption;
    }
    public void setMedicalDescription(String s) {
        medicalOption = s;
    }

    public String getDentalDescription() {
        return dentalOption;
    }
    public void setDentalDescription(String s) {
        dentalOption = s;
    }

    public double getMedicalCost() {
        return medicalOptionCost;
    }
    public void setMedicalCost(double c) {
        medicalOptionCost = c;
    }
```

```java
    public double getDentalCost() {
       return dentalOptionCost;
    }
    public void setDentalCost(double c) {
       dentalOptionCost = c;
    }


    public double getTotalCost() {
       return totalCost;
    }
    public void setTotalCost(double c) {
       totalCost = c;
    }


    public void setPayrollDeduction(double c) {
       payrollDeduction = c;
    }
    public double getPayrollDeduction() {
       return payrollDeduction;
    }


    public boolean getSmokerStatus() {
       return smokerStatus;
    }
    public void setSmokerStatus(boolean s) {
       smokerStatus  = s;
    }
}


package com.star.benefits;

public class EnrollmentException extends Exception {
    // error codes
    public static int UNKNOWN = 0;
    public static int INVAL_PARAM = 1;

    static String[] defaultMessage = {
       "unknown error code",
       "invalid value of input parameter"
    };

    private int errorCode;
```

```java
    public EnrollmentException() {
       super();
    }

    public EnrollmentException(String s) {
       super(s);
    }

    public EnrollmentException(int errorCode, String s) {
       super(s);
       this.errorCode = errorCode;
    }

    public EnrollmentException(int errorCode) {
       super(errorCode >= 0 && errorCode < defaultMessage.length ?
          defaultMessage[errorCode] : "");
       this.errorCode = errorCode;
    }
}
```

Session Bean Class

A session bean class is a Java class that defines the implementation of certain specific methods. The session bean class implements the session bean's business methods. These are the methods that are defined in the remote interface. It also defines implementations of the `ejbCreate` methods that correspond to the `create` methods defined in the home interface, and implementations of the methods defined in the javax.ejb.SessionBean interface.

A session bean class may also implement additional helper methods invoked internally by the previous methods.

In our example, the EnrollmentBean class is the session bean class. Code Example 4.4 shows the skeleton of the EnrollmentBean class:

Code Example 4.4 `EnrollmentBean` Class

```java
public class EnrollmentBean implements SessionBean
{
   // public no-arg constructor
   public EnrollmentBean() { super(); }
```

```
// Implementation of business methods defined in the
// session bean's remote interface.
public EmployeeInfo getEmployeeInfo() { ... }
public Options getCoverageOptions() { ... }
public void setCoverageOption(int choice) { ... }
public Options getMedicalOptions() { ... }
public void setMedicalOption(int choice) { ... }
public Options getDentalOptions() { ... }
public void setDentalOption(int choice) { ... }
public boolean getSmokerStatus() { ... }
public void setSmokerStatus(boolean status) { ... }
public Summary getSummary() { ... }
public void commitSelections() { ... }

// Implementation of the create(...) methods defined in
// the session bean's home interface.
public void ejbCreate(int emplNum) { ... }

// Implementation of the methods defined in the
// javax.ejb.SessionBean interface.
public void ejbRemove() { ... }
public void ejbPassivate() { ... }
public void ejbActivate() { ... }
public void setSessionContext(SessionContext sc) { ... }

// Various helper methods that are used internally by
// the session bean implementation.
private void calculateTotalCostAndPayrollDeduction() { ... }
private void readEnvironmentEntries() { ... }
private static String[] parseClassNames(String list) { ... }
private static void trace(String s) { ... }
}
```

The EnrollmentBean class is a typical example of a session bean class implementation. Notice that we have defined the EnrollmentBean class as `public`; we cannot define it to be `final` or `abstract`. Notice also that it has a `public` constructor that takes no arguments, and that it has no `finalize` method. The EnrollmentBean class does not define the `finalize` method, nor do any of its superclasses. (In fact, according to the specification, a session bean class must define a `public` constructor with no arguments, and it cannot define a `finalize` method.)

The EnrollmentBean class implements the business methods that were declared in the bean's remote interface—the getEmployeeInfo, getSummary, and commitSelections methods, and the methods to get and set various benefits options—plus an ejbCreate method that matches the create method of the home interface (see Session Bean create Methods on page 78 for more information on how these methods are related). The EnrollmentBean class also provides the implementation of the javax.ejb.SessionBean interface methods.

Lastly, EnrollmentBean implements helper methods that are only invoked internally by its business methods. Notice that these methods are declared as private.

Session Bean Business Methods. The session bean class implements the business methods declared by its remote interface. The number and types of parameters and the return value type for these business methods must match those defined in the remote interface. In addition, the throws clauses for the session bean class business methods must not include more checked exceptions than the throws clauses of the corresponding remote interface methods. (Note that the methods in the session bean class can define fewer exceptions than the methods in the remote interface.)

Notice, too, that the business methods must be declared public. They must not be declared final or static.

For example, the EnrollmentBean class defines a number of business methods, including the following.

```
public EmployeeInfo getEmployeeInfo() { ... }
public Options getCoverageOptions() { ... }
public void setCoverageOption(int choice)
        throws EnrollmentException { ... }
```

These methods match the following methods of the Enrollment remote interface.

```
EmployeeInfo getEmployeeInfo()
    throws RemoteException, EnrollmentException;
Options getCoverageOptions()
    throws RemoteException, EnrollmentException;
void setCoverageOption(int choice)
    throws RemoteException, EnrollmentException;
```

Session Bean create Methods. The session bean class defines ejbCreate methods that correspond to the create methods defined in the home interface. For each create method in the home interface, there must an ejbCreate method in the session bean class.

The ejbCreate method has the same number of parameters, and each parameters must be of the same type as those defined in the home interface's corresponding create method. However, the ejbCreate methods differ from the create methods in that they define void as the return value type. (The return value is void because the container does not need any information from the bean to create the object reference that will be returned to the client as the result of the create method. This is in contrast to the entity bean, in which the container needs to embed the primary key returned from the bean's ejbCreate method into the object reference.) The throws clause for each ejbCreate method must not include more checked exceptions than the throws clause of the corresponding create method. However, the throws clause for the ejbCreate method can have fewer exceptions than the corresponding create method.

Like the business methods, the ejbCreate methods must be declared public. They must not be declared final or static.

For example, the EnrollmentBean class declares the following ejbCreate method.

```
public void ejbCreate(int emplnum) throws EnrollmentException;
```

This method corresponds to the create method defined in the EnrollmentHome home interface.

```
Enrollment create(int emplnum) throws RemoteException,
    CreateException, EnrollmentException;
```

SessionBean Interface Methods. A session bean class is required to implement the four methods defined by the javax.ejb.SessionBean interface. The EJB container invokes these methods on the bean instance at specific points in a session bean instance's life cycle. Code Example 4.5 shows the definition of the SessionBean interface.

Code Example 4.5 SessionBean Interface

```
public interface SessionBean extends EnterpriseBean {
    void setSessionContext(SessionContext sessionContext) throws
        EJBException, RemoteException;
    void ejbRemove() throws EJBException, RemoteException;
    void ejbActivate() throws EJBException, RemoteException;
    void ejbPassivate() throws EJBException, RemoteException;
}
```

The container invokes the setSessionContext method before it invokes any other methods on the bean instance. It passes the instance a reference to the SessionContext object. The instance can save the reference and use it during its lifetime to invoke methods on the SessionContext object.

The container invokes the `ejbRemove` method when it is about to remove the instance. This happens either in response to a client's invoking the `remove` method or when a session timeout expires (see Session Object Removal on page 101).

The container invokes the `ejbPassivate` method when passivating an instance and the `ejbActivate` method when activating the instance. The container can passivate an instance to reclaim the resources held by the instance. Passivation and activation are described in Session Object Passivation and Activation on page 110.

4.4.2   EnrollmentBean Session Bean Class Details

In this section, we focus in detail on the EnrollmentBean stateful session bean class to understand how a bean developer implements a session bean class.

We start with the full listing of the source code for EnrollmentBean, and then walk through the individual methods that implement the session bean's functions. Client Developer's Perspective on page 113 explains how a client uses the EnrollmentBean.

Session Bean Class Source Code

Code Example 4.6 shows the complete listing for the EnrollmentBean class.

Code Example 4.6   EnrollmentBean Source Code

```
package com.star.benefits;

import javax.ejb.*;

import javax.naming.Context;
import javax.naming.InitialContext;
import com.star.payroll.Payroll;
import com.star.payroll.PayrollHome;
import java.util.Date;
import java.sql.SQLException;
import javax.sql.DataSource;
import javax.rmi.PortableRemoteObject;

import com.star.benefits.db.DBQueryEmployee;
import com.star.benefits.db.DBQuerySelection;
import com.star.benefits.db.DBInsertSelection;
import com.star.benefits.db.DBUpdateSelection;
```

```
// The Employee class is used internally to represent the employee
// information in the instance's conversational state.
//
class Employee {
    int emplNumber;
    String firstName;
    String lastName;
    Date birthDate;
    Date startDate;
}


// The Selection class is used internally to represent the benefits
// selections in the instance's conversational state.
//
class Selection {
    int emplNumber;
    int coverage;
    String medicalPlanId;
    String dentalPlanId;
    boolean smokerStatus;
}


// EnrollmentBean is a stateful session bean that implements
// the benefits enrollment business process.
//
public class EnrollmentBean implements SessionBean
{
    private final static String[] coverageDescriptions = {
        "Employee Only",
        "Employee and Spouse",
        "Employee, Spouse, and Children"
    };

    // Tables of Java classes that are used for calculation
    // of cost of medical and dental benefits.
    private HealthPlan[] medicalPlans;
    private HealthPlan[] dentalPlans;

    // Portion of the benefits cost paid by the employee. (A real
    // application would read this value from the database.)
    private double employeeCostFactor = 0.10;
```

```java
    // Employee number that uniquely identifies an employee
    private int employeeNumber;

    // Employee information read from database
    private Employee employee;

    // Employee's current benefits selections
    private Selection selection;

    // Indication if bean needs to create a selection record.
    private boolean createSelection;

    // The following variables are calculated values and are
    // used for programming convenience.
    private int age;           // employee's age
    private int medicalSelection = -1;   // index to medicalPlans
    private int dentalSelection = -1;    // index to dentalPlans
    private double totalCost;        // total benefits cost
    private double payrollDeduction;    // payroll deduction

    // JDBC data sources
    private DataSource employeeDS;       // Employee database
    private DataSource benefitsDS;       // Benefits database

    private Payroll payroll;

    // public no-arg constructor
    public EnrollmentBean() { }

    // Business methods follow.

    // Get employee information.
    public EmployeeInfo getEmployeeInfo() {
        return new EmployeeInfo(employeeNumber,
            employee.firstName, employee.lastName);
    }

    // Get coverage options.
    public Options getCoverageOptions() {
        Options opt = new Options(coverageDescriptions.length);
        opt.setOptionDescription(coverageDescriptions);
```

```java
        opt.setSelectedOption(selection.coverage);
        return opt;
    }


    // Set selected coverage option.
    public void setCoverageOption(int choice)
            throws EnrollmentException {

        if (choice >= 0 && choice < coverageDescriptions.length) {
            selection.coverage = choice;
        } else {
            throw new EnrollmentException(
                EnrollmentException.INVAL_PARAM);
        }
    }


    // Get list of available medical options.
    public Options getMedicalOptions() {
        Options opt = new Options(medicalPlans.length);
        for (int i = 0; i < medicalPlans.length; i++) {
            HealthPlan plan = medicalPlans[i];
            opt.setOptionDescription(i, plan.getDescription());
            opt.setOptionCost(i,
                plan.getCost(selection.coverage,
                    age, selection.smokerStatus));
        }
        opt.setSelectedOption(medicalSelection);
        return opt;
    }


    // Set selected medical option.
    public void setMedicalOption(int choice)
            throws EnrollmentException {

        if (choice >= 0 && choice < medicalPlans.length) {
            medicalSelection = choice;
            selection.medicalPlanId =
                medicalPlans[choice].getPlanId();
```

```
      } else {
        throw new EnrollmentException(
          EnrollmentException.INVAL_PARAM);
      }
    }


    // Get list of available dental options.
    public Options getDentalOptions() {
      Options opt = new Options(dentalPlans.length);
      for (int i = 0; i < dentalPlans.length; i++) {
        HealthPlan plan = dentalPlans[i];
        opt.setOptionDescription(i, plan.getDescription());
        opt.setOptionCost(i,
            plan.getCost(selection.coverage,
              age, selection.smokerStatus));
      }
      opt.setSelectedOption(dentalSelection);
      return opt;
    }


    // Set selected dental option.
    public void setDentalOption(int choice)
        throws EnrollmentException {

      if (choice >= 0 && choice < dentalPlans.length) {
        dentalSelection = choice;
        selection.dentalPlanId =
          dentalPlans[choice].getPlanId();
      } else {
        throw new EnrollmentException(
          EnrollmentException.INVAL_PARAM);
      }
    }


    // Get smoker status.
    public boolean getSmokerStatus() {
      return selection.smokerStatus;
    }
```

```
// Set smoker status.
public void setSmokerStatus(boolean status) {
   selection.smokerStatus = status;
}

// Get summary of selected options and their cost.
public Summary getSummary() {
   calculateTotalCostAndPayrollDeduction();
   Summary s = new Summary();
   s.setCoverageDescription(
      coverageDescriptions[selection.coverage]);

   s.setSmokerStatus(selection.smokerStatus);

   s.setMedicalDescription(
      medicalPlans[medicalSelection].getDescription());
   s.setMedicalCost(
      medicalPlans[medicalSelection].getCost(
         selection.coverage, age,
         selection.smokerStatus));

   s.setDentalDescription(
      dentalPlans[dentalSelection].getDescription());
   s.setDentalCost(
      dentalPlans[dentalSelection].getCost(
         selection.coverage, age,
         selection.smokerStatus));

   s.setTotalCost(totalCost);
   s.setPayrollDeduction(payrollDeduction);

   return s;
}

// Update corporate databases with the new selections.
public void commitSelections() {
```

```
                    // Insert new or update existing benefits selection record.
                    if (createSelection) {
                        DBInsertSelection cmd1 = null;
                        try {
                            cmd1 = new DBInsertSelection(benefitsDS);
                            cmd1.setEmplNumber(employeeNumber);
                            cmd1.setCoverage(selection.coverage);
                            cmd1.setMedicalPlanId(selection.medicalPlanId);
                            cmd1.setDentalPlanId(selection.dentalPlanId);
                            cmd1.setSmokerStatus(selection.smokerStatus);
                            cmd1.execute();
                            createSelection = false;
                        } catch (SQLException ex) {
                            throw new EJBException(ex);
                        } finally {
                            if (cmd1 != null)
                                cmd1.release();
                        }
                    } else {
                        DBUpdateSelection cmd2 = null;
                        try {
                            cmd2 = new DBUpdateSelection(benefitsDS);
                            cmd2.setEmplNumber(employeeNumber);
                            cmd2.setCoverage(selection.coverage);
                            cmd2.setMedicalPlanId(selection.medicalPlanId);
                            cmd2.setDentalPlanId(selection.dentalPlanId);
                            cmd2.setSmokerStatus(selection.smokerStatus);
                            cmd2.execute();
                        } catch (SQLException ex) {
                            throw new EJBException(ex);
                        } finally {
                            if (cmd2 != null)
                                cmd2.release();
                        }
                    }

                    // Update information in the payroll system.
                    try {
                        payroll.setBenefitsDeduction(employeeNumber,
                                payrollDeduction);
                    } catch (Exception ex) {
```

```
            throw new EJBException(ex);
        }
    }


// Initialize the state of the EmployeeBean instance.
public void ejbCreate(int emplNum) throws EnrollmentException {
    employeeNumber = emplNum;

    // Obtain values from bean's environment.
    readEnvironmentEntries();

    // Obtain JDBC data sources from the environment.
    getDataSources();

    // Read employee information.
    DBQueryEmployee cmd1 = null;
    try {
        cmd1 = new DBQueryEmployee(employeeDS);
        cmd1.setEmployeeNumber(emplNum);
        cmd1.execute();
        if (cmd1.next()) {
            employee = new Employee();
            employee.emplNumber = emplNum;
            employee.firstName = cmd1.getFirstName();
            employee.lastName = cmd1.getLastName();
            employee.startDate = cmd1.getStartDate();
            employee.birthDate = cmd1.getBirthDate();
        } else {
            throw new EnrollmentException(
                "no employee record");
        }
    } catch (SQLException ex) {
        throw new EJBException(ex);
    } finally {
        if (cmd1 != null)
            cmd1.release();
    }
```

```java
// Read the previous benefits selections.
DBQuerySelection cmd2 = null;
try {
    cmd2 = new DBQuerySelection(benefitsDS);
    cmd2.setEmployeeNumber(emplNum);
    cmd2.execute();
    if (cmd2.next()) {
        selection = new Selection();
        selection.emplNumber = emplNum;
        selection.coverage = cmd2.getCoverage();
        selection.medicalPlanId =
            cmd2.getMedicalPlanId();
        selection.dentalPlanId =
            cmd2.getDentalPlanId();
        selection.smokerStatus =
            cmd2.getSmokerStatus();
        createSelection = false;
    } else {
        // No previous selections exist in
        // the database. Initial selections to
        // default values.
        selection = new Selection();
        selection.emplNumber = emplNum;
        selection.coverage = 0;
        selection.medicalPlanId =
            medicalPlans[0].getPlanId();
        selection.dentalPlanId =
            dentalPlans[0].getPlanId();
        selection.smokerStatus = false;
        createSelection = true;
    }
} catch (SQLException ex) {
    throw new EJBException(ex);
} finally {
    if (cmd2 != null)
        cmd2.release();
}

// Calculate employee's age.
java.util.Date today = new java.util.Date();
age = (int)((today.getTime() -
```

```
            employee.birthDate.getTime()) /
        ((long)365 * 24 * 60 * 60 * 1000));

    // Translate the medical plan ID to an index
    // in the medicalPlans table.
    for (int i = 0; i < medicalPlans.length; i++) {
        if (medicalPlans[i].getPlanId().equals(
            selection.medicalPlanId)) {
            medicalSelection = i;
            break;
        }
    }

    // Translate the dental plan ID to an index
    // in the dentalPlans table.
    for (int i = 0; i < dentalPlans.length; i++) {
        if (dentalPlans[i].getPlanId().equals(
            selection.dentalPlanId)) {
            dentalSelection = i;
            break;
        }
    }
}

// Clean up any resource held by the instance.
public void ejbRemove() {
    try {
        payroll.remove();
    } catch (Exception ex) {
    }
}

// Release state that cannot be preserved across passivation.
public void ejbPassivate() {
    employeeDS = null;
    benefitsDS = null;
}
```

```java
// Reacquire state released before passivation.
public void ejbActivate() {
   getDataSources();
}

public void setSessionContext(SessionContext sc) {}

// Helper methods follow.

// Calculate total benefits cost and payroll deduction.
private void calculateTotalCostAndPayrollDeduction() {
   double medicalCost =
     medicalPlans[medicalSelection].getCost(
       selection.coverage,
       age, selection.smokerStatus);
   double dentalCost =
     dentalPlans[dentalSelection].getCost(
       selection.coverage,
       age, selection.smokerStatus);
   totalCost = medicalCost + dentalCost;
   payrollDeduction = totalCost * employeeCostFactor;
}

// Read and process enterprise bean's environment entries.
private void readEnvironmentEntries() {
   try {
     Context ictx = new InitialContext();

     String medicalPlanList = (String)
       ictx.lookup("java:comp/env/medicalPlans");
     String[] medicalPlanClassNames =
       parseClassNames(medicalPlanList);
     medicalPlans =
       new HealthPlan[medicalPlanClassNames.length];
     for (int i = 0; i < medicalPlanClassNames.length; i++) {
       medicalPlans[i] = (HealthPlan)Class.forName(
         medicalPlanClassNames[i]).newInstance();
     }
```

```
            String dentalPlanList = (String)
                ictx.lookup("java:comp/env/dentalPlans");
            String[] dentalPlanClassNames =
                parseClassNames(dentalPlanList);
            dentalPlans =
                new HealthPlan[dentalPlanClassNames.length];
            for (int i = 0; i < dentalPlanClassNames.length; i++) {
                dentalPlans[i] = (HealthPlan)Class.forName(
                    dentalPlanClassNames[i]).newInstance();
            }

            PayrollHome payrollHome = (PayrollHome)
                PortableRemoteObject.narrow(
                    ictx.lookup("java:comp/env/ejb/PayrollEJB"),
                    PayrollHome.class);
            payroll = (Payroll)payrollHome.create();
        } catch (Exception ex) {
            ex.printStackTrace();
            throw new EJBException(ex);
        }
    }

    private void getDataSources() {
        try {
            Context ictx = new InitialContext();
            employeeDS = (DataSource)ictx.lookup(
                    "java:comp/env/jdbc/EmployeeDB");
            benefitsDS = (DataSource)ictx.lookup(
                    "java:comp/env/jdbc/BenefitsDB");
        } catch (Exception ex) {
            ex.printStackTrace();
            throw new EJBException(ex);
        }
    }

    // Parse : separated class names.
    //
    private static String[] parseClassNames(String list) {
        String[] rv = new String[0];
```

```
    while (list.length() != 0) {
        int x = list.indexOf(':');
        String name;

        if (x < 0) {
            name = list;
            list = "";
        } else {
            name = list.substring(0, x);
            list = list.substring(x + 1);
        }
        if (name.length() == 0) {
            continue;
        }

        String[] orv = rv;
        rv = new String[rv.length + 1];
        for (int i = 0; i < orv.length; i++)
            rv[i] = orv[i];
        rv[rv.length - 1] = name;
    }
    return rv;
  }
}
```

The EnrollmentBean class uses several command beans for database access. Data Access Command Beans on page 102 describes these command beans.

The EnrollmentBean class does not hardcode into the bean class either the set of insurance providers or the calculation of the insurance premium. To facilitate changes to the set of insurance providers and changes to the algorithm to calculate the premium, the IT department of Star Enterprise defined an extensible mechanism for "plugging" the insurance information into the EnrollmentEJB bean. The IT department uses the EJB environment mechanism to configure the set of available plans without the need to recompile the EnrollmentEJB bean.

The IT department of Star Enterprise defined the HealthPlan interface to keep insurance-related logic separate from the session bean code. Developers can change the insurance portion of the business logic and not have to change the session bean code. By keeping the insurance premium logic encapsulated within this HealthPlan interface, it allows developers to change the algorithm that calculates the insurance cost without having to change the session bean code, and to add additional insurance providers without having to change the session bean code.

Code Example 4.7 shows the definition of the HealthPlan interface.

Code Example 4.7   HealthPlan Interface

```
public interface HealthPlan {
   String getPlanId();
   String getDescription();
   double getCost(int coverage, int age, boolean smokerStatus);
}
```

Each insurance plan offered by Star Enterprise to its employees is represented by a class that implements the HealthPlan interface. Each such insurance plan class provides its own implementation for the HealthPlan interface `getCost` method. This method calculates the insurance cost or premium based on the employee's selected coverage category, age, and smoker status. Each insurance plan class also implements the `getPlanID` and `getDescription` methods, which are used by the Enrollment session bean.

Code Example 4.8 provides an example of a class that implements the Health-Plan interface:

Code Example 4.8   Insurance Plan Class Implementing the HealthPlan Interface

```
package com.star.plans;
import com.star.benefits.HeathPlan;

public class PremiumHealthPPOPlan implements HealthPlan {
   public PremiumHealthPPOPlan() { super(); }

   public String getPlanId() { return "PHPPO"; }
   public String getDescription() { return "PremiumHealth PPO"; }
   public double getCost(int coverage, int age,
      boolean smokerStatus) {
         // Calculate the insurance premium based on the
         // coverage category, age, and smoking status.
         ...
         return premium;
   }
}
}
```

The insurance provider (Premium Health Care, in our example) implements this class. By providing its own implementation, the insurance company has the flexibility to use Java code to describe the algorithm that determines the insurance premium based on the employee's coverage category, age, and smoking status. Other insurance providers chosen by Star Enterprise would provide their own implementations of the HealthPlan interface.

The IT department at Star Enterprise uses the EnrollmentEJB bean's environment entries to configure the list of medical and dental plans available to employees. In our example, the deployer sets the `medicalPlans` and `dentalPlans` environment entries to a colon-separated list of Java classes that implement the HealthPlan interface (see Code Example 4.9).

Code Example 4.9   Deployment Descriptor Environment Entries

```
...
<enterprise-beans>
   <session>
      <display-name>Enrollment Bean</display-name>
      <ejb-name>EnrollmentEJB</ejb-name>
      ...
      <env-entry>
         <env-entry-name>medicalPlans</env-entry-name>
         <env-entry-type>java.lang.String</env-entry-type>
         <env-entry-value>com.star.benefits.plans.PremiumHealth
         PPOPlan:com.star.benefits.plans.PremiumHealthHMOPlan:
         com.star.benefits.plans.Kooper</env-entry-value>
      </env-entry>
      <env-entry>
         <env-entry-name>dentalPlans</env-entry-name>
         <env-entry-type>java.lang.String</env-entry-type>
         <env-entry-value>com.star.benefits.plans.MetroDental:
         com.star.benefits.plans.ProvidenceDental</env-entry-value>
      </env-entry>
      ..
   </session>
   ...
```

Session Bean Conversational State

The EnrollmentEJB session object's conversational state consists of the contents of the EnrollmentBean instance variables, including the Java objects reachable from these variables. The `ejbCreate` method initializes the conversational state, the business methods update the state, and the `ejbRemove` method destroys the conversational state.

The conversational state of the Enrollment session object consists of a number of objects; some are primitives (such as `int`, `boolean`, and `double` types) and some are Java classes. The EnrollmentBean class declares these at the beginning, prior to defining the business methods. The following objects comprise the bean's conversational state: medicalPlans, dentalPlans, employeeNumber, employee, selection, recordDoesNotExist, age, medicalSelection, dentalSelection, totalCost, payroll-Deduction, employeeDS, benefitsDS, and payroll.

If the container passivates a session object during the object's lifetime, it moves the conversational state to some secondary storage. It restores the state when the object is later activated. Session Object Passivation and Activation on page 110 describes how a bean developer deals with session object passivation and activation.

Session Object Creation

How is a stateful session object created? The container creates a session object and an instance of the session bean class when the client invokes one of the `create` methods defined in the bean's home interface.

The following details the steps performed by the container.

1. Creates an instance of the session bean class using the constructor that takes no arguments.

2. Invokes the `setSessionContext` method on the instance.

3. Invokes the `ejbCreate` method on the instance.

For the EnrollmentBean, the container uses the following constructor to create a session bean class instance:

```
public EnrollmentBean() { super(); }
```

The container calls the `setSessionContext` method to associate the bean instance with its SessionContext interface. The SessionContext interface provides methods to access runtime properties of the context in which a session bean instance runs. If, during its life cycle, the bean instance needs to invoke the methods of the SessionContext interface, the instance should retain the SessionContext reference in an instance variable as part of its conversational state.

In our example, the setSessionBean method implementation is empty:

```
public void setSessionContext(SessionContext sc) { }
```

The method implementation is empty because the EnrollmentBean instances do not need to access the SessionContext interface during their lifetime. If, however, an instance wants access to the SessionContext reference at a later time, it needs to save this reference, and it does so from within the setSessionContext method. Rather than implementing an empty method, the developer includes code in setSessionContext to save the SessionContext reference. Programmatic Security API on page 364 illustrates the use of the SessionContext interface.

Finally, the container invokes the ejbCreate method on the instance. If the session bean has multiple ejbCreate methods, the container invokes the one with the arguments that match the arguments of the create method invoked by the client. The EnrollmentBean class has only a single create method.

```
public void ejbCreate(int emplNum) throws EnrollmentException {
    ...
}
```

The session bean instance uses the ejbCreate method to initialize its conversational state (the session class instance variables). The instance may retrieve the session bean environment entries, read information from the corporate databases, and initialize the instance variables for later use by the business methods.

The EnrollmentBean instance performs the following in the ejbCreate method: stores the employee number, reads the environment entries, reads and caches the employee record, reads the current benefits selections, and sets up instance variables. (See the code listing for ejbCreate in Code Example 4.6 on page 80.)

- **Stores the employee number.** It stores the employee number passed from the client in the instance variable employeeNumber.

- **Reads the environment entries.** It reads the session bean environment entries using the method readEnvironmentEntries. The environment entries are defined in the deployment descriptor. The deployer configured the values of the java:comp/env/jdbc/EmployeeDB and java:comp/env/jdbc/BenefitsDB environment entries so that the session bean uses the appropriate corporate databases. The deployer also configured the value of the java:comp/env/ejb/PayrollEJB environment entry to the home interface of the dependent enterprise beans (the PayrollEJB bean, in our example). The instance also obtains from the environment entries the names of the classes for the configured medical and dental plans offered by Star Enterprise to its employees. With this information, it builds the `medicalPlans` and `dentalPlans` tables used later by the business methods.

- **Reads and caches the employee record.** Using the DBQueryEmployee command bean, the instance reads the employee record from the database and caches this data in the employee variable. The business methods use this data in their subsequent operations. If the employee record does not exist, the instance throws `EJBException`. `EJBException` is a system-level exception. It indicates to the container that the instance ran into an unexpected error condition from which it cannot recover. When the container catches `EJBException` from an instance, it invokes no other method on the instance and, instead, destroys the instance.

- **Reads current benefits selections.** The instance next uses the DBQuery-Selection command bean to read the user's current benefits selection record from the database into the selection object. If the record does not exist, the instance initializes the selection object with some default values.

- **Sets up instance variables**. The instance sets up various other instance variables used later by the business methods. It calculates the user's age and stores the value in the age variable, and it builds the `medicalPlans` and `dentalPlans` tables that are used to present benefit plan choices to the user.

It is important to note that the work the instance performs in the `ejbCreate` method cannot be moved to the constructor or to the `setSessionContext` method. This is because the container might not have the full execution context for the instance when it invokes the constructor and `setSessionContext` methods. If a session bean developer incorrectly attempts to implement the functionality performed by the `ejbCreate` method in the constructor or the `setSessionContext` method, the execution of either of these latter methods would likely result in a thrown exception.

Session Bean Business Methods

The EnrollmentBean class implements all the business methods defined in the Enrollment remote interface. This section describes the implementation of the `getMedicalOptions`, `setMedicalOption`, and `commitSelections` business methods. These are illustrative implementations of a typical session bean's business methods.

Code Example 4.10 illustrates the implementation of the `getMedicalOptions` method.

Code Example 4.10 `getMedicalOptions` Method Implementation

```
public Options getMedicalOptions() {
   Options opt = new Options(medicalPlans.length);
   for (int i = 0; i < medicalPlans.length; i++) {
      HealthPlan plan = medicalPlans[i];
      opt.setOptionDescription(i, plan.getDescription());
      opt.setOptionCost(i,
         plan.getCost(selection.coverage,
            age, selection.smokerStatus));
   }
   opt.setSelectedOption(medicalSelection);
   return opt;
}
```

The `getMedicalOptions` method creates an Options object and initializes it with the descriptions and costs of the available medical plans. It also sets an indicator to the current medical plan selection. It finishes by returning the initialized Options object to the client. Note that the `getMedicalOptions` method uses the information stored in the instance's conversational state from the execution of the `ejbCreate` method. (For example, the `ejbCreate` method stored the table of the available medical plans in the medicalPlan variable.) This illustrates that the instance's conversational state holds the information across client-invoked methods.

Code Example 4.11 shows the implementation for the `setMedicalOption` method.

Code Example 4.11 `setMedicalOption` Method Implementation

```
public void setMedicalOption(int choice)
   throws EnrollmentException {

   if (choice >= 0 && choice < medicalPlans.length) {
      medicalSelection = choice;
      selection.medicalPlanId =
         medicalPlans[choice].getPlanId();
```

```
    } else {
        throw new EnrollmentException(
            EnrollmentException.INVAL_PARAM);
    }
}
```

The `setMedicalOption` method takes a single input argument. The input argument is an index number into the list of medical plans in the Options object (which was returned by the previously invoked `getMedicalPlans` method). The `setMedicalPlan` method first checks the validity of the input argument. If the argument is valid, `setMedicalPlan` updates the session bean conversational state to reflect the selected medical plan—it updates the selection object, the medicalSelection variable, and the totalCost and payrollDeduction variables.

If the argument is invalid, the method throws `EnrollmentException` to the client. Because `EnrollmentException` is an application-defined exception, it does not cause the container to remove the session object or to roll back the transaction (unlike the system-level exception `EJBException`). The client can continue the enrollment business process by invoking the `setMedicalOption` method with a valid choice.

The `commitSelections` method updates the corporate databases to reflect the user's selection of benefits. Code Example 4.12 shows its implementation:

Code Example 4.12 `commitSelections` Method Implementation

```
public void commitSelections() {
    // Insert new or update existing benefits selection record.
    if (createSelection) {
        DBInsertSelection cmd1 = null;
        try {
            cmd1 = new DBInsertSelection(benefitsDS);
            cmd1.setEmplNumber(employeeNumber);
            cmd1.setCoverage(selection.coverage);
            cmd1.setMedicalPlanId(selection.medicalPlanId);
            cmd1.setDentalPlanId(selection.dentalPlanId);
            cmd1.setSmokerStatus(selection.smokerStatus);
            createSelection = false;
        } catch (SQLException ex) {
            throw new EJBException(ex);
```

```
            } finally {
                if (cmd1 != null)
                    cmd1.release();
            }
        } else {
            DBUpdateSelection cmd2 = null;
            try {
                cmd2 = new DBUpdateSelection(benefitsDS);
                cmd2.setEmplNumber(employeeNumber);
                cmd2.setCoverage(selection.coverage);
                cmd2.setMedicalPlanId(selection.medicalPlanId);
                cmd2.setDentalPlanId(selection.dentalPlanId);
                cmd2.setSmokerStatus(selection.smokerStatus);
            } catch (SQLException ex) {
                throw new EJBException(ex);
            } finally {
                if (cmd2 != null)
                    cmd2.release();
            }
        }
        // Update information in the payroll system.
        try {
            payroll.setBenefitsDeduction(employeeNumber,
                payrollDeduction);
        } catch (Exception ex) {
            throw new EJBException(ex);
        }
    }
```

The commitSelections method updates two databases: the selections table in BenefitsDatabase and, via the PayrollEJB bean, the paycheck table in PayrollDatabase. The EJB container ensures that the update of the multiple databases is performed as a transaction. As you can see, the bean developer does not have to write any code to manage the transaction.

The bean developer used the deployment descriptor to specify that the commitSelections method must run in a transaction. See Chapter 8, Understanding Transactions for more information on how the transaction attributes specified in the deployment descriptor instruct the container to manage transactions on behalf of the enterprise bean.

Session Object Removal

When finished using a session object, a client removes the object by calling the remove method of the remote interface or home interface. The client's invocation of the remove method on the session object or home object causes the container to invoke the ejbRemove method on the session bean instance.

The instance uses the ejbRemove method to release any resources that it has accumulated. For example, the EnrollmentBean bean instance uses the ejbRemove method to remove the Payroll session object, as shown in Code Example 4.13.

Code Example 4.13 Using the ejbRemove Method

```
public void ejbRemove() {
     try {
        payroll.remove();
     } catch (Exception ex) {
     }
}
```

The client invocation of the remove method is the normal way of removing a session object. In our application, EnrollmentWeb invokes the remove method. However, there are other ways to remove a session object.

When a deployer deploys the session bean in an EJB container, the container typically allows the deployer to specify a client inactivity timeout for the session bean. The client inactivity timeout is a specified period of time. If the client does not invoke a session object for the amount of time specified by the timeout value, the container automatically removes the session object. When this happens, the container *may* invoke the ejbRemove method on the session bean instance before it removes the session object. The container is not obligated to invoke the ejbRemove method when the client inactivity timeout occurs.

What circumstances might result in the container *not* invoking the ejbRemove method? If the session bean object is in the passivated state at the time of the removal, the container is not required to activate a passivated session bean instance for the sole purpose of removing the instance. The EJB specification allows the container to skip invoking the ejbActivate method to activate a passivated session bean instance solely to invoke the ejbRemove method on the instance. This enables the container to avoid the overhead of activating the session bean instance. If the session bean objects allocate resources other than Java objects (such as records in a database) and these objects are normally released in ejbRemove, the application should provide a cleanup mechanism to avoid resource leakage because of the missed ejbRemove calls. For example, the application can include a program that periodically cleans up the resources that have not been released by the missed `ejbRemove` calls.

Note that the bean developer does not have to release resource manager connections (such as JDBC connections) in the `ejbRemove` method. The EJB container tracks all resource manager connections held by a session bean instance; the container automatically releases the connections when the instance is removed. This automatic release of JDBC connections is not shown in our example because the EnrollmentEJB bean does not retain open database connections across business methods.

Data Access Command Beans

The EJB specification does not prescribe any specific data access strategy for a session bean. In our example application, the EnrollmentBean class delegates all database operations to *command beans.*

A command bean is a design pattern used frequently in enterprise applications. An application uses a command bean to encapsulate a call to another application or a database call. Note that a command bean is a regular JavaBean, not an enterprise bean. Code Example 4.14 illustrates the use of a command bean.

Code Example 4.14 Using a Command Bean

```
public void commitSelections() {

    // Insert new or update existing benefits selection record.
    if (createSelection) {
        DBInsertSelection cmd1 = null;
        try {
            cmd1 = new DBInsertSelection(benefitsDS);
            cmd1.setEmplNumber(employeeNumber);
            cmd1.setCoverage(selection.coverage);
            cmd1.setMedicalPlanId(selection.medicalPlanId);
            cmd1.setDentalPlanId(selection.dentalPlanId);
            cmd1.setSmokerStatus(selection.smokerStatus);
            createSelection = false;
        } catch (SQLException ex) {
            throw new EJBException(ex);
        } finally {
            if (cmd1 != null)
                cmd1.release();
        }
```

```
    } else {
      DBUpdateSelection cmd2 = null;
      try {
          cmd2 = new DBUpdateSelection(benefitsDS);
          cmd2.setEmplNumber(employeeNumber);
          cmd2.setCoverage(selection.coverage);
          cmd2.setMedicalPlanId(selection.medicalPlanId);
          cmd2.setDentalPlanId(selection.dentalPlanId);
          cmd2.setSmokerStatus(selection.smokerStatus);
      } catch (SQLException ex) {
          throw new EJBException(ex);
      } finally {
          if (cmd2 != null)
              cmd2.release();
      }
    }

    // Update information in the payroll system.
    try {
        payroll.setBenefitsDeduction(employeeNumber,
                payrollDeduction);
    } catch (Exception ex) {
        throw new EJBException(ex);
    }
}
```

The application creates a command bean instance. It then invokes zero or more set methods to pass the input parameters to the intended application or database call. The application then invokes the `execute` method, which makes the actual call to the target application or database. Finally, it invokes zero or more get methods to obtain the values of the output arguments.

The command bean design pattern ensures uniformity with the interface in calling an application or a database. That is, the calling sequence looks the same irrespective of the type of the called application or database. This uniformity makes it possible to use command beans in application development tools.

The EnrollmentBean class uses four command beans for its data access. Descriptions of these command beans and their code follow (Code Examples 4.15 through 4.18).

The `DBQueryEmployee` command bean reads employee information for an employee with a given employee number from a database (Code Example 4.15).

Code Example 4.15 DBQueryEmployee Command Bean

```java
package com.star.benefits.db;

import java.sql.SQLException;
import java.util.Date;
import javax.sql.DataSource;

public class DBQueryEmployee extends DBQueryBean {
    static String statement =
        "SELECT empl_first_name, empl_last_name, empl_birth_date " +
            "empl_start_date, + empl_dept_id " +
        "FROM employees WHERE empl_id = ?";

    public DBQueryEmployee(DataSource ds) throws SQLException {
        super(ds, statement);
    }

    public void setEmployeeNumber(int emplNum) throws SQLException {
        pstmt.setInt(1, emplNum);
    }

    public String getFirstName() throws SQLException {
        return resultSet.getString(1);
    }
    public String getLastName() throws SQLException {
        return resultSet.getString(2);
    }
    public Date getBirthDate() throws SQLException {
        return resultSet.getDate(3);
    }
    public Date getStartDate() throws SQLException {
        return resultSet.getDate(4);
    }
    public int getDepartmentNumber() throws SQLException {
        return resultSet.getInt(5);
    }
}
```

The DBQuerySelection command bean reads the benefits selections for an employee with a given employee number from a database (Code Example 4.16).

Code Example 4.16 DBQuerySelection Command Bean

```java
package com.star.benefits.db;

import java.sql.SQLException;
import javax.sql.DataSource;

public class DBQuerySelection extends DBQueryBean {
   static String statement =
      "SELECT sel_coverage, sel_smoker, " +
         "sel_medical_plan, sel_dental_plan" +
      "FROM Selections WHERE sel_empl = ?";

   public DBQuerySelection(DataSource ds) throws SQLException {
      super(ds, statement);
   }

   public void setEmployeeNumber(int emplNum) throws SQLException {
      pstmt.setInt(1, emplNum);
   }


   public int getCoverage() throws SQLException {
      return resultSet.getInt(1);
   }
   public boolean getSmokerStatus() throws SQLException {
      return resultSet.getString(2).equals("Y");
   }
   public String getMedicalPlanId() throws SQLException {
      return resultSet.getString(3);
   }
   public String getDentalPlanId() throws SQLException {
      return resultSet.getString(4);
   }
}
```

The DBInsertSelection command bean inserts benefits selections into the database (Code Example 4.17).

Code Example 4.17 DBQInsertSelection Command Bean

```
package com.star.benefits.db;

import java.sql.SQLException;
import javax.sql.DataSource;

public class DBInsertSelection extends DBUpdateBean {
    static String statement =
        "INSERT INTO Selections VALUES (?, ?, ?, ?, ?)";

    public DBInsertSelection(DataSource ds) throws SQLException {
        super(ds, statement);
    }

    public void setEmplNumber(int emplNum) throws SQLException {
        pstmt.setInt(1, emplNum);
    }
    public void setCoverage(int cov) throws SQLException {
        pstmt.setInt(2, cov);
    }
    public void setMedicalPlanId(String id) throws SQLException {
        pstmt.setString(3, id);
    }
    public void setDentalPlanId(String id) throws SQLException {
        pstmt.setString(4, id);
    }
    public void setSmokerStatus(boolean st) throws SQLException {
        pstmt.setString(5, st ? "Y" : "N");
    }
}
```

The DBUpdateSelection command bean updates benefits selections in the database (Code Example 4.18).

Code Example 4.18 DBQUpdateSelection Command Bean

```
package com.star.benefits.db;

import java.sql.SQLException;
import javax.sql.DataSource;
```

```java
public class DBUpdateSelection extends DBUpdateBean {
    static String statement =
        "UPDATE Selections SET " +
            "sel_coverage = ?, " +
            "sel_medical_plan = ?, " +
            "sel_dental_plan = ?, " +
            "sel_smoker = ? " +
        "WHERE sel_empl = ?";

    public DBUpdateSelection(DataSource ds) throws SQLException {
        super(ds, statement);
    }

    public void setEmplNumber(int emplNum) throws SQLException {
        pstmt.setInt(5, emplNum);
    }
    public void setCoverage(int cov) throws SQLException {
        pstmt.setInt(1, cov);
    }
    public void setMedicalPlanId(String id) throws SQLException {
        pstmt.setString(2, id);
    }
    public void setDentalPlanId(String id) throws SQLException {
        pstmt.setString(3, id);
    }
    public void setSmokerStatus(boolean st) throws SQLException {
        pstmt.setString(4, st ? "Y" : "N");
    }
}
```

Code Example 4.19 illustrates the command bean's superclasses.

Code Example 4.19 Command Bean Superclasses

```java
package com.star.benefits.db;

import java.sql.Connection;
import java.sql.PreparedStatement;
import java.sql.ResultSet;
import java.sql.SQLException;
import javax.sql.DataSource;
```

```java
public class DBQueryBean {
    protected PreparedStatement pstmt;
    protected ResultSet resultSet = null;
    private Connection con;

    protected DBQueryBean(DataSource ds, String statement)
        throws SQLException
    {
        con = ds.getConnection();
        pstmt = con.prepareStatement(statement);
    }

    public void execute() throws SQLException {
        resultSet = pstmt.executeQuery();
    }

    public boolean next() throws SQLException {
        return resultSet.next();
    }

    public void release() {
        try {
            if (resultSet != null)
                resultSet.close();
            if (pstmt != null)
                pstmt.close();
            if (con != null)
                con.close();
        } catch (SQLException ex) {
        }
    }
}


package com.star.benefits.db;

import java.sql.Connection;
import java.sql.PreparedStatement;
import java.sql.SQLException;
import javax.sql.DataSource;

public class DBUpdateBean {
```

```
    protected PreparedStatement pstmt;
    private Connection con;

    public int execute() throws SQLException {
        int rowCount = pstmt.executeUpdate();
        pstmt.close();
        con.close();
        return rowCount;
    }

    protected DBUpdateBean(DataSource ds, String statement)
        throws SQLException
    {
        con = ds.getConnection();
        pstmt = con.prepareStatement(statement);
    }

    public void release() { }
}
```

Note that some application programmers may prefer to use a command bean to encapsulate the EJB invocation of the setBenefitsDeduction method on the Payroll bean. If so, they would write the commitSelections method of the Enroll-mentBean as shown in Code Example 4.20.

Code Example 4.20 Alternative Implementation of commitSelections Method

```
public void commitSelections() {
    ...
    DeductionUpdateBean cmd = null;
    try {
        cmd = new DeductionUpdateBean(PayrollHome);
        cmd.setEmployee(employeeNumber);
        cmd.setDeduction(payrollDeduction);
        cmd.execute();
    } catch (Exception ex) {
        throw new EJBException();
    } finally {
        if (cmd != null) cmd.release();
    }
}
```

The implementation of the DeductionUpdateBean would create a payroll object, would then invoke the `setBenefitsDeduction` method on the object, and lastly would remove the object.

Database Connections

It is usually good practice to acquire JDBC connections just before they are needed, and to release them as soon as they are not needed. The command beans follow this practice regarding JDBC connections, as follows.

- Each acquires a JDBC connection prior to executing a JDBC statement.

- Once they have established the JDBC connection, each command bean object creates and executes a particular JDBC statement.

- After the statement executes, each releases the JDBC connection.

Adhering to this practice—establishing a JDBC connection, executing the JDBC statement, then releasing the connection—allows the EJB container to maximize the reuse of the physical database connections by multiple session bean instances. It makes it possible for a small number of physical database connections to be serially reused by a large number of session bean instances. This sharing of physical database connections is transparent to the session bean code. The EJB container provides the ability to reuse connections as a service to the enterprise bean applications. This service is usually called *JDBC connection pooling*.

What happens if an instance opens a JDBC connection and holds it across multiple client calls? If it does, the number of open JDBC connections would equal the number of active session bean instances, which in turn is equal to the number of users. When many users simultaneously access the application, the number of open JDBC connections could exceed a system-defined resource limit and potentially cause the application to fail. To avoid application failures resulting from open connection failures, the EJB container would have to passivate some instances so that they would release their connections (see the next section, Session Object Passivation and Activation). The application would run correctly but its performance may be lower because of the overhead of excessive instance passivation and activation.

Session Object Passivation and Activation

A stateful session object lasts for the duration of the business process implemented by the session object. The business process typically spans multiple client-invoked business methods and may last for several minutes, hours, or even days. For example, an employee may start the Benefits Enrollment application, fill in the first two screens, then leave for a meeting that lasts several hours, and, on returning three hours later, complete the remaining steps.

The state of a stateful session object often may occupy a nontrivial amount of main memory on the server. In addition, the state may include expensive resources such as TCP/IP or database connections. (Our example does not show these types of resources.) Because of these factors, it is important that the EJB container be able to reclaim the resources by having the capability to save the state of a stateful session object in some form of secondary memory (such as a database). Later, when the state of the session object is once again needed for the invocation of a business method, the EJB container can restore the state from the saved image.

The process of saving the session object's state to secondary memory is called *passivation*. The process of restoring the state is called *activation*. The container typically passivates a session object when it needs to free resources to process requests from other clients, or when it needs to transfer the session bean instance to a different process for load-balancing purposes. For example, the container passivates the instance by invoking the `ejbPassivate` method in the instance, then serializing the instance and moving it to some secondary storage. When it activates the session object, it restores the session bean instance's state by deserializing the saved image of the passivated instance and then invoking the `ejbActivate` method on the instance.

Recall from the discussion in Understanding Conversational State on page 58, the instance variables of the session bean class maintain the state of a stateful session object. To passivate a session object, the EJB container uses the Java serialization protocol (or another functionally equivalent mechanism) to serialize the state of the instance and save it in secondary storage.

For many session beans, including our example EnrollmentEJB bean, the passivation and activation processes do not require any programming effort from the bean developer. The bean developer only has to ensure that the objects held in the session bean instance variables are serializable at passivation.

In addition to serializable objects, the instance's state may include references to several objects that do not need to be serializable at passivation. These objects are

- References to other enterprise beans' home and remote interfaces

- References to the SessionContext interface

- References to the Java Naming and Dictionary Interface (JNDI) context `java:comp/env` and its subcontexts

- References to the UserTransaction interface

The EJB container recognizes these objects during passivation; therefore, they do not have to be serializable.

Although not prohibited by the EJB specification, the session bean class should not declare fields as transient. This is because the EJB specification does not specify how the EJB container handles transient fields across instance passivation. Although some containers may preserve the values of transient fields across passivation, others may reset the transient fields to their Java language initial default value.

The EJB container allows the session bean class to participate in the session object passivation and activation protocol. For this purpose, the SessionBean interface defines the `ejbPassivate` and `ejbActivate` methods. The EJB container invokes the `ejbPassivate` method just before it passivates the instance. The EJB container invokes the `ejbActivate` method just after it activates the instance.

The session bean instance uses the `ejbPassivate` method to release any expensive resources that can be easily reconstructed at activation, and to ensure that the instance fields contain only serializable objects. For example, an instance must close any open database connections or TCP/IP connections because these objects are not serializable.

The session bean instance uses the `ejbActivate` method to reacquire the resources released by the `ejbPassivate` method so that the instance is ready to accept a client-invoked business method. For example, the instance would reopen the database or TCP/IP connections closed in the `ejbPassivate` method.

The container can invoke the `ejbPassivate` method on a session bean instance at anytime while the instance is not involved in a transaction. Because the bean developer cannot prevent the container from invoking `ejbPassivate`, the bean must be coded to accept `ejbPassivate` at any time between transactions.

Let's look at the implementations of the `ejbPassivate` and `ejbActivate` methods in the EnrollmentBean class in Code Example 4.21.

Code Example 4.21 Implementation of Passivation and Activation

```
// Release resources that cannot be preserved across passivation.
public void ejbPassivate() {
    employeeDS = null;
    benefitsDS = null;
}

// Reacquire resources released in ejbPassivate.
public void ejbActivate() {
    getDataSources();
}
```

```
private void getDataSources() {
    try {
        Context ictx = new InitialContext();
        employeeDS = (DataSource)ictx.lookup(
                "java:comp/env/jdbc/EmployeeDB");
        benefitsDS = (DataSource)ictx.lookup(
                "java:comp/env/jdbc/BenefitsDB");
    } catch (Exception ex) {
        throw new EJBException(ex);
    }
}
}
```

As you can see, the `ejbPassivate` method releases the references of the `employeeDS` and `benefitsDS` objects. This is because the EJB specification does not guarantee that the container can preserve data source objects across passivation. Therefore, it is an error for the bean developer to retain their references in the session bean instance variables.

The session bean uses the `ejbActivate` method to reacquire the data source objects.

4.4.3   Client Developer's Perspective

This section describes the EnrollmentEJB session bean from the perspective of the client developer; that is, it describes how the client application uses the EnrollmentEJB session bean. In our example, the client is the EnrollmentWeb Web application, which consists of several JSPs.

In this section, we focus on the segments of the EnrollmentWeb code relevant to using a session bean. (The examples show only the relevant portions of the code.) We do not show nor do we explain EnrollmentWeb's functions outside of its interaction with the session bean. We do not show how the EnrollmentWeb application generates the HTML pages that are sent to the user's browser, nor do we show how the EnrollmentWeb application processes the user input that the browser sends as HTTP post requests.

Session Object Creation

The application process begins when a user visits the Benefits Web site. The Web container logs in the user and invokes the EnrollmentWeb application, which is the client of the EnrollmentSession bean. The EnrollmentWeb application executes the code segment shown in Code Example 4.22 to create an Enrollment session object. The Enrollment session object drives the conversation with the user and stores the user-specific information from one HTTP request to the next.

Code Example 4.22 Creating a Session Object from a JSP

```
...
import javax.naming.*;
import javax.rmi.PortableRemoteObject;
import com.star.benefits.*;
...
String loginID = request.getUserPrincipal().getName();
int emplNumber = Integer.parseInt(loginID);

InitialContext ictx = new InitialContext();
Object h = ictx.lookup("java:comp/env/ejb/EnrollmentEJB");
EnrollmentHome enrollmentHome = (EnrollmentHome)
    PortableRemoteObject.narrow(h, EnrollmentHome.class);
enrollment = enrollmentHome.create(emplNumber);

session.setAttribute("EnrollmentBean", enrollment);
...
```

Let's look at the EnrollmentWeb code in more detail.

The `getUserPrincipal` method is a servlet API method that obtains the user's login identifier, which is a unique number assigned to each employee. The method returns the login ID that the user entered in the login page displayed to the user by the Web container. EnrollmentWeb then uses the `Integer.parseInt` method to convert the `loginID` string to an integer value representing the user's unique employee number.

Next, EnrollmentWeb must locate the bean's home interface. To locate a session bean's home interface, EnrollmentWeb first needs to obtain a JNDI initial naming context. The code instantiates a new javax.naming.InitialContext object, which our example calls ictx. EnrollmentWeb then uses the context `lookup` method to obtain the Enrollment bean's home interface. Note that the deployer has previously configured the EnrollmentWeb's initial naming context such that the name `java:comp/env/ejb/EnrollmentEJB` resolves to the Enrollment bean's home object.

The `lookup` method returns a `java.lang.Object` type, which the code must then cast to the expected type. Our example casts it to EnrollmentHome. The `javax.rmi.PortableRemoteObject.narrow` method performs type narrowing of the client-side representations of the home and remote interfaces. It makes a client program interoperable with all compliant EJB container implementations. Note that it is not sufficient simply to use the Java `cast` operator; in fact, using the `cast` operator may not work in some container implementations. (Note that the EJB specification requires that applications use the `javax.rmi.PortableRemoteObject.narrow` method to perform type conversion of references of the EJB home and remote interfaces.)

Once EnrollmentWeb obtains a reference to the home interface, it can call a `create` method on that home interface to create a session object. In Code Example 4.22, EnrollmentWeb invokes the home interface `create` method and passes the user's employee number for the method argument. The `create` method returns a reference to the session object that implements the Enrollment remote interface. At this point, EnrollmentWeb can use the session object reference to invoke the bean's business methods. See the next section, Business Method Invocation, for further details.

Lastly, the EnrollmentWeb application stores the session object reference of the Enrollment session object in its HTTP session state. It does this using the servlet API `setAttribute` method. The session object represents the HTTP session for the current user.

Business Method Invocation

The client (that is, the EnrollmentWeb application) invokes the Enrollment object's business methods to accomplish the tasks of the Benefit Enrollment application. This is the business logic of a session bean, and each session bean has its own unique logic.

Code Example 4.23 shows the business logic portion of the EnrollmentWeb code for our example.

Code Example 4.23 Client Business Method Invocation

```
// Get EmployeeInfo.
EmployeeInfo employeeInfo = enrollment.getEmployeeInfo();
...
Options coverageOptions = enrollment.getCoverageOptions();
// Display coverageOptions to user and let him make a selection.
enrollment.setCoverageOption(selection);
...
boolean smokerStatus = enrollment.getSmokerStatus();
// Display smoker status screen to user and let him make a selection.
enrollment.setSmokerStatus(smokerStatus);
...
Options medicalOptions = enrollment.getMedicalOptions();
..
// Display medicalOptions to the user and let him make a selection.
enrollment.setMedicalOption(selection);
...
```

```
Options dentalOptions = enrollment.getDentalOptions();
// Display dentalOptions to the user and let him make a selection.
enrollment.setDentalOption(selection);
...
Summary summary = enrollment.getSummary();
// Display summary of selected choices, and prompt user to confirm.
enrollment.commitSelections();
...
```

The logic in the code mirrors the sequence of the Benefit Enrollment application's HTML screens (see Figure 4.5 on page 62). EnrollmentWeb starts by gathering the necessary data—in this case, the employee data and available coverage options. To accomplish this, EnrollmentWeb first invokes the Enrollment object's getEmployeeInfo method to gather employee information—first and last names—based on the employee's identifier. The getEmployeeInfo method uses the EmployeeInfo helper class to pass this information.

Next, EnrollmentWeb invokes the getCoverageOptions method. This method uses the Options helper class to return the available benefits coverage options. It returns the various coverage options and their descriptions, and the employee's current benefits selection, if any. When EnrollmentWeb receives all the information, it formats the data into an HTML page, with the employee's current coverage option highlighted, and displays the first screen of the Benefits Enrollment application to the user. (This is the Step 1: Select Coverage Category screen.)

The user makes a benefits selection and presses the Next button. EnrollmentWeb calls the setCoverageOption method to test the validity of the selection. If the user makes an invalid selection, the setCoverageOption method throws EnrollmentException, which displays that the error is the result of an invalid parameter. (Recall that because EnrollmentException is an application-defined exception, it does not cause the container to remove the session object.) The setCoverageOption method saves the selection.

EnrollmentWeb then displays the smoker status screen and invokes the getSmokerStatus method. This method returns a Boolean type to EnrollmentWeb indicating the user's smoker status. EnrollmentWeb invokes the setSmokerStatus method to save the user's indicated smoker status. The setSmokerStatus method in turn stores the smoker selection.

Before displaying the third screen in the sequence—the medical options screen—EnrollmentWeb invokes the getMedicalOptions method to extract and return the available medical coverage options. This method uses the Options helper class to return the medical options, with their descriptions and appropriate costs given the user's smoker status. EnrollmentWeb receives the medical coverage information, formats the data into an HTML page, which it then returns to the user's browser so that the Step 3: Medical Options screen is displayed.

The user selects the desired medical coverage, and EnrollmentWeb uses the `setMedicalOption` method to transmit the selection to the benefits application, which saves the selection. The method first checks that the selection is valid; if it is not, it throws the `EnrollmentException` application exception.

Next, EnrollmentWeb retrieves the available dental options by invoking the `getDentalOptions` method. It formats the data into an HTML page and returns the page to the user's browser for display. The user selects a dental option, which EnrollmentWeb saves by invoking the `setDentalOption` method.

Lastly, EnrollmentWeb invokes the `getSummary` method to retrieve the individual data for the user's previously entered coverage selections and to calculate the total cost of all the options. EnrollmentWeb formats the data into an HTML page and returns the page to the user's browser. The user can view his selections, see what each selection costs, and verify the total payroll deduction amount for these benefits. The user can modify his selections at this point or accept them. When accepted, EnrollmentWeb commits the user's coverage selections by invoking the `commitSelections` method.

Session Object Removal

The client (the EnrollmentWeb application) removes the session object at the completion of the enrollment business process after it processes the user's confirmation response; that is, after it invokes the `enrollment.commitSelections` method on the Enrollment session object. This is illustrated as follows.

```
...
enrollment.remove();
session.removeAttribute("EnrollmentBean");
...
```

Note that once EnrollmentWeb removes the stateful session bean, it cannot make additional invocations of the bean's business methods. If EnrollmentWeb attempted to invoke a business method on a stateful session object after it had removed the object, it would receive the `java.rmi.NoSuchObjectException` error.

Use of Object Handles

The EJB architecture allows a session bean client to store an object reference of a session bean's home or remote interface in persistent storage. To do this, a client uses the object's *handle*. The EJB specification defines two interfaces for working with handles.

1. The javax.ejb.Handle interface for the handles of enterprise bean objects

2. The javax.ejb.HomeHandle interface for the handles of the enterprise bean home objects

Code Example 4.24 illustrates the use of a session object handle.

Code Example 4.24 Using a Session Bean Handle

```
...
ObjectOutputStream outputStream = ...;
...
Handle handle = enrollment.getHandle();
outputStream.writeObject(handle);
...
```

Note in this example that the client first obtains the handle by invoking the getHandle method on the session object. The client then serializes the handle into ObjectOutputStream.

At a later point, another client program running in the same client environment can deserialize the handle and create an object from the session object reference. Code Example 4.25 shows how this is done.

Code Example 4.25 Deserializing a Handle

```
...
ObjectInputStream inputStream = ...;
...
Handle handle = (Handle)inputStream.readObject();
Enrollment enrollment = (Enrollment)
      PortableRemoteObject.narrow(handle.getEJBObject(),
            Enrollment.class);
// invoke business methods on enrollment session object
enrollment.getMedicalOptions();
```

Note that the PortableRemoteObject.narrow mechanism, although complicated to use, ensures that the client code works with all EJB containers.

The Benefits Enrollment application does not use handles directly. However, although transparent to the application developer, the Web container running the EnrollmentWeb Web application may use the handle mechanism in several ways, as follows.

- **Maintain a reference to the session object**. EnrollmentWeb maintains a reference to the Enrollment session object in the HTTP session state. If the Web container needs to swap the HTTP session state to secondary storage, it may use the handle mechanism to retain the reference to the session object.

- **Migrate the HTTP session to another process.** The Web container may choose to migrate the HTTP session to another process on the same or different machine. The Web container may use the handle mechanism to migrate the session object reference from one process to another.

- **Store HTTP session data.** The Web container may choose to implement the EnrollmentWeb application as stateless by storing all the HTTP session data in an HTTP cookie. The Web container may use the handle to externalize the session object reference and store it in the cookie.

Note that a container crash invalidates any session handles for session objects that were stored in persistent storage.

Session Object Identity

A stateful session object has a unique identity. The EJB container assigns the identity to the object at the object's creation time. Each invocation of the `create` method on the session bean home interface results in the generation of a new unique identifier.

Unlike the object identity of an entity object, which is visible to the client, the object identifier of a session bean is not available to the client. However, a client may determine if two session object references refer to the same session object by using the `isIdentical` method of the EJBObject interface. Code Example 4.26 illustrates this.

Code Example 4.26 Comparing Session Object References

```
...
Enrollment obj1 = ...;
Enrollment obj2 = ...;
if (obj1.isIdentical(obj2)) {
   // obj1 and obj2 refer to the same session object.
   ...
} else {
   // obj1 and obj2 refer to different session objects.
   ...
}
```

Most session bean client applications, including our example EnrollmentWeb application, typically do not need to compare the references of session objects for identity purposes. Generally, it is only entity bean applications that need to use comparisons for object identity.

4.5   PayrollEJB Stateless Session Bean

The PayrollEJB session bean provides remote access to the PayrollDatabase. Because payroll data is sensitive information, most, if not all, enterprises set up their environments to restrict access to payroll data. The PayrollEJB session bean exists principally to provide applications, such as the Benefits Enrollment application, with restrictive access to the PayrollDatabase. In addition, PayrollEJB may implement an audit trail.

An application that wants to access the payroll information cannot access the PayrollDatabase directly (such as by using JDBC). Instead, an application must use the PayrollEJB session bean to access the information indirectly. By requiring applications to use the PayrollEJB session bean to access the PayrollDatabase, the payroll department restricts the access to the payroll information to the functions defined in the PayrollEJB session bean. In addition, the payroll department can use the EJB declarative security mechanism enforced by the EJB container to restrict access to the individual methods of PayrollEJB to specific applications.

4.5.1   PayrollEJB Stateless Session Bean Parts

Figure 4.11 illustrates the main parts of the PayrollEJB stateless session bean.

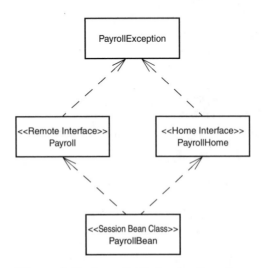

Figure 4.11 PayrollEJB Session Bean Parts

The remote interface is called Payroll. The home interface is called Payroll-Home. The session bean class is called PayrollBean. The methods of the remote and home interfaces throw the application exception `PayrollException`.

PayrollEJB Session Bean Remote Interface

The Payroll remote interface defines the business methods that a client may invoke on the individual session objects. Code Example 4.27 shows the definition of the Payroll remote interface.

Code Example 4.27 Payroll Remote Interface

```
package com.star.payroll;

import javax.ejb.*;
import java.rmi.RemoteException;

public interface Payroll extends EJBObject {
    void setBenefitsDeduction(int emplNumber, double deduction)
        throws RemoteException, PayrollException;
    double getBenefitsDeduction(int emplNumber)
        throws RemoteException, PayrollException;
    double getSalary(int emplNumber)
        throws RemoteException, PayrollException;
    void setSalary(int emplNumber, double salary)
        throws RemoteException, PayrollException;
}
```

The Payroll interface follows the same EJB rules for all enterprise bean remote interfaces.

PayrollEJB Session Bean Home Interface

The PayrollHome home interface defines the `create` method used by the client to create a session object. Code Example 4.28 shows the definition of this interface.

Code Example 4.28 PayrollHome Home Interface

```
import javax.ejb.*;
import java.rmi.RemoteException;

public interface PayrollHome extends EJBHome {
    Payroll create() throws RemoteException, CreateException;
}
```

Notice that PayrollHome defines only one create method, and that this method takes no arguments. Notice also that PayrollHome defines no other methods. According to the EJB specification, the home interface of a stateless session bean must a have a single create method that takes no arguments. The home interface cannot define any other methods.

PayrollEJB Helper Classes

The PayrollEJB session bean uses only one helper class, PayrollException, which defines the payroll-specific exceptions. The Payroll and PayrollHome interfaces are defined to throw the exception PayrollException. Code Example 4.29 shows the definition of the PayrollException class:

Code Example 4.29 PayrollException Helper Class

```
package com.star.payroll;

public class PayrollException extends Exception {
    // error codes
    public static int UNKNOWN = 0;
    public static int INVAL_EMPL_NUMBER = 1;

    static String[] defaultMessage = {
        "unknown error code",
        "invalid employee number"
    };

    int errorCode;

    public PayrollException() { super(); }
    public PayrollException(String s) { super(s); }
    public PayrollException(int errorCode, String s) {
        super(s);
        this.errorCode = errorCode;
    }
    public PayrollException(int errorCode) {
        super(errorCode >= 0 && errorCode < defaultMessage.length ?
            defaultMessage[errorCode] : "");
        this.errorCode = errorCode;
    }
}
```

PayrollEJB Session Bean Class

The PayrollBean class is the PayrollEJB's session bean class. It is defined as shown in Code Example 4.30.

Code Example 4.30 PayrollBean Session Bean Class

```
package com.star.payroll;

import javax.ejb.*;

import javax.naming.*;
import java.sql.*;
import javax.sql.*;


// Payroll is a stateless session bean that provides
// access to the payroll system.
//
public class PayrollBean implements SessionBean
{
    private DataSource ds;

    public void setBenefitsDeduction(int emplNumber,
                            double deduction)
        throws PayrollException
    {
        try {
            Connection con = getConnection();
            PreparedStatement pstmt = con.prepareStatement(
                "UPDATE Paychecks SET " +
                "pay_ded_benefits = ? " +
                "WHERE pay_empl = ?"
            );
            pstmt.setDouble(1, deduction);
            pstmt.setInt(2, emplNumber);
            if (pstmt.executeUpdate() == 0) {
                con.close();
                throw new PayrollException(
                    PayrollException.INVAL_EMPL_NUMBER);
            }
            con.close();
```

```java
        } catch (Exception ex) {
            throw new EJBException(ex);
        }
    }

    public double getBenefitsDeduction(int emplNumber)
        throws PayrollException
    {
        try {
            Connection con = getConnection();
            Statement stmt = con.createStatement();
            PreparedStatement pstmt = con.prepareStatement(
                "SELECT pay_ded_benefits " +
                "FROM Paychecks " +
                "WHERE pay_emp = ?"
            );
            pstmt.setInt(1, emplNumber);
            ResultSet rs = pstmt.executeQuery();
            if (rs.next()) {
                double deduction = rs.getDouble(1);
                con.close();
                return deduction;
            } else {
                con.close();
                throw new PayrollException(
                    PayrollException.INVAL_EMPL_NUMBER);
            }
        } catch (SQLException ex) {
            throw new EJBException(ex);
        }
    }

    public double getSalary(int emplNumber)
        throws PayrollException
    {
        try {
            Connection con = getConnection();
            Statement stmt = con.createStatement();
            PreparedStatement pstmt = con.prepareStatement(
                "SELECT pay_salary " +
                "FROM Paychecks " +
                "WHERE pay_emp = ?"
```

```
      );
      pstmt.setInt(1, emplNumber);
      ResultSet rs = pstmt.executeQuery();
      if (rs.next()) {
         double salary = rs.getDouble(1);
         con.close();
         return salary;
      } else {
         con.close();
         throw new PayrollException(
            PayrollException.INVAL_EMPL_NUMBER);
      }
   } catch (SQLException ex) {
      throw new EJBException(ex);
   }
}

public void setSalary(int emplNumber, double salary)
   throws PayrollException
{
   try {
      Connection con = getConnection();
      PreparedStatement pstmt = con.prepareStatement(
         "UPDATE Paychecks SET " +
         "pay_salary = ? " +
         "WHERE pay_empl = ?"
      );
      pstmt.setDouble(1, salary);
      pstmt.setInt(2, emplNumber);
      if (pstmt.executeUpdate() == 0) {
         con.close();
         throw new PayrollException(
            PayrollException.INVAL_EMPL_NUMBER);
      }
      con.close();
   } catch (Exception ex) {
      throw new EJBException(ex);
   }
}
```

```
public void setSessionContext(SessionContext sc) {}
public void ejbCreate() {}
public void ejbRemove() {}
public void ejbPassivate() { /* never called */ }
public void ejbActivate() { /* never called */ }

private Connection getConnection() {
   try {
      return ds.getConnection();
   } catch (Exception ex) {
      throw new EJBException(ex);
   }
}

private void readEnvironment() {
   try {
      Context ictx = new InitialContext();
      ds = (DataSource)ictx.lookup(
         "java:comp/env/jdbc/PayrollDB");
   } catch (Exception ex) {
      throw new EJBException(ex);
   }
}
}
```

The PayrollBean session bean class is a Java class that defines the implementation of the PayrollEJB session bean. Specifically, it defines the following.

- The business methods that are defined in the Payroll remote interface

- The `ejbCreate` method that corresponds to the `create` method defined in the PayrollHome interface

- The methods defined in the javax.ejb.SessionBean interface

PayrollEJB Business Methods Implementation. The PayrollEJB session bean defines four business methods. The implementations of the four business methods—setSalary, getSalary, setBenefitsDeduction, and getBenefitsDeduction—use JDBC to read or update the underlying PayrollDatabase.

Note that the PayrollBean bean instance acquires a database connection at the start of each business method, and releases the connection at the end of the business method. In this example, the bean developer chose not to hold the database connection across business method invocations; the developer did this to allow the application server's connection pooling mechanism to maximize the reuse of database connections. However, it is also legal to hold the database connection across all business method invocations; that is, to acquire the database connection in the ejbCreate method, use it in the business methods, and then release it in the ejbRemove method.

Recall that a stateless session bean instance does not maintain state for a specific client. The PayrollBean class does not keep any state that is specific to a client (conversational state). The EJB container can use a stateless session bean instance to process (serially) the requests from multiple clients. It can also route each request occurrence from a given client to a different instance, even if that client is running within the context of a transaction. Therefore, instances of a stateless session bean class must not hold any conversational state. (However, they can contain objects that are not specific to a client, such as JDBC data sources, as illustrated in our example.) The client must pass all the state necessary to process a request in the business method arguments.

As the example code illustrates, the paradigm provided by a stateless session bean is essentially procedural programming. This is in contrast to a stateful session bean and an entity bean, both of which provide the object-oriented programming paradigm.

ejbCreate *Method Implementation.* Notice that the PayrollBean leaves the implementation of the ejbCreate method empty.

The container invokes the ejbCreate method after it creates the instance of the PayrollBean class and invokes the setSessionContext method on the instance. The bean developer needs to keep in mind that the container may create instances of a stateless session bean class in no direct relationship to the client-invoked create methods. This differs from a stateful session bean, in which the container creates the instance when a client invokes a create method through the session bean's home interface.

For example, the container may choose to create a fixed number of instances of the stateless session bean at the time that the container starts, and then use these instances to handle all subsequent client-invoked methods. Therefore, the ejbCreate method does not execute in a client context. Because of this, it would be an error for the ejbCreate method to invoke, for example, the getCallerPrincipal method on the associated SessionContext interface.

A stateless session bean typically uses the ejbCreate method to acquire various resources that will be used across subsequently invoked business methods. An example of such a resource would be a TCP/IP connection or a JDBC data source.

SessionBean Method Implementation. The PayrollBean class defines empty implementations of the setSessionContext, ejbRemove, ejbActivate, and `ejbPassivate` *SessionBean interface methods.* PayrollBean is really a simple, uncomplicated bean, and as such it does not need the functionality provided by these container-invoked methods.

The container calls the `setSessionContext` method after it creates the PayrollBean instance and before it invokes the `ejbCreate` method on the instance. If the instance needs to invoke any of the methods that relate to `SessionContext` during its lifetime, it should save the passed `SessionContext` reference in an instance variable, and it should do this from within the `setSessionContext` method.

ejbRemove Method Implementation

The container invokes the `ejbRemove` method before it discards the instance. Once the container invokes the `ejbRemove` method on an instance, it does not invoke any further business methods in the instance. The `ejbRemove` method is typically used to release any resources acquired in the `ejbCreate` method.

Notice the comments in the PayrollBean code for the `ejbActivate` and `ejbPassivate` methods, which indicate that the container never calls the `ejbActivate` and `ejbPassivate` methods. The concept of passivation and activation applies only to stateful session beans; the container thus never calls these methods on a stateless session bean.

Data Access

The PayrollBean class makes direct use of JDBC in its business methods to access the database. Some application developers may prefer encapsulating the data access by using command beans (see Data Access Command Beans on page 102).

If a JDBC call throws an exception, the PayrollBean instance catches the exception and throws `EJBException`. You may notice that the instance does not close the JDBC connection before throwing `EJBException`, even though closing the connection is considered good programming practice. (For example, we always close the JDBC connection in the command beans used by the EnrollmentBean. We do so by calling the `release` method in the `finally` clause.) However, because the container manages resources for bean instances, not closing the JDBC connection does not result in a leak of resources. The container catches `EJBException` and closes all the resources, including JDBC connections, that are held by the instance. Management of resources is one of the services that the EJB container provides on behalf of the enterprise bean instances. The JDBC driver collaborates with the container to achieve the management of resources.

4.5.2   Client Developer's Perspective

In our example application, the EnrollmentEJB session bean is the client of the PayrollEJB session bean.

EnrollmentEJB creates a stateless session object as follows.

```
...
PayrollHome payrollHome = (PayrollHome)
    PortableRemoteObject.narrow(
        ictx.lookup("java:comp/env/ejb/PayrollEJB"),
        PayrollHome.class);
payroll = (Payroll)payrollHome.create();
...
```

A client uses the same API to create a stateless session bean as it does to create a stateful session bean. However, as just discussed in `ejbCreate` Method Implementation on page 127, invoking the `create` method on the home interface of a stateless session bean does not necessarily create a new instance of the session bean class. The implementation of the session bean's home interface `create` method may simply produce an object reference to the (already existing) distributed object that implements the session bean's home interface, and then may return the reference to the client.

After the client creates a stateless session object, it can invoke the object's business methods through the remote interface. For example, the EnrollmentBean invokes the `setBenefitsDeduction` method as follows.

```
...
// Update information in the payroll system.
try {
    payroll.setBenefitsDeduction(employeeNumber, payrollDeduction);
} catch (PayrollException ex) {
    ...
} catch (RemoteException ex) {
    ...
}
...
```

Finally, when the client is done using the Payroll object, it releases it by invoking the `remove` method, as follows.

```
...
try {
      payroll.remove();
} catch (Exception ex) {
}
...
```

Note that all stateless session objects within the same home interface have the same object identity. (However, objects from different home interfaces have different identities.) The following code example shows that two Payroll Bean objects have the same identity (the isIdentical method returns true).

```
Payroll payroll = (Payroll)payrollHome.create();
Payroll payroll2 = (Payroll)payrollHome.create();
if (payroll.isIdentical(payroll2)) {// this test returns true
   ...
} else {
   ...
}
```

This is in contrast to a stateful session bean. Every stateful session object has a unique identity.

4.6   Database Schemas

The Benefits Enrollment application uses three databases. In order for you to understand the example application, this section describes the schemas for these databases.

4.6.1   EmployeeDatabase Schema

The Star Enterprise human resources department maintains information about employees, company departments, and department positions in the Employee Database. The information is stored in three tables. The Employees table within the database holds employee identifying information. Code Example 4.31 shows the SQL CREATE statement defining this table.

Code Example 4.31 Employees Table Schema

```
CREATE TABLE Employees (
    empl_id INT,
    empl_first_name VARCHAR(32),
    empl_last_name VARCHAR(32),
    empl_addr_street VARCHAR(32),
    empl_addr_city VARCHAR(32),
    empl_addr_zip VARCHAR(10),
    empl_addr_state VARCHAR(2),
    empl_dept_id VARCHAR(10),
    empl_start_date DATE,
    empl_position VARCHAR(5),
    empl_birth_date DATE,
    PRIMARY KEY (empl_id)
)
```

The columns of the Employees table contain the following information.

- **empl_id column**—The employee identifier number. This number uniquely identifies each employee, and it is the primary key for these records.

- **empl_first_name and empl_last_name columns**—The employee's first and last names

- **empl_addr_street, empl_addr_city, empl_addr_zip, and empl_addr_state columns**—The employee's complete address

- **empl_dept_id column**—The identifier for the department in which the employee works. This column is a foreign key reference to a row in the Departments table.

- **empl_start_date column**—The employee's start date with the company

- **empl_position column**—The identifier for the employee's current job or position. This column is a foreign key reference to a Positions table record.

- **empl_birth_date column**—The employee's date of birth

The EmployeeDatabase includes two other tables that pertain to the Benefits Enrollment application. The Positions table keeps a description (in the pos_desc column) of each job position within the company. Its primary key is the pos_id column, which contains the position identifier. Code Example 4.32 shows the schema for this table.

Code Example 4.32 Positions Table Schema

```
create table Positions (
   pos_id VARCHAR(5),
   pos_desc VARCHAR(32),
   PRIMARY KEY (pos_id)
)
```

The third relevant table in the EmployeeDatabase is the Departments table, which keeps information about each department within the company. Code Example 4.33 shows the schema for this table.

Code Example 4.33 Departments Table Schema

```
create table Departments (
   dept_id VARCHAR(10),
   dept_desc VARCHAR(32),
   dept_mgr INT,
   PRIMARY KEY (dept_id)
)
```

The columns of the Departments table contain the following data.

- **dept_id column**—The department identifier, unique for each department. This is the primary key for the table.

- **dept_desc column**—A description of the department

- **dept_mgr column**—The empl_id of the current manager of the department

4.6.2   BenefitsDatabase Schema

The BenefitsDatabase schema defines one table, Selections, pertaining to the enrollment application. Code Example 4.34 shows the schema defining the Selections table.

Code Example 4.34 Selections Table Schema

```
create table Selections (
   sel_empl INT,
   sel_coverage INT,
   sel_medical_plan VARCHAR(10),
```

```
sel_dental_plan VARCHAR(10),
sel_smoker CHAR(1),
PRIMARY_KEY (sel_empl)
)
```

The columns of the Selections table hold the following data.

- **sel_empl column**—The employee's identifier number. This is the employee for whom the benefits selections pertain.

- **sel_coverage column**—The type of coverage selected by the employee

- **sel_medical_plan column**—The plan identifier of the employee's selected medical plan

- **sel_dental_plan column**—The plan identifier of the employee's selected dental plan

- **sel_smoker column**—An indicator of whether the employee is a smoker. The allowed values are Y and N.

4.6.3 PayrollDatabase Schema

The PayrollDatabase schema defines one table relevant to the Benefits Enrollment application—the Paychecks table. Code Example 4.35 shows its definition.

Code Example 4.35 Paychecks Table Schema

```
create table Paychecks (
    pay_empl INT,
    pay_salary FLOAT,
    pay_ded_benefits FLOAT,
    PRIMARY KEY (pay_empl)
)
```

This table maintains two amounts (columns): the employee's payroll amount or salary (pay_salary) and the benefits deduction amount (pay_ded_benefits). Its primary key is the employee identifier number, which is held in the pay_empl column.

4.7   Container-Provided Benefits

The previous sections described the tasks required of the session bean developers when developing the Enrollment and Payroll session beans. It is equally interesting to examine the tasks that the bean developers do *not* have to do because of the services provided by the EJB container. These services are distributed programming, concurrency and multithreading, transaction management, security management, resource pooling and other scalability issues, system administration, and high availability.

- **Distributed programming**—Because the EJB container handles distributed programming, the session bean developer doesn't have to deal with the complexity of writing a distributed application. To the developer, the session bean classes are Java classes that require no distributed programming knowledge. The EJB container provides the implementation of the session beans' home and remote interfaces by creating distributed RMI-IIOP objects. This allows the Benefits Enrollment application to be written in the same way regardless of whether the EnrollmentEJB and its client (EnrollmentWeb) are deployed on the same machine or on different machines.

- **Concurrency and multithreading**—The developer can write the session bean classes as if they are used by one user. The EJB container makes it possible for multiple users to execute the benefits application concurrently. How does the container accomplish this? For the EnrollmentEJB stateful session bean, the container creates a private instance of the EnrollmentBean class for each connected user. In the case of the PayrollEJB stateless session bean, the container multiplexes the requests from multiple users across one or more instances of the PayrollBean class. The bean developer does not have to write any thread synchronization code into the application because the EJB container does not allow conflicts resulting from multithreading to arise in the enterprise bean code.

- **Transaction management**—The bean developer does not have to write transaction management code. Note that the EnrollmentBean and PayrollBean classes contain no transaction management-related code. The EJB container automatically wraps the business methods into transactions based on the deployment descriptor information for the bean. For example, the container does the following.

  - Starts a transaction before the execution of the `EnrollmentBean.commit-Selections` method.

- Propagates the transaction to the BenefitsDatabase, the `Payroll-Bean.setBenefitsDeduction` method, and PayrollDatabase.

- Performs a two-phase commit protocol across the two databases when the `EnrollmentBean.commitSelections` method has completed.

- **Security management**—The session bean developer does not have to include security-related code in the respective bean implementations. The Enrollment-Bean and PayrollBean classes contain no security-related code. The deployer and the system administrator set the security management policies using facilities provided by the container. The container enforces these security policies.

- **Resource pooling and other scalability issues**—The session bean developer does not have to deal with scalability issues in the bean's code. In our benefits example, the programmer did not have to deal directly with the issue of simultaneous access by a great number of users—that is, What happens if 10,000 employees all logged in to the benefits application and tried to use it at the same time? If such an event did occur, the EJB container would pool expensive server resources, such as JDBC connections, and this pooling would be transparent to the session bean code. Similarly, if the system happened to be low on memory, the EJB container would passivate some session objects and move them temporarily to secondary storage. Not only is this transparent to the bean, it avoids thrashing and achieves optimal throughput and response time.

- **System administration**—The EJB container provides tools for system administration so that the bean developer does not have to include such code in the application. In the benefits example, the session bean developer didn't have to write code to make the application capable of system administration. The EJB container provides application administration tools that are used by the Star Enterprise IT staff to manage the application at runtime.

- **High availability**—If Star Enterprise is concerned about the availability aspects of the application, it should deploy the application in an EJB container that provides high availability. The session bean developer does not have to do anything different in the bean's code to make the application highly available.

4.8   Conclusion

This chapter provided an in-depth discussion of session beans. It explained the different types of session beans and their state, and showed how session beans fit into a multitiered architecture and how they model business logic.

An extensive employee benefits enrollment example illustrated the different parts of session beans and how to use session beans effectively. The example showed how to use the home and remote interfaces, create and remove session bean instances, employ command beans to encapsulate database access, and utilize session bean activation and passivation. It provided views of session beans from both the application and client developers' perspectives.

Lastly, the chapter summarized the tasks that the container performs for an EJB application. By managing such tasks as distributed programming, concurrency, transaction and security handling, and so forth, the bean developer can focus on the application's business logic.

The next chapter goes into greater detail about the services provided by the EJB container.

CHAPTER 5

Session Bean in Its Container

SESSION beans, like all enterprise beans, reside at runtime within an EJB container. The EJB container manages the session beans and provides numerous system-level services to support its session beans.

This chapter describes the support that an EJB container implements for session beans. Typically, a container provides services to session beans on two occasions: It provides a session bean with services at deployment and, later, it provides runtime services when the session bean is used by a client. These built-in container services simplify application development because the application programmer does not have to develop this portion of the logic as part of the application.

This chapter also describes how the EJB container manages session beans. It describes how the container facilitates locating a session bean's home interface and creating a session object, how it handles a client's invocation of the business methods of the bean, how it handles a session bean that has timed out or is removed, and so forth. This chapter also discusses the special classes that support the distributed object protocol, which the container generates for the bean at runtime.

Although a bean developer will likely find the material in this chapter informative and interesting, this knowledge is not necessary to develop session beans. The container services are present in all EJB containers; they exist "under the covers," and the developer can assume they are there and can treat them like a black box. In most cases, the services are transparent to the bean code; in other cases, the container exposes them as a simple API to the bean. We present a description of the services that the container performs for session beans merely to give the reader an appreciation of the container's work.

Certain things happen in the EJB environment when a session bean is deployed in a container and subsequently invoked by a client. We focus on how the EJB container handles and manages the following: container artifacts, home interface lookup, session object creation, business method invocation, transaction management, passivation and activation, session object removal and time-out, and invocation of other session beans.

- **Container artifacts**—These are the additional classes that the EJB container generates to manage the session bean at runtime and to support the distributed object protocol.

- **Home interface lookup**—A client performs a JNDI lookup of the session bean's home interface.

- **Session object creation**—A client program creates a new session object when it invokes a `create` method on a session bean home object.

- **Business method invocation**—A client program invokes the business methods on the session object.

- **Transaction management**—The container creates and manages a transaction transparently to the session bean class.

- **Passivation and activation**—The container reclaims resources by moving the session object state to secondary memory (passivation). Later, the container restores the session object state (activation) when the session object is needed to handle a client-invoked business method.

- **Session object removal and time-out**—The container removes a session object when the client invokes the `remove` method or when the bean's time-out limit is reached.

- **Invocation of other session beans**—One session bean may be a client of another session bean.

5.1   Container Artifacts

Recall from Container Artifacts on page 35 in Chapter 2 that when a session bean is deployed in an EJB container, the tools provided by the container vendor generate additional classes, called *container artifacts*. The container uses container artifacts to manage the session bean at runtime and to support the distributed object protocol between the client program and the EJB container.

When the container implementation is based on RMI-IIOP, the container tools generate the EnrollmentRMI and EnrollmentHomeRMI distributed object types (Figure 5.1).

EnrollmentRMI and EnrollmentHomeRMI are RMI-IIOP object types. Their instances are distributed CORBA objects that implement the communication between the client and the container. The EnrollmentRMI type provides the implementation of the session bean's remote interface, Enrollment. The EnrollmentHomeRMI type provides the implementation of the session bean's home interface, EnrollmentHome.

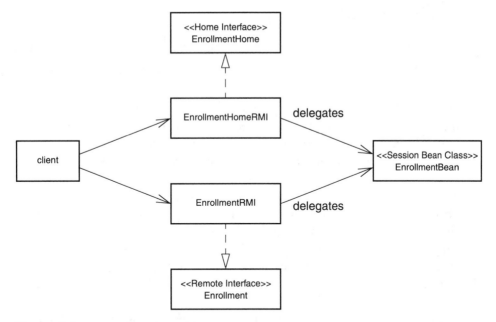

Figure 5.1   Enrollment Class Diagram

We refer to the instances of the EnrollmentRMI object type as *session objects,* and we refer to the instances of the EnrollmentHomeRMI object type as *session bean home objects*. Most containers create a single session bean home object that is shared among all clients, but some containers may use multiple instances of the session bean home object.

The implementation of each RMI-IIOP type consists of multiple Java classes. Although you do not need to know RMI-IIOP details to write an enterprise bean, you may be interested to see the RMI-IIOP specification, which details how to implement RMI-IIOP objects (see Other Sources of Information on page xxii to locate the specification).

5.2   How the Container Manages Session Beans at Runtime

This section illustrates how the EJB container manages the session bean at run-time. We use object interaction diagrams (OIDs) to illustrate the interactions between the client, the distributed objects implemented by the container, and the instances of the session bean class.

5.2.1 EJB Home Interface Lookup

Recall that the client program uses the following code to locate the session bean's home interface.

```
...
Context ictx = new InitialContext();
Object h = ictx.lookup("java:comp/env/ejb/Enrollment");
EnrollmentHome enrollmentHome = (EnrollmentHome)
   PortableRemoteObject.narrow(h, EnrollmentHome.class);
...
```

This code performs a JNDI `lookup` operation and casts the found object to the EnrollmentHome home interface type.

The OID in Figure 5.2 illustrates the EJB container actions that occur "under the covers" when the client initiates a `lookup` operation. An explanation follows the diagram.

1. The client application creates an instance of the InitialContext class, which, because it is part of the JNDI, is defined in the `javax.naming` package.

2. The client invokes the `lookup` operation and passes the method the "`java:comp/env/ejb/EnrollmentEJB`" string as the parameter.

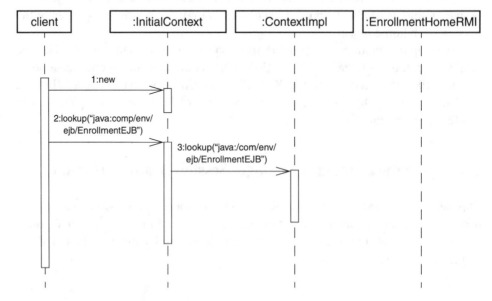

Figure 5.2 Home Interface Lookup OID

3. The InitialContext object delegates the `lookup` operation to a ContextImpl class provided by the EJB container. What causes this to happen? At deployment, the deployer must configure the JNDI name space for the client application. In our example, the deployer configured the JNDI InitialContext object to delegate all JNDI operations for names beginning with the prefix "`java:`" to a ContextImpl class provided by the EJB container. If the client resides on a different machine from the container, this operation may result in a network trip to the container.

The container returns the EnrollmentHomeRMI home object to the client. The client program obtains a reference to the RMI stub for the EnrollmentHomeRMI object. The stub implements the EnrollmentHome interface, which allows the client to invoke subsequently the methods defined in the EnrollmentHome interface on the stub.

Note that the EJB specification requires the client to convert the result of the `lookup` operation by using the `PortableRemoteObject.narrow` method. This is because the home object is a remote object. If the client uses a simple Java `cast` to convert the result of the `lookup` operation, the cast could fail with some EJB container implementations.

5.2.2   Session Object Creation

Let's look at what happens when the client program invokes the `create` method on the session bean home object with the following line of code:

```
enrollment = enrollmentHome.create(emplNumber);
```

The OID diagram that illustrates how the container performs this operation appears in Figure 5.3, and its explanation follows.

1. The client program invokes the `create` operation on EnrollmentHome, which is the RMI stub for the EnrollmentHomeRMI object. The stub forwards the request over RMI-IIOP to the implementation of the EnrollmentHomeRMI object residing in the EJB container. (The figure does not show the forwarding operation.)

2. The implementation of the EnrollmentHomeRMI object creates a new EnrollmentRMI object. Note that this is a distributed RMI-IIOP object, and not a simple Java object.

3. The implementation of the EnrollmentHomeRMI object creates a SessionContext object. The container uses the SessionContext object internally to manage information about the associated EnrollmentBean instance.

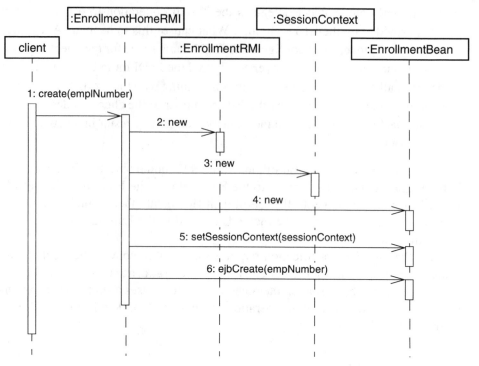

Figure 5.3   Create a Session Object OID

4. The implementation of the EnrollmentHomeRMI object also creates an instance of the EnrollmentBean class using the public constructor that takes no arguments.

5. The implementation of the EnrollmentHomeRMI object then invokes the setSessionContext method on the EnrollmentBean instance to pass the SessionContext object to the instance. The instance may save the reference to the SessionContext object and use it later to communicate with the container.

6. The implementation of the EnrollmentHomeRMI object invokes the matching ejbCreate method on the EnrollmentBean instance. The parameters to the ejbCreate method are the parameters of the client-invoked create method. The session bean instance performs the initialization of its conversational state in the ejbCreate method.

When these operations are complete, the container returns a remote object reference of the EnrollmentRMI distributed object to the client program. The stub implements the Enrollment remote interface.

The create operation does not run in the client's transaction context. There-fore, if a client's transaction rolls back after the client creates a session object, the container does not remove the new session object (such as EnrollmentRMI, in our example) nor does it undo the work of the ejbCreate method. The client can use the session object.

5.2.3 Business Method Invocation

This section discusses how the container manages the execution of the client-invoked business methods. This is probably the heart of an EJB application.

The OID for the business method invocations, as you are about to see, is the most complex of the OID diagrams. It is important to keep in mind that these dia-grams illustrate what the container is doing for the application. Because the con-tainer is responsible for these actions, the application developer's job is greatly simplified. To put it another way, the application developer merely invokes one business method, but the container must manage this with approximately 14 sepa-rate operations. Without the EJB container and environment, the application devel-oper would have to write the code for these 14 operations, a far-from-easy task.

In addition, the case we are examining here is actually a rather simple case. There are two session beans that use just two databases in a transaction. Although one session bean does call another enterprise bean within a transaction, it does not import a client's transactions, nor does it use the SessionSynchronization inter-face. Many real situations are much more complex, involving multiple databases, other enterprise beans, multiple transactions, transaction synchronization, and so forth. In these cases, the container's job is even more complex and involves many more steps.

For our example, let's consider the case when the client invokes the following business method on the Enrollment object:

```
enrollment.commitSelections(selection);
```

The OID diagram in Figure 5.4 illustrates the sequence of actions taken by the container.

1. The client invokes the commitSelections business operation on the RMI stub of the EnrollmentRMI distributed object. In effect, this is an operation on the EnrollmentRMI distributed object and it results in a network call to the container.

2. The container initiates a new transaction. This happens because the bean developer specified the Enrollment session bean to be a bean with container-managed transaction demarcation, and assigned the Requires transaction

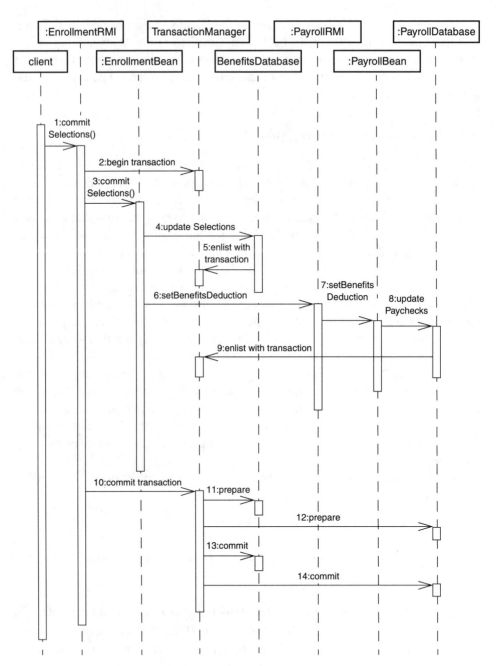

Figure 5.4   Business Method Invocation OID

attribute to the `commitSelections` method. When a bean uses container-managed transaction demarcation, the container evaluates the bean's transaction attribute and determines how to handle the transaction demarcation. If a container-managed bean has the Requires transaction attribute, the container initiates a new transaction if the client is not already participating in a transaction. Note that if the client was already participating in a transaction, the client's invocation of the EnrollmentRMI object propagates the client's transaction to the container, and the container performs the work done by the session bean in the client's current transaction. See Chapter 8, Understanding Transactions for more information. The container also checks if the client is allowed to invoke the business method. If the client is not allowed to invoke the business method, the container throws `RemoteException` to the client. See Chapter 9, Managing Security for information on security management.

3. The EnrollmentRMI object delegates the object invocation to the Enrollment-Bean instance.

4. The EnrollmentBean instance (actually, the DBUpdateBenefits command bean that is used by EnrollmentBean) performs a database operation to update the record in the `Selections` table in the BenefitsDatabase.

5. The DBMS that stores the BenefitsDatabase enlists itself with the transaction started in step 2. This is to ensure that the update to the `Selections` table is included as part of the transaction.

6. The EnrollmentBean instance invokes the PayrollRMI session object via its RMI stub. The container propagates the transaction with the invocation to the PayrollRMI object.

7. The PayrollRMI object delegates the object invocation to the PayrollBean instance.

8. The PayrollBean instance updates the record in the `Paychecks` table in the PayrollDatabase.

9. The DBMS that stores the PayrollDatabase enlists itself with the transaction. This is to ensure that the update to the `Paychecks` table is included as part of the transaction.

10. Before sending a reply to the client, the EnrollmentRMI object commits the transaction.

11–14. The transaction manager coordinates the two-phase commit protocol across the two databases enlisted in the transaction.

After the transaction manager commits the transaction, the EnrollmentRMI object sends the reply to the client. If the commit fails for any reason, the EnrollmentRMI object throws `java.rmi.RemoteException` to the client.

5.2.4   Session Bean Passivation and Activation

Let's assume that the user invoked a business method (such as the `getMedicalOptions` method) and then decided to interrupt his session with the EnrollmentWeb application. For example, the user starts the enrollment process, gets to the page displaying the available medical options, and then, realizing it is time to go to lunch, locks his workstation screen, leaving the application where it is so that he can resume it later. Shortly thereafter, the container detects that the Enrollment session object (recall that the Enrollment session bean is a stateful session bean) has been idle for awhile. At that point, it may decide to reclaim the memory resources by passivating the session object.

The OID diagram in Figure 5.5 illustrates the actions that the container takes to passivate the session object.

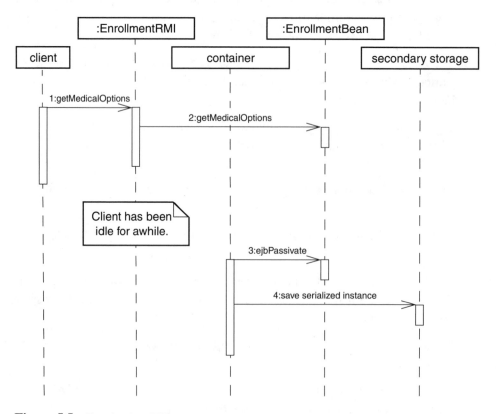

Figure 5.5   Passivation OID

1. The client invokes the `getMedicalOptions` business operation on the RMI stub of the EnrollmentRMI distributed object.

2. The EnrollmentRMI object delegates the object invocation to the Enrollment-Bean instance. At this point, the user leaves for lunch.

3. The container detects that the client has not invoked a method on the session bean object for awhile. If the container needs to reclaim the resources held by the session bean object, the container may choose to passivate the session bean object. The container invokes the `ejbPassivate` method on the Enrollment-Bean instance. The `ejbPassivate` method gives the instance a chance to prepare its conversational state for passivation.

4. The container saves the serialized instance of the EnrollmentBean's state to secondary storage.

Later, when the user comes back from lunch and resumes his session with the EnrollmentWeb application, the container activates the passivated object. It does this by taking the actions illustrated in Figure 5.6.

1. The user returns from lunch and resumes the EnrollmentWeb application from the point at which he invoked the `getMedicalOptions` business operation on the RMI stub of the EnrollmentRMI distributed object. Now the user submits the form that results in the invocation of the `setMedicalOption` method on the session object.

2. The EnrollmentRMI object tells the container (this is an internal communication within the container) to activate the object invocation and the state of the EnrollmentBean instance.

3. The container loads into main memory the serialized instance of Enrollment-Bean that it had previously stored in secondary storage.

4. The container invokes the `ejbActivate` method on the EnrollmentBean instance. The EnrollmentBean instance at this point has been notified that it has been activated and it can perform whatever operations it deems necessary to transfer itself to a state in which it can accept the invocation of a business method.

5. The EnrollmentRMI object delegates the `setMedicalOption` object invocation to the EnrollmentBean instance.

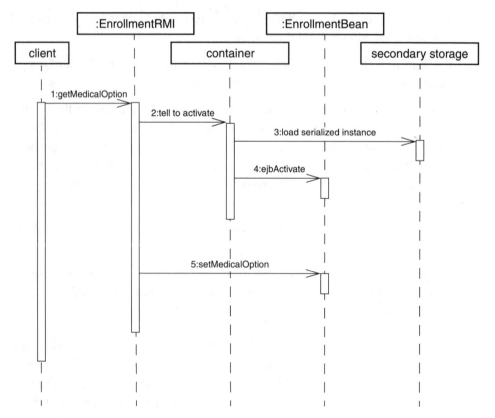

Figure 5.6 Activation OID

5.2.5 Session Object Removal

The client invokes the `remove` method on the RMI stub for the EnrollmentRMI object to remove the session bean instance. This is shown in the following code segment:

```
enrollment.remove();
```

The client call to the `remove` method causes the container to invoke the following sequence of actions, as illustrated in Figure 5.7.

1. The client invokes the `remove` operation on the RMI stub that implements the Enrollment interface. This is an operation on the EnrollmentRMI distributed object and results in a network call to the container.

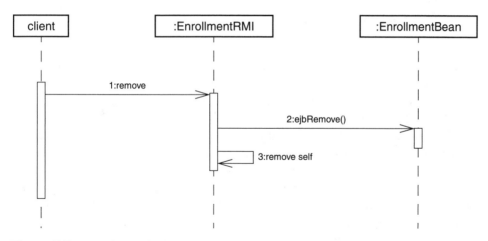

Figure 5.7 Session Bean Removal OID

2. The EnrollmentRMI object invokes the `ejbRemove` method in the Enrollment-
   Bean instance to give the instance a chance to release the resources held in its
   conversational state. The JVM will eventually garbage collect the Enrollment-
   Bean instance and all objects reachable from the instance.

3. The EnrollmentRMI object removes itself. At that point, a client is no longer
   able to use the EnrollmentRMI object.

If a client attempts to invoke a business method on a session object after the
object has been removed, the client receives `java.rmi.Remote.NoSuchObject-`
`Exception`.

A client cannot remove a session object while the object is participating in a
transaction. That is, the `remove` method cannot be called when the object is participating in a transaction; this throws `javax.ejb.RemoveException` to the client.

A client may also remove a session object using the `Enrollment-`
`Home.remove(Handle handle)` method. Handles are discussed in Use of Object
Handles on page 117 in Chapter 4.

The container has the option of invoking the `ejbRemove` method on an
instance after the life of the session bean instance has expired, even without a
prior `remove` method call from the client. See the section Session Bean Timeout,
which follows.

Lastly, the `remove` operation does not run in the client's transaction context.
Therefore, if a client's transaction rolls back after the client removed a session
object, the container does not restore the removed session object (such as EnrollmentRMI in our example) nor does it undo the work of the `ejbRemove` method.

5.2.6   Session Bean Timeout

In some cases, a client may create a session object but then may never call the `remove` method on this object. To handle these occurrences, the container typically uses a time-out mechanism to remove session objects automatically that are no longer used by clients. The deployer usually sets the time-out.

The container must be able to remove a session bean without waiting for the `remove` method invocation because it needs, eventually, to deallocate the resources that it allocated for the session object, such as the space on secondary storage to store the serialized image of the session bean instance. Essentially, if a client has not invoked the session object for a specified period of time, the container implicitly removes the session object. Keep in mind, however, that a session bean time-out never occurs while a session object is in a transaction.

When the container removes the session object because of the time-out, it may choose to call or not to call the `ejbRemove` method on the session bean instance. The state of the session object determines whether the container invokes the `ejbRemove` method. If a session object is not in the "passive" state, the container invokes the `ejbRemove` method. If the session object is in the passive state (in other words, it has been passivated by the container), the container may simply reclaim the secondary storage allocated for the session object, and not call the `ejbRemove` method. Therefore, the developer must design the application to tolerate the case that the `ejbRemove` method is not called when a session object is removed.

In addition, if a client attempts to invoke a business method on a session object already removed by the container, the client receives `java.rmi.Remote.NoSuchObjectException`.

5.3   Conclusion

This chapter described how an EJB container manages a session bean during runtime. It explained the container artifacts and covered the container's handling of session bean creation, business method invocation, session bean activation and passivation, session bean removal, and session bean time-out.

This completes the discussion on session beans. The next chapters focus on entity beans.

CHAPTER 6

Understanding Entity Beans

AN entity bean is a component that encapsulates the implementation of a business entity or a business process. The encapsulation of a business entity or process is typically independent from the client application that uses the entity bean. As a result, an entity bean can be reused by many client applications.

This chapter focuses on understanding the basics of entity beans from a programming point of view. It describes the client view of an entity bean (which is the view of the developer of an application that uses an entity bean) and the view of the developer of the entity bean itself. We also describe the life cycle of entity bean class instances and show how the container manages the instances at runtime.

Clients of entity beans, similar to session bean clients, use the methods of the home and remote interfaces. However, because there are differences in the life cycle of an entity object from that of a session object, an entity bean client takes a different approach to using the home interface methods for creating and removing entity objects. In addition, each entity object has a unique identity, which allows the home interface to define find methods for locating entity bean instances.

A bean developer must write the implementation of the entity bean's business logic in addition to the life cycle-related methods defined by the home interface. The bean developer is also concerned with entity object persistence. The state of an entity object is stored in a resource manager. The entity bean methods access the state in the resource manager using either container-managed persistence (CMP) or bean-managed persistence (BMP).

This chapter also provides a description of how the container manages entity bean instances. Although not all developers need to know this information, it is interesting to see what happens beneath the surface during the various method invocations, passivation and activation, and transactions.

6.1   Client View of an Entity Bean

We begin by explaining the client view of an entity bean. This is the view seen by an application developer who uses an entity bean in a client application. Note that the client application developer is typically different from the developer (or company) that developed the bean.

An entity bean is a component that provides to its client a true object-oriented abstraction of a business entity or a business process. For example, a real-life business entity may be an account, employee, customer, and so forth. A business process, on the other hand, can be the process of granting a loan approval, opening a bank account, scheduling a meeting, and so forth. When an entity bean is used to implement a business entity or process, each individual business entity or process is represented by an entity object.

Five concepts define the client view of an entity bean. These concepts are

1. Home interface

2. Remote interface

3. Primary key and object identity

4. Life cycle of an entity object

5. Handles

In the following sections, we explain and illustrate how a client uses the home and remote interfaces to manipulate entity objects. We also discuss the role of the primary key in the client view, and explain the life cycle of an entity bean and the use of handles.

6.1.1   Home Interface

A client uses the home interface to manage the life cycle of individual entity objects. Life cycle operations involve creating, finding, and removing entity objects. Specifically, the client uses the home interface methods to create new entity objects, and to find and remove existing entity objects.

In addition, a client can use the home interface to obtain the javax.ejb.EJBMeta-Data interface for the entity bean and to obtain a handle for the home interface.

Although the signatures of the `create` and find methods may be different for each entity bean, the life cycle operations are uniform across all entity beans. This uniformity makes it easier for a client developer to use entity beans supplied by other developers.

Let's look at the example AccountHome interface (Code Example 6.1).

Code Example 6.1   AccountHome Interface

```
import java.rmi.RemoteException;
import javax.ejb.CreateException;
import javax.ejb.FinderException;

public interface AccountHome extends javax.ejb.EJBHome {
   // create methods
   Account create(String lastName, String firstName)
      throws RemoteException, CreateException, BadNameException;
   Account create(String lastName)
      throws RemoteException, CreateException;
   ...

   // find methods
   Account findByPrimaryKey(AccountKey primaryKey)
      throws RemoteException, FinderException;
   Collection findInActive(Date sinceWhen)
      throws RemoteException, FinderException, BadDateException;
   ...
}
```

The next sections explain the client's use of the home interface.

Locating the Home Interface

The client must first obtain the home interface to use it. A client obtains the home interface for the AccountEJB entity bean from the client's environment using JNDI, as follows:

```
Context initCtx = new InitialContext();
AccountHome accountHome = (AccountHome)PortableRemoteObject.narrow(
      initCtx.lookup("java:comp/env/ejb/CheckingAccountEJB"),
      AccountHome.class);
```

The deployer configured the home interface in the JNDI name space. Note that the client must use the `PortableRemoteObject.narrow` method to cast the value returned from JNDI to the home interface type.

create Methods

An entity bean home interface defines zero or more `create` methods. Each `create` method represents a different way to create a new entity object. The number and types of the input parameters of the `create` methods are entity bean specific. The return value type for all `create` methods is always the entity bean's remote interface.

Returning to our example, the client can use the AccountHome interface to create new Account objects, as follows.

```
Account account1 = accountHome.create("Matena", "Vlada");
Account account2 = accountHome.create("Stearns", "Beth");
```

It is important to understand that when the client invokes a `create` operation, the entity bean creates the representation of the entity object's state in a resource manager. This is in contrast to invoking a `create` method on a session bean. Invoking a `create` method on a session bean results "only" in the creation of a session bean instance; it does not result in the creation of persistent state in a resource manager.

It is possible for a home interface to define no `create` methods, and there are times when this approach is useful and preferable. Because the entity object's state exists in the resource manager independently from the entity bean and its container (Entity Object Persistence on page 163 explains how a resource manager manages the state of an entity object), it is possible to create or remove an entity object directly in the resource manager. An application is not limited to going through the entity bean and its container to create or remove the object. For example, an application can use SQL statements to create or remove an Account object in a relational database. There may be situations when the bean developer does not want to allow the entity bean clients to create entity objects, and instead wants to ensure that the entity objects are created solely by other means. In such a case, the entity bean's home interface would have zero `create` methods. This is discussed in more detail in Using Entity Beans with Preexisting Data on page 212.

In Chapter 7, Entity Bean Application Example, the EmployeeEJB and the ProvidenceEJB entity beans illustrate entity bean home interfaces with no `create` methods. See EmployeeHome Home Interface on page 248 and ProvidencePlanHome Home Interface on page 310.

Find Methods

The home interface defines one or more find methods. A client uses the find methods to look up entity objects that meet given criteria.

All entity bean home interfaces define a `findByPrimaryKey` method to allow the client to find an entity object by its primary key. The `findByPrimaryKey` method takes a single input parameter with a type that is the entity bean's primary key type. The return value type is the entity bean's remote interface.

Our example AccountEJB client may use the `findByPrimaryKey` method, as follows.

```
AccountKey pk = new AccountKey();
pk.setAccountNumber("100-300-423");

try {
    Account account = accountHome.findByPrimaryKey(pk);
} catch (NoSuchObjectException ex) {
    // account with the given primary key does not exist
}
```

If the `findByPrimaryKey` method completes successfully, the client knows that the entity object with the given primary key exists. If the entity object does not exist when the client invokes the `findByPrimaryKey` method, then the method throws `java.rmi.NoSuchObjectException` to the client.

In addition to the required `findByPrimaryKey` method, the home interface may include additional find methods. The number and types of the input arguments of these additional find methods are entity bean specific. A find method's return value type is either the entity bean's remote interface or java.util.Collection. Find methods that can potentially find more than one entity object should define the return value type as a java.util.Collection. Find methods that can return at most one entity object should define the return value type as the remote interface type.

The following example illustrates using a find method, `findInActive`, that may return more than one entity object.

```
Date sinceDate = ...;
Collection inActiveAccounts = accountHome.findInActive(sinceDate);
Iterator it = inActiveAccounts.iterator();
while (it.hasNext()) {
    Account acct = (Account)PortableRemoteObject.narrow(it.next(),
                               Account.class);
    // do something with acct
    acct.debit(100.00);
}
```

The `findInActive` method returns a collection of accounts that have been inactive since a given date. The client uses an iterator to obtain the individual entity objects returned in the Collection. Note that the client must use the `PortableRemoteObject.narrow` operation to cast an object retrieved from the collection to the entity bean's remote interface type.

remove **Methods**

All entity bean home interfaces extend the javax.ejb.EJBHome interface, which defines two `remove` methods. A client uses the EJBHome `remove` methods to remove the entity objects specified by the method's input parameter.

The `void remove(Object primaryKey)` method is used to remove an entity object by a given primary key. The `void remove(Handle handle)` method is used to remove an entity object identified by a given handle.

The following code illustrates using a `remove` method.

```
AccountKey pk = new AccountKey();
pk.setAccountNumber("100-300-423");
accountHome.remove(pk);
```

It is important to understand that successful execution of a `remove` method results in the removal of the representation of the entity object's state from the resource manager that stores the state. In the previous example, the `remove` method results in the removal of the specified account record from the database.

6.1.2   Remote Interface

There are several ways for a client to get a reference to an existing entity object's remote interface. The client can do the following.

- Receive the reference as a result of a `create` method.

- Find the entity object using a find method defined in the entity bean's home interface.

- Obtain the reference from the entity object's handle.

- Receive the reference as a parameter in a method call. This can be an input parameter or a method result.

Once the client obtains the reference to the entity bean's remote interface, the client can do a number of things with that reference.

- Invoke business methods on the entity object through the remote interface.

- Obtain a reference to the entity bean's home interface.

- Pass the reference in a parameter or as a result of a remote method call.

- Obtain the entity object's primary key.

- Obtain the entity object's handle.

- Remove the entity object.

Code Example 6.2 shows the definition of the Account remote interface.

Code Example 6.2   Account Interface

```
import java.rmi.RemoteException;
public interface Account extends javax.ejb.EJBObject {
    double getBalance() throws RemoteException;
    void credit(double amount) throws RemoteException;
    void debit(double amount)
        throws RemoteException, InsufficientFundsException;
    ...
}
```

Code Example 6.3 illustrates using the remote interface.

Code Example 6.3   Using the Remote Interface

```
// Somehow obtain a reference to an Account object.
Account acct = ...;

// Invoke business methods.
double balance = acct.getBalance();
acct.debit(200.00);
acct.credit(300.00);

// Obtain the primary key.
AccountKey pk = (AccountKey)acct.getPrimaryKey();

// Obtain the home interface.
AccountHome home = (AccountHome)PortableRemoteObject.narrow(
                   acct.getEJBHome(), AccountHome.class);
```

```
// Obtain the entity object's handle.
Handle handle = acct.getHandle();

// Pass the entity object as a parameter in a remote call.
// (Foo is an enterprise bean's remote or home interface).
Foo foo = ...;      // Foo
foo.someMethod(acct, ...);

// Remove the entity object.
acct.remove();
```

Note that although we used the `PortableRemoteObject.narrow` operation to convert the result of the `getEJBHome` method to the AccountHome type, we use a simple Java `cast` to convert the result of the `getPrimaryKey` method to the AccountKey type. We did not have to use the `PortableRemoteObject.narrow` method for the type conversion of the primary key object because the primary key object is not a remote object. In contrast, we had to use the more complex `PortableRemoteObject.narrow` method for the type conversion of the home interface object because the home interface object is a reference to a remote object.

6.1.3   Primary Key and Object Identity

Every entity object has an identity unique within the scope of its home interface. The primary key determines this identity. If two entity objects with the same home interface have the same primary key, they are considered identical entity objects. If they have a different primary key, they are considered different entity objects.

A client can test if two entity object references refer to the same entity object using the `isIdentical` method. The following code segment illustrates using the `isIdentical` method to compare two object references to determine whether they are identical.

```
Account acct1 = ...;
Account acct2 = ...;

if (acct1.isIdentical(acct2)) {
      // acct1 and acct2 refer to the same entity object
} else {
      // acct1 and acct2 refer to different entity objects
}
```

Alternatively, if the client obtains two entity object references from the same home interface, it can determine if these objects are identical by comparing their primary keys.

```
AccountHome accountHome = ...;
Account acct1 = accountHome.findOneWay(...);
Account acct2 = accountHome.findAnotherWay(...);

if (acct1.getPrimaryKey().equals(acct2.getPrimaryKey())) {
    // acct1 and acct2 refer to the same entity object
} else {
    // acct1 and acct2 refer to different entity objects
}
```

Note that comparing primary keys is only valid when comparing objects obtained from the same home interface. When objects are obtained from different home interfaces, the client must use the `isIdentical` method on one of the objects to perform the comparison.

6.1.4   Entity Object Life Cycle

Figure 6.1 illustrates an entity object's life cycle, as seen from the perspective of a client. In the diagram, the term *referenced* means that the client holds an object reference for the entity object.

Figure 6.1 illustrates the following points about an entity object's life cycle.

- Creating an entity object.

  - A client can create an entity object by invoking a `create` method defined in the entity bean's home interface.

  - It is possible to create an entity object without involving the entity bean or its container. For example, using a direct database insert can create the representation of the entity object's state in the resource manager (that is, in the database).

- Finding an entity object. A client can look up an existing entity object using a find method defined in the home interface.

- Invoking business methods. A client that has an object reference for the entity object can invoke business methods on the entity object.

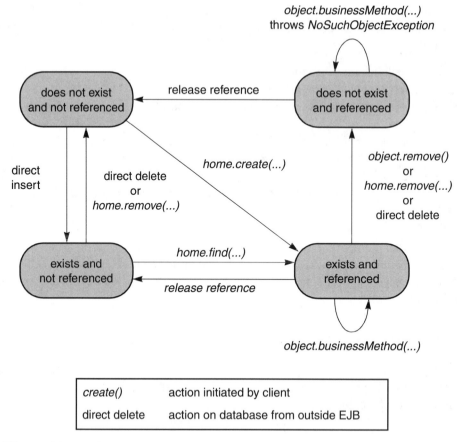

Figure 6.1   Client View of an Entity Object Life Cycle

- Understanding the life cycle. The life cycle of the entity object is independent from the life cycle of the client-held object references. This means that an entity object is not removed when it is no longer referenced by a client. Likewise, the existence of an object reference does not ensure the existence of the entity object.

- Removing an entity object.

    - A client can remove an entity object using one of the `remove` methods defined in the home and remote interfaces. If a client attempts to invoke a business method on an entity object after the object has been removed, the client receives `NoSuchObjectException`.

- It is possible to remove an entity object without involving the entity bean or its container. For example, using a direct database delete can remove the representation of the entity object's state from the resource manager (the database). If a client attempts to invoke a business method on an entity object after its state has been removed from the database, the client receives `NoSuchObjectException`.

Entity objects are considered to be, in general, persistent objects. An entity object can be accessed concurrently through multiple JVMs. The lifetime of an entity object is not limited by the lifetime of the Java Virtual Machine (JVM) process in which the entity bean instances execute.

Although the crash of the JVM may result in the rollback of current transactions, it does not destroy previously created entity objects, nor does it invalidate the references to the remote and home interfaces held by clients.

An entity object remains accessible to its clients as long as the representation of its state is maintained in the resource manager, or until a reconfiguration of the bean or container invalidates the object references and handles held by the clients. This can happen, for example, when the entity bean is uninstalled from the container, or if the container is reconfigured to listen on a different network address.

Multiple clients can access the same entity object concurrently. If so, the container uses transactions to isolate the clients' work from each other. This is explained in Concurrent Invocation of an Entity Object on page 209.

6.1.5   Entity Bean Handle

An entity object's handle is an object that identifies an entity object on a network. Because a handle class extends the java.io.Serializable interface, a client may serialize the handle and save it in stable storage. The client may later use the serialized handle, even in a different JVM, to reobtain a reference to the entity object identified by the handle.

When a client has a reference to an entity object's remote interface, the client can obtain the entity object's handle by invoking the `getHandle` method on the remote interface.

When a client has an entity object's handle, the client can obtain a reference to an entity object's remote interface by invoking the `getEJBObject` method on the handle. The client code must use the `javax.rmi.PortableRemoteObject.narrow` method to convert the result of the `getEJBObject` method invoked on a handle to the entity bean's remote interface type.

Code Example 6.4 illustrates the use of a handle.

Code Example 6.4 Using a Handle

```
// A client obtains a handle of an Account entity object and
// stores the handle in stable storage.
ObjectOutputStream stream = ...;
Account account = ...;
Handle handle = account.getHandle();
stream.writeObject(handle);

// A client can read the handle from stable storage, and use the
// handle to resurrect an object reference to the
// Account entity object.
ObjectInputStream stream = ...;
Handle handle = (Handle) stream.readObject(handle);
Account account = (Account)javax.rmi.PortableRemoteObject.narrow(
        handle.getEJBObject(), Account.class);
account.debit(100.00);
```

The EJB specification also allows a client to obtain a handle for the object that implements the home interface. The client can use the home handle to store a reference to an entity bean's home interface in stable storage and later recreate the reference. Home interface handle functionality may be useful when a client needs to use the home interface at some future time, but might not know the JNDI name of the home interface at that time.

A handle object for a home interface implements the javax.ejb.HomeHandle interface. The client code must use the `javax.rmi.PortableRemote-Object.narrow` method to convert the result of the `getEJBHome` method invoked on a handle to the home interface type.

6.2 Bean Developer View of an Entity Bean

The bean developer has a different view of an entity bean than that of the client. Essentially, the bean developer is responsible for the implementation of the methods defined in the bean's remote and home interfaces, plus the callback methods of the EntityBean interface. The developer needs to know how to implement correctly the methods defined by the home interface (the find and `create` methods), the business methods, and the methods defined by the EntityBean interface. These method implementations access the state of the entity objects maintained in a resource manager. As a result, the bean developer needs to understand entity object state and persistence to implement the entity bean methods optimally.

We begin this section by describing entity object state and persistence. The entity object state is managed by a resource manager. Management of state is separate from the container's management of entity bean instances. The developer can use either the CMP or the BMP approach to access object state. The advantages and drawbacks of these two persistence approaches are discussed in detail.

This section also describes different approaches to using the `ejbLoad` and `ejbStore` methods. The container invokes these methods on the bean implementation. The developer can use these methods to utilize the container's cache management capabilities and to maximize performance (see Using the `ejbLoad` and `ejbStore` Methods on page 196).

We conclude this section with a discussion on how the container manages multiple client invocations on an entity object.

6.2.1   Entity Object Persistence

The methods of an entity bean class access the object's state in a resource manager. It is important to understand that most resource managers (such as relational databases) manage entity objects' state externally to the bean instances (Figure 6.2).

Separating the state of the entity objects from the instances of the entity bean class has the following advantages:

- Facilitates persistence and transactions.

    - Separating an entity object's state from the bean class instance allows the entity object's state to be persistent. Separation permits the life cycle of the entity object's state to be independent from the life cycle of the entity bean class instances and from the life cycle of the JVMs in which the instances are created.

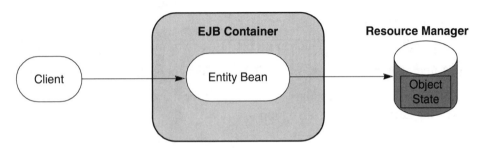

Figure 6.2   Entity Object's State Managed by Resource Manager

- The resource manager, instead of the entity bean or the EJB container, is responsible for the implementation of the ACID properties. Recall that ACID stands for the four key principles that pertain to transactions: atomicity, consistency, isolation, and durability.

- Promotes the implementation of the EJB server.

  - Separation makes it possible to implement the entity object's state to be accessible concurrently from multiple JVMs, even when the JVMs run on different network nodes. This is essential to a high-end implementation of an EJB server.

  - It makes it possible to implement a highly available EJB server. Should a node of the JVM be unavailable, another JVM can access the entity object's state.

- Improves accessibility between Java and non-Java applications.

  - It makes it possible to externalize an entity object's state in a representation suitable for non-Java applications. For example, if a relational database keeps the state of entity objects, the state is available to any application that can access the database via SQL statements.

  - It makes it possible to present data residing in an enterprise's databases as entity beans. Similarly, it allows the creation of an entity bean façade on top of the client interfaces of the enterprise's non-Java application. This client-view entity bean of the enterprise's preexisting data or applications makes it easier to develop and integrate new Java applications with the legacy data or applications.

The entity bean architecture is flexible regarding the choice of the type of resource manager in which to store an entity object's state. Examples of resource managers in which the state of an entity bean can be stored are

- A relational database system
- An application system, such as an ERP system or mainframe application
- A nonrelational database, such as a hierarchical or an object-oriented database
- Some form of fast secondary-memory resource manager that may be provided by the EJB container as an option

The state of most entity beans is typically stored in a resource manager external to the EJB container—these are the database or application systems noted in the first three examples just presented. The fast secondary memory integrated with the EJB container is a special example. If provided, it typically is used only for storing the state of short-lived entity objects with states that are not accessed by other applications running outside the EJB container.

Because a resource manager maintains the state of an entity object, an entity bean instance must use an API to access the state of the associated entity object. (Associating an instance with an entity object is called *object activation,* and it is explained in Entity Bean Instance Life Cycle on page 174.) An entity bean instance can access the state of its associated entity object using two access styles: BMP and CMP.

Bean-Managed Persistence

When an entity bean uses BMP, the bean uses a resource manager-specific interface (API) to access state. (BMP is an approach to managing entity object state persistence in which the entity bean itself manages the access to the underlying state in a resource manager.) Figure 6.3 shows three different entity bean classes (Account-Bean, AccountBean2, and AccountBean3). Each class accesses a different resource

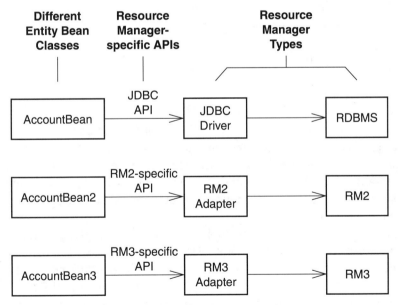

Figure 6.3   Entity Beans Using BMP to Access Different Resource Managers

manager type. For example, a bean uses JDBC to access state if the state is stored in a relational database. In Figure 6.3, AccountBean uses the JDBC API to access state stored in the relational database management system (RDBMS). If the state is stored in a different type of database, the bean uses a different API to access the state, and the API is specific to the resource manager. Thus, AccountBean2 uses an API specific to the RM2 adapter for its RM2-type database. This means that if an entity bean uses BMP, the bean code is, in general, dependent on the type of the resource manager.

For example, the AccountBean entity bean class may use JDBC to access the state of the Account entity objects in a relational database, as Code Example 6.5 illustrates.

Code Example 6.5   Using the JDBC API to Access State

```
public class AccountBean implements EntityBean {
    ...
  public void debit(double amount) {
    Connection con = ...;
    PreparedStatement pstmt = con.prepareStatement(
       "UPDATE Account SET acct_balance = acct_balance - ? " +
       "WHERE acct_number = ?"
    );
    pstmt.setDouble(1, amount);
    pstmt.setString(2, (String)ctx.getPrimaryKey());
    pstmt.execute();
    con.close();
  }
}
```

In the example, the implementation of the debit method obtains the primary key of the Account entity object currently associated with the instance. The method uses the JDBC API to update the account balance. Note that in a real-life application development, the bean developer would likely use some data access tools, such as command beans, on top of JDBC rather than coding JDBC directly in the entity bean class.

BMP's main advantage is it simplifies deploying the entity bean. When an entity bean uses BMP, no deployment tasks are necessary to adapt the bean to the resource manager type or to the database schema used within the resource manager. At the same time, this is also the main disadvantage of BMP, because an entity bean using BMP is, in general, dependent on the resource manager type and the database schema. This dependency makes the entity bean less reusable across different operational environments.

However, an entity bean using BMP can achieve some degree of independence of the entity bean code from the resource manager type and the database schema. This can be accomplished, for example, by using "portable" data access components when developing the BMP entity bean. Essentially, the entity bean class uses the data access components to access the entity object's state. The data access components would provide deployment interfaces for customizing the data access logic to different database schemas, or even to a different resource manager type, without requiring changes to the entity bean's code.

Figure 6.4 shows the AccountBean entity bean using three different APIs to access three different resource manager types. This example is very much like Figure 6.3, with one significant difference. Notice that instead of three separate entity beans (AccountBean, AccountBean2, and AccountBean3) implementing access to the resource manager APIs, a single entity bean class, AccountBean, using data access components can access the different resource manager-specific APIs. The data access components support all three resource manager types.

On the surface, this is similar to CMP, which is explained next. There is, however, a significant difference between CMP and the data access component approach. The CMP approach allows the EJB container to provide a sophisticated persistence manager that can cache the entity object's state in the container. The caching strategy implemented by the persistence manager can be tuned without making modifications to the entity bean's code. It is important to note that the CMP cache may be shared by multiple instances of the same entity bean or even

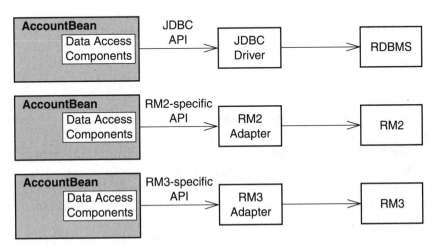

Figure 6.4   Entity Beans Using Data Access Components to Access Resource Managers

by instances of different entity beans. This contrasts with the data access components approach, in which it is not possible, in general, to build a cache that can be shared by multiple instances.

Container-Managed Persistence

CMP enables the development of entity beans with implementations that can be used with multiple resource manager types and database schemas. The CMP architecture allows ISVs to develop entity beans that can be adapted at deployment to work with customers' preexisting data. Because different customers use different resource manager types and have different database schemas, the deployer needs to adapt an entity bean to each customer's resource manager type and its database schema. However, the entity bean developer does not have to write a different implementation of the bean for each customer.

CMP is essentially a resource manager-type independent data access API that is tailored for use by entity beans. In the EJB 1.0 and 1.1 specifications, the CMP API depends on mapping the instance variables of an entity bean class to the data items representing an entity object's state in the resource manager. For example, the same AccountBean coded using CMP looks as follows (Code Example 6.6).

Code Example 6.6   AccountBean Entity Bean Using CMP

```
public class AccountBean implements EntityBean {
   // container-managed fields
   public String accountNumber;
   public double balance;
   ...
   public void debit(double amount) {
      balance = balance - amount;
   }
}
```

At deployment, the deployer uses tools to generate code that implements the mapping of the instance fields to the data items in the resource manager.

Figure 6.5 shows how an entity bean using CMP utilizes the different resource manager-specific APIs to access data in the respective resource managers. Notice that only one entity bean class is required, regardless of the resource manager type. Based on the mapping done by the deployer, CMP generates the appropriate data access code for the resource manager API.

Note that the EJB 2.0 specification significantly extends the functionality of CMP. (Refer to *Enterprise JavaBeans 2.0 Specification, Public Draft,* for more information.) To support the new functionality in EJB 2.0, the CMP API is

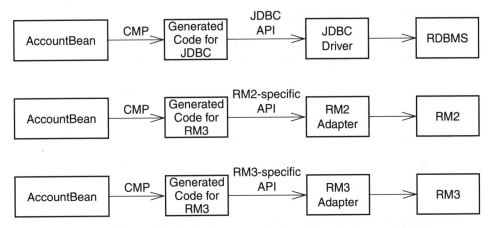

Figure 6.5   AccountBean Entity Bean Using CMP to Access Resource Managers

enhanced. Rather than relying solely on mapping data items comprising state to instance fields, it now provides an API in which an instance uses explicit get and set accessor methods to access the data items comprising the entity object's state.

For example, the same AccountBean coded using EJB 2.0 CMP would look as shown in Code Example 6.7.

Code Example 6.7   AccountBean Entity Bean Using EJB 2.0 CMP

```
public abstract class AccountBean implements EntityBean {
   // Accessor methods for container-managed fields

   public abstract String getAccountNumber();    // accountNumber
   public abstract void setAccountNumber(String v);

   public abstract double getBalance();          // balance
   public abstract void setBalance(double v);
   ...
   // Business methods
   public void debit(double amount) {
      setBalance(getBalance() - amount);
   }
}
```

Because the EJB 2.0 specification was not finalized at the time this book was printed, we discuss only the EJB 1.1 field-based approach to CMP.

6.2.2   Entity Bean Class Methods

The bean developer's primary focus is the development of the entity bean class. The bean developer is responsible for writing the implementation of the following methods.

- Business methods from the remote interface

- `create` methods from the home interface

- Find methods from the home interface

- The container callback methods defined in the javax.ejb.EntityBean interface

The following subsections describe these methods in more detail. Entity Bean Instance Life Cycle on page 174 explains when and in what context the EJB container invokes these methods.

Entity Bean Business Methods

The bean developer implements in the entity bean class the business methods declared by the entity bean's remote interface. The rules for the business method implementations of an entity bean are similar to those for a session bean implementation. The number and types of parameters and the return value type for these business methods must match those defined in the remote interface. In addition, the `throws` clause for the entity bean class business methods must not include more checked exceptions than the `throws` clause of the corresponding remote interface methods. (Note that the methods in the entity bean class can define fewer exceptions than the methods in the remote interface.)

Notice, too, that the business methods must be declared `public`. They must not be declared `final` or `static`.

Recall that the Account remote interface defines the following business methods.

```
double getBalance() throws RemoteException;
void credit(double amount) throws RemoteException;
void debit(double amount)
    throws RemoteException, InsufficientFundsException;
```

The bean developer implements these same business methods in the Account-Bean class, as follows.

```
public double getBalance() { ... }
public void credit(double amount) { ... }
public void debit(double amount)
    throws InsufficientFundsException { ... }
```

Entity Bean create Methods

The entity bean class defines ejbCreate methods that correspond to the create methods defined in the home interface. For each create method in the home interface, the bean developer implements an ejbCreate method in the entity bean class. Remember that an entity bean may choose *not* to expose the create functionality to clients, in which case the entity bean home interface defines no create methods, and, of course, the bean developer does not implement an ejbCreate method in the bean class.

The ejbCreate method has the same number of parameters, and each parameter must be of the same type as those defined in the home interface's corresponding create method. However, the ejbCreate methods differ from the create methods in that they define the bean's primary key type as their return value type. The throws clause for each ejbCreate method must not include more checked exceptions than the throws clause of the corresponding create method. However, the ejbCreate method throws clause can have fewer exceptions than the corresponding create method.

Like the business methods, the ejbCreate methods must be declared public. They must not be declared final or static.

For example, the Account home interface declares the following create methods.

```
Account create(String lastName, String firstName)
    throws RemoteException, CreateException, BadNameException;
Account create(String lastName)
    throws RemoteException, CreateException;
```

The bean developer implements these corresponding ejbCreate methods in the AccountBean class.

```
public AccountKey ejbCreate(String lastName, String firstName)
    throws BadNameException;
public AccountKey ejbCreate(String lastName);
```

The bean developer must also implement an ejbPostCreate method to correspond to each ejbCreate method. Of course, if there are no ejbCreate methods, then the bean developer does not implement any ejbPostCreate methods.

An `ejbPostCreate` method has the same input parameters, number and type, as the `ejbCreate` method, but its return type is void. When creating a new entity instance, the EJB container first invokes the `ejbCreate` method, then it invokes the matching `ejbPostCreate` method (see Invocation of the `create` Method on page 177).

If an instance needs to pass a reference of the entity object that is being created to another enterprise bean, it must do so in the `ejbPostCreate` method, not in the `ejbCreate` method. For example, the `ejbPostCreate` method may pass the created Account object to the Customer object as an argument in the `addAccount` method.

```
public class AccountBean implements EntityBean {
    EntityContext ctx;

    public ejbCreate(Customer cust) {
        // This would be an ERROR because it is illegal to
        // invoke ctx.getEJBObject from an ejbCreate method.
        cust.addAccount((Account)ctx.getEJBObject());
        ...
    }
    public ejbPostCreate(Customer cust) {
        cust.addAccount((Account)ctx.getEJBObject());
    }
    ...
}
```

Entity Bean Find Methods

The bean developer must also implement in the entity bean class find methods that correspond to those defined in the home interface. Recall that an entity bean's home interface defines one or more find methods, which a client uses to locate entity objects.

At a minimum, the developer implements an `ejbFindByPrimaryKey` method corresponding to the `findByPrimaryKey` method, which is defined by all entity bean home interfaces. This method looks up a single entity object using the object's primary key. The developer also implements `ejbFind` methods that correspond to any additional find methods, such as those that return multiple objects, defined by the home interface. Each find method implementation has the same number of parameters, and each parameter is of the same type as the corresponding home interface find method.

The entity bean class implementations of the find methods differ in some respects from the home interface definition. In the home interface, the result type of find methods that return single objects, whether the `findByPrimaryKey` or another find method, is the entity bean's remote interface. The result type of the corresponding `ejbFind` methods is the entity bean's primary key type. Similarly, in the home interface, the result type of find methods returning multiple objects is a collection (java.util.Collection) of objects implementing the remote interface. In the implementation class, the result type of the corresponding `ejbFind` methods that return multiple objects is a collection (java.util.Collection) of objects of the bean's primary key type.

Finally, similar to the `create` methods, the `throws` clause for each `ejbFind` method must not include more checked exceptions than the `throws` clause of the corresponding find method. However, the `ejbFind` method `throws` clause can have fewer exceptions than the corresponding find method. The `ejbFind` methods must be declared `public`. They must not be declared `final` or `static`.

For example, the AccountHome interface defines the `findByPrimaryKey` method and an additional method, `findInActive`, which returns multiple objects.

```
import java.util.Collection;

Account findByPrimaryKey(AccountKey primaryKey)
        throws RemoteException, FinderException;
Collection findInActive(Date sinceWhen)
    throws RemoteException, FinderException, BadDateException;
```

The bean developer implements these methods in the entity bean class as follows.

```
public AccountPrimaryKey ejbFindByPrimaryKey
    (AccountPrimaryKey primkey) throws FinderException { ... };
public Collection ejbFindInActive(Date sinceWhen)
    throws BadDateException { ... };
```

EntityBean Interface Methods

An entity bean class is required to implement the methods defined by the javax.ejb.EntityBean interface. The EJB container invokes these methods on the bean instance at specific points in an entity bean instance's life cycle.

Code Example 6.8 shows the definition of the EntityBean interface methods.

Code Example 6.8 EntityBean Interface

```
public interface EntityBean extends EnterpriseBean {
    public void setEntityContext(EntityContext ctx)
        throws EJBException, RemoteException;
    public void unsetEntityContext()
        throws EJBException, RemoteException;
    public void ejbRemove()
        throws RemoveException, EJBException, RemoteException;
    public void ejbActivate() throws EJBException, RemoteException;
    public void ejbPassivate() throws EJBException, RemoteException;
    public void ejbLoad() throws EJBException, RemoteException;
    public void ejbStore() throws EJBException, RemoteException;
}
```

6.2.3 Entity Bean Instance Life Cycle

Every entity bean instance has a life cycle that starts from its time of creation and continues through its removal. The EJB container manages the life cycle for every instance of an entity bean class.

Bean developers that code the entity bean class manually need to know what happens during an entity bean's life cycle and how that life cycle is managed by the container. On the other hand, bean developers who use an EJB-aware application development tool in general do not need to know most of this information because the application development tool may provide a simpler abstraction.

Instance Life Cycle Diagram

Figure 6.6 illustrates the life cycle of an entity bean instance.

Figure 6.6 shows that an entity bean instance is in one of the following three states:

1. **Does-not-exist state**—Denotes that the container has not yet created an instance or the container has discarded the instance.

2. **Pooled state**—An instance is in the pooled state when it is not associated with a particular entity object identity.

3. **Ready state**—An instance is in the ready state when the instance is associated with an entity object identity.

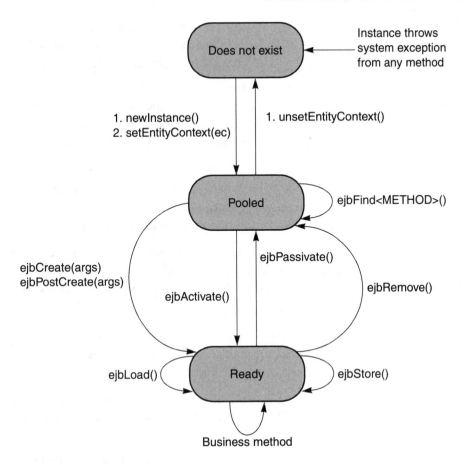

Figure 6.6 Life Cycle of an Entity Bean Instance

There are defined characteristics to each entity instance state. Plus, transitions between states happen as a result of certain actions. The EJB container drives the state transition in response to client-invoked methods from the home and remote interfaces, and in response to container-internal events, such as transaction commit, exceptions, or resource management.

- An instance's life begins when the container creates the instance using newInstance or the new operator. The container then invokes the setEntityContext method to pass the instance a reference to its EntityContext object. At this point, the instance transitions to the pooled state.

- While in the pooled state, the instance is not associated with an entity object identity. As a result, all instances in the pooled state are considered equivalent. The container can perform the following actions with an instance in the pooled state.

  - Execute an `ejbFind<METHOD>` method in response to a client-invoked `find<METHOD>` through the home interface. Note that the instance does not move to the ready state during the execution of the `ejbFind<METHOD>` method.

  - Associate the instance with an existing entity object by invoking the `ejbActivate` method on the instance. A successful execution of the `ejbActivate` method transitions the instance to the ready state.

  - Use the instance to create a new entity object by invoking the `ejbCreate` and `ejbPostCreate` methods on the instance. Successfully executing the `ejbCreate` and `ejbPostCreate` methods transitions the instance to the ready state.

  - Discard the instance by invoking the `unsetEntityContext` method on the instance. By doing so, the container notifies the instance that it will invoke no other methods on the instance.

- When the instance is in the ready state, it is associated with an entity object. The container can perform the following actions on an instance in the ready state.

  - Invoke the `ejbLoad` method on the instance. The `ejbLoad` method instructs the instance to synchronize any cached representation it maintains of the entity object's state from the entity object's state in the resource manager. (Typically, the bean reads the data from the database.) The instance remains in the ready state.

  - Invoke the `ejbStore` method on the instance. The `ejbStore` method instructs the instance to synchronize the entity object's state in the resource manager with updates to the state that may have been cached in the instance. (Typically, the bean writes the changed data to the database.) The instance remains in the ready state.

  - Invoke a business method in response to a client-invoked method in the remote interface. The instance remains in the ready state.

  - Invoke the `ejbPassivate` method on the instance and move the instance to the pooled state.

- Invoke the `ejbRemove` method on the instance in response to a client-in-voked `remove` method. The `ejbRemove` method transitions the instance to the pooled state.

- If an instance throws and does not catch a system exception (that is, an exception that is a subclass of java.lang.RuntimeException), the container catches the exception and transitions the instance to the does-not-exist state.

Invocation of the `create` Method

This section uses OID diagrams to illustrate what happens when an entity object is created with BMP or CMP. Figure 6.7 illustrates creating an entity object with BMP.

1. The client starts a transaction using the `begin` method of the UserTransaction interface.

2. The client invokes a `create` method on the home object. The home object is implemented by the container.

3. The home object invokes the matching `ejbCreate` method on the entity bean instance.

4. The bean instance creates a representation of the entity object state in the database.

5. The database system registers itself with the transaction service, which is a synonym for *transaction manager.*

6. The home object creates the entity object. The entity object is a distributed object that implements the entity bean's remote interface.

7. The home object invokes the matching `ejbPostCreate` method on the bean instance.

8. The home object creates a transaction synchronization object.

9. The home object registers the transaction synchronization object with the transaction service.

10. The client invokes a business method on the newly created entity object in the same transaction context as the `create` method.

11. The entity object delegates the invocation to the bean instance.

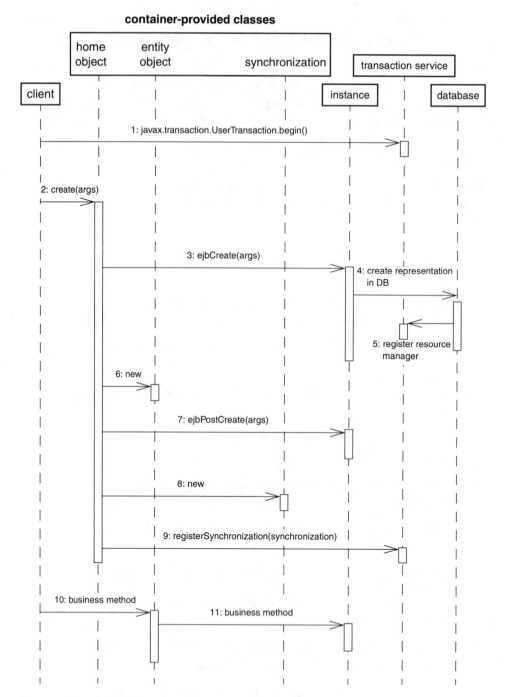

Figure 6.7   OID of Creation of Entity Object with BMP

When the client eventually attempts to commit the transaction, the transaction service orchestrates the commit protocol, as described in Transaction Commit OID on page 188.

Note that creation of the entity object is considered part of the transaction. If the transaction fails, the representation of the object's state in the database is automatically deleted and the entity object does not exist.

Figure 6.8 shows the OID for the creation of an entity object with CMP.

1. The client starts a transaction using the `begin` method of the UserTransaction interface.

2. The client invokes a `create` method on the home object.

3. The home object invokes the matching `ejbCreate` method on the entity bean instance. The bean instance initializes its CMP fields using the data passed in the arguments of the `ejbCreate` method.

4. The home object extracts the values of the CMP fields.

5. The home object uses the extracted CMP values to create the representation of the entity object state in the database.

6. The database system registers itself with the transaction service.

7. The home object creates the entity object. The entity object is a distributed object that implements the entity bean's remote interface.

8. The home object invokes the matching `ejbPostCreate` method on the bean instance.

9. The home object creates a transaction synchronization object.

10. The home object registers the transaction synchronization object with the transaction service.

11. The client invokes a business method on the newly created entity object in the same transaction context as the `create` method.

12. The entity object delegates the invocation to the bean instance.

Invocation of the `remove` Method

The next two figures illustrate removing entity objects. Figure 6.9 shows the steps that take place when removing an entity object with BMP, and Figure 6.10 shows the equivalent steps for removing an entity object with CMP.

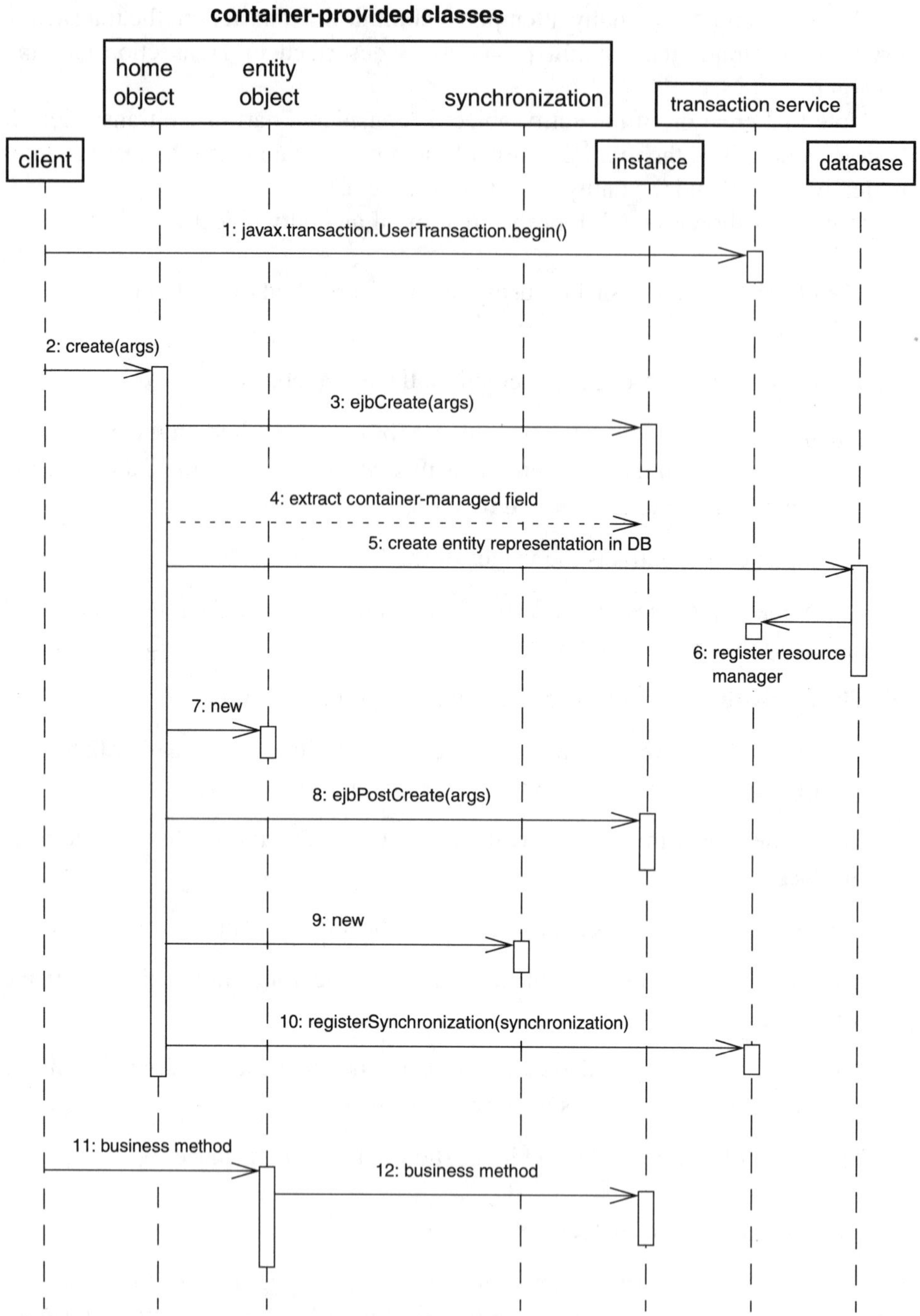

container-provided classes

home object   entity object   synchronization   transaction service

client   instance   database

1: javax.transaction.UserTransaction.begin()

2: create(args)

3: ejbCreate(args)

4: extract container-managed field

5: create entity representation in DB

6: register resource manager

7: new

8: ejbPostCreate(args)

9: new

10: registerSynchronization(synchronization)

11: business method

12: business method

Figure 6.8   OID of Creation of Entity Object with CMP

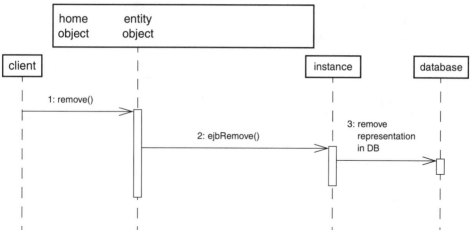

Figure 6.9   OID of Removal of an Entity Object with BMP

1. The client invokes the `remove` method on the entity object.

2. The entity object invokes the `ejbRemove` method on the bean instance.

3. The instance removes the representation of the entity object state from the database.

Note that the diagram does not illustrate the transaction-related interactions between the container, transaction service, and the database. The removal of the object's state representation from the database (step 3 in the diagram) is included as part of the transaction in which the `remove` method is executed. If the transaction fails, the object's state is not removed from the database, and the entity object continues to exist.

1. In Figure 6.10, the client invokes the `remove` method on the entity object.

2. The entity object invokes the `ejbRemove` method on the bean instance.

3. The entity object removes the representation of its state from the database.

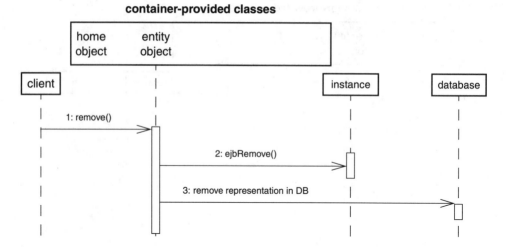

Figure 6.10 OID of Removal of Entity Object with CMP

Invocation of Find Methods

This section illustrates find method invocations on entity beans. Figure 6.11 shows the OID for a find method invocation on an entity bean instance with BMP. In contrast, Figure 6.12 shows the execution of a find method on an entity instance with CMP.

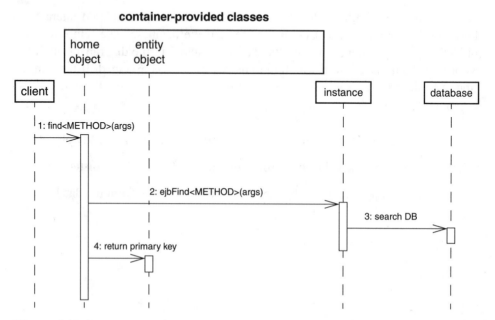

Figure 6.11 OID of Find Method Execution on a Bean-Managed Entity Instance

1. The client invokes a find method on the home object.

2. The home object invokes the matching ejbFind method on a bean instance.

3. The bean instance searches the database to find the object (or objects) that match the finder's criteria. The instance returns the primary key (or collection of keys) from the ejbFind method.

4. The home object converts the returned primary key to an entity object reference (or collection of entity object references) and returns it to the client.

Note that the diagram does not illustrate the transaction-related interactions between the container, transaction service, and the database. The database search (step 3 in the diagram) is included as part of the transaction in which the find method executes. Depending on the isolation level, the found objects may be protected from deletion by other transactions.

1. The client invokes a find method on the home object (Figure 6.12).

2. The home object searches the database to find the object (or objects) that match the find method's criteria.

3. The home object converts the primary key of the found object to an entity object reference and returns it to the client. If the find method finds more than one object, a collection of entity object references is returned to the client.

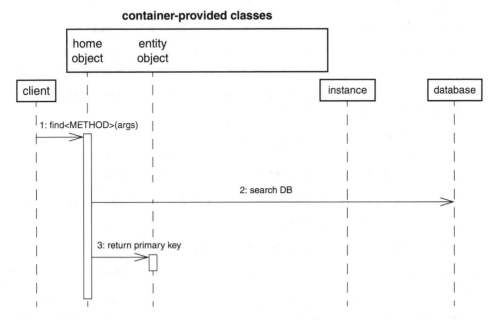

Figure 6.12 OID of Find Method Execution on a Container-Managed Entity Instance

Passivation and Activation OID

The EJB architecture allows the EJB container to passivate an instance during a transaction. Figures 6.13 and 6.14 show the sequence of object interactions that occur for entity bean passivation and activation. Figure 6.13 is the OID for passivation and reactivation of an entity instance with BMP. Figure 6.14 represents the same operations for an entity instance with CMP.

1. The client invokes the last business method before passivation occurs.

2. The entity object delegates the business method to the bean instance.

3. The container decides to passivate the instance while the instance is associated with a transaction. (The reason for passivation may be, for example, that the container needs to reclaim the resources held by the instance.) The container invokes the `ejbStore` method on the instance.

4. The instance writes any cached updates made to the entity object state to the database.

5. The container invokes the `ejbPassivate` method in the instance. The instance should release any resources that it does not need into the pooled state. The instance is now in the pooled state. The container may use the instance to run find methods, activate the instance for another object identity, or release the instance through the `unsetEntityContext` method.

6. The client invokes another business method on the entity object.

7. The entity object allocates an instance from the pool. (The allocated instance could be the same instance or a different instance than the one that was associated with the object identity prior to passivation.) The container invokes the `ejbActivate` method in the instance.

8. The container invokes the `ejbLoad` method in the instance. Note that the container implements the entity object. Therefore, the `ejbActivate` and `ejbLoad` calls invoked in steps 7 and 8 are in fact invoked by the container.

9. The instance uses the `ejbLoad` method to read the object state, or parts of the object state, from the database.

10. The entity object delegates the business method to the instance.

11. The client invokes the next business method on the entity object.

12. Because the instance is in the ready state, the entity object can delegate the business method to the instance.

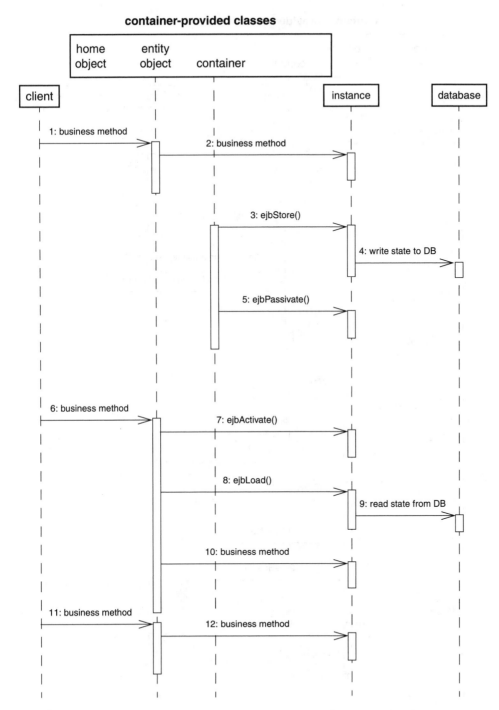

Figure 6.13 OID of Passivation and Reactivation of a Bean-Managed Entity Instance

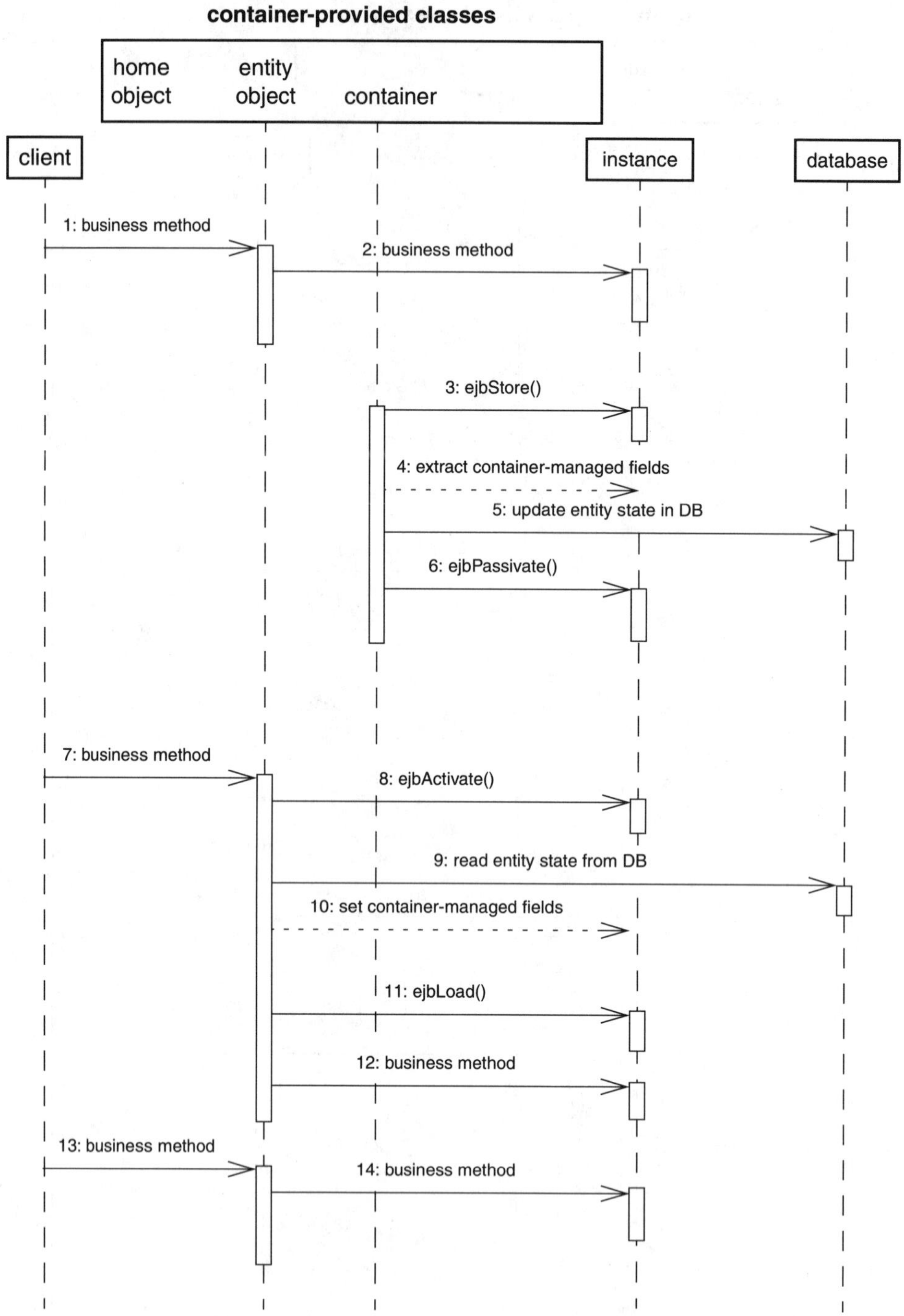

Figure 6.14 OID of Passivation and Reactivation of an Entity Instance with CMP

1. The client invokes the last business method before passivation occurs.

2. The entity object delegates the business method to the bean instance.

3. The container decides to passivate the instance while the instance is associated with a transaction. (The reason for passivation may be, for example, that the container needs to reclaim the resources held by the instance.) The container invokes the `ejbStore` method on the instance.

4. The container extracts the values of the CMP fields from the instance.

5. The container updates the object state in the database with the extracted values of the CMP fields.

6. The container invokes the `ejbPassivate` method in the instance. The instance should release any resources that it does not need into the pooled state. The instance is now in the pooled state. The container may use the instance to run find methods, activate the instance for another object identity, or release the instance through the `unsetEntityContext` method.

7. The client invokes another business method on the entity object.

8. The entity object allocates an instance from the pool. (The instance could be the same instance or a different instance than the one that was associated with the object identity prior to passivation.) The container invokes the `ejbActivate` method in the instance.

9. The container reads the object state from the database.

10. The container sets the CMP fields of the instance with the values read from the database.

11. The container invokes the `ejbLoad` method in the instance. Note that the container implements the entity object. Therefore, the `ejbActivate` and `ejbLoad` calls invoked in steps 8 and 11 (and the work in steps 9 and 10) are in fact invoked by the container.

12. The entity object delegates the business method to the instance.

13. The client invokes the next business method on the entity object.

14. Because the instance is in the ready state, the entity object can delegate the business method to the instance.

Transaction Commit OID

This section describes the operations that occur during transaction commit. Figure 6.15 shows the object interactions of the transaction commit protocol for an entity instance with BMP.

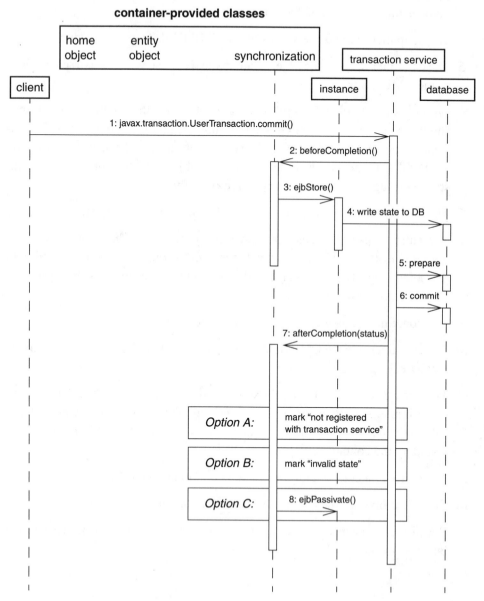

Figure 6.15   OID of Transaction Commit Protocol for a Bean-Managed Entity Instance

1. After invoking methods on an entity bean, the client attempts to commit the transaction by invoking the `commit` method on the UserTransaction interface.

2. The transaction service invokes the `beforeCompletion` method on a transaction synchronization object implemented by the container.

3. The container invokes the `ejbStore` method on the bean instance used by the transaction.

4. The instance writes any cached updates made to the entity object state to the database.

5. The transaction service performs the prepare phase of the two-phase commit protocol. This step is skipped if the database is the only resource manager enlisted with the transaction and the transaction service implements the one-phase commit optimization.

6. The transaction service performs the commit phase of the two-phase commit protocol.

7. The transaction service invokes the `afterCompletion` method on the synchronization object.

8. If the container chooses commit option C (see Commit Options on page 194), the container invokes the `ejbPassivate` method in the instance.

Figure 6.16 shows the equivalent interactions of the transaction commit protocol for an entity instance with CMP.

1. After invoking methods on an entity bean, the client attempts to commit the transaction by invoking the `commit` method on the UserTransaction interface.

2. The transaction service invokes the `beforeCompletion` method on a transaction synchronization object implemented by the container.

3. The container invokes the `ejbStore` method on the bean instance used by the transaction.

4. The container extracts the values of the CMP fields from the instance.

5. The container updates the object state in the database with the extracted values of the CMP fields.

6. The transaction service performs the prepare phase of the two-phase commit protocol. This step is skipped if the database is the only resource manager enlisted with the transaction and the transaction service implements the one-phase commit optimization.

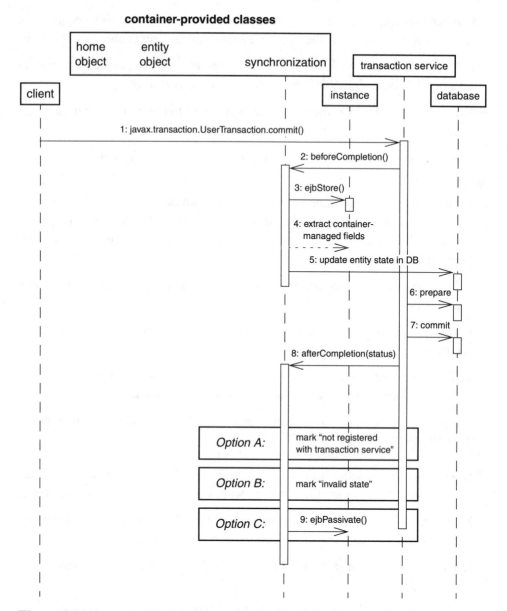

Figure 6.16 OID of Transaction Commit Protocol for CMP Entity Instance

7. The transaction service performs the commit phase of the two-phase commit protocol.

8. The transaction service invokes the `afterCompletion` method on the synchronization object.

9. If the container chooses commit option C, the container invokes the `ejbPassivate` method in the instance.

Start of Next Transaction OID

This section describes the operations that occur at the start of the next transaction. Figure 6.17 shows the object interactions at the start of the next transaction for an entity instance with BMP.

1. The client starts the next transaction by invoking the `begin` method on the UserTransaction interface.

2. The client then invokes a business method on the entity object that implements the remote interface.

3. If the container uses commit option C, it allocates an instance from the pool and invokes the `ejbActivate` method on it.

4. If the container uses commit options B or C, it invokes the `ejbLoad` method on the instance.

5. The instance uses the `ejbLoad` method to read the object state, or parts of the object state, from the database. (This happens only if the container uses commit options B or C.)

6. The database system registers itself with the transaction service. (This happens only if the container uses commit options B or C.)

7. The entity object creates a Synchronization object.

8. The entity object registers the Synchronization object with the transaction service.

9. The entity object delegates the invocation of the business method to the instance.

10. The client invokes the next business method in the same transaction.

11. The entity object delegates the invocation to the instance.

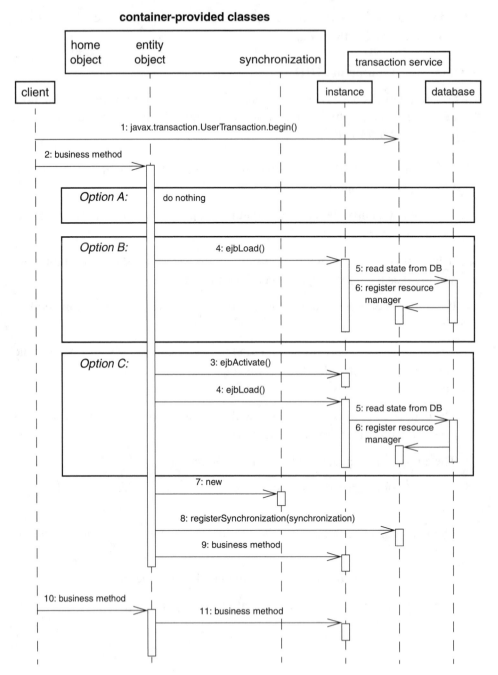

Figure 6.17 OID of Next Transaction for a Bean-Managed Entity Instance

Figure 6.18 shows the object interactions at the start of the next transaction for an entity instance with CMP.

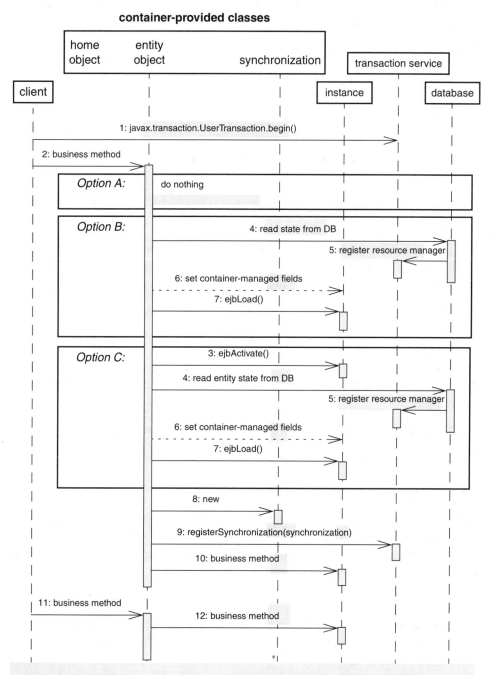

Figure 6.18 OID of Next Transaction for a Container-Managed Entity Instance

1. The client starts the next transaction by invoking the `begin` method on the UserTransaction interface.

2. The client then invokes a business method on the entity object that implements the remote interface.

3. If the container uses commit option C, it allocates an instance from the pool and invokes the `ejbActivate` method on it.

4. If the container uses commit options B or C, it reads the values of the container-managed fields from the database.

5. The database system registers itself with the transaction service. (This happens only if the container uses commit options B or C.)

6. The container sets the container-managed fields in the instance with the values read from the database. (This happens only if the container uses commit options B or C.)

7. The container invokes the `ejbLoad` method on the instance. The implementation of the `ejbLoad` method is typically empty for instances with CMP. (This happens only if the container uses commit options B or C.)

8. The entity object creates a Synchronization object.

9. The entity object registers the Synchronization object with the transaction service.

10. The entity object delegates the invocation of the business method to the instance.

11. The client invokes the next business method in the same transaction.

12. The entity object delegates the invocation to the instance.

Commit Options

The entity bean protocol gives the container the flexibility to select the disposition of the instance state at transaction commit. This flexibility allows the container to manage optimally the caching of the entity object's state and the association of an entity object identity with the enterprise bean instances.

The container selects from the following commit options.

- **Option A**—The container caches a "ready" instance between transactions. The container ensures that the instance has exclusive access to the state of the object in the persistent storage. Because of this exclusive access, there is no need for the container to synchronize the instance's state from the persistent storage at the beginning of the next transaction.

- **Option B**—The container caches a "ready" instance between transactions. In contrast to option A, the container does not ensure that the instance has exclusive access to the state of the object in the persistent storage. Therefore, the container must synchronize the instance's state from the persistent storage at the beginning of the next transaction by invoking the `ejbLoad` method on the instance.

- **Option C**—The container does not cache a "ready" instance between transactions. The container returns the instance to the pool of available instances after a transaction has completed. When the entity object is reinvoked in the next transaction, the container must activate an instance from the pool to handle the invocation.

Table 6.1 provides a summary of the commit options. As you can see, for all three options, the container synchronizes the instance's state with the persistent storage at transaction commit.

Table 6.1   Summary of Commit Options

Option	Write Instance State to Database	Instance Stays Ready	Instance State Remains Valid
A	Yes	Yes	Yes
B	Yes	Yes	No
C	Yes	No	No

A container can implement some or all of the three commit options. If the container implements more than one option, the deployer can typically specify which option will be used for each entity bean. The optimal option depends on the expected workload.

- If there is a low probability that a client will access an entity object again, using option C will result in returning the instance to the pooled state as quickly as possible. The container can immediately reuse the instance for other object identities rather than allocating new instances.

- If there is a high probability that a client may access an entity object again, using Option B will result in retaining the instance associated with an object identity in the ready state. Retaining the instance in the ready state saves the `ejbPassivate` and `ejbActivate` transitions on each client transaction to the same entity object.

- Option A can be used instead of option B to improve performance further by skipping the `ejbLoad` synchronization call on the next transaction. Note that option A can be used only if it can be guaranteed that no other program can modify the underlying state in the database.

The selection of the commit option is transparent to the entity bean implementation. The entity bean works correctly regardless of the commit option chosen by the container. The bean developer writes the entity bean in the same way.

The object interaction diagrams in Transaction Commit OID on page 188 and Start of Next Transaction OID on page 191 illustrate the commit options in detail.

6.2.4 Using the `ejbLoad` and `ejbStore` Methods

In this section, we explain how an entity bean can best utilize the `ejbLoad` and `ejbStore` methods in the entity bean class implementation. The container invokes the `ejbLoad` and `ejbStore` methods uniformly on the instances of both BMP and CMP entity beans. However, using the `ejbLoad` and `ejbStore` methods typically differs between BMP and CMP entity beans.

Using `ejbLoad` and `ejbStore` with BMP

Recall from earlier in this chapter that the state of an entity object is kept in a resource manager. Typically, the resource manager resides on a different network node than the EJB container in which the entity bean accessing the state is deployed. (This is the typical case: The EJB container is part of a middle-tier server. However, there are EJB containers integrated with the resource managers that store the entity object's state. Oracle 8i is an example of the latter case. Oracle 8i integrates the EJB container directly with the RDBMS.) Because the implementation of a business method typically accesses the entity object's state, each invocation of a business method normally results in a network trip to the resource manager. If a transaction includes multiple business method invocations, the resulting multiple calls to the resource manager over the network may increase the transaction overhead.

Figure 6.19 shows the OID for a transaction with three calls to entity bean business methods. The business methods either read or update the entity object's state stored in the resource manager. Together with the data commit at the end of the transaction, this one transaction includes a total of four network calls to the resource manager.

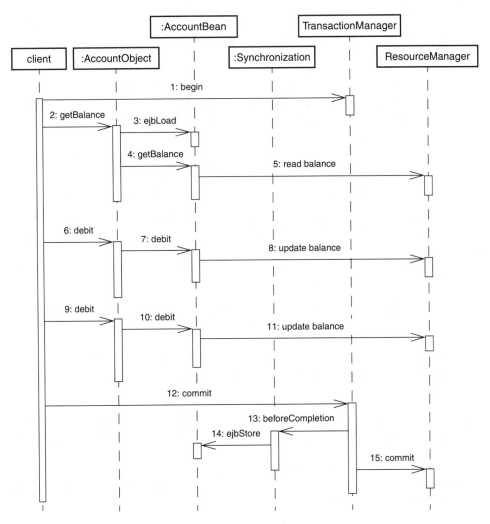

Figure 6.19 Multiple Invocations to the Resource Manager

1. The client starts a transaction by invoking the begin method. This initiates the appropriate actions from the transaction manager to create a new transaction.

2. The client, working within the transaction context, invokes the getBalance business method on the Account remote interface.

3. AccountObject, which implements the Account remote interface, in turn invokes the ejbLoad method on the AccountBean instance. In our example, the instance does no work in the ejbLoad method.

4. AccountObject invokes the `getBalance` method on the AccountBean instance that corresponds to the `getBalance` method invoked by the client through the Account remote interface.

5. The `getBalance` method must access the entity object's state stored in the resource manager; that is, it must read in the account balance information stored in the database. As a result, AccountBean initiates a network call to access these values from the resource manager.

6. The client invokes the `debit` method on the Account remote interface.

7. The AccountObject invokes the `debit` method on the entity bean instance.

8. The `debit` method performs the `debit` operation by updating the account balance in the resource manager. This is the second network call to the resource manager.

9. The client invokes the `debit` method a second time.

10. The previous process (steps 6 and 7) repeats: AccountObject invokes the `debit` method on the entity bean instance.

11. The `debit` method performs the `debit` operation by updating the account balance in the resource manager. This is the third network call to the resource manager.

12. The work of the transaction is now complete and the client invokes the `commit` method on the transaction manager.

13. The client's invocation causes the transaction manager first to call the `beforeCompletion` method in the Synchronization object implemented by the container.

14. The container invokes the `ejbStore` method on the instance. In our example, the instance does no work in the `ejbStore` method.

15. The transaction manager completes the transaction by committing the results in the resource manager. This constitutes the fourth network call.

Many bean developers will want to reduce the overhead of accessing the resource manager multiple times in a transaction. To accomplish this, the EJB architecture allows the entity bean instance to cache the entity object's state, or part of its state, within a transaction. (Some containers may allow the instance to cache the entity object's state even between transactions. Such a container would use commit option A described in Commit Options on page 194.) Rather than making repeated calls to the resource manager to access the object's state, the instance loads the object's state from the resource manager at the beginning of a transaction and caches it in its instance variables.

To facilitate caching, the EJB container invokes the `ejbLoad` method on the instance prior to the first business method invocation in a transaction. The instance can utilize the `ejbLoad` method to load the entity object's state, or part of its state, into the instance's variables. Then, subsequently invoked business methods in the instance can read and update the cached state instead of making calls to the resource manager. When the transaction ends, the EJB container invokes the `ejb-Store` method on the instance. If the previously invoked business methods updated the state cached in the instance variables, the instance uses the `ejbStore` method to synchronize the entity object's state in the resource manager with the cached state. Note that AccountBean in Figure 6.19 did not take advantage of the `ejbLoad` and `ejbStore` methods although the methods were called by the container.

Figure 6.20 shows the OID diagram illustrating the use of cached state for the same account balance and debit transactions in Figure 6.19.

1. The client starts a transaction by invoking the `begin` method. This initiates the appropriate actions from the transaction manager to create a new transaction.

2. The client, working within the transaction context, invokes the `getBalance` business method on the Account remote interface.

3. Before any business methods execute, AccountObject invokes the `ejbLoad` method on the AccountBean instance. Recall that the AccountObject class was generated by the container tools.

4. From the `ejbLoad` method, AccountBean accesses the resource manager and reads the object's state into its instance's variables.

5. AccountObject then invokes the corresponding `getBalance` method on the AccountBean instance.

6. The client does the first invocation of the `debit` method on the Account remote interface.

7. AccountObject invokes the `debit` method on the AccountBean instance.

8. The client does the second invocation of the `debit` method on the Account remote interface.

9. AccountObject invokes the `debit` method on the AccountBean class.

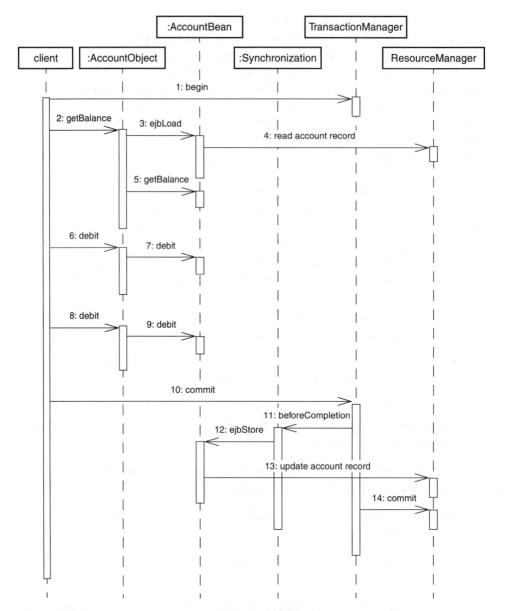

Figure 6.20 Caching State in BMP Entity Bean's Instance Variables

10. The actual work of the transaction completes and the client invokes the `commit` method on the transaction manager.

11. The transaction manager invokes the `beforeCompletion` method to signal the container (via the Synchronization interface) that the transaction is starting its commit process.

12. The container invokes the `ejbStore` method on the AccountBean instance so that it properly synchronizes the object's state in the resource manager with the updated state cached in the instance variables.

13. AccountBean sends changed state cached in its instance variables to the resource manager, which updates its copy of the entity object's state.

14. The transaction manager invokes the `commit` method on the resource manager to save all state changes and to end the transaction.

The container invokes the `ejbLoad` and `ejbStore` methods—plus the business methods between the `ejbLoad` and `ejbStore` methods—in the same transaction context. When, from these methods, the entity bean instance accesses the entity object's state in the resource manager, the resource manager properly associates all the multiple resource manager accesses with the transaction (see steps 4 and 13).

Note that the container also invokes the `ejbStore` and `ejbLoad` methods during instance passivation and activation. The OIDs in Passivation and Activation OID on page 184 illustrate this.

Because the container needs a transaction context to drive the `ejbLoad` and `ejbStore` methods on an entity bean instance, caching of the entity object's state in the instance variable works reliably only if the entity bean methods execute in a transaction context.

The `ejbLoad` and `ejbStore` methods must be used with great caution for entity beans with methods that do not execute with a defined transaction context. (These would be entity beans with methods that use the transaction attributes Not-Supported, Never, and Supports.) If the business methods can execute without a defined transaction context, the instance should cache only the state of immutable entity objects. For these entity beans, an instance can use the `ejbLoad` method to cache the entity object's state, but the `ejbStore` method should always be a noop.

Using `ejbLoad` and `ejbStore` with CMP

Caching of entity object state works differently with CMP. An entity bean with CMP typically does not use the `ejbLoad` and `ejbStore` methods to manage the caching of the entity object's state in the instance variables. Instead, the entity bean relies on the container. The container performs suitable cache management when it maps the container-managed fields to the data items comprising the state representation in the resource manager.

Essentially, the EJB container makes it appear that the entity object's state loads into the container-managed fields at the beginning of a transaction, and that changes to values of the container-managed fields automatically propagate to the entity object's state in the resource manager at the end of the transaction. The business methods simply access the container-managed fields as if the entity object's state is maintained directly in the fields rather than in the resource manager.

The container performs the loading and saving of the state transparently to the entity bean's code. The container decides the following, typically using information provided by the deployer.

- The parts of the state that it "eagerly" loads at the beginning of a transaction (just before the container invokes the `ejbLoad` call on the instance).

- The parts of the state that it "lazily" reads from the resource manager, according to when the business methods need these parts.

The container propagates the updates made to the container-managed fields to the resource manager immediately after it invokes the `ejbStore` method (Figure 6.21).

1. The client starts a transaction by invoking the `begin` method. This initiates the appropriate actions from the transaction manager to create a new transaction.

2. The client, working within the transaction context, invokes the `getBalance` business method on the Account remote interface.

3. Before any business methods execute, AccountObject reads the entity object state for the resource manager. Recall that the container tools generated the AccountObject class.

4. AccountObject sets the values of the CMP fields in the AccountBean instance.

5. AccountObject invokes the `ejbLoad` method on the AccountBean instance.

6. AccountObject then invokes the corresponding `getBalance` method on the AccountBean instance.

7. The client does the first invocation of the `debit` method on the Account remote interface.

8. AccountObject invokes the `debit` method on the AccountBean instance.

9. The client does the second invocation of the `debit` method on the Account remote interface.

10. AccountObject invokes the `debit` method on the AccountBean instance.

11. The actual work of the transaction completes and the client invokes the `commit` method on the transaction manager.

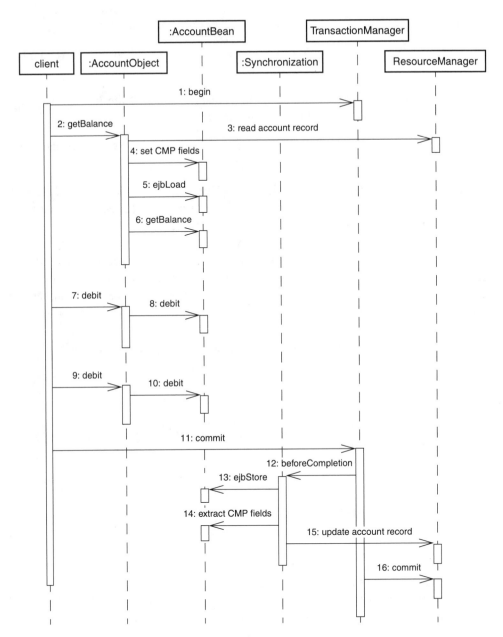

Figure 6.21 Caching with CMP Entity Beans

12. The transaction manager invokes the `beforeCompletion` method to signal the Container (via the Synchronization interface) that the transaction is starting its commit process.

13. The container invokes the `ejbStore` method on the AccountBean instance.

14. The container extracts the updated values of the CMP fields from the Account-Bean instance.

15. The container updates the representation of the account state in the resource manager with the extracted values from the CMP fields.

16. The transaction manager invokes the `commit` method on the resource manager to save all state changes and to end the transaction.

As noted at the start of this section, an entity bean with CMP typically does not use `ejbLoad` and `ejbStore` to manage caching of state. (This means that the method implementations in the entity bean class are left empty.)

When and how would an entity bean with CMP use the `ejbLoad` and `ejb-Store` methods? An entity bean with CMP could use the `ejbLoad` method to compute values derived from the container-managed fields. It would then use the `ejbStore` method to update the container-managed fields with the updated derived values. The entity bean's business methods can then directly use the derived values.

Code Example 6.9 illustrates using `ejbLoad` and `ejbStore` in CMP entity beans.

Code Example 6.9   Using `ejbLoad` and `ejbStore` in CMP Entity Beans

```
public class AccountBean implements EntityBean {
    // container-managed fields
    String acct_number;
    double balance;// balance in native currency

    // fields containing values derived from CMP fields
    double balanceInEuros;
    ...

    public double getBalance() {
        return balanceInEuros;
    }

    public void debit(double amountInEuros) {
        balanceInEuros = balanceInEuros - amountInEuros;
    }
```

```
public void credit(double amountInEuros) {
   balanceInEuros = balanceInEuros + amountInEuros;
}

public void ejbLoad() {
   balanceInEuros = balance * conversionFactor;
}

public ejbStore() {
   balance = balanceInEuros / conversionFactor;
}
}
}
```

AccountBean in Code Example 6.9 is designed for new applications that use the Euro as the common currency for all currency calculations. Therefore, the methods of the Account remote interface expect currency amounts in Euros. However, the legacy account information stored in the resource manager uses the country's native currency. The CMP AccountBean implements the `ejbLoad` and `ejbStore` methods to perform the conversions from the native currency to Euros and vice versa.

Although each business method could do the currency conversions itself, using the `ejbLoad` and `ejbStore` methods is a convenience that isolates the currency conversion logic from the rest of the business logic.

6.2.5 Designing the Entity Bean Remote Interface

The entity bean developer is responsible for the design of the bean's remote interface. The entity bean developer needs to consider carefully how the bean's clients might use the methods of the remote interface.

We describe three different approaches to the design of the entity bean's remote interface, and discuss the trade-offs with each approach.

Accessor Methods for Individual Attributes

The entity bean developer can choose to define the remote interface methods to promote individual access to each persistent attribute. With this style, the entity bean developer defines separate accessor methods in the remote interface for each individual attribute. Code Example 6.10 illustrates this approach.

Code Example 6.10 Accessor Methods for Individual Attributes

```
public interface Selection extends EJBObject {
    Employee getEmployee() throws RemoteException;
    int getCoverage() throws RemoteException;
    Plan getMedicalPlan() throws RemoteException;
    Plan getDentalPlan() throws RemoteException;
    boolean getSmokerStatus() throws RemoteException;
    void setEmployee(Employee v) throws RemoteException;
    void setCoverage(int v) throws RemoteException;
    void setMedicalPlan(Plan v) throws RemoteException;
    void setDentalPlan(Plan v) throws RemoteException;
    void setSmokerStatus(boolean v) throws RemoteException;
}
```

This style may be useful when the entity bean may have many attributes and most clients need access to only a few attributes at a time, but the set of attributes used by each client is not known a priori. The client retrieves only the attributes needed.

This style should be used only when the clients are other enterprise beans that are part of the same application and reside in the same EJB container. Several drawbacks make this style less suitable for use by entity beans that are accessed by remote clients. These drawbacks are the following.

- Each client invocation of an accessor method results in a network call, reducing the performance of the application.

- If several attributes need to be updated in a transaction, the client must use client-side transaction demarcation to make the invocation of the individual set methods atomic. The transaction is also open across several network calls, further reducing overall performance by increasing lock contention on the underlying data and by adding the overhead of additional network trips for the transaction demarcation.

In addition, it may be cumbersome for the implementation of the set methods in the entity bean class to validate business logic if the validation involves the values of several attributes. For example, let's suppose that SelectionEJB needs to enforce the following business rule: If the value of coverage is equal to 2, the value of dentalPlan must not be null. The client performs the following sequence of calls.

```
sel.setCoverage(1);
sel.setDentalPlan(null);
// sel is in a consistent state now

sel.setCoverage(2); // Does this throw an exception?
sel.setDentalPlan(somePlan);
// sel is in a consistent state now
```

When the client performs a sequence of set method invocations, the target entity object may be temporarily in an inconsistent state, such as the case after the `sel.setCoverage(2)` call. Unfortunately, the entity bean cannot know that the client is just about to invoke the next set method to make the state consistent again. This makes it difficult, if not impossible, for the entity bean to check the business rule.

Unless the application requires the use of individual access methods, we recommend that the bean developer use one of the two other styles described next for the design of an entity bean's remote interface.

Accessing All Attributes in One Value Object

As an alternative to accessing attributes individually, the developer can define the remote interface methods to access all attributes in one call. This is a good approach when client applications typically need to access most or all of the attributes of the entity bean. The client makes one method call and that method transfers all individual attributes in a single value object.

This style is illustrated by the Employee and Selection entity bean remote interfaces used in the example in Chapter 7. The following code example illustrates the Selection interface.

```
public interface Selection extends EJBObject {
    SelectionCopy getCopy()
        throws RemoteException, SelectionException;
    void updateFromCopy(SelectionCopy copy)
        throws RemoteException, SelectionException;
}
```

The value object is also used as the argument of the `create` method defined in the home interface.

```
public interface SelectionHome extends EJBHome {
    Selection create(SelectionCopy copy)
        throws RemoteException, CreateException;
    ...
}
```

The SelectionCopy class is a value object used for passing all the persistent attributes of the SelectionEJB entity bean between the client and the bean. Its definition is in SelectionCopy Value Object on page 253.

Accessing Separate Value Objects

In some cases, the developer may choose to apportion the individual attributes into subsets (the subsets can overlap) and then define methods that access each subset. This design approach is particularly useful when the entity bean has a large number of individual attributes, but the typical client programs need to access only small subsets of these attributes. The entity bean developer defines multiple value objects, one for each subset of attributes. Each value object meets the needs of a client use case; each value object contains the attributes required by a client's use of that entity bean.

Defining the appropriate value objects and suitable business methods for the individual use case has two benefits. First, because the business method typically suggests the intended use case, it makes it easier for the client programmer to learn how to use the entity bean. Second, it optimizes the network traffic because the client is sent only the data that it needs, and the data is transferred in a single call.

The BankAccount remote interface in Code Example 6.11 illustrates this style.

Code Example 6.11 Using Multiple Value Objects

```
public interface BankAccount extends EJBObject {
    // Use case one
    Address getAddress()
       throws RemoteException, BankAccountException;
    void updateAddress(Address changedAddress)
       throws RemoteException, BankAccountException;

    // Use case two
    Summary getSummary()
       throws RemoteException, BankAccountException;

    // Use case three
    Collection getTransactionHistory(Date start, Date end)
       throws RemoteException, BankAccountException;
    void modifyTransaction(Transaction tran)
         throws RemoteException, BankAccountException;
```

```
// Use case four
void credit(double amount)
   throws RemoteException;
void debit(double amount)
   throws RemoteException, InSufficientFundsException;
}
```

The developer of this entity bean recognized three different client use cases for the bean, for which the bean defines the following value objects.

- One type of client uses the bean to obtain and update the address information.

- Another client type uses the entity bean for account summary information.

- A third client type uses the entity bean to view and possibly edit transaction history.

The design of the entity bean reflects this usage; it defines the value objects Address, Summary, and Transaction for the three different client use cases. The developer has tailored the BankAccount remote methods for the three client use cases.

A fourth client type uses the entity bean to perform debit and credit transactions on the account. The fourth use case does not define any value objects.

Other entity beans in the example also use this style of defining an entity bean's remote interface. See the Plan entity remote interface in Plan Remote Interface on page 270.

6.2.6   Concurrent Invocation of an Entity Object

Recall that an entity object differs from a session object in terms of its client invocation. Only a single client can use a session object, and the client must ensure that it invokes the methods on the object serially. In contrast, multiple clients can concurrently invoke an entity object. However, each client must invoke the methods of the entity object serially.

Although the entity object appears as a shared object that the clients can invoke concurrently, the bean developer does not have to design the entity bean class to be multithreading safe. The EJB container synchronizes multiple access to the entity object. The bean developer depends on the EJB container for appropriate synchronization to an entity object when multiple clients concurrently access the object. This section explains how the EJB container dispatches methods invoked by multiple clients through the entity object's remote interface to the entity bean instances so that the potentially concurrent execution of multiple client requests does not lead to the loss of the entity object's state integrity.

An EJB container may employ one of two typical implementation strategies to synchronize concurrent access from multiple clients to an entity object. It is important to note that, from the bean developer's perspective, it makes no difference which strategy the container uses. The bean developer implements the same code for the entity object regardless of the container synchronization strategy.

One implementation strategy essentially delegates the synchronization of multiple clients to the resource manager. It works as follows.

1. When a client-invoked method call reaches the container, the container first determines the target transaction context in which to invoke the business method. Chapter 8, Understanding Transactions describes the rules for determining the transaction context for the invoked business method (see Declarative Transaction Demarcation on page 337).

2. The container attempts to locate an entity object instance that is in the ready state and already associated with the target entity object identity and the target transaction context. If such an instance exists, the container dispatches the business method on the instance.

3. If there are bean instances in the ready state associated with the target entity object identity, but none are in the target transaction context, the container can take an instance not currently associated with a transaction context, invoke the `ejbLoad` method on the instance, and then dispatch the business method on it. The instance stays associated with the transaction context until the end of the transaction. Ending the transaction causes the container to invoke `ejbStore` on the instance; note that `ejbStore` executes in the transaction context.

4. If there are no bean instances in the ready state suitable for dispatching the business method, the container activates an instance in the pooled state by invoking the `ejbActivate` and `ejbLoad` methods, and then dispatches the business method on the instance. The instance remains associated with the transaction context, as described in the previous step.

Note that when the container uses this implementation strategy, the container may concurrently dispatch multiple invocations to the same entity object by using a different instance of the entity bean class for each invocation (see Figure 6.22).

In Figure 6.22, the two Account 100 instances are associated with the same Account 100 entity object, but each instance is in a different transaction context. Because the transaction context is associated with an instance's access to the

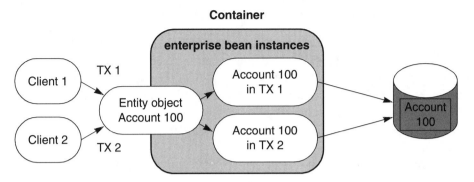

Figure 6.22 Multiple Clients Using Multiple Instances to Access an Entity Object

resource manager, the resource manager performs the synchronization of the updates from the multiple bean instances to the entity object's state based on the transaction context. An EJB container using this implementation strategy uses commit options B or C described in Commit Options on page 194.

The second implementation strategy places a greater burden for the synchronization of client calls on the container. With this strategy, the EJB container acquires exclusive access to the entity object's state in the database. The container activates a single instance and serializes the access from multiple transactions to this instance (see Figure 6.23). The container can use any of the commit options A, B, or C if it employs this single-instance strategy.

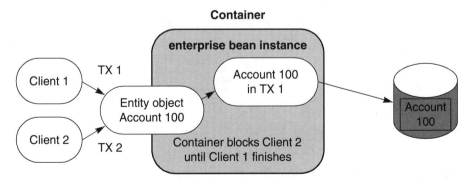

Figure 6.23 Multiple Clients Using Single Instance to Access an Entity Object

6.2.7   Using Entity Beans with Preexisting Data

It is important to understand that the representation of an entity object in the resource manager may preexist the deployment of an entity bean. For example, a bank may have been using nonobject-based applications that store account records in a database system. The bank then later developed or purchased an EJB application that includes the AccountEJB entity bean. The AccountEJB entity bean provides the object-oriented EJB client view of the same account database records (see Figure 6.24).

The new EJB application seamlessly coexists with the legacy nonobject-based application, as follows.

- An account record created by a legacy application is visible to the EJB application as an Account object. From the perspective of the EJB application, an Account object exists even if a `create` method of the entity bean home interface did not create it.

- Similarly, if the EJB application creates a new Account object, the legacy application can access the state of the entity object because it is a record in the database.

- If the EJB application changes the Account object by invoking methods of the Account remote interface, these changes are visible to a legacy application as changes to the account record in the database.

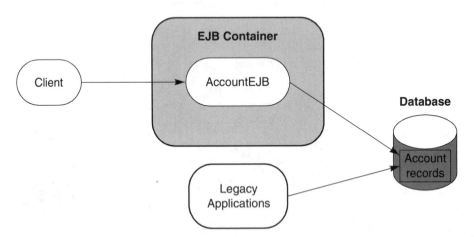

Figure 6.24   Access to Preexisting Data Shared with Legacy Applications

- Similarly, if the legacy application changes the account record in the database, the changes are visible to the EJB application as changes to the state of the Account object.

- If the legacy application deletes an account record from the database, the EJB application is no longer able to access the corresponding Account object.

- If the EJB application removes an Account object, the object removal operation causes the deletion of the corresponding account record from the database. The legacy application is no longer able to access the record.

- The resource manager's (database system) transaction mechanism allows the EJB application to be used concurrently with the legacy application.

6.3 Conclusion

This chapter presented the fundamental concepts of entity beans. In particular, it described the two views of entity beans: the client view and the bean developer view. It also described how the container manages the life cycle of an entity bean instance, and how the bean developer can make optimal use of the container's management of object state and persistence.

The next chapter presents the same benefits enrollment example that was used earlier to illustrate session beans, but it is rewritten as an application that uses entity beans. The example application illustrates all of the concepts discussed in this chapter with "real-world" code. It illustrates many of the techniques for using entity beans to develop and integrate applications for different customers with different environments.

CHAPTER 7

Entity Bean
Application Example

THIS chapter uses an example of a distributed application to illustrate how enterprise applications use entity beans. The example application is typical of applications that include components built by multiple organizations. The chapter shows how the different organizations develop the respective components of the application and how, ultimately, the customer deploys the entire application.

The example application illustrates the following.

- **The techniques for using entity beans to develop applications for different customers with different operational environments.** An ISV uses entity beans in the development of an application so that it can sell the application to as broad a range of customers and operational environments as possible. Our example illustrates the following.

    - How the ISV uses entity beans with CMP to integrate its application with the customer's existing applications and database

    - How the ISV uses the entity bean client-view API as the integration points with the different third-party components

- **The techniques for integrating application software parts from multiple vendors into a single application.** We illustrate the following.

    - How an ISV enables the customer to extend the application by adding components from other vendors

    - How other vendors structure their components to facilitate the integration of their components with the first ISV

- **The implementation of several entity beans to illustrate the various issues of the entity bean architecture.** Entity beans use different styles to implement their persistence; thus, we illustrate the use of both CMP and BMP. In addition, we illustrate different strategies for implementing entity bean state, including the following:

  - An entity bean with a state that is implemented in a database using JDBC. This is the PremiumHealthPlanEJB entity bean.

  - An entity bean with a state that is implemented by other entity beans. This is the WrapperPlanEJB entity bean.

  - An entity bean with a state that is stored in a remote Web server accessible using XML over HTTP. This is the ProvidencePlanBeanEJB entity bean.

- **Various design approaches for an entity bean's remote interface, plus the advantages each approach offers to different applications.** The developer should design the remote interface so that its methods support the intended client use cases.

- **The techniques for caching an entity object's persistent state.** The example illustrates how to use the instance variables of an entity bean class, along with the `ejbLoad` and `ejbStore` methods, to cache the entity object's persistent state.

- **The correct approach that a client application (such as EnrollmentBean) takes to use the entity bean client-view API.**

- **The use of an entity bean to aggregate the function of multiple other entity beans into a single component.** WrapperPlanEJB is an entity bean that performs just such a function. Aggregation simplifies the development of an application that needs to access multiple entity beans because the application can access their functions through the single aggregate bean.

- **The correspondence of entity beans to database rows.** In particular, an entity object does not always correspond to a single row in a database. The example illustrates that the state of an entity object can map to multiple rows in possibly multiple tables in the database. In addition, we show that it is not necessary to expose as entity beans the business objects that are not intended to be invoked from other applications. These objects could be implemented as dependent objects of the entity beans with which they are associated. For example, the Doctor object is implemented as a dependent object of the Plan entity object.

- **The techniques for "subclassing" an entity bean with CMP to create an entity bean with BMP.** The subclass implements the data access methods.

- **The packaging of enterprise beans into J2EE standard files.** The example illustrates packaging the entity beans and their dependent parts into the standard ejb-jar file and the J2EE enterprise application archive file (`.ear` file).

- **The parts of an application that do *not* have to be developed.** The example code is also interesting in what it does not include. The reader will see no transaction or security management-related code. The deployment descriptors describe declaratively the transaction and security requirements for entity beans. Transaction management is described in Chapter 8, Understanding Transactions and Chapter 9, Managing Security, describes security management.

- **A discussion on application integration techniques involving entity beans.**

This chapter begins with the description of the problem. Then, to give you a feel for the scope of the application, it describes the application components from a high level. This is followed by detailed information on each part of the application, from the perspective of the vendor that developed the part.

7.1   Application Overview

Our example application illustrates the development and deployment of an enterprise application that consists of components developed by multiple vendors. We illustrate how using entity beans in the application facilitates the integration of the components from different vendors.

7.1.1   Problem Description

The example entity bean application implements a benefits self-service application. An employee uses this application to select and enroll in the benefits plans offered by the company. From the end user perspective, the application is identical to the application described in Chapter 4, Working with Session Beans, which in that case was a benefits application built using session beans. However, the following are the key differences in the design of the two applications.

- Wombat Inc. developed the core of the application. Wombat is an ISV that specializes in the development of benefits applications used by enterprises. Wombat wants to sell its application to as many different enterprises as it can. This means that its application must work in a myriad of different operational environments. In contrast, Star Enterprise's IT department developed the application illustrated in Chapter 4. Because that application was only intended to be used within Star Enterprise's own environment, it was developed with no regard for the application's portability to operational environments other than that of Star Enterprise.

- The application described in this chapter allows dynamic changes to the configuration of the available medical and dental plans. For example, a benefits administrator at Star Enterprise can add and remove medical and dental plans to the benefits application. In contrast, the application in Chapter 4 requires redeployment to change the configuration of the available plans.

- Star Enterprise uses a payroll system from Aardvark (another ISV) that is a mainframe application. External programs cannot directly access the payroll system or its database. The PayrollEJB enterprise bean from Aardvark provides the integration interfaces so that other applications can access the payroll system.

- The application described in this chapter dynamically interacts with the plan providers; that is, with the insurance companies. For example, a plan provider can change the premium calculation formula and manage the list of doctors participating in the offered plans, and the application reflects these changes. In contrast, the application in Chapter 4 requires redeployment to change this information.

7.1.2   Main Parts of the Application

The example application presented here consists of multiple enterprise beans, Web applications, and databases. Typical for an application such as this, some parts already existed at Star Enterprise, whereas multiple outside organizations developed the other parts. Figure 7.1 illustrates the logical parts of the application. It is followed by a brief description.

The section Summary of the Integration Techniques on page 329 discusses how to use the EJB architecture to integrate these parts at deployment.

The application consists of four principal parts, and these parts come from four different sources.

1. The preexisting employee and payroll parts in the Star Enterprise operational environment

2. The Wombat benefits application, which consists of multiple enterprise beans and Web applications

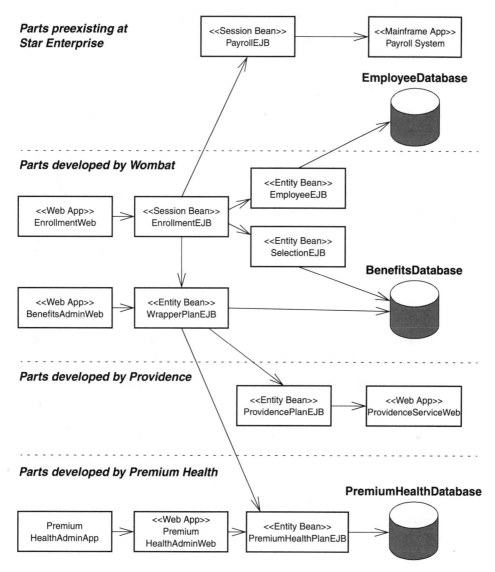

Figure 7.1   Logical Parts of the Entity Bean Benefits Application

3. The enterprise bean and Web application parts developed by Premium Health Insurance

4. The enterprise bean and Web application parts developed by Providence Insurance

Prior to the deployment of Wombat's benefits application, Star Enterprise utilized the EmployeeDatabase, Payroll System, and PayrollEJB parts. These parts pertain to the following aspects of Star Enterprise's business.

- EmployeeDatabase contains information about Star Enterprise employees.

- Payroll System is a mainframe application that Star Enterprise uses for its payroll.

- PayrollEJB is a stateless session bean that provides nonpayroll applications with secure access to the payroll system. Nonpayroll applications, including Wombat's benefits application, use PayrollEJB as the payroll integration interface.

Wombat, an ISV, has implemented the bulk of the benefits application. Wombat develops multiple Web applications and enterprise beans, as follows.

- EnrollmentWeb is a Web application that implements the presentation logic for the benefits enrollment process. A Wombat customer's employees (such as Star Enterprise employees when the application is deployed at Star Enterprise) access EnrollmentWeb via a browser.

- BenefitsAdminWeb is a Web application that implements the presentation logic for business processes used by the customer's benefits administration department. The benefits administration department uses BenefitsAdminWeb, for example, to customize the portfolio of plans offered to the employees.

- EnrollmentEJB is a stateful session bean that implements the benefits enrollment business process. It uses several entity beans to perform its function.

- EmployeeEJB is an entity bean that encapsulates access to the customer's (Star Enterprise, in this example) employee information. It is an entity bean with CMP, and its main role is to allow deployment binding with the customer's employee database.

- SelectionEJB is an entity bean that encapsulates the benefits selections chosen by each employee.

- WrapperPlanEJB is an entity bean that aggregates the medical and dental plans from multiple providers (that is, from the insurance companies). It is the integration point between the benefits application and the plan entity beans provided by the insurance companies.

- BenefitsDatabase stores the information used by the SelectionEJB and WrapperPlanEJB entity beans.

Wombat defines what an insurance provider needs to do to integrate its plan information with Wombat's benefits application. This integration technique is explained in the section Benefits Plan Integration Approach on page 268. Our example shows the parts developed by two insurance providers: Premium Health and Providence. For the sake of illustration, Premium Health and Providence use very different techniques to implement access to their plan information.

Premium Health provides PremiumHealthPlanEJB, PremiumHealthAdmin-Web, PremiumHealthDatabase, and PremiumHealthAdminApp.

- PremiumHealthPlanEJB is an entity bean that implements the interfaces defined by Wombat. PremiumHealthPlanEJB allows the Wombat benefits application to access the information about the medical and dental plans offered by Premium Health.

- PremiumHealthAdminWeb is a Web application that allows Premium Health to update remotely the benefits information stored in PremiumHealthDatabase at Star Enterprise.

- PremiumHealthDatabase is a database residing at Star Enterprise that stores the data used by PremiumHealthPlanEJB.

- PremiumHealthAdminApp is an application that Premium Health uses to upload and modify the plan information in PremiumHealthDatabase.

Providence provides the ProvidencePlanEJB entity bean and Providence-ServiceWeb Web application.

- ProvidencePlanEJB allows the Wombat benefits application to access information about the medical and dental plans offered by Providence. Providence-PlanEJB communicates using XML over HTTP with ProvidenceServiceWeb located at Providence. This enables the benefits application to get on-line the information about the medical and dental plans offered by Providence.

- ProvidenceServiceWeb is a Web application located at the Providence site. It is used by applications running at customer sites, including the benefits application running at Star Enterprise, to obtain the current plan information for the plans offered by Providence.

7.1.3 Distributed Deployment

Star Enterprise has deployed the benefits application across multiple servers, including six servers within its own enterprise intranet. The benefits application also communicates with two servers located at the insurance companies. The deployment configuration is shown in Figure 7.2.

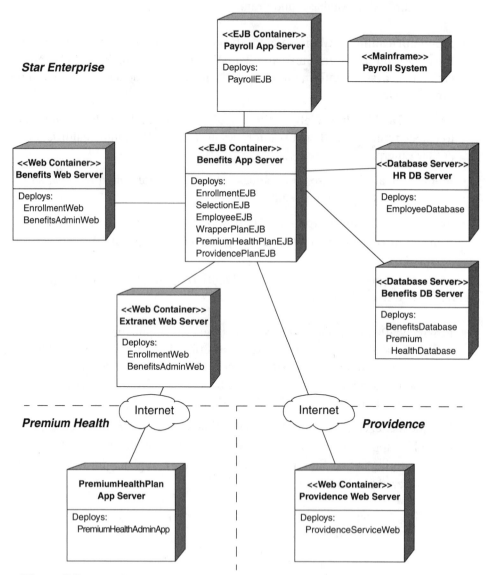

Figure 7.2 Benefits Application Deployment

The benefits application is spread across six servers within Star Enterprise's own physical confines. The benefits department has deployed the EnrollmentWeb and BenefitsWeb Web applications on the Benefits Web server. It has deployed the enterprise beans EnrollmentEJB, SelectionEJB, EmployeeEJB, WrapperPlanEJB, PremiumHealthPlanEJB, and ProvidencePlanEJB on the Benefits App server. BenefitsDatabase and PremiumHealthDatabase are stored on the Benefits Database server. The enterprise bean PayrollEJB is deployed on the Payroll App server, which in turn provides the connection to the payroll system on the mainframe. EmployeeDatabase is stored on the Human Resources (HR) Database server. The PremiumHealthAdminWeb Web application is deployed on the extranet Web server that Star Enterprise uses for communication with its trading partners.

The deployment diagram also illustrates the two servers that are physically located outside Star Enterprise. The PremiumHealthPlan App server is located at Premium Health, and the Providence Web server is located at Providence. The PremiumHealthPlan App server runs the PremiumHealthAdminApp application that communicates with PremiumHealthAdminWeb located at Star Enterprise. This application updates the health plan information stored at Star Enterprise. The Providence Web server hosts the ProvidenceServiceWeb Web application, which is invoked by the ProvidencePlanEJB deployed at Star Enterprise.

Figure 7.2 illustrates deploying Web applications and enterprise beans across multiple server machines. This is just one deployment scenario. It is possible to deploy the application on fewer machines without modification to its components. For example, the Benefits Web server, Benefits App server, Benefits Database server, and Human Resources Database server can all be part of the same J2EE server installed on a single server machine. The example illustrates the more distributed deployment scenario because it reflects the traditional division of "information ownership" by multiple departments within a large enterprise. It also illustrates the power and flexibility of the EJB architecture for developing and deploying distributed applications.

7.2 Preexisting Parts at Star Enterprise

This section describes the relevant software and systems at Star Enterprise that preexisted the deployment of Wombat's benefits application.

7.2.1 EmployeeDatabase

The human resource department at Star Enterprise maintains the information about employees and the company departments in EmployeeDatabase. The information is stored in multiple tables. The `Employees` table within the database is relevant to the benefits application. Code Example 7.1 shows the SQL `CREATE` statement that defines this table.

Code Example 7.1 Employees Table Definition

```
CREATE TABLE Employees (
    empl_id INT,
    empl_first_name VARCHAR(32),
    empl_last_name VARCHAR(32),
    empl_addr_street VARCHAR(32),
    empl_addr_city VARCHAR(32),
    empl_addr_zip VARCHAR(10),
    empl_addr_state VARCHAR(2),
    empl_dept_id VARCHAR(10),
    empl_start_date DATE,
    empl_position VARCHAR(5),
    empl_birth_date DATE,
    ...
    PRIMARY KEY ( empl_id )
)
```

Note that Wombat has no knowledge of the schema of EmployeeDatabase, nor does it need that knowledge. Wombat must code its benefits application as generically as possible. Its primary consideration is that the application work regardless of an individual customer's schema and type of DBMS. If Wombat coded the benefits application using the Star Enterprise schema, the application would be unusable by other customers who are likely to have a different schema or even a different type of DBMS.

7.2.2   Payroll System

Star Enterprise's Payroll System is a mainframe application. It consists of a collection of CICS TP programs.

Prior to the deployment of Wombat's benefits application, Star Enterprise needed to give its nonmainframe applications access to payroll information. To accomplish this, Star Enterprise purchased a mainframe connectivity product from vendor Aardvark.

Aardvark sells enterprise beans that provide access to popular mainframe applications, including the Payroll System used by Star Enterprise. Star Enterprise bought Aardvark's PayrollEJB enterprise bean to enable access to the Payroll System from Java applications.

Aardvark packages the client-view interface files for its enterprise bean products into JAR files. Because Aardvark wants to encourage others to build products utilizing Aardvark's enterprise beans, it makes these client-view JAR files available to other ISVs. With the JAR files, other vendors can create Java applications that communicate with Aardvark's enterprise beans. The JAR file `payroll_ejb_client.jar` contains the client view of PayrollEJB. Wombat, an ISV, uses the `payroll_ejb_client.jar` file in its benefits application to access the customer's Payroll System.

Star Enterprise deployed Aardvark's mainframe connectivity product and PayrollEJB.

Aardvark supplies PayrollEJB, which is a stateless session bean. The external interface of the mainframe Payroll System is a procedural interface, and therefore Aardvark defined its Java representation using a stateless session bean.

Code Example 7.2 shows the definition for the Payroll interface, which is the PayrollEJB remote interface.

Code Example 7.2 Payroll Remote Interface

```
package com.aardvark.payroll;

import javax.ejb.*;
import java.rmi.RemoteException;

public interface Payroll extends EJBObject {
    void setBenefitsDeduction(int emplNumber, double deduction)
        throws RemoteException, PayrollException;
    double getBenefitsDeduction(int emplNumber)
        throws RemoteException, PayrollException;
    double getSalary(int emplNumber)
        throws RemoteException, PayrollException;
    void setSalary(int emplNumber, double salary)
        throws RemoteException, PayrollException;
}
```

Code Example 7.3 gives the definition of the PayrollHome home interface.

Code Example 7.3 PayrollHome Home Interface

```
package com.aardvark.payroll;

import javax.ejb.*;
import java.rmi.RemoteException;

public interface PayrollHome extends EJBHome {
    Payroll create() throws RemoteException, CreateException;
}
```

The implementation of PayrollEJB's PayrollBean class uses Aardvark's mainframe connectivity product. The mainframe connectivity product integrates with the EJB container as a resource adapter using the Connector architecture to communicate with the Payroll System TP programs on the mainframe. (Refer to the *Java 2 platform, Enterprise Edition Connector Specification.* See Other Sources of Information on page xxii for the complete reference to this specification. Also note that the Connector API, although public, is not yet the final version.)

Code Example 7.4 shows the implementation of the PayrollBean class.

Code Example 7.4 PayrollBean Class

```
package com.aardvark.payroll.impl;

import javax.ejb.*;

import javax.naming.Context;
import javax.naming.InitialContext;
import javax.naming.NamingException;

import javax.resource.cci.ConnectionFactory;
import javax.resource.cci.Connection;
import javax.resource.cci.MappedRecord;
import javax.resource.cci.RecordFactory;
import javax.resource.cci.InteractionSpec;
import javax.resource.cci.Interaction;

import javax.resource.ResourceException;

import com.aardvark.payroll.PayrollException;

public class PayrollBean implements SessionBean {
    // Mainframe connection factory
    private ConnectionFactory connectionFactory;

    public void setBenefitsDeduction(int emplNumber,
            double deduction) throws PayrollException
    {
        Connection cx = null;
        try {
            // Obtain connection to mainframe.
            cx = getConnection();
```

```java
      // Create an interaction object.
      Interaction ix = cx.createInteraction();

      InteractionSpecImpl ixSpec = new InteractionSpecImpl();

      // Set the name of the TP program to be invoked.
      ixSpec.setFunctionName("SETPAYROLL_DEDUCTION");

      // Specify that we will be sending input parameters
      // to the TP program, but are expecting to receive
      // no output parameters.
      ixSpec.setInteractionVerb(InteractionSpec.SYNC_SEND);

      RecordFactory rf = ix.getRecordFactory();

      // Create an object that knows how to
      // format the input parameters.
      MappedRecord input =
          rf.createMappedRecord("PAYROLLINFO_DEDUCTION");
      input.put("EMPLOYEENUMBER", new Integer(emplNumber));
      input.put("DEDUCTION", new Double(deduction));

      // Execute invokes the TP program, passing it
      // the input parameters.
      ix.execute(ixSpec, input);
   } catch (ResourceException ex) {
      throw new EJBException(ex);
   } finally {
      try {
         if (cx != null) cx.close();
      } catch (ResourceException ex) {
      }
   }
}

public double getBenefitsDeduction(int emplNumber)
   throws PayrollException
{
   Connection cx = null;
   try {
      cx = getConnection();
      Interaction ix = cx.createInteraction();
```

```
        InteractionSpecImpl ixSpec = new InteractionSpecImpl();
        ixSpec.setFunctionName("GETPAYROLLDATA");
        ixSpec.setInteractionVerb(
           InteractionSpec.SYNC_SEND_RECEIVE);

        RecordFactory rf = ix.getRecordFactory();

        MappedRecord input =
           rf.createMappedRecord("EMPLOYEEINFO");
        input.put("EMPLOYEENUMBER", new Integer(emplNumber));

        EmployeeRecord employee = new EmployeeRecordImpl();

        if (ix.execute(ixSpec, input, employee))
           return employee.getBenefitsDeduction();
        else
           throw new PayrollException(
              PayrollException.INVAL_EMPL_NUMBER);
     } catch (ResourceException ex) {
        throw new EJBException(ex);
     } finally {
        try {
           if (cx != null) cx.close();
        } catch (ResourceException ex) {
        }
     }
}

public void setSalary(int emplNumber, double salary)
   throws PayrollException
{
   Connection cx = null;
   try {
      cx = getConnection();
      Interaction ix = cx.createInteraction();

      InteractionSpecImpl ixSpec = new InteractionSpecImpl();
      ixSpec.setFunctionName("SETPAYROLL_SALARY");
      ixSpec.setInteractionVerb(InteractionSpec.SYNC_SEND);

      RecordFactory rf = ix.getRecordFactory();
```

```
      MappedRecord input =
         rf.createMappedRecord("PAYROLLINFO_SALARY");
      input.put("EMPLOYEENUMBER", new Integer(emplNumber));
      input.put("SALARY", new Double(salary));

      ix.execute(ixSpec, input);
   } catch (ResourceException ex) {
      throw new EJBException(ex);
   } finally {
      try {
         if (cx != null) cx.close();
      } catch (ResourceException ex) {
      }
   }
}

public double getSalary(int emplNumber)
   throws PayrollException
{
   Connection cx = null;
   try {
      cx = getConnection();
      Interaction ix = cx.createInteraction();

      InteractionSpecImpl ixSpec = new InteractionSpecImpl();
      ixSpec.setFunctionName("GETPAYROLLDATA");
      ixSpec.setInteractionVerb(
         InteractionSpec.SYNC_SEND_RECEIVE);

      RecordFactory rf = ix.getRecordFactory();

      MappedRecord input =
         rf.createMappedRecord("EMPLOYEEINFO");
      input.put("EMPLOYEENUMBER", new Integer(emplNumber));

      EmployeeRecord employee = new EmployeeRecordImpl();

      if (ix.execute(ixSpec, input, employee))
         return employee.getSalary();
      else
         throw new PayrollException(
            PayrollException.INVAL_EMPL_NUMBER);
```

```
      } catch (ResourceException ex) {
         throw new EJBException(ex);
      } finally {
         try {
            if (cx != null) cx.close();
         } catch (ResourceException ex) {
         }
      }
   }

   public void ejbCreate() {}
   public void ejbRemove() {}
   public void ejbPassivate() {}
   public void ejbActivate() {}
   public void setSessionContext(SessionContext sc) {}

   private Connection getConnection() {
      try {
         Connection cx = connectionFactory.getConnection();
         return cx;
      } catch (ResourceException ex) {
         throw new EJBException(ex);
      }
   }

   private void readEnvironment() {
      try {
         Context nc = new InitialContext();

         connectionFactory = (ConnectionFactory)nc.lookup(
            "java:comp/env/eis/ConnectionFactory");
      } catch (NamingException ex) {
         throw new EJBException(ex);
      }
   }
}
```

Let's look at the implementation of the setBenefitsDeduction method. It first obtains a Connection object to use for communication with the mainframe. It uses the Connection object to create an Interaction object. The Interaction object is used for a single interaction with the mainframe.

The `setBenefitsDeduction` method then creates an InteractionSpecImpl object and sets on it the name of the target TP mainframe program. It also specifies the direction of the interaction. In our case, the `SYNC_SEND` verb indicates that arguments pass only to the mainframe.

The `setBenefitsDeduction` method next creates a MappedRecord object and uses the `put` methods to set the values of input arguments to be sent to the target mainframe program.

Finally, the `setBenefitsDeduction` method invokes the `execute` method on the Interaction object, which causes the resource adapter to send the input arguments to the `SETPAYROLL_DEDUCTION` program on the mainframe. "Under the covers," the EJB container and the mainframe resource adapter propagate the transaction from the PayrollBean instance to the mainframe TP program. The developer of the PayrollBean did not have to write any transaction-related code to enable this propagation of the transaction.

Refer to CCI Interface Classes on page 401 in Appendix B for a more detailed description of the classes that implement the common client interface (CCI).

7.3   Parts Developed by Wombat

Wombat Inc. is an ISV specializing in the development of applications for enterprises to use to administer benefits plans (such as medical and dental insurance plans). One Wombat application is a Web-based self-service Benefits Enrollment application. Employees of an enterprise use the application to make selections from multiple medical and dental plans offered to them by their employer.

Wombat's goal is to develop a single, generic Benefits Enrollment application and sell it to many customer enterprises. The Benefits Enrollment application is not an isolated application: It uses data provided by other applications or databases that exist in the customers' operational environment. This presents a challenge for Wombat: Every customer is likely to have a different implementation of the application or data with which the Benefits Enrollment application needs to integrate. For example, the enrollment application needs access to a database that contains information about employees. It also needs access to the payroll system so that it can update benefits-related paycheck deductions. In addition, the enrollment application needs to be integrated at the customer site with the plan-specific components provided by the insurance companies.

Wombat uses entity bean components to integrate the Benefits Enrollment application with applications or databases from other parties.

7.3.1   Overview of the Wombat Parts

Wombat develops the Web applications and enterprise beans, which are illustrated in Figure 7.3. Each application and enterprise bean is detailed throughout this section.

- **EnrollmentWeb**—A Web application that implements the presentation logic for the benefits enrollment process. A customer's employees use Enroll-mentWeb to enroll into the offered medical and dental plans.

- **BenefitsAdminWeb**—A Web application that implements the presentation logic for business processes used by the customer's benefits administration department. The benefits administration department uses this Web application to configure and customize the medical and dental plans offered to the employees.

- **EnrollmentEJB**—EnrollmentEJB is a stateful session bean that implements the benefits enrollment business process.

- **EmployeeEJB**—EmployeeEJB is an entity bean that encapsulates access to a customer's employee information. It is an entity bean with CMP so that it can accommodate the different representations of employee databases at different customer sites. CMP allows deployment binding with the customer's employee database.

- **SelectionEJB**—SelectionEJB is an entity bean that encapsulates the benefits selections chosen by each employee.

- **WrapperPlanEJB**—WrapperPlanEJB is an entity bean that aggregates the medical and dental plans from multiple providers (that is, insurance companies). It takes the different plans from multiple providers and "wraps" them into

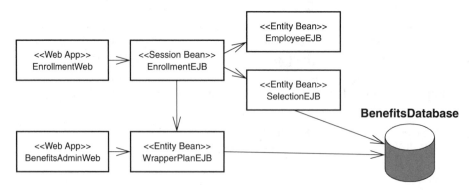

Figure 7.3   Web Applications and Enterprise Beans Developed by Wombat

a single component, thus simplifying application development. WrapperPlanE-JB insulates the rest of the enrollment application from the configuration of the individual medical and dental plans. Without this entity bean, the application would have to be coded to handle several different health plans; with this entity bean, the application has to deal only with a single component.

The enterprise beans developed by Wombat store information in BenefitsDatabase. Wombat designed the BenefitsDatabase schema, and at deployment the customer creates the database at his own site. Wombat also allows the customer to choose a different schema as a deployment option.

The following sections describe in greater detail the parts developed by Wombat.

7.3.2   EnrollmentEJB Session Bean

EnrollmentEJB is a stateful session bean that implements the benefits enrollment business process. EnrollmentEJB's home and remote interfaces are the same as in the Chapter 4, Working with Session Beans example. However, although an IT developer at Star Enterprise defined the interfaces in the session bean chapter, Wombat defined the home and remote interfaces shown in this chapter.

Code Example 7.5 shows the EnrollmentEJB's home interface definition.

Code Example 7.5   EnrollmentHome Home Interface Defined by Wombat

```
package com.wombat.benefits;

import javax.ejb.*;
import java.rmi.RemoteException;

public interface EnrollmentHome extends EJBHome {
    Enrollment create(int emplnum) throws RemoteException,
        CreateException, EnrollmentException;
}
```

Code Example 7.6 shows the definition of the EnrollmentEJB's remote interface.

Code Example 7.6 Enrollment Remote Interface Defined by Wombat

```java
package com.wombat.benefits;

import javax.ejb.*;
import java.rmi.RemoteException;

public interface Enrollment extends EJBObject {
   EmployeeInfo getEmployeeInfo()
      throws RemoteException, EnrollmentException;
   Options getCoverageOptions()
      throws RemoteException, EnrollmentException;
   void setCoverageOption(int choice)
      throws RemoteException, EnrollmentException;
   Options getMedicalOptions()
      throws RemoteException, EnrollmentException;
   void setMedicalOption(int choice)
      throws RemoteException, EnrollmentException;
   Options getDentalOptions()
      throws RemoteException, EnrollmentException;
   void setDentalOption(int choice)
      throws RemoteException, EnrollmentException;
   boolean getSmokerStatus()
      throws RemoteException, EnrollmentException;
   void setSmokerStatus(boolean status)
      throws RemoteException, EnrollmentException;
   Summary getSummary()
      throws RemoteException, EnrollmentException;
   void commitSelections()
      throws RemoteException, EnrollmentException;
}
```

The implementation of the EnrollmentBean session bean class is similar to the implementation illustrated in Chapter 4. However, there are some key differences, as follows.

- EnrollmentEJB in Chapter 4 uses command beans to access the employee's database. EnrollmentEJB in this chapter uses the EmployeeEJB entity bean to encapsulate access to the employee information. Because the EmployeeEJB entity bean is implemented with CMP, the deployer can bind the EmployeeEJB bean with the customer's employee database in a standard way.

- EnrollmentEJB in Chapter 4 uses command beans to access the benefits selections in BenefitsDatabase. EnrollmentEJB in this chapter uses the SelectionEJB entity bean to encapsulate the access to the employees' current selections. This approach is advantageous because the benefits selection access is available, via the Selection and SelectionHome client-view interfaces, to other applications regardless of their location on the network. For example, the Star Enterprise IT department can develop other applications that use the Selection and SelectionHome client-view interfaces to access the employees' benefits selections. In addition, because Wombat also provides a CMP version of the SelectionEJB entity bean (the SelectionBeanCMP class), a customer can customize the format in which the selections are stored, or even store them in a nonrelational database.

- EnrollmentEJB uses the WrapperPlanEJB entity bean to access the medical and dental plans currently offered to the employees. WrapperPlanEJB integrates the medical and dental plans provided by multiple insurance companies with the enrollment application. WrapperPlanEJB offers the same advantages as SelectionEJB: Other Star Enterprise applications can use WrapperPlanEJB to access the available medical and dental plans. The applications do not have to be concerned with the multiple plan entity beans provided by the the individual insurance companies.

Code Example 7.7 illustrates the source code for the EnrollmentBean session bean class, as it has been implemented for the example in this chapter. (Note that this implementation of EnrollmentBean differs from the implementation in Chapter 4.)

Code Example 7.7 EnrollmentBean Class Implementation

```
package com.wombat.benefits;

import javax.ejb.*;

import javax.naming.Context;
import javax.naming.InitialContext;
import com.wombat.plan.Plan;
import com.wombat.plan.PlanHome;
import com.wombat.plan.PlanInfo;
import com.aardvark.payroll.Payroll;
import com.aardvark.payroll.PayrollHome;
import java.util.Collection;
```

```java
import java.util.Iterator;
import javax.rmi.PortableRemoteObject;


// PlanCache is a helper class that encapsulates the access
// to a Plan object. It caches PlanInfo associated with
// the Plan object to avoid remote calls to the plan.
//
class PlanCache {
   private Plan plan;
   private PlanInfo planInfo;

   public PlanCache(Plan plan, PlanInfo planInfo) {
      this.plan = plan;
      this.planInfo = planInfo;
   }

   public Plan getPlan() {
      return plan;
   }
   public PlanInfo getPlanInfo() {
      return planInfo;
   }

   public String getPlanId() {
      return planInfo.getPlanId();
   }
   public String getPlanName() {
      return planInfo.getPlanName();
   }
   public int getPlanType() {
      return planInfo.getPlanType();
   }
   public double getCost(int coverage, int age, boolean smoker) {
      try {
         return plan.getCost(coverage, age, smoker);
      } catch (Exception ex) {
         throw new EJBException("getCost failed");
      }
   }
}
```

```java
// EnrollmentBean implements the benefits enrollment
// business process.
public class EnrollmentBean implements SessionBean
{
    private final static String[] coverageDescriptions = {
        "Employee Only",
        "Employee and Spouse",
        "Employee, Spouse, and Children"
    };

    // Tables of Java classes that are used for calculation of
    // of cost of medical and dental benefits
    private PlanCache[] medicalPlans;
    private PlanCache[] dentalPlans;

    // Portion of the benefits cost paid by the employee
    // (A real-life application would read this value from some
    // benefits plan configuration database.)
    private double employeeCostFactor = 0.10;

    // Employee number that uniquely identifies an employee
    private int employeeNumber;

    private EmployeeHome employeeHome;
    private Employee employee;
    private EmployeeCopy employeeCopy;

    private SelectionHome selectionHome;
    private Selection selection;
    private SelectionCopy selCopy;

    // Indication if a selection record exist for an employee
    private boolean recordDoesNotExist = false;

    // The following variables are calculated values and are
    // used for programming convenience.
    private int age;          // employee's age
    private int medicalSelection = -1;   // index to medicalPlans
    private int dentalSelection = -1;    // index to dentalPlans
    private double totalCost;      // total benefits cost
    private double payrollDeduction;    // payroll deduction
```

```java
private Payroll payroll;
private PayrollHome payrollHome;

private PlanHome planHome;

// public no-arg constructor
public EnrollmentBean() { }

// Business methods follow

// Get employee information.
public EmployeeInfo getEmployeeInfo() {
    return new EmployeeInfo(employeeNumber,
        employeeCopy.getFirstName(),
        employeeCopy.getLastName());
}

// Get coverage options.
public Options getCoverageOptions() {
    Options opt = new Options(coverageDescriptions.length);
    opt.setOptionDescription(coverageDescriptions);
    opt.setSelectedOption(selCopy.getCoverage());
    return opt;
}

// Set selected coverage option.
public void setCoverageOption(int choice)
        throws EnrollmentException {
    if (choice >= 0 && choice < coverageDescriptions.length) {
        selCopy.setCoverage(choice);
    } else {
        throw new EnrollmentException(
            EnrollmentException.INVAL_PARAM);
    }
}

// Get list of available medical options.
public Options getMedicalOptions() {
    Options opt = new Options(medicalPlans.length);
```

```
      for (int i = 0; i < medicalPlans.length; i++) {
         PlanCache plan = medicalPlans[i];
         opt.setOptionDescription(i, plan.getPlanName());
         opt.setOptionCost(i, plan.getCost(
            selCopy.getCoverage(),
            age, selCopy.getSmokerStatus()));
      }
      opt.setSelectedOption(medicalSelection);
      return opt;
   }


   // Set selected medical option.
   public void setMedicalOption(int choice)
         throws EnrollmentException
   {
      if (choice >= 0 && choice < medicalPlans.length) {
         medicalSelection = choice;
         selCopy.setMedicalPlan(medicalPlans[choice].getPlan());
      } else {
         throw new EnrollmentException(
            EnrollmentException.INVAL_PARAM);
      }
   }


   // Get list of available dental options.
   public Options getDentalOptions() {
      Options opt = new Options(dentalPlans.length);
      for (int i = 0; i < dentalPlans.length; i++) {
         PlanCache plan = dentalPlans[i];
         opt.setOptionDescription(i, plan.getPlanName());
         opt.setOptionCost(i, plan.getCost(
            selCopy.getCoverage(),
            age, selCopy.getSmokerStatus()));
      }
      opt.setSelectedOption(dentalSelection);
      return opt;
   }
```

```java
// Set selected dental option.
public void setDentalOption(int choice)
    throws EnrollmentException
{
   if (choice >= 0 && choice < dentalPlans.length) {
      dentalSelection = choice;
      selCopy.setDentalPlan(dentalPlans[choice].getPlan());
   } else {
      throw new EnrollmentException(
         EnrollmentException.INVAL_PARAM);
   }
}


// Get smoker status.
public boolean getSmokerStatus() {
   return selCopy.getSmokerStatus();
}


// Set smoker status.
public void setSmokerStatus(boolean status) {
   selCopy.setSmokerStatus(status);
}


// Get summary of selected options and their cost.
public Summary getSummary() {
   calculateTotalCostAndPayrollDeduction();
   try {
      Summary s = new Summary();
      s.setCoverageDescription(
         coverageDescriptions[selCopy.getCoverage()]);
      s.setSmokerStatus(selCopy.getSmokerStatus());
      s.setMedicalDescription(
         medicalPlans[medicalSelection].getPlanName());
      s.setMedicalCost(
         medicalPlans[medicalSelection].getCost(
            selCopy.getCoverage(),
            age, selCopy.getSmokerStatus()));
      s.setDentalDescription(
         dentalPlans[dentalSelection].getPlanName());
```

```
      s.setDentalCost(
         dentalPlans[dentalSelection].getCost(
            selCopy.getCoverage(),
            age, selCopy.getSmokerStatus())));
      s.setTotalCost(totalCost);
      s.setPayrollDeduction(payrollDeduction);
      return s;
   } catch (Exception ex) {
      throw new EJBException(ex);
   }
}


// Update corporate databases with the new selections.
public void commitSelections() {
   try {
      if (recordDoesNotExist) {
         selection = selectionHome.create(selCopy);
         recordDoesNotExist = false;
      } else {
         selection.updateFromCopy(selCopy);
      }

      // Update information in the payroll system.
      payroll.setBenefitsDeduction(employeeNumber,
         payrollDeduction);
   } catch (Exception ex) {
      throw new EJBException(ex);
   }
}

// Initialize the state of the EmployeeBean instance.
public void ejbCreate(int emplNum) throws EnrollmentException {
   employeeNumber = emplNum;

   // Obtain values from the bean's environment.
   readEnvironmentEntries();

   try {
      Collection coll;
      Iterator it;
```

```
coll = planHome.findMedicalPlans();
medicalPlans = new PlanCache[coll.size()];
it = coll.iterator();
for (int i = 0; i < medicalPlans.length; i++) {
   Plan plan = (Plan)PortableRemoteObject.narrow(
         it.next(), Plan.class);
   medicalPlans[i] = new PlanCache(
      plan, plan.getPlanInfo());
}

coll = planHome.findDentalPlans();
dentalPlans = new PlanCache[coll.size()];
it = coll.iterator();
for (int i = 0; i < dentalPlans.length; i++) {
   Plan plan = (Plan)PortableRemoteObject.narrow(
         it.next(), Plan.class);
   dentalPlans[i] = new PlanCache(
      plan, plan.getPlanInfo());
}

try {
   employee = employeeHome.findByPrimaryKey(
         new Integer(emplNum));
} catch (ObjectNotFoundException ex) {
   throw new EnrollmentException(
      "employee not found");
}
employeeCopy = employee.getCopy();

selection = selectionHome.findByEmployee(employee);
if (selection == null) {
   // This is the first time that the employee
   // runs this application. Use values
   // for the selections.
   selCopy = new SelectionCopy();
   selCopy.setEmployee(employee);
   selCopy.setCoverage(0);
   selCopy.setMedicalPlan(medicalPlans[0].getPlan());
   selCopy.setDentalPlan(dentalPlans[0].getPlan());
   selCopy.setSmokerStatus(false);
   recordDoesNotExist = true;
```

```
    } else {
       selCopy = selection.getCopy();
    }

    // Calculate employee's age.
    java.util.Date today = new java.util.Date();
    age = (int)((today.getTime() -
       employeeCopy.getBirthDate().getTime()) /
         ((long)365 * 24 * 60 * 60 * 1000));

    // Translate the medical plan id to an index
    // in the medicalPlans table.
    String medicalPlanId = (String)
       selCopy.getMedicalPlan().getPrimaryKey();
    for (int i = 0; i < medicalPlans.length; i++) {
       if (medicalPlans[i].getPlanId().
             equals(medicalPlanId)) {
          medicalSelection = i;
          break;
       }
    }

    // Translate the dental plan id to an index
    // in the dentalPlans table.
    String dentalPlanId = (String)
       selCopy.getMedicalPlan().getPrimaryKey();
    for (int i = 0; i < dentalPlans.length; i++) {
       if (dentalPlans[i].getPlanId().
             equals(dentalPlanId)) {
          dentalSelection = i;
          break;
       }
    }

    // Create a payroll session object.
    payroll = (Payroll)payrollHome.create();
  } catch (Exception ex) {
    throw new EJBException(ex);
  }
}
```

```java
// Clean up any resource held by the instance.
public void ejbRemove() {
   try {
      payroll.remove();
   } catch (Exception ex) {
   }
}

public void ejbPassivate() {}
public void ejbActivate() {}
public void setSessionContext(SessionContext sc) {}

// Helper methods follow

// Calculate total benefits cost and payroll deduction.
private void calculateTotalCostAndPayrollDeduction() {
   try {
      double medicalCost =
         medicalPlans[medicalSelection].getCost(
            selCopy.getCoverage(),
            age, selCopy.getSmokerStatus());

      double dentalCost =
         dentalPlans[dentalSelection].getCost(
            selCopy.getCoverage(),
            age, selCopy.getSmokerStatus());

      totalCost = medicalCost + dentalCost;
      payrollDeduction = totalCost * employeeCostFactor;
   } catch (Exception ex) {
      throw new EJBException(ex);
   }
}

// Read and process enterprise bean's environment entries.
private void readEnvironmentEntries() {
   try {
      Context ictx = new InitialContext();
      planHome = (PlanHome)
               PortableRemoteObject.narrow(ictx.lookup(
                     "java:comp/env/ejb/PlanEJB"),
                  PlanHome.class);
```

```
        employeeHome = (EmployeeHome)
                PortableRemoteObject.narrow(ictx.lookup(
                        "java:comp/env/ejb/EmployeeEJB"),
                    EmployeeHome.class);
        selectionHome = (SelectionHome)
                PortableRemoteObject.narrow(ictx.lookup(
                        "java:comp/env/ejb/SelectionEJB"),
                    SelectionHome.class);
        payrollHome = (PayrollHome)
                PortableRemoteObject.narrow(ictx.lookup(
                        "java:comp/env/ejb/PayrollEJB"),
                    PayrollHome.class);
    } catch (Exception ex) {
        throw new EJBException(ex);
    }
  }
}
```

The EnrollmentBean class illustrates how applications typically use the entity bean client-view interfaces. Recall that EnrollmentEJB is a client of the EmployeeEJB, SelectionEJB, and WrapperPlanEJB entity beans.

For example, let's look how EnrollmentEJB uses the SelectionEJB entity bean. In the `ejbCreate` method, notice that EnrollmentEJB uses the `findByPrimaryKey` method to look up an existing Selection object, as follows.

```
selection = selectionHome.findByEmployee(employee);
```

After EnrollmentEJB obtains an object reference to the Selection object, it invokes a business method on the object. Here, it invokes the Selection object's `getCopy` method to read the current benefit selection values.

```
selCopy = selection.getCopy();
```

In the `commitSelections` method, EnrollmentEJB either creates a new Selection object by invoking the `create` method on the SelectionHome interface, or it updates the existing Selection object by invoking the `updateFromCopy` business method on the Selection object, as follows.

```
if (recordDoesNotExist) {
    selection = selectionHome.create(selCopy);
    recordDoesNotExist = false;
```

```
} else {
    selection.updateFromCopy(selCopy);
}
```

Note that EnrollmentEJB does not need to remove Selection objects. If it did, however, it would use the following code fragment.

```
selection.remove();
```

Alternatively, EnrollmentEJB could use the SelectionHome interface to remove a Selection object identified by its primary key.

```
selectionHome.remove(new Integer(employeeNumber));
```

EnrollmentEJB uses the other entity beans in much the same manner.

7.3.3   EmployeeEJB Entity Bean

EmployeeEJB is an entity bean with CMP. It provides an object-oriented view of the employee data used by the Benefits Enrollment application. Its main role is to allow the integration between the benefits application and customer's employee data.

Because Wombat does not impose rules on a customer regarding how it stores the information about its employees, it must give its customers the means to integrate the application with the customer's employee data. Wombat uses the CMP mechanism to allow the deployer to bind EmployeeEJB with an existing employee database.

However, Wombat designs the Employee and EmployeeHome interfaces to meet the needs of the Benefits Enrollment application.

EmployeeEJB's Primary Key

Wombat uses the employee number as the primary key for the EmployeeEJB entity bean. Its type is the class java.lang.Integer. Note that it would be an error if the employee number was the Java primitive int. This is because the EJB specification requires that the primary key type for an entity bean be a Java class. Furthermore, this specification implies that primitive types that are not Java classes cannot be used directly for the primary key type.

Employee Remote Interface

Code Example 7.8 shows the Employee remote interface definition.

Code Example 7.8   Employee Remote Interface

```
package com.wombat.benefits;

import javax.ejb.*;
import java.rmi.RemoteException;
import java.util.Date;

public interface Employee extends EJBObject {
    EmployeeCopy getCopy()
        throws RemoteException, EmployeeException;
    void updateFromCopy(EmployeeCopy copy)
        throws RemoteException, EmployeeException;
}
```

The enrollment application needs access to each employee's employee number, first name, last name, and date of birth. To exchange information efficiently between the employee object and the client application (the client is Enrollment-Bean in our example application), Wombat defines the `getCopy` and `update-FromCopy` methods. The `getCopy` method returns all the employee attributes to the client, and the `updateFromCopy` method updates the employee object using the modified values passed by the client.

The `getCopy` and `updateFromCopy` methods use the EmployeeCopy class, which is defined in Code Example 7.9.

Code Example 7.9   EmployeeCopy Class

```
package com.wombat.benefits;

import java.util.Date;

public class EmployeeCopy implements java.io.Serializable {
    private int employeeNumber;
    private String firstName;
    private String lastName;
    private Date birthDate;

    public int getEmployeeNumber() { return employeeNumber; }
    public String getFirstName() { return firstName; }
    public String getLastName() { return lastName; }
    public Date getBirthDate() { return birthDate; }
```

```
      public void setEmployeeNumber(int v) { employeeNumber = v; }
      public void setFirstName(String v) { firstName = v; }
      public void setLastName(String v) { lastName = v; }
      public void setBirthDate(Date v) { birthDate = v; }
   }
```

Note that the EmployeeCopy class implements the java.io.Serializable interface so that its instances can be passed by value over RMI-IIOP. Refer to the EmployeeBean class in Code Example 7.11 on 249 to see how a client uses the information returned in the EmployeeCopy object.

EmployeeHome Home Interface

Code Example 7.10 shows the EmployeeHome interface definition.

Code Example 7.10   EmployeeHome Home Interface

```
   package com.wombat.benefits;

   import javax.ejb.*;
   import java.rmi.RemoteException;

   public interface EmployeeHome extends EJBHome {
      // find methods
      Employee findByPrimaryKey(Integer employeeNumber)
         throws RemoteException, FinderException;
   }
```

The EmployeeHome interface defines only the mandatory findByPrimaryKey method. It defines no create methods because the Wombat Benefits Enrollment application does not need to create new employee objects in the customer databases.

EmployeeBean Entity Bean Class

The EmployeeBean class illustrates how simple it is to develop an entity bean with CMP. Notice that the entity bean contains no database operations. Summary of the Integration Techniques on page 329 describes how the deployer binds the container-managed fields with the columns of the preexisting EmployeeDatabase at Star Enterprise. Note also that the entity bean class contains no implementations of any find methods, although the home interface defines the findByPrimaryKey method. Because the EmployeeEJB is an entity bean with CMP, the implementations of find methods have to be supplied at deployment. Wombat describes in the deployment descriptor those objects that the find methods are supposed to return. The deployer then implements the find methods to return the specified objects.

Code Example 7.11 shows the source code of the EmployeeBean entity bean class.

Code Example 7.11 EmployeeBean Class Implementation

```
package com.wombat.benefits;

import javax.ejb.*;
import java.util.Date;

public class EmployeeBean implements EntityBean {
    //
    // Container-managed fields
    //
    public int employeeNumber;
    public String firstName;
    public String lastName;
    public Date birthDate;

    public EmployeeCopy getCopy() {
        EmployeeCopy ec = new EmployeeCopy();
        ec.setEmployeeNumber(employeeNumber);
        ec.setFirstName(firstName);
        ec.setLastName(lastName);
        ec.setBirthDate(birthDate);
        return ec;
    }

    public void updateFromCopy(EmployeeCopy ec)
        throws EmployeeException
    {
        if (ec.getEmployeeNumber() != employeeNumber) {
            throw new EmployeeException(
                "can't change primary key");
        } else {
            firstName = ec.getFirstName();
            String newLastName = ec.getLastName();
```

```
            if (newLastName == null ||
               newLastName.length() == 0)
               throw new EmployeeException(
                       "last name can't be blank");
           lastName = newLastName;
           birthDate = ec.getBirthDate();
       }
   }


   //
   // There are no ejbCreate(...) methods.
   //

   //
   // Methods from EntityBean interface
   //
   public void setEntityContext(EntityContext ctx) {}
   public void unsetEntityContext() {}
   public void ejbRemove() {}
   public void ejbActivate() {}
   public void ejbLoad() {}
   public void ejbStore() {}
   public void ejbPassivate() {}
}
```

The implementation of an entity bean class of an entity bean with CMP is generally straightforward. The EmployeeBean class is a good example of a straightforward implementation. Its updateFromCopy method provides a good illustration of a simple business rule validation. The method checks that the new last name is not blank. It throws an exception if the client passes an empty string for the value for last name.

However, there are some important things to note about the implementation of an entity bean class, particularly concerning container-managed fields and the primary key. The employeeNumber, lastName, firstName, and birthDate fields are container-managed fields of the entity bean class. The EJB specification mandates that the container-managed fields be defined as public, even though a client program never directly accesses them. These fields must be public so that the container can move the data between the fields and the database to keep the content of the fields synchronized with the information in the database.

The example also illustrates that the primary key of an entity object is not allowed to change. Changing an entity object's primary key would result in confusion about object identity in a distributed application. The entity object should throw an exception if a client attempts to change the primary key. For example, the `updateFromCopy` method throws `EmployeeException` if a client attempts to change its primary key.

7.3.4   SelectionEJB Entity Bean

There are two approaches for dealing with entity bean persistence. An entity bean can use either BMP or CMP. To provide a choice to its customers, Wombat developed two versions of the SelectionEJB entity bean. One uses CMP and the other uses BMP.

Wombat first developed the SelectionEJBCMP entity bean as an entity bean with CMP. An entity bean with CMP can be developed independently from the underlying database schema. With CMP, the deployer binds the database table columns to the entity bean fields at deployment by using tools provided by the container. Wombat's SelectionEJBCMP entity bean is independent from the schema of the database that stores the persistent state of the Selection objects. It is even independent from the type of the database in which the state of the Selection objects are stored. Selection objects can be stored in a relational database or a nonrelational database.

After developing the SelectionEJBCMP entity bean, Wombat defines the SelectionEJB entity bean with BMP. This entity bean uses a default relational database schema defined by Wombat. The benefit of using the default schema is simpler deployment, because the deployer does not have to set up the binding between the container-managed fields and the database schema. The Selection-Bean entity bean class is a subclass of the SelectionBeanCMP entity bean class. The Java class hierarchy is illustrated in Figure 7.4.

Wombat defines both the container-managed and bean-managed entity beans so that it can support customers who want to use a custom database schema and those content to use the Wombat-supplied default database schema. Wombat expects that most customers will use the default schema. Customers using the default database schema can use the SelectionEJB entity bean. Customers who want to use a custom database schema can use the SelectionEJBCMP entity bean and define their own binding of the SelectionEJBCMP container-managed fields to the schema.

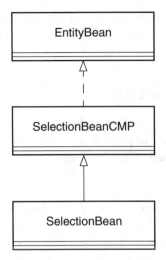

Figure 7.4   Entity Bean Persistence Class Hierarchy

SelectionEJB's Primary Key

Wombat uses the employee number as the primary key for the SelectionEJB entity bean. The type of the primary key is java.lang.Integer.

Selection Remote Interface

Wombat designed SelectionEJB's remote interface to meet the needs of its client, the EnrollmentEJB session bean. The remote interface uses the SelectionCopy value object to pass the information between the SelectionEJB entity bean and its client. It uses the getCopy and updateFromCopy design pattern that was also used in the Employee remote interface.

The Selection interface definition is shown in Code Example 7.12.

Code Example 7.12   Selection Interface Definition

```
package com.wombat.benefits;

import javax.ejb.*;
import java.rmi.RemoteException;
import com.wombat.plan.Plan;

public interface Selection extends EJBObject {
    SelectionCopy getCopy()
        throws RemoteException, SelectionException;
```

```
        void updateFromCopy(SelectionCopy copy)
            throws RemoteException, SelectionException;
    }
```

The Selection interface defines methods to obtain and update an employee's benefits selection. In the Wombat benefits application, the EnrollmentEJB session bean, which is the client of SelectionEJB, uses the getCopy method to obtain a copy of the employee's benefits selection and the updateFromCopy method to change the selection.

The Selection interface uses the SelectionCopy value object, which is defined in Code Example 7.13.

Code Example 7.13   SelectionCopy Value Object

```
    package com.wombat.benefits;

    import com.wombat.plan.Plan;

    public class SelectionCopy {
        private Employee employee;
        private int coverage;
        private Plan medicalPlan;
        private Plan dentalPlan;
        private boolean smokerStatus;

        public Employee getEmployee() { return employee; }
        public int getCoverage() { return coverage; }
        public Plan getMedicalPlan() { return medicalPlan; }
        public Plan getDentalPlan() { return dentalPlan; }
        public boolean getSmokerStatus() { return smokerStatus; }
        public void setEmployee(Employee v) { employee = v; }
        public void setCoverage(int v) { coverage = v; }
        public void setMedicalPlan(Plan v) { medicalPlan = v; }
        public void setDentalPlan(Plan v) { dentalPlan = v; }
        public void setSmokerStatus(boolean v) { smokerStatus = v; }
    }
```

The SelectionCopy class defines private fields to hold the information about an employee's benefits selection. It also defines public access methods (that is, the get and set methods) for each field.

The CoverageCategory interface (Code Example 7.14) defines the integer values that represent the different coverage categories.

Code Example 7.14 CoverageCategory Interface

```java
package com.wombat.benefits;

public class CoverageCategory {
    public static final int EMPLOYEE_ONLY = 0;
    public static final int EMPLOYEE_SPOUSE = 1;
    public static final int EMPLOYEE_SPOUSE_CHILDREN = 2;
}
```

SelectionHome Home Interface

Code Example 7.15 shows the definition for the SelectionHome home interface.

Code Example 7.15 SelectionHome Home Interface

```java
package com.wombat.benefits;

import javax.ejb.*;
import java.rmi.RemoteException;
import com.wombat.plan.Plan;
import java.util.Collection;

public interface SelectionHome extends EJBHome {
    // create methods
    Selection create(SelectionCopy copy)
        throws RemoteException, CreateException;

    // find methods
    Selection findByPrimaryKey(Integer emplNumber)
        throws RemoteException, FinderException;
    Selection findByEmployee(Employee employee)
        throws RemoteException, FinderException;
    Collection findByPlan(Plan plan)
        throws RemoteException, FinderException;
}
```

Notice how the SelectionHome interface uses the SelectionCopy object as the argument of the `create` method. A client uses this method to create an entity object that stores an employee's benefits selections from a copy of the information passed by the client.

The SelectionHome interface also defines three entity bean find methods. The mandatory findByPrimaryKey method finds the Selection object by the employee number. The findByEmployee method finds the Selection object for a given Employee object. The findByPlan find method finds a collection of Selection objects that contain a reference to a given plan.

The benefits application does not use the findByEmployee and findByPlan methods. Wombat includes these definitions so that other applications developed by Wombat customers can reuse SelectionEJB more easily. (We include them to illustrate how to implement more complex find methods.)

SelectionBeanCMP Entity Bean Class

Code Example 7.16 illustrates the SelectionBeanCMP entity bean class implementation.

Code Example 7.16   SelectionBeanCMP Entity Bean Class Implementation

```
package com.wombat.benefits;

import javax.ejb.*;

import javax.naming.Context;
import javax.naming.InitialContext;

import com.wombat.plan.Plan;
import com.wombat.plan.PlanType;

public class SelectionBeanCMP implements EntityBean
{
    // Container-managed fields
    public int coverage;
    public boolean smokerStatus;
    public Employee employee;
    public Plan medicalPlan;
    public Plan dentalPlan;
    public Integer employeeNumber;    // primary key field

    // Values obtained from environment
    boolean checkPlanType;
```

```java
// Helper methods
//
void updateCoverage(int v) throws SelectionException {
   switch (coverage) {
   case CoverageCategory.EMPLOYEE_ONLY:
   case CoverageCategory.EMPLOYEE_SPOUSE:
   case CoverageCategory.EMPLOYEE_SPOUSE_CHILDREN:
      coverage = v;
      break;
   default:
      throw new SelectionException(
         SelectionException.INVAL_COVERAGE);
   }
}

void updateMedicalPlan(Plan p) throws SelectionException {
   if (checkPlanType) {
      int type;
      try {
         type = p.getPlanType();
      } catch (Exception ex) {
         throw new EJBException(ex);
      }
      if (type != PlanType.MEDICAL)
         throw new SelectionException(
            SelectionException.INVAL_PLAN_TYPE);
   }
   medicalPlan = p;
}

void updateDentalPlan(Plan p) throws SelectionException {
   if (checkPlanType) {
      int type;
      try {
         type = p.getPlanType();
      } catch (Exception ex) {
         throw new EJBException(ex);
      }
      if (type != PlanType.DENTAL)
         throw new SelectionException(
            SelectionException.INVAL_PLAN_TYPE);
```

```
      }
      dentalPlan = p;
   }

   void updateSmokerStatus(boolean v) { smokerStatus = v; }

   // Business methods from remote interface
   //
   public SelectionCopy getCopy() {
      SelectionCopy copy = new SelectionCopy();
      copy.setEmployee(employee);
      copy.setCoverage(coverage);
      copy.setMedicalPlan(medicalPlan);
      copy.setDentalPlan(dentalPlan);
      copy.setSmokerStatus(smokerStatus);
      return copy;
   }

   public void updateFromCopy(SelectionCopy copy)
      throws SelectionException
   {
      try {
         if (!employeeNumber.equals(
            copy.getEmployee().getPrimaryKey()))
            throw new SelectionException(
               "can't change primary key");
      } catch (java.rmi.RemoteException ex) {
         throw new EJBException(ex);
      }
      updateMedicalPlan(copy.getMedicalPlan());
      updateDentalPlan(copy.getDentalPlan());
      updateSmokerStatus(copy.getSmokerStatus());
      updateCoverage(copy.getCoverage());
   }

   // create(...) methods from home interface
   //
   public Integer ejbCreate(SelectionCopy copy)
      throws SelectionException, CreateException
   {
      employee = copy.getEmployee();
```

```
      try {
         employeeNumber = (Integer)employee.getPrimaryKey();
      } catch (java.rmi.RemoteException ex) {
         throw new EJBException(ex);
      }
      updateMedicalPlan(copy.getMedicalPlan());
      updateDentalPlan(copy.getDentalPlan());
      updateSmokerStatus(copy.getSmokerStatus());
      updateCoverage(copy.getCoverage());
      return null; // ejbCreate returns null in CMP beans
   }

   public void ejbPostCreate(SelectionCopy copy) {}

   // Methods from EntityBean interface
   //
   public void setEntityContext(EntityContext ctx) {
      readEnvironment();
   }
   public void unsetEntityContext() {}
   public void ejbRemove() {}
   public void ejbActivate() {}
   public void ejbLoad() {}
   public void ejbStore() {}
   public void ejbPassivate() {}

   // Helper methods
   private void readEnvironment() {
      try {
         Context ictx = new InitialContext();
         Boolean val = (Boolean)ictx.lookup(
               "java:comp/env/checkPlanType");
         checkPlanType = val.booleanValue();
      } catch (Exception ex) {
         throw new EJBException(ex);
      }
   }
}
```

First, let's examine the container-managed fields: coverage, smokerStatus, employee, medicalPlan, dentalPlan, and employeeNumber. Notice that the `employee`, `medicalPlan`, and `dentalPlan` fields are references to other enterprise beans (Employee and Plan, respectively). The EJB specification allows the container-managed fields to include references to other enterprise beans. Allowing container-managed fields to include references to other enterprise beans has two benefits.

1. It simplifies the development of the SelectionBeanCMP methods because they can work directly with object references rather than having to convert object references to primary keys.

2. It avoids hard-coding the database representation of the relationships to the other entity beans into the SelectionBeanCMP class. It leaves a deployer free to choose how to represent the relationships in the underlying database schema.

See SelectionBean Entity Bean Class on page 260 for an explanation of how Wombat implemented the representation of the entity object relationships in the SelectionBean class.

Let's take a closer look at the implementation of the SelectionBeanCMP methods. The SelectionBeanCMP class implements three sets of methods.

1. The business methods defined in the Selection remote interface

2. The `ejbCreate` and `ejbPostCreate` methods that correspond to the `create` method defined in the SelectionHome interface

3. The container callbacks defined in the EntityBean interface

The SelectionBeanCMP class follows the EJB specification rules and does not implement the `ejbFind` methods corresponding to the `find` methods defined in the SelectionHome interface.

The business methods and the `ejbCreate` method read and write the container-managed fields. The container loads and stores the contents of the container-managed fields according to the rules defined in the EJB specification. The business methods can assume that the contents of the container-managed fields are always up-to-date, even if other transactions change the underlying selection record in the database.

The code for the business methods demonstrates how an enterprise might implement simple business rules. For example, the `updateCoverage` method checks that the value of the coverage field is an allowed value, whereas the `updateMedicalPlan` method optionally checks that the value of `medicalPlan` is indeed a medical plan, rather than a dental plan. The `getCopy`, `updateFromCopy`, and `ejbCreate` methods illustrate how the entity bean class can implement handling value objects passed between the entity bean and the client. The Selection-BeanCMP class (within its `setEmployee` and `updateFromCopy` methods) enforces the rule that a client cannot change the primary key of a Selection object.

The SelectionBeanCMP class (within the `readEnvironment` helper method) makes access to the environment entry available with the key `java:comp/env/checkPlanType`. The value of the entry parameterizes the business logic of the bean. If the value of the environment entry is true, the `setMedicalPlan` and `setDentalPlan` methods check that the value of the plan to be set is indeed of the expected plan type. If the value is false, they do not perform these checks. The application assembler sets the value of the environment entry at application assembly. Wombat made the plan type checks optional to allow the application assembler to improve performance by omitting the checks if the clients of SelectionEJB are known to set the plan types correctly. (We added this somewhat artificial optional check to illustrate how to use the enterprise bean environment entries to parameterize the business logic at application assembly or deployment.)

The `ejbCreate` method sets up the container-managed fields from the values passed to it in the method parameter. After the `ejbCreate` method completes, the container extracts the values of the container-managed fields and creates a representation of the selection object in the database. Note that `ejbCreate` returns a null value even though the return value type is declared to be the primary key type. According to the EJB specification, the container ignores the value returned from an `ejbCreate` method of an entity bean with CMP. However, the EJB specification requires that the type of the `ejbCreate` method be the primary key type to allow a subclass of the SelectionBeanCMP class to be an entity bean with BMP. The SelectionBean class illustrates this use of "subclassing."

Notice that most of the container callbacks inherited from the EntityBean interface have an empty implementation. More complex entity beans with CMP may use nonempty implementations of these callback methods. See WrapperPlanBeanCMP Entity Bean Class on page 275 for an illustration of the use of the `ejbLoad` method in an entity bean with CMP.

SelectionBean Entity Bean Class

There are many possible ways to implement an entity bean's persistence—that is, its database access code. The SelectionBean class illustrates one such way: It uses subclassing to convert an entity bean with CMP into an entity bean with BMP. This is accomplished by subclassing the SelectionBeanCMP entity bean class. Although in our example we manually coded the SelectionBean class, most real development and deployment scenarios use tools to generate the database access code automatically. Code Example 7.17 shows the implementation of the SelectionBean class.

Code Example 7.17 SelectionBean Class Implementation

```java
package com.wombat.benefits;

import javax.ejb.*;

import javax.naming.InitialContext;
import javax.naming.Context;
import java.sql.Connection;
import java.sql.PreparedStatement;
import java.sql.ResultSet;
import java.sql.SQLException;
import javax.sql.DataSource;
import java.util.Vector;
import java.util.Collection;
import javax.rmi.PortableRemoteObject;

import com.wombat.plan.Plan;
import com.wombat.plan.PlanHome;
import com.wombat.plan.PlanInfo;
import com.wombat.plan.PlanType;

public class SelectionBean extends SelectionBeanCMP
{
    private EntityContext entityContext;
    private DataSource ds;
    private EmployeeHome employeeHome;
    private PlanHome planHome;

    //
    // create(...) methods from home interface
    //
    public Integer ejbCreate(SelectionCopy copy)
        throws SelectionException, CreateException
    {
        super.ejbCreate(copy);
        try {
            Connection con = getConnection();
            PreparedStatement pstmt = con.prepareStatement(
                "INSERT INTO Selections " +
                "VALUES (?, ?, ?, ?, ?)"
            );
```

```java
        pstmt.setInt(1, employeeNumber.intValue());
        pstmt.setInt(2, coverage);
        pstmt.setString(3, (String)medicalPlan.getPrimaryKey());
        pstmt.setString(4, (String)dentalPlan.getPrimaryKey());
        pstmt.setString(5, smokerStatus ? "Y" : "N");
        if (pstmt.executeUpdate() == 1) {
            con.close();
            return employeeNumber;
        } else {
            con.close();
            throw new CreateException();
        }
    } catch (SQLException ex) {
        throw new EJBException(ex);
    } catch (java.rmi.RemoteException ex) {
        throw new EJBException(ex);
    }
}


public Integer ejbFindByPrimaryKey(Integer employeeNumber)
    throws FinderException
{
    try {
        Connection con = getConnection();
        PreparedStatement pstmt = con.prepareStatement(
            "SELECT sel_empl " +
            "FROM Selections " +
            "WHERE sel_empl = ?"
        );
        pstmt.setInt(1, employeeNumber.intValue());
        ResultSet rs = pstmt.executeQuery();
        if (rs.next()) {
            con.close();
            return employeeNumber;
        } else {
            con.close();
            throw new ObjectNotFoundException();
        }
    } catch (SQLException ex) {
        throw new EJBException(ex);
    }
}
```

```java
public Integer ejbFindByEmployee(Employee employee)
        throws FinderException
{
   try {
      return ejbFindByPrimaryKey(
         (Integer)employee.getPrimaryKey());
   } catch (java.rmi.RemoteException ex) {
      throw new EJBException(ex);
   }
}


public Collection ejbFindByPlan(Plan plan)
{
   try {
      PlanInfo planInfo = plan.getPlanInfo();
      int planType = planInfo.getPlanType();
      String planId = (String)planInfo.getPlanId();
      String columnName = (planType == PlanType.MEDICAL) ?
         "sel_medical_plan" : "sel_dental_Plan";

      Connection con = getConnection();
      PreparedStatement pstmt = con.prepareStatement(
         "SELECT sel_empl " +
         "FROM Selections " +
         "WHERE " + columnName + " = ?"
      );
      pstmt.setString(1, planId);
      ResultSet rs = pstmt.executeQuery();

      Vector vec = new Vector();
      while (rs.next()) {
         int emplnum = rs.getInt(1);
         vec.add(new Integer(emplnum));
      }
      con.close();
      return vec;
   } catch (Exception ex) {
      throw new EJBException(ex);
   }
}
```

```java
//
// Methods from EntityBean interface
//

public void setEntityContext(EntityContext ctx) {
    readEnvironment();
    super.setEntityContext(ctx);
}

public void ejbRemove() {
    super.ejbRemove();
    try {
        Connection con = getConnection();
        PreparedStatement pstmt = con.prepareStatement(
            "DELETE FROM Selections " +
            "WHERE sel_empl = ?"
        );
        pstmt.setInt(1, employeeNumber.intValue());
        pstmt.executeUpdate();
        con.close();
    } catch (Exception ex) {
        throw new EJBException(ex);
    }
}

public void ejbLoad() {
    try {
        String medicalPlanId;
        String dentalPlanId;
        employeeNumber =
            (Integer)entityContext.getPrimaryKey();
        employee =
            employeeHome.findByPrimaryKey(employeeNumber);

        Connection con = getConnection();
        PreparedStatement pstmt = con.prepareStatement(
            "SELECT sel_coverage, sel_smoker, " +
                "sel_medical_plan,  sel_dental_plan" +
            "FROM Selections " +
            "WHERE sel_empl = ?"
        );
```

```java
        pstmt.setInt(1, employeeNumber.intValue());
        ResultSet rs = pstmt.executeQuery();
        if (rs.next()) {
            coverage = rs.getInt(1);
            smokerStatus = rs.getString(2).equals("Y");
            medicalPlanId = rs.getString(3);
            dentalPlanId = rs.getString(4);
            con.close();
        } else {
            throw new NoSuchEntityException();
        }
        medicalPlan = planHome.findByPlanId(medicalPlanId);
        dentalPlan = planHome.findByPlanId(dentalPlanId);
    } catch (Exception ex) {
        throw new EJBException(ex);
    }
    super.ejbLoad();
}

public void ejbStore() {
    super.ejbStore();
    try {
        Connection con = getConnection();
        PreparedStatement pstmt = con.prepareStatement(
            "UPDATE Selections SET " +
            "sel_coverage = ?, " +
            "sel_medical_plan = ?, " +
            "sel_dental_plan = ?, " +
            "sel_smoker = ? " +
            "WHERE sel_empl = ?"
        );
        pstmt.setInt(1, coverage);
        pstmt.setString(2, (String)medicalPlan.getPrimaryKey());
        pstmt.setString(3, (String)dentalPlan.getPrimaryKey());
        pstmt.setString(4, smokerStatus ? "Y" : "N");
        pstmt.setInt(5, employeeNumber.intValue());
        pstmt.executeUpdate();
        con.close();
    } catch (Exception ex) {
        throw new EJBException(ex);
    }
}
```

```
//
// Helper methods
//

private Connection getConnection() {
   try {
      return ds.getConnection();
   } catch (Exception ex) {
      throw new EJBException(ex);
   }
}

private void readEnvironment() {
   try {
      Context ictx = new InitialContext();

      planHome = (PlanHome)
         PortableRemoteObject.narrow(ictx.lookup(
            "java:comp/env/ejb/PlanEJB"),
            PlanHome.class);
      employeeHome = (EmployeeHome)
         PortableRemoteObject.narrow(ictx.lookup(
            "java:comp/env/ejb/EmployeeEJB"),
            EmployeeHome.class);
      ds = (DataSource)
         ictx.lookup("java:comp/env/jdbc/BenefitsDB");
   } catch (Exception ex) {
      throw new EJBException(ex);
   }
}
}
```

The SelectionBean class defines the following methods:

- The ejbCreate method. This method overrides the ejbCreate method in the SelectionBeanCMP superclass.

- All the find methods defined in the SelectionHome interface

- The ejbLoad, ejbStore, ejbRemove, and setEntityContext container call-backs inherited from the EntityBean interface. These callbacks override the same-name methods in the superclass.

Invoking Superclass Methods. These methods (`ejbCreate`, `ejbLoad`, `ejbStore`, `ejbRemove`, and `setEntityContext`) invoke their corresponding overridden method in the superclass. The timing of the invocation of the same-name super-class method is significant: The order in which a method invokes the same-name method in the superclass relative to the database operations performed in the method is important.

The `ejbCreate`, `ejbRemove`, and `ejbStore` methods invoke the method in the superclass *before* they perform the database operations. The `ejbLoad` method calls `ejbLoad` in the superclass *after* it performs the database operations. The order of operation ensures the proper synchronization between the values of the container-managed fields, as seen by the superclass methods, and the values of the fields stored in the database.

`NoSuchEntityException`. Note that the `ejbLoad` method throws `NoSuchEntity-Exception` if the representation of the entity object has been removed from the database and the entity bean expects that the representation exists. `NoSuchEntityException` provides more information to the container than the generic exception `EJBException` thrown on other database errors. If the bean throws `NoSuchEntityException`, the container throws `java.rmi.NoSuchObject-Exception` to the client to indicate that the reason for a failed method was the removal of the entity object's representation from the database.

Representing Object References in a Database. Note how the `ejbCreate`, `ejb-Load`, and `ejbStore` methods handle object references to other entity beans maintained in the container-managed fields (that is, the `employee`, `medicalPlan`, and `dentalPlan` fields defined in the SelectionBeanCMP class). The object references are represented as foreign keys in the `Selections` database table. However, use of a foreign key is only one possible mechanism for representing an object reference. WrapperPlanEJB Entity Bean on page 268 describes an entity bean that illustrates how serialized object handles can be used to represent object references in persistent storage.

Automatic Closing of Connections on Uncaught Exceptions. Although it is a good practice to ensure that a bean always closes its database connections, we illustrate that it is not necessary to close a database connection when the bean throws a runtime exception from a method. If the developer has not closed a database connection when a method throws a runtime exception (for example, `EJBException`) and the exception is not caught within the bean, the EJB container will automatically release the connection when it catches the exception. The container will also remove the instance from its pool because the values of the instance's variables may be in an inconsistent state after the thrown exception.

7.3.5   WrapperPlanEJB Entity Bean

The WrapperPlanEJB entity bean aggregates the medical and dental plans provided by multiple insurance providers into a single entity bean. Aggregation hides the complexity of managing the configuration of plans from multiple providers, and is a benefit for applications that need to access these plans. An example of such an application is the EnrollmentEJB session bean.

Wombat uses the same approach with persistence for WrapperPlanEJB as it did for SelectionEJB. Wombat first defines the WrapperPlanEJBCMP entity bean with CMP. Wombat then subclasses the WrapperPlanBeanCMP entity bean class to create the WrapperPlanBean entity bean class with BMP. This allows the customer to choose between using the WrapperPlanEJB entity bean, which uses the default BenefitsDatabase schema, and the WrapperPlanEJBCMP entity bean, which allows the customer to define a custom database schema or to store the entity bean's state in a nonrelational database.

Benefits Plan Integration Approach

Wombat wants to allow its customers to configure the benefits application with multiple medical and dental plans that may be provided by multiple insurance companies. Therefore, Wombat designed the benefits application to access plan information from multiple sources.

Wombat uses EJB client-view interfaces as the contract between the benefits application and the software from the individual insurance companies. Wombat defines the Plan remote interface and the PlanHome home interface to be the standard interfaces for integrating the plan information from an insurance company with the benefits application. If an insurance provider wants to support the benefits application, the insurance provider (or application integrator) must develop an enterprise bean that uses the Plan and PlanHome interfaces as its client-view interfaces.

Figure 7.5 illustrates the ProvidencePlanEJB developed by Providence (Providence is an insurance company). Note that the "interface implementation" notation in the diagram does not represent the interface implementation in the Java language sense. Instead, it shows that the remote and home interfaces of the ProvidencePlanEJB entity bean are the Plan and PlanHome interfaces, or their subinterfaces.

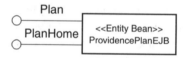

Figure 7.5   ProvidencePlanEJB

Aggregation of Plans into a Single Entity Bean

Although enterprise beans from all the insurance providers have a uniform client view (that is, they implement the Plan and PlanHome interfaces), dealing with these multiple enterprise beans can be a tedious task for application programmers. It is tedious because the programmer must know where to locate all the enterprise beans and how to deal with the situation in which enterprise beans are added or removed.

To simplify this task, Wombat develops the WrapperPlanEJB entity bean. WrapperPlanEJB aggregates all the configured enterprise beans from multiple insurance providers into what looks like a single entity bean to the application programmer (Figure 7.6).

The Plan objects implemented by WrapperPlanEJB "wrap" the Plan objects implemented by the entity beans from the individual insurance providers. The implementation of the WrapperPlanEJB business methods delegates to the wrapped plan. The find methods implemented in WrapperPlanEJB aggregate the find methods in the individual plan entity beans. WrapperPlanEJB "hides" the primary key of the wrapped plan. The primary keys visible to a WrapperPlanEJB's client are customer-assigned plan identifiers that must be unique within the scope of the WrapperPlanHome interface. In our example, the Star Enterprise benefits administration department assigns these primary keys.

A client program deals only with the single WrapperPlanEJB, regardless of how many different insurance providers are used by the customer. A client of the WrapperPlanEJB entity bean uses the Plan and PlanHome interfaces to access the aggregated insurance plan information.

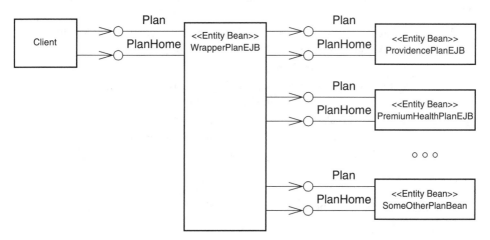

Figure 7.6 WrapperPlanEJB Aggregation of Enterprise Beans

The EnrollmentBean class in EnrollmentEJB Session Bean on page 233, which is a WrapperPlanEJB's client, illustrates that the existence of multiple insurance providers is transparent to the client application. The following statement from the EnrollmentBean class finds all the configured medical plans (or, more accurately, their wrapper Plan objects) for all the currently enabled medical plans.

```
coll = planHome.findMedicalPlans();
```

Plan Remote Interface

The plan entity beans provided by the individual insurance providers must use the Plan interface as their remote interface. The WrapperPlanEJB entity bean developed by Wombat also uses the Plan interface as its remote interface. Code Example 7.18 illustrates the definition of the Plan interface.

Code Example 7.18   Plan Remote Interface

```
package com.wombat.plan;

import javax.ejb.*;
import java.rmi.RemoteException;
import java.util.Collection;

public interface Plan extends EJBObject {
    PlanInfo getPlanInfo()
        throws RemoteException, PlanException;
    int getPlanType() throws RemoteException, PlanException;

    double getCost(int coverage, int age, boolean smokerStatus)
        throws RemoteException, PlanException;
    Collection getAllDoctors()
        throws RemoteException, PlanException;
    Collection getDoctorsByName(Doctor template)
        throws RemoteException, PlanException;
    Collection getDoctorsBySpecialty(String specialty)
        throws RemoteException, PlanException;
}
```

The Plan interface methods perform the following operations.

- The getPlanInfo method returns a PlanType value object that contains the plan attributes. The PlanType class is described later in this section (see Code Example 7.20 on page 272).

- The getPlanType method returns an integer value. The value is equal to PlanType.MEDICAL if the plan is a medical plan, and it is equal to Plan-Type.DENTAL if the plan is a dental plan.

- The getCost method returns the monthly premium charged by the plan provider. The premium depends on the coverage category, age, and smoker status.

- The getAllDoctors method returns a collection of Doctor objects that participate in the plan. The Doctor class is described later.

- The getDoctorsByName method returns a collection of participating doctors whose names match the information in the template supplied as a method argument.

- The getDoctorsBySpecialty method returns all the doctors of a given specialty.

Code Example 7.19 illustrates the definition of the PlanInfo class.

Code Example 7.19 PlanInfo Class

```
package com.wombat.plan;

public class PlanInfo implements java.io.Serializable {
    String planId;
    String planName;
    int planType;

    public String getPlanId() { return planId; }
    public String getPlanName() { return planName; }
    public int getPlanType() { return planType; }

    public void setPlanId(String v) { planId = v; }
    public void setPlanName(String v) { planName = v; }
    public void setPlanType(int v) { planType = v; }
}
```

The PlanInfo class is part of the Plan remote interface. The getPlanInfo method uses the PlanInfo class to pass a set of plan attributes to the client. The attributes are the following.

- PlanId—This is the unique identifier of the plan. It should be the same as the primary key of the Plan entity object.

- PlanName—This is a short name for the plan. The GUI portion of the application uses this name for display.

- PlanType—This is either `PlanType.MEDICAL` or `PlanType.DENTAL`.

Code Example 7.20 illustrates the PlanType class, which defines the integer values representing the plan types.

Code Example 7.20   PlanType Class

```
package com.wombat.plan;

public class PlanType {
    public static final int MEDICAL = 1;
    public static final int DENTAL = 2;
}
```

The Doctor class is used to pass information about participating doctors. Note that we do not implement the Doctor class as an entity bean, but instead implement it as a value object that is passed through the Plan interface. Why do we do this? Our application does not need to view a Doctor object as an entity object. For example, the client does not have the need to invoke methods on the Doctor objects, nor to compare Doctor objects for identity. Rather, the application sees a Doctor object as only a piece of information available through the Plan entity objects. Therefore, we decided not to implement the Doctor class as an entity bean. The Doctor class is shown in Code Example 7.21.

Code Example 7.21   Implementation of the Doctor Class

```
package com.wombat.plan;

public class Doctor implements java.io.Serializable {
    String lastName;
    String firstName;
    String specialty;
    String hospital;
    int practiceSince;

    // public get/set methods
```

```
    public String getLastName() { return lastName; }
    public void setLastName(String v) { lastName = v; }
    public String getFirstName() { return firstName; }
    public void setFirstName(String v) { firstName = v; }
    public String getSpecialty() { return specialty; }
    public void setSpecialty(String v) { specialty = v; }
    public String getHospital() { return hospital; }
    public void setHospital(String v) { hospital = v; }
    public int getPracticeSince() { return practiceSince; }
    public void setPracticeSince(int v) { practiceSince = v; }
}
```

PlanHome Home Interface

The plan entity beans provided by the individual insurance providers must extend
the PlanHome interface in their home interfaces. At the same time, the Wrapper-
PlanHome interface of the WrapperPlanEJB entity bean developed by Wombat
also extends the PlanHome interface. Code Example 7.22 shows the definition of
the PlanHome interface.

Code Example 7.22 PlanHome Home Interface

```
package com.wombat.plan;

import javax.ejb.*;
import java.rmi.RemoteException;
import java.util.Collection;

public interface PlanHome extends EJBHome {
    // find methods
    Plan findByPlanId(String planID)
        throws RemoteException, FinderException;
    Collection findMedicalPlans()
        throws RemoteException, FinderException;
    Collection findDentalPlans()
        throws RemoteException, FinderException;
    Collection findByDoctor(Doctor template)
        throws RemoteException, FinderException;
}
```

The PlanHome interface defines the find methods used by the benefits application. The find methods include the following.

- The findByPlanId method returns the Plan object for a given plan identifier. The plan identifier is a primary key that uniquely identifies the plan.

- The findMedicalPlans method returns all the medical plans configured in this home interface. The objects in the returned Collection implement the Plan interface.

- The findDentalPlans method returns all the dental plans configured in this home interface. The objects in the returned Collection implement the Plan interface.

- The findByDoctor method returns all the plans configured in this home interface that include a specified doctor in their preferred doctors list. A template is used to specify the doctor and to perform a partial match using first and last names. The objects in the returned Collection implement the Plan interface.

Note that the PlanHome interface does not define the findByPrimaryKey method. Although it is expected that most plan providers will use the plan identifier as the primary key, not defining findByPrimaryKey in the PlanHome interface allows the plan provider to choose the primary key type if necessary. The plan provider must define the findByPrimaryKey method in the subinterface of the PlanHome interface.

The PlanHome interface defines no create methods. create methods are not needed because the benefits application does not create new medical and dental plans in the individual entity beans supplied by the insurance companies. An insurance provider that wants to use the entity bean home interface as the mechanism for creating new insurance plans should define the create methods in a subinterface of the PlanHome interface. The PremiumHealthPlanHome home interface of the PremiumHealthPlanEJB entity bean illustrates extending the home interface for the purpose of creating a new insurance plan, as does the WrapperPlanHome home interface (described in the next section). See Premium-HealthPlanHome Home Interface on page 294.

WrapperPlanEJB's Remote Interface

The WrapperPlanEJB uses the com.wombat.plan.Plan interface as its remote interface (see Code Example 7.18, which lists the Plan remote interface).

WrapperPlanHome Home Interface

The WrapperPlanHome interface is the home interface of the WrapperPlanEJB entity bean. Code Example 7.23 shows its definition.

Code Example 7.23   WrapperPlanHome Home Interface

```
package com.wombat.benefits;

import javax.ejb.*;
import java.rmi.RemoteException;
import com.wombat.plan.Plan;
import com.wombat.plan.PlanHome;

public interface WrapperPlanHome extends PlanHome {
   Plan create(Plan planRef, String wrapperPlanId)
      throws RemoteException, CreateException;
   Plan findByPrimaryKey(String pkey)
       throws RemoteException, FinderException;
}
```

The WrapperPlanHome interface extends the PlanHome interface and defines a single `create` method. The BenefitsAdminWeb Web application uses this `create` method to add a new plan to the plans currently configured for the Benefits Enrollment application. The `plan` argument is an object reference to an actual medical or dental plan object provided by an insurance company. `wrapperPlanId` is a primary key for the plan visible to the WrapperPlanEJB clients. The customer (Star Enterprise's benefits administrator, in our example) chooses this key. See BenefitsAdminWeb Web Application on page 287 for the description of the BenefitsAdminWeb Web application.

WrapperPlanBeanCMP Entity Bean Class

WrapperPlanBeanCMP is an interesting entity bean class from the perspective of its persistence. Its persistence state consists of two parts. Container-managed fields implement one part of its persistent state (these fields are ultimately bound to columns in a database table, which we illustrate in the WrapperPlanBean class), whereas delegation to the wrapped actual Plan object implements the other part. Our example implementation also illustrates caching of some of the state obtained from the wrapped bean. Delegating and caching can be considered a form of BMP in which the access to the state is made by calls to the wrapped Plan objects.

Code Example 7.24 below illustrates the implementation of the WrapperPlanBeanCMP class.

Code Example 7.24   WrapperPlanBeanCMP Class Implementation

```
package com.wombat.benefits;

import javax.ejb.*;
import java.rmi.RemoteException;
import java.util.Collection;
import com.wombat.plan.Plan;
import com.wombat.plan.PlanInfo;
import com.wombat.plan.Doctor;
import com.wombat.plan.PlanException;

public class WrapperPlanBeanCMP implements EntityBean {

    // container-managed fields
    public String wrapperPlanId;
    public Plan plan;

    // cached attributes of the wrapped plan
    public int planType;
    public String planName;

    //
    // Business methods from WrapperPlan interface
    //

    public PlanInfo getPlanInfo() {
        PlanInfo pi = new PlanInfo();
        pi.setPlanId(wrapperPlanId);
        pi.setPlanType(planType);
        pi.setPlanName(planName);
        return pi;
    }

    public int getPlanType() throws PlanException {
        return planType;
    }

    public double getCost(int coverage, int age,
            boolean smokerStatus) throws PlanException {
```

```java
      try {
         return plan.getCost(coverage, age, smokerStatus);
      } catch (RemoteException ex) {
         throw new EJBException(ex);
      }
   }

   public Collection getAllDoctors() throws PlanException {
      try {
         return plan.getAllDoctors();
      } catch (RemoteException ex) {
         throw new EJBException(ex);
      }
   }

   public Collection getDoctorsByName(Doctor template)
         throws PlanException {
      try {
         return plan.getDoctorsByName(template);
      } catch (RemoteException ex) {
         throw new EJBException(ex);
      }
   }

   public Collection getDoctorsBySpecialty(String specialty)
         throws PlanException {
      try {
         return plan.getDoctorsBySpecialty(specialty);
      } catch (RemoteException ex) {
         throw new EJBException(ex);
      }
   }

   //
   // Methods from the home interface WrapperPlanHome
   //
   public String ejbCreate(Plan plan, String wrapperPlanId) {
      // Set container-managed fields.
      this.wrapperPlanId = wrapperPlanId;
      this.plan = plan;
      return null;
   }
```

```
public void ejbPostCreate(Plan plan, String wrapperPlanId) {
   updateCachedFields();
}


//
// Methods from javax.ejb.EntityBean interface
//
public void setEntityContext(EntityContext ctx) {}
public void unsetEntityContext() {}
public void ejbRemove() {}
public void ejbActivate() {}
public void ejbLoad() {
   updateCachedFields();
}
public void ejbStore() {}
public void ejbPassivate() {}

private void updateCachedFields() {
   try {
      PlanInfo planInfo = plan.getPlanInfo();
      this.planType = planInfo.getPlanType();
      this.planName = planInfo.getPlanName();
   } catch (Exception ex) {
      throw new EJBException(ex);
   }
}
}
```

The WrapperPlanBeanCMP class defines two container-managed fields: wrapperPlanId and plan. The wrapperPlanId field is a customer-assigned primary key that identifies a particular plan at a customer enterprise. The plan field is an object reference to the actual Plan object implemented by an entity bean supplied by the insurance providers. In our example, this is one of the entity beans provided by Premium Health or Providence.

The WrapperPlanBeanCMP class also defines two fields that are cached values obtained from the wrapped actual plan. These fields are planType and planName. We discuss their use later in this section.

In addition to the fields, the WrapperPlanBeanCMP class implements the business methods defined in the PlanHome remote interface, the ejbCreate method that corresponds to the create method defined in the WrapperPlanHome interface, and the container callbacks defined in the EntityBean interface.

The `getCost`, `getAllDoctors`, `getDoctorsByName`, and `getDoctorsBy-Specialty` methods delegate to the same-name method of the actual Plan object using the `plan` object reference.

The `getPlanInfo` method returns the plan attributes cached in the instance fields. `planId` in the PlanInfo object is `wrapperPlanId`. Returning the key in this manner means that the client of the WrapperPlanEJB bean does not see the primary key of the actual plan object provided by the insurance company.

The `getPlanType` method returns the value of the `planType` field.

It is important to note how and when we set the values of the cached fields. Note how we manage the `planType` and `planName` fields. These fields contain cached values of the wrapped actual plan state. We set the cached fields in the `ejbPostCreate` and `ejbLoad` methods. We use the `ejbPostCreate` method to set the values for the first time. (Alternatively, we could have used the `ejbCreate` method to set the values.) Because other programs may change the objects from which the cached fields are obtained, we use the `ejbLoad` method to refresh the values of the cached fields. The container invokes the `ejbLoad` method before it dispatches the first business method on an instance of the WrapperPlanBeanCMP class in each transaction unless the container is certain that the values have not changed in the underlying objects. The `ejbLoad` method ensures that the instance has a chance to refresh the values of the cached fields before the container dispatches a business method on the instance. See Transaction Commit OID on page 188 in Chapter 6, Understanding Entity Beans for a discussion of transaction commit options.

WrapperPlanBean Entity Bean Class

The WrapperPlanBean class is the BMP version of the WrapperPlanBeanCMP entity bean class. The WrapperPlanBean class extends the WrapperPlanBeanCMP class and implements the data access logic using the BenefitsDatabase default schema defined by Wombat (see BenefitsDatabase on page 288).

Code Example 7.25 shows the implementation of the WrapperPlanBean class.

Code Example 7.25 WrapperPlanBean Class Implementation

```
package com.wombat.benefits;

import javax.ejb.*;

import javax.naming.InitialContext;
import javax.naming.Context;
import java.sql.Connection;
import java.sql.PreparedStatement;
```

```java
import java.sql.ResultSet;
import java.sql.SQLException;
import javax.sql.DataSource;
import java.util.Vector;
import java.util.Collection;
import javax.rmi.PortableRemoteObject;
import java.io.ObjectOutputStream;
import java.io.ObjectInputStream;
import java.io.ByteArrayOutputStream;
import java.io.ByteArrayInputStream;

import com.wombat.plan.Plan;
import com.wombat.plan.PlanHome;
import com.wombat.plan.PlanInfo;
import com.wombat.plan.PlanType;
import com.wombat.plan.Doctor;

public class WrapperPlanBean extends WrapperPlanBeanCMP {
    private EntityContext entityContext;
    private DataSource ds;

    public String ejbCreate(Plan plan, String wrapperPlanId) {
        super.ejbCreate(plan, wrapperPlanId);

        // Perform database insert.
        try {
            byte[] serHandle = planToSerHandle(plan);

            Connection con = getConnection();
            PreparedStatement pstmt = con.prepareStatement(
                "INSERT INTO Wrapper_Plans VALUES (?, ?, ?)"
            );
            pstmt.setString(1, this.wrapperPlanId);
            pstmt.setBytes(2, serHandle);
            pstmt.setInt(3, this.plan.getPlanType());
            pstmt.executeUpdate();
            con.close();
            return wrapperPlanId;
        } catch (Exception ex) {
            throw new EJBException(ex);
        }
    }
```

```java
public String ejbFindByPrimaryKey(String planID)
   throws ObjectNotFoundException
{
   try {
      Connection con = getConnection();
      PreparedStatement pstmt = con.prepareStatement(
         "SELECT cfg_wrapper_planid " +
         "FROM Wrapper_Plans " +
         "WHERE cfg_wrapper_planid = ?"
      );
      pstmt.setString(1, planID);
      ResultSet rs = pstmt.executeQuery();
      if (rs.next()) {
         con.close();
         return planID;
      } else {
         con.close();
         throw new ObjectNotFoundException();
      }
   } catch (SQLException ex) {
      throw new EJBException(ex);
   }
}


public String ejbFindByPlanId(String planID)
   throws ObjectNotFoundException
{
      return ejbFindByPrimaryKey(planID);
}


public Collection ejbFindMedicalPlans() {
   return findPlans(PlanType.MEDICAL);
}


public Collection ejbFindDentalPlans() {
   return findPlans(PlanType.DENTAL);
}


public Collection ejbFindByDoctor(Doctor template) {
   try {
      Vector vec = new Vector();
```

```java
        Connection con = getConnection();
        PreparedStatement pstmt = con.prepareStatement(
            "SELECT cfg_wrapper_planid, cfg_act_plan_handle " +
            "FROM Wrapper_Plans "
        );
        ResultSet rs = pstmt.executeQuery();

        while (rs.next()) {
            String wrapperPK = rs.getString(1);
            byte[] serHandle = rs.getBytes(2);
            Plan plan = serPlanHandleToRef(serHandle);
            Collection coll =
                plan.getDoctorsByName(template);
            if (coll.size() > 0)
                vec.add(wrapperPK);
        }
        con.close();
        return vec;
    } catch (Exception ex) {
        throw new EJBException(ex);
    }
}

public void setEntityContext(EntityContext ctx) {
    readEnvironment();
    super.setEntityContext(ctx);
}

public void ejbRemove() {
    super.ejbRemove();

    try {

        Connection con = getConnection();
        PreparedStatement pstmt = con.prepareStatement(
            "DELETE FROM Wrapper_Plans " +
            "WHERE cfg_wrapper_planid = ?");
        pstmt.setString(1, wrapperPlanId);
        pstmt.executeUpdate();
        con.close();
    } catch (Exception ex) {
```

```java
            throw new EJBException(ex);
        }
    }

    public void ejbLoad() {
        try {
            byte[] serHandle;

            wrapperPlanId =
                (String)entityContext.getPrimaryKey();

            // Load plan handle from database.
            Connection con = getConnection();

            PreparedStatement pstmt = con.prepareStatement(
                "SELECT cfg_act_plan " +
                "FROM Wrapper_Plans " +
                "WHERE cfg_wrapper_planid = ?");
            pstmt.setString(1, wrapperPlanId);
            ResultSet rs = pstmt.executeQuery();
            if (rs.next()) {
                serHandle = rs.getBytes(1);
                con.close();
            } else {
                throw new NoSuchEntityException();
            }

            // Convert handle to plan reference.
            plan = serPlanHandleToRef(serHandle);
        } catch (Exception ex) {
            throw new EJBException(ex);
        }
        super.ejbLoad();
    }

    //
    // Helper methods
    //

    private Connection getConnection() {
```

```java
      try {
         return ds.getConnection();
      } catch (Exception ex) {
         throw new EJBException(ex);
      }
   }

   private void readEnvironment() {
      try {
         Context ictx = new InitialContext();
         ds = (DataSource)
            ictx.lookup("java:comp/env/jdbc/BenefitsDB");
      } catch (Exception ex) {
         throw new EJBException(ex);
      }
   }

   private static Plan serPlanHandleToRef(byte[] serHandle) {
      try {
         ObjectInputStream inp = new ObjectInputStream(
            new ByteArrayInputStream(serHandle));
         Handle handle = (Handle)inp.readObject();
         return (Plan)PortableRemoteObject.narrow(
            handle.getEJBObject(), Plan.class);
      } catch (Exception ex) {
         throw new EJBException(ex);
      }
   }

   private static byte[] planToSerHandle(Plan plan) {
      try {
         ByteArrayOutputStream barr =
            new ByteArrayOutputStream();
         ObjectOutputStream out =
            new ObjectOutputStream(barr);
         Handle handle = plan.getHandle();
         out.writeObject(handle);
         return barr.toByteArray();
      } catch (Exception ex) {
         throw new EJBException(ex);
      }
   }
```

```
private Collection findPlans(int planType) {
    try {
        Vector vec = new Vector();
        Connection con = getConnection();
        PreparedStatement pstmt = con.prepareStatement(
            "SELECT cfg_wrapper_planid " +
            "FROM Wrapper_Plans " +
            "WHERE cfg_plan_type = ?"
        );
        pstmt.setInt(1, planType);
        ResultSet rs = pstmt.executeQuery();

        while (rs.next()) {
            String pkey = rs.getString(1);
            vec.add(pkey);
        }
        con.close();
        return vec;
    } catch (Exception ex) {
        throw new EJBException(ex);
    }
}
}
```

The WrapperPlanBean class defines the following methods:

- The `ejbCreate` method, which corresponds to the `create` method defined in the WrapperPlanHome interface

- All the find methods defined in the PlanHome interface

- The `ejbLoad`, `ejbRemove`, and `setEntityContext` container callbacks that override the same-name callbacks in the superclass

The same principles apply to invoking these methods for the WrapperPlan-Bean class as for the SelectionBean class. Refer to Invoking Superclass Methods on page 267 for more information.

The WrapperPlanBean class is of particular interest because it uses an entity object handle to deal with the persistence of the object references to the actual plan entity objects implemented by the insurance companies. The WrapperPlan-Bean class uses handles to store entity object references in persistent storage. Its `ejbCreate` and `ejbLoad` methods illustrate the code to persist an entity object handle. The `ejbCreate` method obtains a handle for the `plan` object reference, serializes it, and stores it in the `cfg_act_Plan_handle` database column. The `ejbLoad` method reads the handle from the `cfg_act_Plan_handle` database column and deserializes it to obtain the object reference to the Plan entity object. The size of a serialized handle depends on how the container implements handles. It is typically on the order of hundreds of bytes.

Note that Wombat does not override the `ejbStore` method in the Wrapper-PlanBean class. This is because Wombat knows that the business methods of the WrapperPlanBeanCMP class do not modify the container-managed fields. Therefore, there is no need to update the database when the container invokes `ejbStore` on the instance.

Using a handle is not the only way to represent an entity object reference in persistent storage. A handle's main advantage is that the program storing the handle does not need to know the JNDI name of the home interface of the entity object. However, a handle's main disadvantage is that the handle is a binary object not understood outside the Java environment that created the handle. (This means, for example, that the handle is stored as a VARBINARY data type, which is opaque to SQL queries.) In addition, the serialized handle may become invalid after a container reconfiguration. Other ways of storing an object reference in persistent storage include the following.

- Store the primary key of the entity object (if all the saved object references have the same home interface).

- Store both the name of the JNDI home interface and the primary key of the entity object (if the saved object references have different home interfaces).

The second approach (storing both the JNDI home interface name and primary key) would be more suitable for our application because the wrapped actual plans have different home interfaces. A real-life application would probably use this approach rather than the handle-based approach to avoid storing opaque binary handles in the relational schema.

Notice that the `Wrapper_Plans` table maintains the plan type indication in the `cfg_plan_type` database column. Keeping the plan type in its own database column enables a more efficient implementation of the `ejbFindMedicalPlans` and `ejbFindDentalPlans` methods. Without this database column, the find methods would have to iterate over all rows in the `Wrapper_Plans` table and invoke the `getPlanType` method on all the actual Plan objects to find the set of all the configured medical or dental plans.

`plan_intf.jar` JAR File

A JAR file is a standard file format for packaging a collection of compiled Java classes into a unit that can be loaded and executed in a JVM. One use of a JAR file is for packaging libraries.

To allow the insurance companies or application integrators to develop the enterprise beans that implement the Plan and PlanHome interfaces, Wombat creates and publishes the `plan_intf.jar` JAR file. The `plan_intf.jar` JAR file contains all the class files that an entity bean that implements the Plan and PlanHome interfaces needs at compile time and at runtime.

The `plan_intf.jar` file contains the following class files.

```
com.wombat.plan.Plan.class
com.wombat.plan.PlanHome.class
com.wombat.plan.PlanType.class
com.wombat.plan.PlanInfo.class
com.wombat.plan.Doctor.class
com.wombat.plan.PlanException.class
```

7.3.6   EnrollmentWeb Web Application

The EnrollmentWeb Web application is a set of JSP. See the example in Chapter 4, Working with Session Beans, for a description of the EnrollmentWeb Web application.

7.3.7   BenefitsAdminWeb Web Application

The BenefitsAdminWeb Web application is a set of JSP used by the customer's benefits administration department to administer its benefits plans. The BenefitsAdminWeb Web application does the following work.

- It finds all the deployed plan beans from the insurance companies.

- It assumes that all the home interfaces of the deployed plans are located in a specified JNDI context.

- It uses the find methods in the WrapperPlanHome interface to find all the plans that are currently configured for use by the Benefits Enrollment application.

- It displays the information to the plan administrator and lets her modify the set of configured plans.

If the plan administrator modifies the set of plans, the BenefitsAdminWeb Web application uses the WrapperPlanHome interface to add and remove the configured plans. The skeleton code for adding a plan is illustrated next (we show only the parts that are relevant to the use of the WrapperPlanEJB entity bean).

```
...
// Select a plan to add to the set of configured plans. The plan
// is the object reference to the plan to be added.
Plan plan = ...;

// Let the plan administrator select a primary key that will
// be seen by the clients.
String wrapperPkey = ...;

// Create a wrapper entity object for the plan.
Plan wrapperPlan = WrapperPlanHome.create(wrapperPkey, plan);
...
```

After the `create` method completes, the created wrapper plan entity object becomes available to the Benefits Enrollment application.

If a plan administrator wishes to remove a plan from the list of configured plans, she invokes the `remove` method on the WrapperPlanHome interface, passing it the wrapper plan primary key, as follows.

```
...
WrapperPlanHome.remove(wrapperPkey);
...
```

7.3.8   BenefitsDatabase

Wombat defines the default schema for BenefitsDatabase, which stores the persistent state of SelectionEJB and WrapperPlanEJB. BenefitsDatabase contains two tables: the `Selections` table and the `Wrapper_Plans` table. The SelectionEJB and WrapperPlanEJB entity beans access these tables.

If a customer chooses to use a different database schema than the default schema, the customer needs to use the entity beans with CMP rather than the entity beans with BMP. That is, the customer uses the SelectionEJBCMP and WrapperPlanEJBCMP entity beans instead of the SelectionEJB and WrapperPlanEJB beans. In addition, the customer must define a custom persistence mechanism that does not use BenefitsDatabase.

The Selections table contains the employee's current benefits selections. Code Example 7.26 shows the SQL definition of this table.

Code Example 7.26   Selections Table

```
CREATE TABLE Selections (
    sel_empl INT,
    sel_coverage INT,
    sel_medical_plan VARCHAR(32),
    sel_dental_plan VARCHAR(32),
    sel_smoker INT,
    PRIMARY KEY (sel_empl)
)
```

The columns of the Selections table contain the following data.

- **sel_empl column**—The employee number identifying the employee.

- **sel_coverage column**—The coverage selection. sel_coverage accepts three possible values.

  - 0 means "employee only"

  - 1 means "employee and spouse"

  - 2 means "employee, spouse, and children"

- **sel_medical_plan column**—The primary key of the medical plan selected by the employee.

- **sel_dental_plan column**—The primary key of the dental plan selected by the employee.

- **sel_smoker column**—The indication whether the employee is a smoker. The allowed values are Y and N.

The Wrapper_Plans table contains information about the plans configured for the Benefits Enrollment application. Code Example 7.27 shows the SQL definition for this table.

Code Example 7.27 Wrapper_Plans Table

```
CREATE TABLE Wrapper_Plans (
    cfg_wrapper_planid VARCHAR(32),
    cfg_act_plan VARBINARY(1024),
    cfg_plan_type INT,
    PRIMARY KEY (cfg_wrapper_planid)
)
```

The columns of the Wrapper_Plans table contain the following data.

- **cfg_wrapper_planid column**—Identifies the primary key for the wrapper plan. The customer's benefits department (such as Star Enterprise) assigns the wrapper primary key.

- **cfg_act_plan column**—Identifies the serialized handle of the entity object representing the actual medical or dental plan implemented by an entity bean provided by an insurance company.

- **cfg_plan_type column**—Provides a means for the WrapperPlanEJB entity bean to optimize the implementation of the find methods. There are two possible values for cfg_plan_type.

  - 1 indicates the plan is a medical plan

  - 2 indicates the plan is a dental plan

7.3.9 Packaging of Parts

This section describes how Wombat packages its benefits application for distribution to customers.

benefits.ear File

Wombat packages the benefits application as a single J2EE enterprise application archive file, which it names benefits.ear. (A .ear file is an enterprise application archive resource file.) Figure 7.7 depicts the contents of the benefits.ear file.

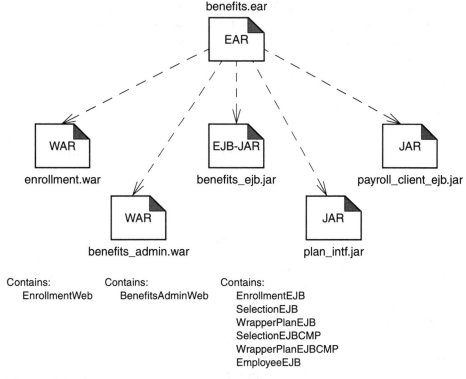

Figure 7.7 Contents of the `benefits.ear` File

The `benefits.ear` file contains the following parts.

- The `enrollment.war` file with the EnrollmentWeb Web application. (A `war` file is a Web archive file.) The EnrollmentWeb Web application consists of several JSP.

- The `benefits_admin.war` file with the BenefitsAdminWeb Web application. The BenefitsAdminWeb Web application consists of several JSP.

- The `benefits_ejb.jar` file. This is the ejb-jar file that contains the enterprise beans developed by Wombat (see the next section for details).

- The `plan_intf.jar` JAR file that contains the Plan and PlanHome interface files with their dependent classes and interfaces. The `benefits_ejb.jar` file should note the dependency on this JAR file in the manifest file of the `benefits_ejb.jar` file.

- The `payroll_client_ejb.jar` file. This is the JAR file with the client view of the Aardvark PayrollEJB session bean. Wombat needs this file to compile the EnrollmentEJB classes, and the EnrollmentEJB classes need this JAR file at runtime. The `benefits_ejb.jar` file should note this dependency in the manifest file of the `benefits_ejb.jar` file.

`benefits_ejb.jar` File

The `benefits_ejb.jar` file is an ejb-jar file that contains the enterprise beans developed by Wombat. Code Example 7.28 lists the classes that the file contains.

Code Example 7.28   Contents of the `benefits_ejb.jar` File

```
com.wombat.benefits.CoverageCategory.class
com.wombat.benefits.Employee.class
com.wombat.benefits.EmployeeBean.class
com.wombat.benefits.EmployeeCopy.class
com.wombat.benefits.EmployeeException.class
com.wombat.benefits.EmployeeHome.class
com.wombat.benefits.EmployeeInfo.class
com.wombat.benefits.Enrollment.class
com.wombat.benefits.EnrollmentBean.class
com.wombat.benefits.EnrollmentException.class
com.wombat.benefits.EnrollmentHome.class
com.wombat.benefits.Options.class
com.wombat.benefits.Selection.class
com.wombat.benefits.SelectionBean.class
com.wombat.benefits.SelectionBeanCMP.class
com.wombat.benefits.SelectionCopy.class
com.wombat.benefits.SelectionException.class
com.wombat.benefits.SelectionHome.class
com.wombat.benefits.Summary.class
com.wombat.benefits.WrapperPlanBean.class
com.wombat.benefits.WrapperPlanBeanCMP.class
com.wombat.benefits.WrapperPlanHome.class
```

7.4   Parts Developed by Premium Health

Premium Health is one of the insurance companies that provides insurance plans to the employees of Star Enterprise. It develops its own Web application and enterprise beans that are intended for deployment at its customer sites.

7.4.1   Overview

Premium Health develops the parts illustrated in Figure 7.8. Premium Health expects its customers to deploy the PremiumHealthAdminWeb, PremiumHealth-PlanEJB, and PremiumHealthDatabase parts at their own customer sites. A company such as Star Enterprise that contracts with Premium Health deploys the three parts at its own site. However, the PremiumHealthAdminApp is deployed at the Premium Health site, not at the customer site.

PremiumHealthAdminWeb is a Web application deployed at the customer site. Premium Health uses it to administer remotely the plan information stored and used at the customer site.

PremiumHealthPlanEJB is an entity bean that implements the Plan and Plan-Home interfaces. Recall that Wombat developed these interfaces to provide a standard way for an insurance company to integrate its coverage plans with Wombat's benefits application.

PremiumHealthDatabase is a database that stores the plan information used by the PremiumHealthPlan bean.

PremiumHealthAdminApp is an application deployed at the Premium Health site. Premium Health uses the application to upload and modify the plan information at the customer sites.

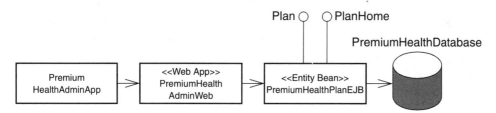

Figure 7.8   Parts Developed by Premium Health

7.4.2   PremiumHealthPlanEJB EntityBean

The PremiumHealthPlanEJB entity bean implements the business logic for the medical and dental plans provided by Premium Health to its customers. It uses the Plan remote interface and the PremiumHealthPlanHome home interface. This section describes the remote and home interfaces, and the entity bean implementation class.

PremiumHealthPlanEJB Remote Interface

PremiumHealthPlanEJB uses the com.wombat.plan.Plan interface as its remote interface (see Code Example 7.18).

PremiumHealthPlanHome Home Interface

The PremiumHealthPlanHome interface extends the PlanHome interface and adds a single `create` method. Code Example 7.29 shows the definition of this home interface.

Code Example 7.29 PremiumHealthPlanHome Home Interface

```
package com.premiumhealth.plan;

import javax.ejb.*;
import java.rmi.RemoteException;
import com.wombat.plan.Plan;
import com.wombat.plan.PlanHome;

public interface PremiumHealthPlanHome extends PlanHome {
    Plan create(Plan planRef, String planName,
        int planType)throws RemoteException, CreateException;
    Plan findByPrimaryKey(String planId)
        throws RemoteException, FinderException;
}
```

The PremiumHealthAdminWeb Web application invokes the `create` method when adding a new plan to the list of the available plans administered by Premium Health and offered to a given customer enterprise.

PremiumHealthPlanBean Entity Bean Class

The PremiumHealthPlanBean entity bean class defines the implementation of the plan business logic. Code Example 7.30 shows the implementation of the PremiumHealthPlanBean class.

Code Example 7.30 PremiumHealthPlanBean Entity Bean Class

```
package com.premiumhealth.plan;

import javax.ejb.*;
import java.util.Vector;
import java.util.Collection;
import com.wombat.plan.Plan;
import com.wombat.plan.PlanHome;
import com.wombat.plan.PlanInfo;
import com.wombat.plan.PlanType;
```

```java
import com.wombat.plan.PlanException;
import com.wombat.plan.Doctor;
import java.sql.SQLException;
import javax.sql.DataSource;
import javax.naming.InitialContext;
import javax.naming.Context;

import com.premiumhealth.plan.db.DBDeletePremiumByPlanId;
import com.premiumhealth.plan.db.DBQueryPremium;

import com.premiumhealth.plan.db.DBDeleteDoctorByPlanId;
import com.premiumhealth.plan.db.DBQueryAllDoctors;
import com.premiumhealth.plan.db.DBQueryDoctorByName;
import com.premiumhealth.plan.db.DBQueryDoctorBySpecialty;

import com.premiumhealth.plan.db.DBInsertPlan;
import com.premiumhealth.plan.db.DBDeletePlan;
import com.premiumhealth.plan.db.DBUpdatePlan;
import com.premiumhealth.plan.db.DBQueryPlan;
import com.premiumhealth.plan.db.DBQueryPlanByDoctor;
import com.premiumhealth.plan.db.DBQueryPlanByType;

public class PremiumHealthPlanBean implements EntityBean {

    // Cached persistent state
    String planId;    // primary key
    int planType;
    String planName;

    // Other instance variables
    DataSource ds;
    EntityContext ctx;

    // Business methods from the remote interface
    // com.wombat.plan.Plan

    public PlanInfo getPlanInfo() {
        PlanInfo pi = new PlanInfo();
        pi.setPlanId(planId);
        pi.setPlanType(planType);
        pi.setPlanName(planName);
        return pi;
    }
```

```java
public int getPlanType() { return planType; }

public double getCost(int coverage, int age,
        boolean smokerStatus) throws PlanException
{
    DBQueryPremium cmd = null;
    try {
        cmd = new DBQueryPremium(ds);
        cmd.setPlanId(planId);
        cmd.setAge(age);
        cmd.setSmokerStatus(smokerStatus ? "Y" : "N");
        cmd.setCoverage(coverage);
        cmd.execute();
        if (!cmd.next()) {
            throw new PlanException(
                "premium information unavailable");
        }
        double amount = cmd.getAmount();
        return amount;
    } catch (SQLException ex) {
        throw new EJBException(ex);
    } finally {
        if (cmd != null) cmd.release();
    }
}

public Collection getAllDoctors()
{
    DBQueryAllDoctors cmd = null;
    try {
        cmd = new DBQueryAllDoctors(ds);
        cmd.setPlanId(planId);
        cmd.execute();

        Vector vec = new Vector();
        while (cmd.next()) {
            Doctor doc = new Doctor();
            doc.setFirstName(cmd.getFirstName());
            doc.setLastName(cmd.getLastName());
            doc.setSpecialty(cmd.getSpecialty());
            doc.setHospital(cmd.getHospital());
```

```
            doc.setPracticeSince(cmd.getPracticeSince());
            vec.add(doc);
         }
         return vec;
      } catch (SQLException ex) {
         throw new EJBException(ex);
      } finally {
         if (cmd != null) cmd.release();
      }
   }


   public Collection getDoctorsByName(Doctor template)
   {
      DBQueryDoctorByName cmd = null;
      try {
         cmd = new DBQueryDoctorByName(ds);
         cmd.setPlanId(planId);
         cmd.setFirstName(template.getFirstName() + "%");
         cmd.setLastName(template.getLastName() + "%");
         cmd.execute();

         Vector vec = new Vector();
         while (cmd.next()) {
            Doctor doc = new Doctor();
            doc.setFirstName(cmd.getFirstName());
            doc.setLastName(cmd.getLastName());
            doc.setSpecialty(cmd.getSpecialty());
            doc.setHospital(cmd.getHospital());
            doc.setPracticeSince(cmd.getPracticeSince());
            vec.add(doc);
         }
         return vec;
      } catch (SQLException ex) {
         throw new EJBException(ex);
      } finally {
         if (cmd != null) cmd.release();
      }
   }
```

```java
public Collection getDoctorsBySpecialty(String specialty)
{
    DBQueryDoctorBySpecialty cmd = null;
    try {
        cmd = new DBQueryDoctorBySpecialty(ds);
        cmd.setPlanId(planId);
        cmd.setSpecialty(specialty);
        cmd.execute();

        Vector vec = new Vector();
        while (cmd.next()) {
            Doctor doc = new Doctor();
            doc.setFirstName(cmd.getFirstName());
            doc.setLastName(cmd.getLastName());
            doc.setSpecialty(cmd.getSpecialty());
            doc.setHospital(cmd.getHospital());
            doc.setPracticeSince(cmd.getPracticeSince());
            vec.add(doc);
        }
        return vec;
    } catch (SQLException ex) {
        throw new EJBException(ex);
    } finally {
        if (cmd != null) cmd.release();
    }
}


// Methods from the home interface
// com.wombat.plan.PremiumHealthPlanHome

public String ejbCreate(String planId, String planName,
        int planType)
{
    this.planId = planId;
    this.planName = planName;
    this.planType = planType;

    DBInsertPlan cmd = null;
    try {
        cmd = new DBInsertPlan(ds);
        cmd.setPlanId(planId);
```

```
        cmd.setPlanType(planType);
        cmd.setPlanDescr(planName);
        cmd.execute();
        return planId;
    } catch (SQLException ex) {
        throw new EJBException(ex);
    } finally {
        if (cmd != null) cmd.release();
    }
}


public void ejbPostCreate(String planId, String planName,
        int planType) {}


// Find methods

public String ejbFindByPrimaryKey(String planId)
    throws FinderException
{
    DBQueryPlan cmd = null;
    try {
        cmd = new DBQueryPlan(ds);
        cmd.setPlanId(planId);
        cmd.execute();

        Vector vec = new Vector();
        if (cmd.next()) {
            return planId;
        } else {
            throw new ObjectNotFoundException();
        }
    } catch (SQLException ex) {
        throw new EJBException(ex);
    } finally {
        if (cmd != null) cmd.release();
    }
}

public String ejbFindByPlanId(String planId)
    throws FinderException
```

```
{
    return ejbFindByPrimaryKey(planId);
}

public Collection ejbFindMedicalPlans()
{
    DBQueryPlanByType cmd = null;
    try {
        cmd = new DBQueryPlanByType(ds);
        cmd.setPlanType(PlanType.MEDICAL);
        cmd.execute();

        Vector vec = new Vector();
        while (cmd.next()) {
            vec.add(cmd.getPlanId());
        }
        return vec;
    } catch (SQLException ex) {
        throw new EJBException(ex);
    } finally {
        if (cmd != null) cmd.release();
    }
}

public Collection ejbFindDentalPlans()
{
    DBQueryPlanByType cmd = null;
    try {
        cmd = new DBQueryPlanByType(ds);
        cmd.setPlanType(PlanType.DENTAL);
        cmd.execute();

        Vector vec = new Vector();
        while (cmd.next()) {
            vec.add(cmd.getPlanId());
        }
        return vec;
    } catch (SQLException ex) {
        throw new EJBException(ex);
```

```
      } finally {
         if (cmd != null) cmd.release();
      }
   }

   public Collection ejbFindByDoctor(Doctor template)
   {
      DBQueryPlanByDoctor cmd = null;
      try {
         cmd = new DBQueryPlanByDoctor(ds);
         cmd.setFirstName(template.getFirstName() + "%");
         cmd.setLastName(template.getLastName() + "%");
         cmd.execute();

         Vector vec = new Vector();
         while (cmd.next()) {
            vec.add(cmd.getPlanId());
         }
         return vec;
      } catch (SQLException ex) {
         throw new EJBException(ex);
      } finally {
         if (cmd != null) cmd.release();
      }
   }

   //
   // Methods from the javax.ejb.EntityBean interface
   //

   public void setEntityContext(EntityContext ctx) {
      this.ctx = ctx;
      readEnvironment();
   }

   public void unsetEntityContext() {}

   public void ejbRemove()
   {
      DBDeletePlan cmd = null;
      DBDeletePremiumByPlanId cmd2 = null;
      DBDeleteDoctorByPlanId cmd3 = null;
```

```java
        try {
            // Delete dependent premium information.
            cmd2 = new DBDeletePremiumByPlanId(ds);
            cmd2.setPlanId(planId);
            cmd2.execute();

            // Delete dependent doctor information.
            cmd3 = new DBDeleteDoctorByPlanId(ds);
            cmd3.setPlanId(planId);
            cmd3.execute();

            // Delete plan record.
            cmd = new DBDeletePlan(ds);
            cmd.setPlanId(planId);
            cmd.execute();
        } catch (SQLException ex) {
            throw new EJBException(ex);
        } finally {
            if (cmd != null) cmd.release();
            if (cmd2 != null) cmd2.release();
            if (cmd3 != null) cmd3.release();
        }
    }

    public void ejbActivate() {
        planId = (String)ctx.getPrimaryKey();
    }

    public void ejbPassivate() { planId = null; }

    public void ejbLoad()
    {
        DBQueryPlan cmd = null;
        try {
            cmd = new DBQueryPlan(ds);
            cmd.setPlanId(planId);
            cmd.execute();
            if (!cmd.next()) {
                throw new NoSuchEntityException();
            }
            planName = cmd.getPlanDescr();
            planType = cmd.getPlanType();
```

```
        } catch (SQLException ex) {
            throw new EJBException(ex);
        } finally {
            if (cmd != null) cmd.release();
            }
    }

    public void ejbStore()
    {
        DBUpdatePlan cmd = null;
        try {
            cmd = new DBUpdatePlan(ds);
            cmd.setPlanId(planId);
            cmd.setPlanType(planType);
            cmd.setPlanDescr(planName);
            cmd.execute();
            } catch (SQLException ex) {
                throw new EJBException(ex);
            } finally {
                if (cmd != null) cmd.release();
                }
    }

    private void readEnvironment() {
        try {
            Context ictx = new InitialContext();
            ds = (DataSource)ictx.lookup(
                "java:comp/env/jdbc/PremiumHealthDB");
        } catch (Exception ex) {
            throw new EJBException(ex);
        }
    }
}
```

The PremiumHealthPlanBean class is a typical entity bean class with BMP. As such, it manages its own database access by making use of command beans. See Data Access Command Beans on page 102 for an explanation of command beans.

The entity object caches some parts of the persistent state (planType and planName) to reduce the number of database accesses. The entity object does not cache other parts of the PremiumHealthPlanEJB state. For example, it does not cache the doctor information. Instead, the entity object's business methods access the database directly when doctor information is needed.

Refer to Data Access Command Beans on page 406 to see the implementations of the different data access command beans used by the entity example.

7.4.3   HelperEJB Session Bean

The HelperEJB is a stateless session bean that the PremiumHealthAdminWeb application uses to create and maintain the benefits information in the database. We do not show its implementation in the book because it is not relevant to the rest of the application.

7.4.4   PremiumHealthAdminWeb Web Application

The PremiumHealthAdminWeb Web application is a set of servlets that the Premium Health insurance company uses to maintain plan information at its customer sites. The PremiumHealthAdminWeb Web application is deployed at the customer site. Premium Health sends XML requests over the Internet to make on-line updates to the plan information at the customer site.

The PremiumHealthAdminWeb Web application uses PremiumHealthPlanEJB and HelperEJB to perform the updates to the plan information.

We briefly mention the Web application only because it is one part of the entire example. The Web application consists of servlets, and these servlets are important to EJB. We do not discuss the Web application and servlets in more detail because the focus of this book is Enterprise JavaBeans.

7.4.5   PremiumHealthAdminApp

PremiumHealthAdminApp is an application deployed at Premium Health. PremiumHealthAdminApp acts as the client of the PremiumHealthAdminWeb Web application. It is used to upload and maintain the plan information at the customer sites.

We do not describe the architecture and implementation of PremiumHealthAdminApp in this book.

7.4.6   PremiumHealthDatabase

PremiumHealthDatabase is a relational database that exists at the customer site. It contains the plan information needed by the PremiumHealthPlanEJB entity bean. Using the PremiumHealthAdminWeb Web application, the Premium Health insurance company updates the plan information in the database via the Internet.

The PremiumHealthDatabase schema defines three tables. The Plans table contains the plans offered by Premium Health. The Premium table contains the information about the plan premium. The Doctor table contains the information about the participating doctors.

Code Example 7.31 shows the definition of the Plans table.

Code Example 7.31 Plans Table

```
CREATE TABLE Plans (
    plan_id VARCHAR(32),
    plan_descr VARCHAR(32),
    plan_type INT,
    PRIMARY KEY (plan_id)
)
```

The columns of the Plans table contain the following data.

- **plan_id column**—Contains the unique identifier for the plan

- **plan_descr column**—Holds a short description of the plan suitable for display within a GUI form

- **plan_type column**—Indicates whether the plan is a medical or dental plan. When equal to 1, the plan is a medical plan; when equal to 2, the plan is a dental plan.

Code Example 7.32 shows the SQL statements defining the Premium table.

Code Example 7.32 Premium Table

```
CREATE TABLE Premium (
    prem_plan_id VARCHAR(32),
    prem_age INT,
    prem_smoker_status CHAR(1),
    prem_coverage INT,
    prem_amount DECIMAL(6.2),
    PRIMARY KEY (prem_plan_id, prem_age, prem_smoker_status,
        prem_coverage)
)
```

The columns of the `Premium` table contain information that the application uses to calculate an employee's premium deduction. An employee's premium amount is determined by the selected plan, his or her age, smoker status, and extent of coverage. The columns of the `Premium` table hold the following data.

- **prem_plan_id column**—Holds the unique identifier of the plan

- **prem_age column**—Indicates the age of the employee

- **prem_smoker_status column**—Indicates whether the employee is a smoker. The allowed values are Y and N.

- **prem_coverage column**—Indicates the coverage category selected by the employee

- **prem_amount column**—Holds the amount of the plan premium

Code Example 7.33 shows the SQL definition of the `Doctors` table.

Code Example 7.33 Doctors Table

```
CREATE TABLE Doctors (
    doc_id INT,
    doc_plan_id VARCHAR(32),
    doc_first_name VARCHAR(32),
    doc_last_name VARCHAR(32),
    doc_specialty VARCHAR(32),
    doc_hospital VARCHAR(32),
    doc_practice_since INT,
    PRIMARY KEY (doc_id, doc_plan_id)
)
```

The columns of the `Doctors` table hold information about the different doctors affiliated with a particular plan. These columns contain the following data.

- **doc_id column**—An identifier for a particular doctor

- **doc_plan_id column**—The identifier for a particular plan

- **doc_first_name column**—The doctor's first name

- **doc_last_name column**—The doctor's last name

- **doc_specialty column**—A short description of the doctor's field of specialty

- **doc_hospital column**—The name of the hospital with which the doctor is affiliated

- **doc_practice_since column**—The year when the doctor first began his practice

The doc_id and doc_plan_id columns together uniquely identify a row in the Doctors table, and this is noted as the primary key. Note that the database is not in normalized form. Because of this, it would be possible (although not desirable) to have the same doctor listed in different plans with inconsistent information.

7.4.7   Packaging

This section describes the packaging of the parts developed by Premium Health.

premiumhealth.ear Archive File

Premium Health packages the parts that support the benefits application as a single J2EE enterprise application archive file, which it names premiumhealth.ear. Figure 7.9 depicts the contents of the premiumhealth.ear file.

The premiumhealth.ear file contains the following parts.

- **premiumhealth_admin.war file**—This Web application archive file contains the PremiumHealthAdminWeb Web application. The Web application consists of several servlets. A war file is a Web archive resource file that contains the class files for servlets and JSPs.

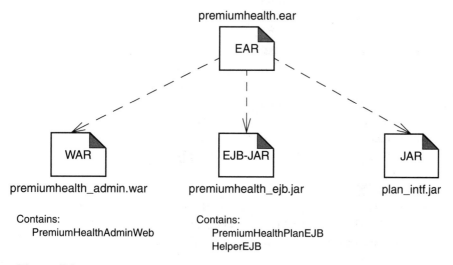

Figure 7.9   Premium Health's Enterprise Application Archive File

- **premiumhealth_ejb.jar file**—This ejb-jar file contains the enterprise beans (PremiumHealthPlanEJB and HelperEJB) developed by Premium Health.

- **plan_intf.jar file**—This is the JAR file published by Wombat. Because the PremiumHealthPlanEJB depends on the contents of this JAR file at runtime, it is included in the premiumhealth.ear file. The Class-Path attribute in the manifest of the premiumhealth_ejb.jar file lists this dependency on the plan_intf.jar file.

premiumhealth_ejb.jar File

The premiumhealth_ejb.jar file is an ejb-jar file that contains the enterprise beans developed by Premium Health. Code Example 7.34 shows the Java class files contained by the file.

Code Example 7.34 premiumhealth_ejb.jar File

```
com.premiumhealth.plan.PremiumHealthPlan.class
com.premiumhealth.plan.PremiumHealthPlanBean.class
com.premiumhealth.plan.PremiumHealthPlanException.class
com.premiumhealth.plan.PremiumHealthPlanHome.class

com.premiumhealth.plan.db.DBDeletePlan.class
com.premiumhealth.plan.db.DBDeletePremiumByPlanId.class
com.premiumhealth.plan.db.DBDeleteDoctorByPlanId.class
com.premiumhealth.plan.db.DBInsertPlan.class
com.premiumhealth.plan.db.DBQueryAllDoctors.class
com.premiumhealth.plan.db.DBQueryBean.class
com.premiumhealth.plan.db.DBQueryDoctorsByName.class
com.premiumhealth.plan.db.DBQueryDoctorsBySpecialty.class
com.premiumhealth.plan.db.DBQueryPlan.class
com.premiumhealth.plan.db.DBQueryPlanByDoctor.class
com.premiumhealth.plan.db.DBQueryPlanByType.class
com.premiumhealth.plan.db.DBQueryPremium.class
com.premiumhealth.plan.db.DBUpdateBean.class
com.premiumhealth.plan.db.DBUpdatePlan.class

com.premiumhealth.helper.Helper.class
com.premiumhealth.helper.HelperBean.class
com.premiumhealth.helper.HelperException.class
com.premiumhealth.helper.HelperHome.class
```

7.5   Parts Developed by Providence

Providence is another insurance provider that interoperates with Wombat's benefits application. Providence, however, differs radically from Premium Health in its approach to exchanging information with its customers. Although Premium Health maintains a database with the plan information at each customer site, Providence maintains the plan data at its own site. An application that needs to access the Providence plan data must access the Providence Web site to obtain the plan data.

7.5.1   Overview

Figure 7.10 illustrates the main parts developed by Providence. ProvidencePlanEJB is an entity bean that enables Providence's plan to be integrated with the Wombat benefits application. Providence accomplishes this by defining ProvidencePlanEJB's remote and home interfaces to be compatible with the Plan and PlanHome interfaces defined by Wombat. ProvidencePlanEJB uses HTTP and XML to communicate with ProvidenceServiceWeb to obtain the Providence plan information.

ProvidenceServiceWeb is a Web application deployed at the Providence site. Customers access it remotely from their own sites to obtain up-to-date plan information.

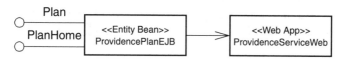

Figure 7.10 Providence's Benefits Plan Parts

7.5.2   ProvidencePlanEJB EntityBean

The ProvidencePlanEJB entity bean uses the Plan remote interface and the ProvidencePlanHome home interface. This section describes these two interfaces as well as the entity bean implementation class.

ProvidencePlanEJB Remote Interface

ProvidencePlanEJB uses the com.wombat.plan.Plan interface as its remote interface (see Code Example 7.18).

ProvidencePlanHome Home Interface

The ProvidencePlanHome interface is the home interface for ProvidencePlanEJB. This interface extends the Wombat PlanHome interface. It neither defines nor overrides any methods (see Code Example 7.35).

Code Example 7.35   ProvidencePlanHome Home Interface

```
package com.providence.plan;

import java.rmi.RemoteException;
import javax.ejb.FinderException;

public interface ProvidencePlanHome
        extends com.wombat.plan.PlanHome {
    Plan ejbFindByPrimaryKey(String planId)
        throws RemoteException, FinderException;
}
```

ProvidencePlanBean Entity Bean Class

The ProvidencePlanBean class demonstrates the implementation of an entity bean with a persistent state that is not stored directly in a local database. Instead, the state is obtained by making requests to a remote application. In our case, the remote application is the ProvidenceServiceWeb Web application at the Providence site. The communication is over HTTP in the XML format. Code Example 7.36 shows the implementation of the ProvidencePlanBean entity bean class.

Code Example 7.36   ProvidencePlanBean Class

```
package com.providence.plan;

import javax.ejb.*;
import java.rmi.RemoteException;
import java.util.Vector;
import java.util.Collection;
import java.util.Iterator;
import javax.naming.Context;
import javax.naming.InitialContext;
import com.wombat.plan.Plan;
import com.wombat.plan.PlanHome;
import com.wombat.plan.PlanInfo;
```

```java
import com.wombat.plan.PlanType;
import com.wombat.plan.PlanException;
import com.wombat.plan.Doctor;

import com.providence.plan.cb.GetCostBean;
import com.providence.plan.cb.GetPlansBean;
import com.providence.plan.cb.GetPlanInfoBean;
import com.providence.plan.cb.GetDoctorsBean;
import com.providence.plan.cb.HttpCommandBeanException;

public class ProvidencePlanBean implements EntityBean {
    EntityContext ctx;
    String baseURL;

    String planId;
    String planName;
    int planType;

    // Business methods from the remote interface
    // com.wombat.plan.Plan

    public PlanInfo getPlanInfo() {
        PlanInfo pi = new PlanInfo();
        pi.setPlanId(planId);
        pi.setPlanName(planName);
        pi.setPlanType(planType);
        return pi;
    }

    public int getPlanType() { return planType; }

    public double getCost(int coverage, int age,
        boolean smokerStatus)
    {
        GetCostBean cmd = null;
        try {
            cmd = new GetCostBean();
            cmd.setBaseURL(baseURL);
            cmd.setPlanId(planId);
            cmd.setCoverage(coverage);
            cmd.setAge(age);
```

```java
            cmd.setSmoker(smokerStatus);
            cmd.execute();
            return cmd.getCost();
        } catch (HttpCommandBeanException ex) {
            throw new EJBException(ex);
        } finally {
            if (cmd != null) cmd.release();
        }
    }

    public Collection getAllDoctors()
    {
        GetDoctorsBean cmd = null;
        try {
            cmd = new GetDoctorsBean();
            cmd.setBaseURL(baseURL);
            cmd.setPlanId(planId);
            cmd.execute();

            Vector vec = new Vector();
            while (cmd.next()) {
                Doctor doc = new Doctor();
                doc.setLastName(cmd.getLastName());
                doc.setFirstName(cmd.getFirstName());
                doc.setSpecialty(cmd.getSpecialty());
                doc.setPracticeSince(cmd.getPracticeSince());
                doc.setHospital(cmd.getHospital());
                vec.add(doc);
            }
            return vec;
        } catch (HttpCommandBeanException ex) {
            throw new EJBException(ex);
        } finally {
            if (cmd != null)
                cmd.release();
        }
    }
```

```java
public Collection getDoctorsByName(Doctor template) {
    GetDoctorsBean cmd = null;
    try {
        cmd = new GetDoctorsBean();
        cmd.setBaseURL(baseURL);
        cmd.setPlanId(planId);
        cmd.setLastName(template.getLastName());
        cmd.setFirstName(template.getFirstName());

        cmd.execute();
        Vector vec = new Vector();
        while (cmd.next()) {
            Doctor doc = new Doctor();
            doc.setLastName(cmd.getLastName());
            doc.setFirstName(cmd.getFirstName());
            doc.setSpecialty(cmd.getSpecialty());
            doc.setPracticeSince(cmd.getPracticeSince());
            doc.setHospital(cmd.getHospital());
            vec.add(doc);
        }
        return vec;
    } catch (HttpCommandBeanException ex) {
        throw new EJBException(ex);
    } finally {
        if (cmd != null)
            cmd.release();
    }
}

public Collection getDoctorsBySpecialty(String specialty) {
    GetDoctorsBean cmd = null;
    try {
        cmd = new GetDoctorsBean();
        cmd.setBaseURL(baseURL);
        cmd.setPlanId(planId);
        cmd.setSpecialty(specialty);
        cmd.execute();

        Vector vec = new Vector();
        while (cmd.next()) {
            Doctor doc = new Doctor();
```

```
                  doc.setLastName(cmd.getLastName());
                  doc.setFirstName(cmd.getFirstName());
                  doc.setSpecialty(cmd.getSpecialty());
                  doc.setPracticeSince(cmd.getPracticeSince());
                  doc.setHospital(cmd.getHospital());
                  vec.add(doc);
              }
              return vec;
          } catch (HttpCommandBeanException ex) {
              throw new EJBException(ex);
          } finally {
              if (cmd != null) cmd.release();
          }
      }


      // Find methods

      public String ejbFindByPrimaryKey(String planId)
          throws ObjectNotFoundException
      {
          GetPlansBean cmd = null;
          try {
              cmd = new GetPlansBean();
              cmd.setBaseURL(baseURL);
              cmd.setPlanId(planId);
              cmd.execute();

              Vector vec = new Vector();
              if (cmd.next()) {
                  return planId;
              } else {
                  throw new ObjectNotFoundException();
              }
          } catch (HttpCommandBeanException ex) {
              throw new EJBException(ex);
          } finally {
              if (cmd != null) cmd.release();
          }
      }
```

```java
public String ejbFindByPlanId(String planId)
   throws ObjectNotFoundException
{
   return ejbFindByPrimaryKey(planId);
}

public Collection ejbFindMedicalPlans()
{
   GetPlansBean cmd = null;
   try {
      cmd = new GetPlansBean();
      cmd.setBaseURL(baseURL);
      cmd.setPlanType("medical");
      cmd.execute();

      Vector vec = new Vector();
      while (cmd.next()) {
         vec.add(cmd.getPlanId());
      }
      return vec;
   } catch (HttpCommandBeanException ex) {
      throw new EJBException(ex);
   } finally {
      if (cmd != null) cmd.release();
   }
}

public Collection ejbFindDentalPlans()
{
   GetPlansBean cmd = null;
   try {
      cmd = new GetPlansBean();
      cmd.setBaseURL(baseURL);
      cmd.setPlanType("dental");
      cmd.execute();

      Vector vec = new Vector();
      while (cmd.next()) {
         vec.add(cmd.getPlanId());
      }
      return vec;
```

```java
        } catch (HttpCommandBeanException ex) {
           throw new EJBException(ex);
        } finally {
           if (cmd != null) cmd.release();
        }
    }

    public Collection ejbFindByDoctor(Doctor template)
    {
        GetPlansBean cmd = null;
        try {
           cmd = new GetPlansBean();
           cmd.setBaseURL(baseURL);
           cmd.setLastName(template.getLastName());
           cmd.setFirstName(template.getFirstName());
           cmd.execute();

           Vector vec = new Vector();
           while (cmd.next()) {
              vec.add(cmd.getPlanId());
           }
           return vec;
        } catch (HttpCommandBeanException ex) {
           throw new EJBException(ex);
        } finally {
           if (cmd != null) cmd.release();
        }
    }


    //
    // Methods from the javax.ejb.EntityBean interface
    //

    public void setEntityContext(EntityContext ctx) {
        this.ctx = ctx;
        readEnvironment();
    }

    public void unsetEntityContext() {}
```

```java
public void ejbRemove() throws RemoveException {
   throw new RemoveException(
      "application is not allowed to remove plan");
}

public void ejbActivate() {
   planId = (String)ctx.getPrimaryKey();
}

public void ejbPassivate() { planId = null; }

public void ejbLoad()
{
   GetPlanInfoBean cmd = null;
   try {
      cmd = new GetPlanInfoBean();
      cmd.setBaseURL(baseURL);
      cmd.setPlanId(planId);
      cmd.execute();
      planName = cmd.getPlanName();
      planType = cmd.getPlanType();
   } catch (HttpCommandBeanException ex) {
      throw new EJBException(ex);
   } finally {
      if (cmd != null) cmd.release();
   }
}

public void ejbStore() {}

private void readEnvironment() {
   try {
      Context ictx = new InitialContext();
      baseURL = (String)ictx.lookup(
         "java:comp/env/ProvidenceServiceWebURL");
   } catch (Exception ex) {
      throw new EJBException(ex);
   }
}
}
```

The ProvidencePlanBean class depends on several command beans to perform the invocation of the HTTP requests to ProvidenceServiceWeb.

The `ejbLoad` method loads the basic information about a plan and caches it in the `planName` and `planType` instance fields. Although the ProvidencePlanBean methods are assigned the NotSupported transaction attribute, we use the `ejbLoad` method to cache the plan information. Although in general it is not possible to use the `ejbLoad` and `ejbStore` methods to cache information for entity beans with nontransactional methods (see Using the `ejbLoad` and `ejbStore` Methods on page 196), it is possible to use the `ejbLoad` method to cache information that is immutable, such as the plan name and plan type.

A business method obtains other information, such as doctor lists, directly from ProvidenceServiceWeb when needed. The ProvidencePlanBean class also implements the find methods defined in PlanHome interface.

Note that the ProvidencePlanBean class obtains the URL of the Providence-ServiceWeb from an environment entry of ProvidencePlanEJB entity bean.

HTTP Command Beans

Code Examples 7.37 through 7.42 illustrate the implementation of the command beans that make the HTTP calls to ProvidenceServiceWeb.

The command beans use the APIs defined in the `org.w3.dom` and `org.xml.sax` packages to process XML. They use the `java.net` package to make HTTP calls to ProvidenceServiceWeb. This book does not describe the use of these APIs. XML Message Formats on page 326 describes the format of the message.

Code Example 7.37   HttpCommandBean Command Bean

```
package com.providence.plan.cb;

import java.io.InputStream;
import java.net.URL;
import org.w3c.dom.Element;
import org.w3c.dom.NodeList;
import org.xml.sax.Parser;
import org.xml.sax.InputSource;

import com.sun.xml.tree.XmlDocumentBuilder;

public class HttpCommandBean {
    private String baseURL;
    private String params = "";
```

```java
private int paramCount = 0;
private Element elem;

public void setBaseURL(String url) {
   this.baseURL = url;
}

public void release() {
}

protected void addParam(String name, String value) {
   if (paramCount == 0)
      params = "?" + name + "=" + value;
   else
      params = params + "&" + name + "=" + value;
   paramCount++;
}

protected void addParam(String name, int value) {
   addParam(name, String.valueOf(value));
}

protected void addParam(String name, double value) {
   addParam(name, String.valueOf(value));
}

protected void callServer() throws HttpCommandBeanException
{
   try {
      URL u = new URL(baseURL + params);
      Object xmlReply = u.getContent();

      XmlDocumentBuilder builder =
         new XmlDocumentBuilder();
      Parser parser = new com.sun.xml.parser.Parser();

      parser.setDocumentHandler(builder);
      builder.setParser(parser);
      builder.setDisableNamespaces(true);
      parser.parse(new InputSource((InputStream)xmlReply));
      elem = builder.getDocument().getDocumentElement();
```

```java
      } catch (Exception ex) {
          throw new HttpCommandBeanException(ex);
      }
  }

  protected static String getElementValue(Element elem,
          String tagName)
  {
      NodeList li = elem.getElementsByTagName(tagName);
      if (li.getLength() == 1) {
          return li.item(0).getFirstChild().getNodeValue();
      } else {
          return null;
      }
  }

  protected Element getTopElement() {
      return elem;
  }
}
```

Code Example 7.38   GetCostBean Command Bean

```java
package com.providence.plan.cb;

import org.w3c.dom.Element;
import org.w3c.dom.NodeList;

public class GetCostBean extends HttpCommandBean {
   public GetCostBean() {
      super();
      addParam("method", "calc-cost");
   }

   public void setCoverage(int coverage) {
      addParam("coverage", coverage);
   }
   public void setPlanId(String planId) {
      addParam("plan-id", planId);
   }
```

```
    public void setAge(int age) {
        addParam("age", age);
    }
    public void setSmoker(boolean smoker) {
        addParam("smoker", smoker ? "Y" : "N");
    }

    public void execute() throws HttpCommandBeanException {
        callServer();
    }

    public double getCost() {
        String s = getElementValue(getTopElement(), "cost");
        return Double.parseDouble(s);
    }
}
```

Code Example 7.39   GetDoctorsBean Command Bean

```
package com.providence.plan.cb;

import org.w3c.dom.Element;
import org.w3c.dom.NodeList;

public class GetDoctorsBean extends HttpCommandBean {
    private NodeList list;
    private int listLength;
    private int listIndex = -1;
    private Element elem;

    public GetDoctorsBean() {
        super();
        addParam("method", "get-doctors");
    }

    public void setPlanId(String planId) {
        addParam("plan-id", planId);
    }
    public void setLastName(String lastName) {
        addParam("last-name", lastName);
    }
```

```java
        public void setFirstName(String firstName) {
           addParam("first-name", firstName);
        }
        public void setSpecialty(String specialty) {
           addParam("specialty", specialty);
        }

        public void execute() throws HttpCommandBeanException {
           callServer();
           list = getTopElement().getElementsByTagName("doctor");
           listLength = list.getLength();
        }

        public String getLastName() {
           return getElementValue(elem, "last-name");
        }
        public String getFirstName() {
           return getElementValue(elem, "first-name");
        }
        public String getSpecialty() {
           return getElementValue(elem, "specialty");
        }
        public int getPracticeSince() {
           return Integer.parseInt(
              getElementValue(elem, "practice-since"));
        }
        public String getHospital() {
           return getElementValue(elem, "hospital");
        }

        public boolean next() {
           if (++listIndex < listLength) {
              elem = (Element)list.item(listIndex);
              return true;
           } else {
              return false;
           }
        }
     }
```

Code Example 7.40   GetPlanInfoBean Command Bean

```
package com.providence.plan.cb;

import org.w3c.dom.Element;
import org.w3c.dom.NodeList;

import com.wombat.plan.PlanType;

public class GetPlanInfoBean extends HttpCommandBean {
   public GetPlanInfoBean() {
      super();
      addParam("method", "get-plan-info");
   }

   public void setPlanId(String planId) {
      addParam("plan-id", planId);
   }

   public void execute() throws HttpCommandBeanException {
      callServer();
   }

   public String getPlanId() {
      return getElementValue(getTopElement(), "plan-id");
   }
   public String getPlanName() {
      return getElementValue(getTopElement(), "plan-name");
   }
   public int getPlanType()
      throws HttpCommandBeanException
   {
      return convertPlanType(
         getElementValue(getTopElement(), "plan-type"));
   }

   static private int convertPlanType(String s)
       throws HttpCommandBeanException
   {
      if (s.equals("Medical"))
         return PlanType.MEDICAL;
```

```
        else if (s.equals("Dental"))
            return PlanType.DENTAL;
        else
            throw new HttpCommandBeanException(
                "Bad plan type from server");
    }
}
```

Code Example 7.41   GetPlansBean Command Bean

```
package com.providence.plan.cb;

import org.w3c.dom.Element;
import org.w3c.dom.NodeList;

public class GetPlansBean extends HttpCommandBean {
    private NodeList list;
    private int listLength;
    private int listIndex = -1;
    private Element elem;

    public GetPlansBean() {
        super();
        addParam("method", "get-plans");
    }

    public void setLastName(String lastName) {
        addParam("last-name", lastName);
    }
    public void setFirstName(String firstName) {
        addParam("first-name", firstName);
    }
    public void setSpecialty(String specialty) {
        addParam("specialty", specialty);
    }
    public void setPlanId(String planId) {
        addParam("plan-id", planId);
    }
    public void setPlanType(String planType) {
        addParam("plan-type", planType);
    }
```

```
   public void execute() throws HttpCommandBeanException {
      callServer();
      list = getTopElement().getElementsByTagName("plan-id");
      listLength = list.getLength();
   }

   public String getPlanId() {
      return elem.getFirstChild().getNodeValue();
   }

   public boolean next() {
      if (++listIndex < listLength) {
         elem = (Element)list.item(listIndex);
         return true;
      } else {
         return false;
      }
   }
}
```

Code Example 7.42   HttpCommandBeanException Command Bean

```
package com.providence.plan.cb;

public class HttpCommandBeanException extends java.lang.Exception {
   private Exception causeException = null;

   public HttpCommandBeanException() {
   }

   public HttpCommandBeanException(String message) {
      super(message);
   }

   public HttpCommandBeanException(Exception  ex) {
      super();
      causeException = ex;
   }

   public Exception getCausedByException() {
      return causeException;
   }
}
```

XML Message Formats

XML stands for eXtensible Markup Language. XML is the industry standard used both for documents and for exchange of data between organizations. The structure of an XML document is defined using *document type description* (DTD).

The following DTD defines the formats of the XML messages returned from ProvidenceServiceWeb to ProvidencePlanEJB. Code Example 7.43 shows the DTD for Providence's messages.

Code Example 7.43   XML DTD for Providence

```
<!ELEMENT plan-ids (plan-id*)>
<!ELEMENT plan-id (#PCDATA)>

<!ELEMENT plans (plan*)>
<!ELEMENT plan (plan-id, plan-name, plan-type)>
<!ELEMENT plan-name (#PCDATA)>
<!ELEMENT plan-type (#PCDATA)>

<!ELEMENT premium-quote (coverage, age, smoker, cost)>
<!ELEMENT coverage (#PCDATA)>
<!ELEMENT age (#PCDATA)>
<!ELEMENT smoker (#PCDATA)>
<!ELEMENT cost (#PCDATA)>

<!ELEMENT doctors (doctor*)>
<!ELEMENT doctor (last-name, first-name, specialty,
        practice-since, hospital)>
<!ELEMENT last-name (#PCDATA)>
<!ELEMENT first-name (#PCDATA)>
<!ELEMENT specialty (#PCDATA)>
<!ELEMENT practice-since (#PCDATA)>
<!ELEMENT hospital (#PCDATA)>
```

In conjunction with the previous DTD, Table 7.1 describes the HTTP requests and XML replies between ProvidencePlanBean and the ProvidenceServiceWeb Web application.

Table 7.1 describes the HTTP requests sent by the ProvidencePlanBean class methods and the corresponding XML replies sent by ProvidenceServiceWeb. The arguments ID, LN, FN, SP, CV, AG, and SM are, respectively, the plan identifier, doctor's last name, doctor's first name, doctor's specialty, coverage category, age, and smoker status.

Table 7.1   XML Replies to Providence HTTP Requests

Method	Query String in Request	Returned XML
ejbFindByPrimaryKey	method=get-plans&plan-id=ID	plan-ids
ejbFindMedicalPlans	method=get-plans&plan-type=medical	plan-ids
ejbFindDentalPlans	method=get-plans&plan-type=dental	plan-ids
ejbFindByDoctor	method=get-plans?last-name= LN&first-name=FN	plan-ids
ejbLoad	method=get-plan-info&plan-id=ID	plan
getAllDoctors	method=get-doctors&plan-id=ID	doctors
getDoctorsByName	method=get-doctors&plan-id= ID&lastname=LN&firstname=FN	doctors
getDoctorsBySpecialty	method=get-doctors&plan-id= ID&specialty=SP	doctors
getCost	method=calc-cost&plan-id= ID&coverage=CV&age=AG&smoker=SM	cost

For example, the getDoctorsByName method may send the following request to ProvidenceServiceWeb to find all the doctors whose last names start with the string Ford and who participate in the plan identified by plan ID PRUD-01.

```
http://serviceweb.Providence.com/star/plans?method=get-
doctors&plan-id=PRUD-01&last-name=Ford&first-name=
```

ProvidenceServiceWeb may send the following reply to this request.

```
<doctors>
        <doctor>
                <last-name>Ford</last-name>
                <first-name>Harrison</first-name>
                <specialty>Surgeon</specialty>
                <practice-since>1990</practice-since>
                <hospital>Stanford</hospital>
        </doctor>
        <doctor>
                <last-name>Ford</last-name>
                <first-name>Betty</first-name>
                <specialty>Pediatrics</specialty>
                <practice-since>1992</practice-since>
                <hospital>Palo Alto Clinic</hospital>
        </doctor>
</doctors>
```

We assumed in the example that the environment entry `java:comp/env/ProvidenceServiceWebURL` of ProvidencePlanEJB was set to `http://service-web.providence.com/star/plans`, the URL at which ProvidenceServiceWeb maintains the plan information for the plans that it offers to Star Enterprise.

7.5.3   ProvidenceServiceWeb Web Application

ProvidenceServiceWeb is a Web application that consists of a number of servlets. The servlets handle the HTTP requests sent by ProvidencePlanBean instances. They return the requested plan information in XML format. This book does not describe the design of ProvidenceServiceWeb.

7.5.4   Packaging

This section describes the packaging of the parts developed by Providence.

`providence.ear` Archive File

Providence packages the parts that support the benefits application as a single J2EE enterprise application archive file, which it names `providence.ear`. Figure 7.11 depicts the contents of the `providence.ear` file.

The `providence.ear` file contains two parts.

1. **`providence_ejb.jar` file**—This ejb-jar file contains the ProvidencePlanEJB enterprise bean developed by Providence.

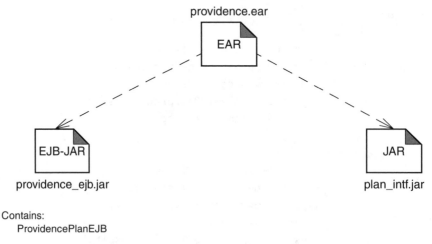

Figure 7.11 Providence's Enterprise Application Archive File

2. `plan_intf.jar` **file**—This is the JAR file published by Wombat. Because ProvidencePlanEJB depends on the contents of this JAR file at runtime, it is included in the `providence.ear` file. The Class-Path attribute in the manifest of the `providence_ejb.jar` file lists this dependency on the `plan_intf.jar` file.

`providence_ejb.jar` File

The `providence_ejb.jar` file is an ejb-jar file that contains the enterprise beans developed by Providence. Code Example 7.44 shows the Java class files contained by the file.

Code Example 7.44 `providence_ejb.jar` File

```
com.providence.plan.ProvidencePlan.class
com.providence.plan.ProvidencePlanBean.class
com.providence.plan.ProvidencePlanHome.class

com.providence.plan.db.GetCostBean.class
com.providence.plan.db.GetDoctorsBean.class
com.providence.plan.db.GetPlanInfoBean.class
com.providence.plan.db.GetPlansBean.class
com.providence.plan.db.HttpCommandBean.class
com.providence.plan.db.HttpCommandBeanException.class
```

7.6   Summary of the Integration Techniques

The complete benefits application includes parts developed by several companies. This section discusses the techniques used to integrate these different parts into an operational application. As the discussion proceeds, notice how the EJB architecture simplifies the integration of components from multiple organizations.

We start the discussion by focusing on the key integration points. These are the points at which the parts developed by different organizations come together. Figure 7.12 illustrates these integration points.

The application illustrates the following three different techniques for integrating components.

1. The client developer relies on the bean provider to publish the EJB client-view interfaces. This is the case with Wombat's EnrollmentEJB, which is dependent on PayrollEJB from Aardvark. EnrollmentEJB's dependency is as a client of PayrollEJB.

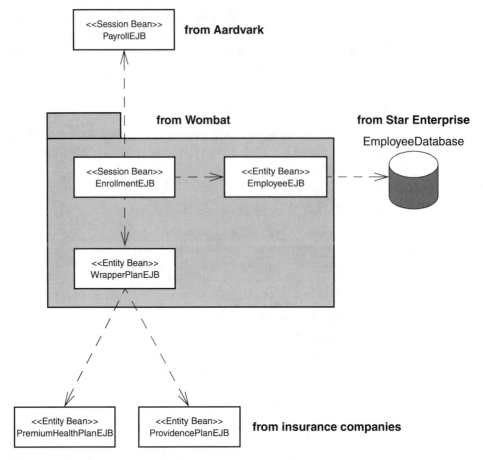

Figure 7.12 Integration of the Benefits Application Parts

2. The bean provider relies on the client provider to publish the EJB client-view interfaces so that it can develop an entity bean that can be integrated with the client application. This is the case with integration of the WrapperPlanEJB from Wombat with the individual plan entity beans, such as ProvidencePlan-EJB and PremiumHealthEJB, from the insurance companies. WrapperPlan-EJB is the client of the ProvidencePlanEJB and PremiumHealthEJB entity beans.

3. The bean provider uses CMP to allow the integration with its customers' existing databases or applications. This is the case with the integration of Wombat's EmployeeEJB with the preexisting EmployeeDatabase at Star Enterprise.

The following subsections explain these different techniques in more detail.

7.6.1 Bean Provider Publishes EJB Client-View Interfaces

Let's look at how to integrate EnrollmentEJB from Wombat with PayrollEJB from vendor Aardvark. PayrollEJB implements the remote access to Star Enterprise's Payroll System and can be used by nonpayroll applications to access the Payroll System. For example, EnrollmentEJB uses PayrollEJB to update the payroll information at the end of the benefits enrollment process.

The following six steps describe the integration of these two enterprise beans. Note that in our scenario, PayrollEJB preexisted the development of Wombat's benefits application.

1. Aardvark implements PayrollEJB.

2. Aardvark creates the `payroll_ejb_client.jar` JAR file, which contains the client-view interfaces and classes for PayrollEJB's client view. Aardvark makes the `payroll_ejb_client.jar` file available to companies that have a need to invoke PayrollEJB.

3. Star Enterprise deploys PayrollEJB at its site. When it deploys PayrollEJB, it also makes the PayrollEJB's home object available to other applications in the JNDI name space.

4. Wombat obtains the `payroll_ejb_client.jar` file from Aardvark. The class EnrollmentBean imports the package `com.aardvark.payroll` and uses the Payroll and PayrollHome interfaces to invoke PayrollEJB.

5. Wombat declares the dependency on PayrollEJB interfaces using the EJB reference mechanism. The EJB reference is an environment entry in the EnrollmentEJB's deployment descriptor.

6. When the deployer at Star Enterprise deploys the application from Wombat, he discovers the EJB reference to PayrollEJB. He resolves the EJB reference by linking it to the PayrollEJB's home object, which was created in step 3.

Keep in mind that the `payroll_ejb_client.jar` file created by Aardvark and used by Wombat contains all the Java class files that comprise the PayrollEJB's client view. Wombat needs the `payroll_ejb_client.jar` file when compiling the EnrollmentBean class. Because the EnrollmentEJB classes need access to the `payroll_ejb_client.jar` file at runtime, Wombat includes the `payroll_ejb_client.jar` file in the `benefits.ear` file. (The `benefits.ear` file contains the parts of the applications developed by Wombat.)

7.6.2 Client Provider Publishes EJB Client-View Interfaces

Let's look at how Wombat's Benefits Enrollment application integrates with the individual plan entity beans provided by the insurance companies. This is a good illustration of how a bean developed by one vendor implements the EJB client-view interfaces defined by another vendor.

1. Wombat designs the Plan and PlanHome interfaces. Wombat assumes that these interfaces will be implemented by the plan entity beans developed by the individual insurance companies. Wombat packages the class files for these interfaces with their dependent class files in the `plan_intf.jar` file, and makes the `plan_intf.jar` file available to the insurance companies.

2. Wombat develops the Benefits Enrollment application. The WrapperPlanBean component functions as the client of the plan entity beans developed by the insurance providers. WrapperPlanEJB uses the Plan and PlanHome interfaces to invoke the individual plan beans. (The fact that WrapperPlanBean also implements the Plan and PlanHome interface in its client view is irrelevant to the discussion here.)

3. An insurance company, such as Providence, obtains the `plan_intf.jar` file from Wombat. Providence implements the ProvidencePlanEJB entity bean so that its remote and home interfaces are compatible with the Plan and PlanHome interfaces.

4. The deployer at Star Enterprise deploys the Wombat Benefits Enrollment application.

5. The deployer at Star Enterprise deploys the ProvidencePlanEJB entity bean from Providence so that the home interface of ProvidencePlanEJB is made available to the BenefitsAdminWeb Web application. The deployer does this by binding the home interface object to an entry in the JNDI context that BenefitsAdminWeb uses to find all the deployed plan beans.

6. The BenefitsAdminWeb Web application finds the home interface of ProvidencePlanEJB at runtime, displays all the individual plans offered by Providence to Star Enterprise, and allows the Star Enterprise's benefits plan administrator to add one or more of the benefits plans to the list of plans aggregated by the WrapperPlanEJB entity bean. The benefits plan administrator adds the Providence benefits plans by calling the `create` method on the WrapperPlanEJB's home interface. This creates wrapper plan objects that are then used by the EnrollmentEJB bean.

Although the discussion of the integration of the benefits application with the individual plan beans seems complicated, in reality it is not. The apparent complication is the result of Wombat's action combining the integration of the individual plans with their aggregation into a single entity bean (WrapperPlanEJB) at one time.

7.6.3   Use of Container-Managed Persistence

In this section, we look at how the bean provider can use CMP to integrate the application with existing databases and customer applications.

1. The customer (Star Enterprise, in this case) has EmployeeDatabase. Star Enterprise created EmployeeDatabase before the deployment of the Wombat benefits application. The designer of the EmployeeDatabase schema had no knowledge of the Wombat application. Many Star Enterprise applications use EmployeeDatabase to obtain employee information.

2. Wombat develops the benefits application. It develops the EmployeeEJB entity bean that provides the application's interface to the customer's employee data. The remainder of the Wombat application, including the EnrollmentEJB session bean, uses the EmployeeEJB client-view interfaces to access the customer's employee data. It is important to note that Wombat had no knowledge of the Star Enterprise's EmployeeDatabase schema when developing the EmployeeEJB entity bean. Wombat had to design the EmployeeEJB bean so that it works with many customers' employee databases.

3. When Star Enterprise deploys the Wombat application, the deployer has to bind the container-managed fields of EmployeeEJB to columns in the EmployeeDatabase database, which stores the Star Enterprise's employee information. The deployer may either use the tools provided by the container vendor or manually write code that performs the binding. For example, the deployer could write code to subclass the EmployeeBean class to create an entity bean with BMP, as illustrated with the SelectionEJB and WrapperPlanEJB entity beans.

CMP allows not only the integration of an EJB application with a relational database, but also the integration of an EJB application with non-EJB applications. For example, the EmployeeEJB bean can be integrated with an ERP system that a customer uses to manage its employee information. Because most ERP systems do not expose the database schema to third-party applications, the third-party applications need to invoke the integration interfaces published by the ERP vendor rather than accessing the ERP system's database directly. For example, if the benefits application needed to be integrated with an ERP system, the deployment-generated classes that implement the EmployeeEJB bean's CMP would make calls to the ERP applications rather than directly accessing the database used by the ERP system.

7.7 Conclusion

We have now completed our examination of entity beans. This chapter presented an employee Benefits Enrollment application that is very similar to the example presented earlier. However, this example was built and deployed using entity beans when appropriate, rather than relying completely on session beans.

The example application clearly illustrated the differences, from a developer's point of view, of using entity beans. It focused on the various techniques for working with entity beans, such as caching persistent state, aggregating application functionality into a single component, subclassing techniques, and so forth, and how best to use the features of these types of beans.

This chapter showed how entity beans are more appropriate for applications that must be easily adapted for different customers with different operational environments. Typically, these are applications built by ISVs rather than applications developed by an enterprise's in-house IT department.

CHAPTER 8

Understanding Transactions

THE EJB architecture provides for two kinds of transaction demarcation: container-managed transaction demarcation and bean-managed transaction demarcation. This chapter covers the essential aspects of transactions necessary for a typical application developer to know.

With the *container-managed transaction demarcation* approach, the EJB container does the bulk of the work of managing transactions for the programmer. This greatly simplifies the application developer's work when programming transactional applications. However, even though the container does the majority of the work, the bean provider or application assembler must still provide transaction-related instructions to the container. Part of this chapter describes how the example application described in Chapter 7, Entity Bean Application Example utilizes *transaction attributes,* which are special attributes set in the deployment descriptor to instruct the container on how to manage transactions for the benefits application.

This chapter also discusses *bean-managed transaction demarcation*. With this approach, the bean developer manages transaction boundaries programmatically from within the application code. The Benefits Enrollment application does not use bean-managed transaction demarcation. Instead, we discuss appropriate scenarios for using bean-managed transaction demarcation.

Application programmers benefit from developing their applications on platforms that support transactions. A transaction-based system simplifies application development because it frees the developer from the complex issues of failure recovery and multiuser programming. In addition, the EJB architecture does not limit transactions to single databases or single sites. The EJB architecture supports distributed transactions that can simultaneously update multiple databases across multiple sites.

How is this accomplished? The EJB architecture permits the work of an application to, typically, be divided into a series of units. Each unit of work is a separate transaction. While the application progresses, the underlying system ensures that each unit of work—each transaction—fully completes without interference from other processes. If not, the system rolls back the transaction, completely undoing whatever work the transaction had performed.

The EJB architecture allows enterprise beans to utilize a declarative style of transaction management that differs from the traditional transaction management style. With declarative management, the enterprise bean application declares transaction attributes in the deployment descriptor. These transaction attributes describe how to partition the work of an application into separate, discrete units of work. The transaction attributes indicate to the container how it should apply transaction management to the execution of the bean's methods.

Using the traditional transaction management approach, the application was responsible for managing all aspects of a transaction. This entailed such operations as

- Explicitly starting the transaction

- Committing or rolling back the transaction

- Suspending and resuming the transaction association, particularly for applications that need more sophisticated transaction demarcation

A developer is required to have more programming expertise to be able to write an application that is responsible for managing a transaction from start to finish. The code for such an application is more complex, and thus more difficult to write, and it is easy for "pilot error" to occur (for example, a programmer may forget to commit a transaction). Furthermore, it is hard to reuse components that programmatically manage transaction boundaries as building blocks for applications with additional components.

With declarative transaction management, the container manages most if not all aspects of the transaction for the application. The container handles starting and ending the transaction, plus it maintains its context throughout the life of the transaction. The container automatically propagates the transaction context into invoked enterprise beans and resource managers, based on the declarative instructions in the deployment descriptor. This greatly simplifies an application developer's responsibilities and tasks, especially for transactions in distributed environments. In addition, it means that the components are reusable as building blocks for other applications, which are composed of multiple components.

8.1   Declarative Transaction Demarcation

Most applications are best off using the container-managed transaction demarcation feature. This feature is commonly referred to as *declarative transaction demarcation* or *declarative transactions*. For this feature to work, application developers set up transaction attributes separate from their code: A transaction attribute is associated with each enterprise bean method. The EJB container uses these attributes to determine how it should handle transaction demarcation for that method. As a result, the application programmer does not need to include transaction demarcation code in the application.

8.1.1   Transaction Attributes

When a client invokes a method of an enterprise bean using the enterprise bean's home or remote interface, the container interposes on the method invocation to inject the container services. One of the services that the container injects is transaction demarcation.

The bean developer or application assembler uses the deployment descriptor to specify how the container should manage transaction demarcation. Essentially, the deployment descriptor allows the bean developer or application assembler to specify a transaction attribute for each method of the remote and home interfaces.

Keep in mind that there are some limitations on the methods to which transaction attributes may be assigned. The deployment descriptor may not assign a transaction attribute to all of the methods of the home and remote interfaces. For example, a session bean may define a transaction attribute only for the business methods defined in the bean's remote interface; it may not assign transaction attributes to the methods of the home interface. In addition, it may not assign transaction attributes to the methods defined in the EJBObject interface because the container implements these methods. Therefore, it is meaningless to define a transaction attribute for them.

Like a session bean, an entity bean may also define a transaction attribute for each of the business methods in the bean's remote interface. In addition, an entity bean may define transaction attributes for the `create` and find methods defined in the home interface, and for the `remove` methods inherited from the EJBObject and EJBHome interfaces. However, an entity bean may not define transaction attributes for all other methods defined in the EJBObject and EJBHome interfaces. Because the container implements these other methods, it would be meaningless for the entity bean to define a transaction attribute for them.

There is one implication of this rule that is important to note. The `create` and `remove` methods of an entity bean have transaction attributes, but the `create` and `remove` methods of a session bean do not have transaction attributes. The container treats the `create` and `remove` methods of a session bean as if they had the NotSupported transaction attribute.

8.1.2 Transaction Attribute Values

A transaction attribute may have one of six values:

1. Required

2. RequiresNew

3. Supports

4. NotSupported

5. Mandatory

6. Never

The following sections describe how transaction attributes are used. Table 8.1 on page 342 summarizes these transaction attributes.

Required Transaction Attribute

The Required transaction attribute is typically used for the bean methods that update databases or other transaction-capable resource managers. The Required transaction attribute ensures that all the updates from the method are performed atomically, and that the updates done by the enterprise bean method can be included in a larger transaction. A transaction is required in such scenarios to achieve application correctness.

How does the container interpret and apply the Required transaction attribute? If a method is assigned the Required transaction attribute, the container executes the method with a transaction context so that one of two events occurs.

1. If the method caller is already associated with a transaction context, the container includes the execution of the method in the client's existing transaction context.

2. If the method caller is not associated with a transaction context, the container starts a transaction before the execution of the method, and it commits the transaction after the method has completed.

The EnrollmentBean in the application in Chapter 7 uses the Required transaction attribute for the `commitSelections` method. By using this attribute for this method, the application ensures that the updates to BenefitsDatabase and the Payroll System are performed as a single transaction.

RequiresNew Transaction Attribute

The RequiresNew transaction attribute, like the Required attribute, is typically used for methods that update databases. However, methods that use the RequiresNew attribute should have the database updates committed regardless of the outcome of the caller's transaction.

The container applies the RequiresNew transaction attribute somewhat differently than the Required attribute. The container always executes a method that is assigned the RequiresNew transaction attribute in a new transaction context. This means that the container starts a new transaction before it executes the method, and it commits the transaction after the method completes. If the method caller is already associated with a transaction context at the time it calls the method, the container suspends the association for the duration of the new transaction.

In what situations would the RequiresNew transaction attribute be useful? An application service provider may want to track, for marketing or billing purposes, the applications that each of its users has executed. Use of the RequiresNew attribute enables the application service provider to implement such tracking. The service provider uses the enterprise bean ApplicationStatistics for collecting the application use information. Each time a user invokes an application, the application in turn invokes the `recordUsage` method on the ApplicationStatistics bean. The `recordUsage` method is assigned the RequiresNew transaction attribute to ensure that it records the use information even if the actual application rolls back its transaction. In contrast, if the Required attribute were used for the `recordUsage` method and the application rolled back its transaction, there would be no record that the user ran the application.

Supports Transaction Attribute

The Supports transaction attribute is used when a method does not absolutely require a transaction. When a method is assigned the Supports transaction attribute, the method's transaction context depends on the transaction context of the method caller. The container executes the method with or without a transaction context depending on whether the method caller is associated with a transaction context.

If the caller is associated with a transaction context, the container includes the method execution in the caller's transaction. (In this case, the container's execution of the method is the same as if the method had been assigned the Required transaction attribute.)

If the caller is not associated with a transaction context, the container executes the method in a manner that transaction semantics are not defined by the EJB specification. (In this case, the container's execution of the method is the same as if the method had been assigned the NotSupported transaction attribute.)

When would you use the Supports transaction attribute? You typically use this attribute for those methods in which atomicity of multiple updates from within the method is not an issue. These cases include methods that make no updates (directly or indirectly via other enterprise beans) to data. Or, they perform only a single data update operation that is guaranteed to be atomic by other mechanisms (such as atomicity of a SQL statement). The Supports attribute allows the container to avoid the overhead of using a transaction for executing a method when a transaction is not needed. At the same time, it tells the container to include the work of the method into the client's transaction when this is required.

NotSupported Transaction Attribute

A method may also be assigned the NotSupported transaction attribute. When a method is assigned the NotSupported attribute, the container invokes the method in a manner that transaction semantics are not defined by the EJB specification. Normally, the EJB specification allows the container to invoke a method with no transaction context, or in some container-specific local transaction context.

When a caller invokes a method with the NotSupported transaction attribute, and the caller is associated with a transaction context defined by the EJB specification, the container suspends the caller's transaction association for the duration of the method.

When would you use the NotSupported transaction attribute? There are two cases when you typically use the NotSupported transaction attribute. You would assign the NotSupported attribute to those methods of an enterprise bean that use resource managers not capable of interfacing with an external transaction coordinator, or when the correct application semantics do not depend on performing resource manager access in a transaction.

When an enterprise bean uses resource managers incapable of interfacing with an external transaction coordinator, the container cannot propagate the transaction context into the resource managers. Using the NotSupported transaction attribute for the bean's methods instructs the container that the application developer has taken into consideration the dependency on the less capable transaction manager.

Our example application uses the NotSupported attribute for the methods of the ProvidencePlanBean enterprise bean. ProvidencePlanBean uses the HTTP protocol to communicate with the Providence Web site. Because the HTTP protocol does not support propagating a transaction, the Providence assembler or bean developer assigned the NotSupported transaction attribute to all the methods of the ProvidencePlanBean enterprise bean. The bean developer designed the ProvidencePlanBean such that its communication with the Providence Web site does not require a transaction for its correctness.

Mandatory Transaction Attribute

When a method is assigned the Mandatory transaction attribute, the container first checks that the caller is associated with a transaction context. If the caller is *not* associated with a transaction context, the container throws the `javax.transaction.TransactionRequired` exception to the caller. If the client is associated with a transaction, the container performs the method invocation in the same way as for the Required attribute: The container includes the execution of the method in the client's existing transaction context.

When do you use the Mandatory transaction attribute? Use this attribute for a method for which an application assembly error would occur if the method was invoked by a caller without a transaction context.

Never Transaction Attribute

When a method is assigned the Never transaction attribute, the container first checks that the caller is associated with a transaction context. If the caller is associated with a transaction context, the container throws `java.rmi.RemoteException` to the client. If the caller is not associated with a transaction, the container invokes the method in the same way as the NotSupported attribute.

You use the Never attribute when you want the container to ensure that a transactional client does not invoke an enterprise bean method that is not capable of transaction.

Summary of Transaction Attributes

Table 8.1 provides a summary of the transaction context that the EJB container passes to an invoked business method. The table also illustrates the transaction context that the container passes to the resource managers called by the invoked business method. As illustrated, the transaction context passed by the container is a function of the transaction attribute plus the client's transaction context.

In Table 8.1, T1 represents a transaction passed with the client request, whereas T2 represents a transaction initiated by the container. Keep in mind that the enterprise bean's business method may invoke other enterprise beans, via their home and remote interfaces. When this occurs, the transaction indicated beneath the column entitled Transaction Associated with Business Method is passed as part of the client context to the target enterprise bean.

Table 8.1   Summary of Transaction Attributes

Transaction Attribute	Client's Transaction	Transaction Associated with Business Method	Transaction Associated with Resource Managers
Required	None	T2	T2
	T1	T1	T1
RequiresNew	none	T2	T2
	T1	T2	T2
Supports	None	None	None
	T1	T1	T1
NotSupported	None	None	None
	T1	None	None
Mandatory	None	Error	NA
	T1	T1	T1
Never	None	None	None
	T1	Error	NA

Note on Transaction Attributes for Entity Beans

As explained in Using the `ejbLoad` and `ejbStore` Methods on page 196, an entity bean may use the `ejbLoad` and `ejbStore` methods to perform caching of data. For this caching to work correctly, the container must combine the `ejbLoad` method, the business methods, and the `ejbStore` method into a single transaction.

This means that, if the bean depends on the `ejbLoad` and `ejbStore` methods to manage caching, it should not be using the NotSupported, Supports, and Never transaction attributes.

8.1.3   Transaction Attributes for Sample Application

Table 8.2 shows the transaction attributes used for methods of the entity bean sample application, the application in Chapter 7. Following the table is an explanation of why these attributes were assigned in this manner.

Wombat assigned the Required transaction attribute to the `commitSelections` method defined in the Enrollment remote interface. The `commitSelections` method updates multiple databases, and therefore Wombat uses a transaction to achieve atomicity of the multiple updates. Wombat assigned the Supports attribute to all other methods of the Enrollment remote interface because these methods do not require a transaction for their correctness (the methods only read data from the database).

Table 8.2   Sample Application for Method Transaction Attributes

Enterprise Bean Name	Method Name	Transaction Attribute
Enrollment	getEmployeeInfo, getCoverageOptions, setCoverageOption, getMedicalOptions, setMedicalOption, getDentalOptions, setDentalOption, getSmokerStatus, setSmokerStatus, getSummary	Supports
	commitSelections	Requires
Selection	getCopy, updateFromCopy, remove	Requires
SelectionHome	findByPrimaryKey, findByEmployee, findByPlan, remove	Requires
WrapperPlan	getPlanInfo, getPlanType, getCost, getAllDoctors, getDoctorsByName, getDoctorsBySpecialty, remove	Requires
WrapperPlanHome	findByPlanId, findByPrimaryKey, findMedicalPlans, findDentalPlans, findByDoctor, create, remove	Requires
Employee	getCopy, updateFromCopy, remove	Requires
EmployeeHome	findByPrimaryKey, remove	Requires
PremiumHealthPlan	getPlanInfo, getPlanType, getCost, getAllDoctors, getDoctorsByName, getDoctorsBySpecialty, remove	Requires
PremiumHealth-PlanHome	findByPlanId, findByPrimaryKey, findMedicalPlans, findDentalPlans, findByDoctor, create, remove	Requires
ProvidencePlan	getPlanInfo, getPlanType, getCost, getAllDoctors, getDoctorsByName, getDoctorsBySpecialty, remove	NotSupported
ProvidencePlan-Home	findByPlanId, findByPrimaryKey, findMedicalPlans, findDentalPlans, findByDoctor, remove	NotSupported
Payroll	setSalary, getSalary, setBenefitsDeduction, getBenefitsDeduction	Supports

Wombat assigned the Required transaction attribute to all the methods of all the entity beans. Using the Required attribute is typical for methods of an entity bean because it guarantees that the container includes the execution of the ejbLoad method, the business methods, and the ejbStore method in a single transaction. See Using the ejbLoad and ejbStore Methods on page 196.

Similarly, Premium Health assigned the Required transaction attribute to all the methods of the PremiumHealthPlanEJB. These methods access Premium-HealthDatabase.

Providence assigned the NotSupported transaction attribute to all the methods of the ProvidenceEJB enterprise bean. Providence did so because these methods invoke the ProvidenceServiceWeb application using the HTTP protocol, which does not propagate a transaction context from the client to the Web server. Providence designed the ProvidenceEJB enterprise bean and the ProvidenceService-Web application so that they work correctly without transaction propagation.

8.2   Programmatic Transaction Demarcation

The preferred way to demarcate transactions in EJB applications is to use transaction attributes. By using transaction attributes, the bean developer does not have to manage transaction boundaries programmatically in the enterprise bean's code. However, although declarative transaction demarcation via transaction attributes works in most cases, there are situations in which the declarative demarcation does not provide the required functionality, or in which declarative demarcation is awkward to use (such as when it forces the application developer to partition the application unnaturally into multiple enterprise beans to achieve the required transaction demarcation).

This section discusses when and how the application developer should use programmatic transaction demarcation to control transaction boundaries programmatically. The application developer may control the transaction boundaries programmatically either in the client code for the enterprise bean, or directly in the enterprise bean business methods. The following sections describe the usage of these techniques.

8.2.1   Transaction Demarcated by a Client

Typically, an enterprise bean client (such as a Web application or a stand-alone Java client application) does not manage transaction boundaries. Instead, the client invokes methods on an enterprise bean, and the EJB container in which the target enterprise bean is deployed automatically manages transactions based on the values of the transaction attributes for the invoked method. This container-provided transaction demarcation is transparent to the client. The client either sees a successful completion of the invoked method, or, if an error occurs, receives the `java.rmi.RemoteException` exception from the invoked method.

Certain situations require the client to demarcate transactions programmatically. Typically in these situations, the client needs to combine the invocation of multiple methods into a single transaction. The methods can be on the same enterprise bean or they can be on multiple beans. For this to work, the client needs to demarcate transactions programmatically, which the client accomplishes using the javax.transaction.UserTransaction interface. (The javax.transaction.UserTransaction interface is part of the Java Transaction API (JTA). More information about JTA is available at `http://java.sun.com/j2ee/docs.html`.) The client obtains the javax.transaction.UserTransaction interface from its environment using the JNDI name `java:comp/UserTransaction`.

The MyServlet servlet, which transfers funds from one bank account to another, illustrates this. Figure 8.1 shows the OID for the interactions that occur during MyServlet's operation.

MyServlet executes the funds transfer in a single transaction by using the TransferFunds Java Bean component. (Note that TransferFunds is not an enterprise bean.) However, as far as the discussion of transactions is concerned, the TransferFunds bean is considered part of the servlet. Code Example 8.1 shows the MyServlet code.

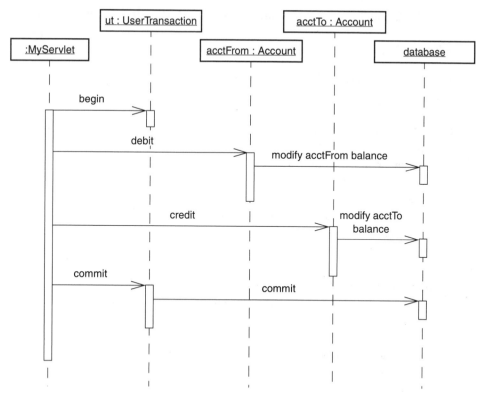

Figure 8.1 MyServlet OID

Code Example 8.1   MyServlet Class

```
public class MyServlet extends HttpServlet {
   public void service(ServletRequest req, ServletResponse resp) {
      ...
      TransferFunds transferFunds = new TransferFunds();
      transferFunds.setAccountFrom(...);
      transferFunds.setAccountTo(...);
      transferFunds.setAmount(...);
      try {
         transferFunds.execute();
      } catch (TransferException ex) {
         ...
      }
      ...
   }
}
```

Code Example 8.2 shows the code for the TransferFunds JavaBean.

Code Example 8.2   TransferFunds JavaBean Class

```
import javax.transaction.*;
...

public class TransferFunds {
   String accountNumberFrom;
   String accountNumberTo;
   double amount;

   public void setAccountFrom(String accountNumber) {
      accountNumberFrom = accountNumber;
   }

   public void setAccountTo(String accountNumber) {
      accountNumberTo = accountNumber;
   }

   public void setAmount(double amt) {
         amount = amt;
   }
```

```
public void execute() throws TransferException
{
    UserTransaction ut = null;

    try {
        ...
        AccountHome h1 = ...;
        AccountHome h2 = ...;
        Account acctFrom = h1.findByPrimaryKey(
                            accountNumberFrom);
        Account acctTo = h2.findByPrimaryKey(
                            accountNumberTo);

        // Obtain the UserTransaction interface.
        Context initCtx = new InitialContext();
        ut = (UserTransaction)initCtx.lookup(
                "java:comp/UserTransaction");

        // Perform the transfer.
        ut.begin();
        acctFrom.debit(amount);
        acctTo.credit(amount);
        ut.commit();
        // Transfer was completed.
    } catch (Exception ex) {
        try {
            if (ut != null)
                ut.rollback();
        } catch (Exception ex) {
        }
        // Transfer was not completed.
        throw new TransferException(ex);
    }
}
```

Let's take a closer look at the implementation of the execute method of the
TransferFunds JavaBean. The servlet client uses the execute method to accomplish a number of tasks. The client code works as described in the next paragraph,
assuming that it does not encounter any failures.

First, the client obtains the remote interfaces for the two accounts, `acctFrom` and `acctTo`, involved in the transaction. The client then uses the JNDI API to obtain a reference to the UserTransaction interface from the servlet's environment. Once the client obtains the reference, it starts a transaction using the `begin` method of the UserTransaction interface. The client then debits the `acctFrom` account and credits the `acctTo` account. Finally, the client commits the transaction using the `commit` method of the UserTransaction interface.

However, what is even more interesting is how the `execute` method deals with failures. Notice that the `execute` method wraps all its statements in a `try` block. If the execution of the statements in the `try` block raises an exception, then this executes the block of code in the `catch` clause. The block of code in the `catch` clause attempts to roll back the in-progress transaction started by the `execute` method and throws `TransferException` to the caller.

If the servlet container crashes before the transaction is committed, the transaction manager will automatically roll back all updates performed by the `execute` method. For example, if the `execute` method debited `acctFrom` before the servlet container crashed, the transaction manager instructs the database that stores `acctFrom` to roll back the changes caused by the `debit` operation.

8.2.2   Transaction Demarcation by a Session Bean

A session bean can use the UserTransaction interface to demarcate transactions programmatically. However, an entity bean cannot use the UserTransaction interface. In this section we describe a typical scenario in which the session bean developer uses the UserTransaction interface to demarcate a transaction rather than relying on the declarative transaction demarcation via transaction attributes.

The J2EE platform does not allow a stand-alone Java application to use the UserTransaction interface. How can a stand-alone Java application perform multiple invocations to an enterprise bean within a single transaction if it cannot use the UserTransaction interface? The application can use the bean-managed transaction demarcation feature of the EJB specification to combine multiple client-invoked methods into a single transaction. It would be impossible for a stand-alone Java application to achieve this—combining multiple client-invoked methods into a single transaction—with declarative transaction demarcation.

We illustrate this using the session bean example from Chapter 4. Let's assume that a stand-alone Java client application uses the EnrollmentEJB session bean in that example. Let's further assume, for the sake of this illustration, that the logic of the Benefits Enrollment application requires that all data access performed by the multiple steps of the entire enrollment business process be part of a single transaction. (This is not a very realistic example!)

In such a scenario, the application developer would design the EnrollmentEJB session bean as a bean with bean-managed transaction demarcation. The developer would modify the EnrollmentBean class (described in EnrollmentBean Session Bean Class Details on page 80) to obtain and use the UserTransaction interface in the `ejbCreate` and `commitSelections` methods, as illustrated in Code Example 8.3.

Code Example 8.3   EnrollmentBean Class with Bean-Managed Transaction
Demarcation

```
public class EnrollmentBean implements SessionBean
{
   UserTransaction ut = null;
   ...
   public void ejbCreate(int emplNum) throws EnrollmentException
   {
      // Obtain the UserTransaction interface from the
      // session bean's environment.
      Context initCtx = new InitialContext();
      ut = (UserTransaction)initCtx.lookup(
               "java:comp/UserTransaction");

      // Start a transaction.
      ut.begin();

      // The rest of the ejbCreate method
      employeeNumber = emplNum;
         ...
   }
   ...
   public void commitSelections() {

      // Insert new or update existing benefits selection record.
      if (recordDoesNotExist) {
         benefitsDAO.insertSelection(selection);
         recordDoesNotExist = false;
      } else {
         benefitsDAO.updateSelection(selection);
      }
```

```
// Update information in the payroll system.
try {
    payroll.setBenefitsDeduction(employeeNumber,
                                   payrollDeduction);
} catch (Exception ex) {
    throw new EJBException(ex);
}

// Commit the transaction started in ejbCreate.
try {
    ut.commit();
} catch (Exception ex) {
    // Handle exception from commit.
    ...
}
}
...
}
```

The `ejbCreate` method starts a transaction that then spans all the methods invoked by the client application. The `commitSelections` method commits the transaction after the client application has completed its work. Figures 8.2 and 8.3 show the OIDs for these transaction operations.

The OID diagrams illustrate the interactions between the Enrollment session object and the transaction manager that take place via the UserTransaction interface. They also illustrate the interactions between the transaction manager and the corporate databases.

The Enrollment session object starts the transaction by invoking the `begin` method on the UserTransaction interface. This causes the container to include the access to the corporate databases performed by the Enrollment object as part of the transaction. As the OID diagram illustrates, the container enlists the corporate databases with the transaction.

In addition, when the Enrollment object invokes the Payroll object, the container propagates the transaction context to the Payroll object to include the payroll deduction update as part of the transaction.

Finally, the Enrollment object commits the transaction by invoking the `commit` method on the UserTransaction interface. The transaction manager instructs the corporate databases to commit the changes made by the transaction. If the corporate databases are located on multiple servers, the transaction manager performs the two-phase commit protocol.

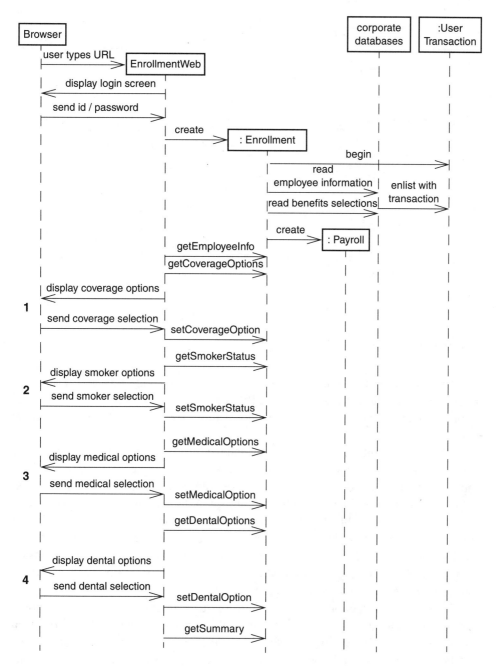

Figure 8.2   Transaction OID, Part One

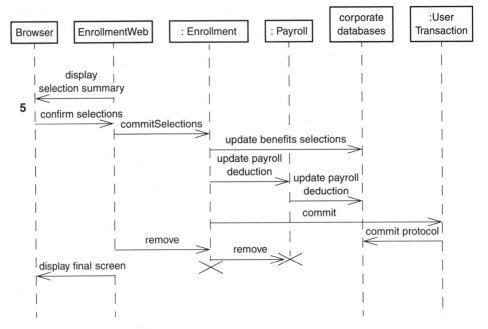

Figure 8.3 Transaction OID, Part Two

All the accesses to the corporate databases between the `UserTransaction.begin` method invoked in the `ejbCreate` method and the `UserTransaction.commit` method invoked at the end of the `commitSelections` method are part of a single transaction.

What are the pitfalls of using bean-managed transaction demarcation? As we stated earlier, bean-managed transaction demarcation is typically used to combine multiple client-invoked methods into a single transaction. This means that a transaction is "in progress" across a client's multiple interactions with the application. The transaction may block other transactions because a transaction causes the resource managers to hold locks on the data accessed by the transaction. If a user works slowly, or leaves the application in the middle of the in-progress transaction, the transaction may block all other users' transactions that need access to the data now locked by the slow user's transaction.

Therefore, transactions that span multiple user interactions with an application should be used only in environments with a small population of well-behaved users. And, just as important, they should always be used with a great deal of care.

For example, it would be very unusual if a Web-based application—with its multitude of unregulated users—used transactions that span user interactions. For this reason, the benefits applications described in Chapter 4 and in Chapter 7 do not use transactions that span interactions with the user.

8.2.3   Pitfalls of Using Programmatic Transaction Demarcation

The developer using programmatic transaction demarcation needs to be very careful in the placement of the `begin`, `commit`, and `rollback` calls in the application code.

- The programmer must ensure that `begin` is not called when the application is already associated with a transaction. J2EE does not support nested transactions.

- The programmer must ensure that the application will eventually commit or roll back the transaction. This may be nontrivial if the application code has many execution paths and Java exceptions are thrown. If the application does not commit or roll back a transaction, the transaction manager will eventually time-out the transaction and roll it back. Before the time-out expires, the locks held by the transaction may block other transactions from making progress.

Therefore, an application developer should use declarative transaction demarcation whenever possible, and apply programmatic transaction demarcation only for those cases for which declarative transaction demarcation does not work. The container implements declarative transaction demarcation and properly handles all the application execution paths.

8.3   Conclusion

This chapter explained the different transaction attributes defined by the EJB architecture. It showed how to apply these attributes with declarative transaction demarcation. The chapter also explained and demonstrated how to do transaction demarcation by clients and by session beans.

From here, we move to the issues surrounding security. Chapter 9, Managing Security, describes how to handle security from the point of view of application developers and deployers.

Managing Security

SECURITY is of paramount importance for an enterprise. The EJB architecture provides comprehensive support for security management. This support is particularly useful given the wide variety of protocols and security mechanisms that enterprises may employ today.

This chapter describes the EJB security environment from the point of view of an application developer. In particular, it discusses how an application developer handles security. It also focuses on how the deployer maps this security view to the actual security management infrastructure of the enterprise.

In today's environment, it is commonplace for EJB applications to control important business functions in the enterprise. Enterprise beans routinely have access to confidential data in the enterprise. To ensure the continued integrity and confidentiality of this data, it is important that only authorized users be permitted to invoke enterprise bean methods. An authorized user is a user whose position or role in the enterprise necessitates that he perform the business function implemented by the method, or it may be someone whose managerial responsibilities necessitate access to these business functions. For example, in the case of our example entity bean application in Chapter 7, it is important to ensure that confidential employee information, such as an employee's payroll data, is accessible only to the users who are authorized to access the information (for example, the payroll department).

The basic security management problem that confronts an application developer is the diversity of security management approaches. Different enterprises manage security in many different ways in their operational environments. Most often, the goal of an application developer is to develop an application that can be deployed in multiple operational environments. When each such operational environment uses different security mechanisms and policies, it becomes a real challenge to address the security needs of the application.

Because both the application developer and the deployer potentially share the responsibilities for security management, a fine line must be maintained between the two because there are trade-offs when one or the other takes responsibility for implementing security policies. On the one hand, when the application developer designs and codes the security policies into the application, it is easier for the deployer to deploy the application if the policies meet the needs of the operational environment. However, the same application is no longer reusable across multiple operational environments.

On the other hand, if the application developer leaves the security of the application to the deployer, the deployer must be familiar with the intimate details of the application to secure it in the operational environment.

The EJB architecture is designed so that the deployer bears the most burden for securing an application. At the same time, the EJB architecture makes the deployer's job easier. The security support in the EJB architecture allows the application developer to pass certain security-related information to the deployer. This information frees the deployer from having to understand the intimate details of the application in order to secure it.

The EJB architecture carefully apportions the responsibility for the security of EJB applications across the multiple EJB roles. The following sections describe the security responsibilities of the individual EJB roles.

9.1   Responsibilities of the System Administrator

The system administrator is responsible for the overall security configuration of the enterprise's network environment. Although most of the system administrator's tasks are independent from specific applications deployed in the enterprise, these security administration tasks affect the deployment of EJB applications.

In this section, we describe the security administration procedures relevant to the discussion of EJB application security. Keep in mind that the EJB specification does not define or require these procedures; rather, these procedures are typically used in enterprise environments.

The following system administration tasks are relevant to the deployment of an EJB application.

- **Administering security principals**—A security principal roughly corresponds to a user account. Administering security principals includes such tasks as adding and removing user accounts, adding a user account to the appropriate user groups, and so forth. A user group represents a group of users that has a certain set of privileges. A user account may belong to multiple user groups.

- **Managing the necessary principal mappings on the enterprise's network**—Principal mapping is required in certain circumstances when related applications run in different security domains. For example, the system administrator must manage principal mapping when an application running in one security domain invokes an application or a database in a different security domain, and each security domain has its own set of security principals.

- **Integrating the EJB container into the enterprise's secure network environment**

Let's look at some of the tasks that a system administrator at Star Enterprise may perform that are relevant to the deployment of the benefits application described in Chapter 7.

9.1.1 Administering Users and Security Principals

To begin, the Star Enterprise system administrator manages the user accounts and user groups. When a new employee starts her job, the system administrator creates a user account for the employee. Depending on the employee's role in the enterprise, the system administrator adds the user account to the appropriate user groups. For example, Mary Smith joins the benefits administration department as the department director. The system administrator creates a user account for Mary Smith and adds her user account to the *employees, payroll-department,* and *directors* user groups.

The user account information is used both for *authentication* and *authorization* purposes. Authentication takes place at the time a user connects to the system. For example, when Mary Smith logs in to her computer, she first needs to authenticate herself—prove that she is indeed Mary Smith—to the enterprise network security manager.

After she authenticates herself, Mary's session is associated with a security token. The security token represents the information from her user account, including the user groups to which the user account belongs, and it allows applications and servers to check authorizations. When Mary invokes an application or a database on the enterprise's network, the security token is passed along with the request to the target application or database. The target application or database server uses the passed security token to check whether Mary Smith is authorized to access the requested application or data.

9.1.2 Managing Principal Mapping

Passing the security token works only if the target application or database system understands the security token. If the target application or database system is in a different security domain, then it may not understand the token. Such a situation necessitates one of two solutions:

1. The user needs to log in to the target system. Mary Smith has to log in a second time directly to the target application or database system.

2. The enterprise security infrastructure maps the security token associated with Mary Smith's original session with her computer to another security token that is usable on the target system.

This second technique is called *principal mapping* and it is managed by the system administrator. Principal mapping allows Mary Smith to use a single password only across the entire set of applications and database systems at Star Enterprise.

In our benefits application example, the Payroll System is an application running on a mainframe. The Payroll System does not understand the security token received from the network on which Mary Smith's computer resides. In order for the Payroll System to recognize Mary Smith—or any other user from that network—as an authorized user, the Payroll App Server EJB container (see Figure 7.2 on page 222) needs to perform principal mapping on the calls coming to the mainframe payroll application.

For the EJB container to perform principal mapping, the system administrator must have already set up the principal mapping. The principal mapping maps all clients of PayrollEJB to a single mainframe user. From the perspective of the mainframe, all instances of PayrollBean use the identity of a single mainframe user, which we'll call *payroll user*, to invoke the mainframe Payroll System. Within the mainframe environment, the payroll user is authorized to access all the information needed by PayrollEJB.

Figure 9.1 illustrates mapping of principals.

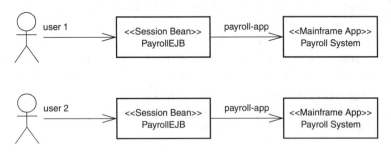

Figure 9.1   Principal Mapping

9.2   Responsibilities of the Container Provider

In EJB applications, the container bears most of the responsibility for enforcing application security at runtime. The EJB container is responsible for a number of tasks related to authentication and security principals. In addition, the container is responsible for tasks pertaining to the management of security in a multiapplication and multidomain environment.

The EJB container provider is responsible for providing the security mechanisms applicable to the target operational environment. Because the EJB container is typically an integral part of the security infrastructure of the operational environment, the EJB container interacts with the other parts of the operational environment to implement the security mechanisms.

9.2.1   Authentication and Authorization Tasks

There are several areas in which the container handles authentication and authorization tasks.

- **Authenticating principals**—Typically, the user accounts and the definitions of the user groups in the operational environment are stored in some external directory system rather than directly in the container. User accounts and groups are kept in an external directory from the container because all enterprise applications use this information, not just the EJB applications running in the container. Therefore, the container must be able to interface in a secure manner with the user account information. An enterprise may use either a proprietary protocol or standard protocol, such as Kerberos, for this purpose.

- **Enforcing method permissions**—The EJB container enforces the method permissions defined in the application's deployment descriptor. The EJB container dispatches a client-invoked method on an enterprise bean only if the client has been assigned a security role that has permission to invoke the target method. Otherwise, the container throws an exception to the client.

- **Controlling access to resource managers**—Many enterprise beans access resource managers such as databases. The EJB container is responsible for managing the authentication protocol with the resource manager based on the deployer's instructions.

9.2.2   Managing Multiple Applications and Domains

The container also has tasks related to managing security among multiple applications and multiple domains. Many enterprise environments run multiple applications, often across different security domains. The container, to ensure that no security breaches occur among the different applications, is responsible for the following tasks.

- **Ensuring the integrity of concurrent applications**—The container may execute multiple applications at the same time, may handle invocations from multiple clients at the same time, and may cache sensitive data in meory. The container ensures that this concurrent activity does not result in a security breach. The container must isolate the running applications and users from each other so that information is not "leaked" via the container from one application to another. In addition, the container ensures that data access by one user is not exposed to another user. The container should be implemented to be safe from security attacks.

- **Mapping principals between domains**—When clients from one security domain invoke enterprise beans in a different security domain, or the beans invoke other enterprise beans or other types of applications that are in different security domains, the container participates in the protocol for mapping the principals between the domains.

- **Keeping an audit trail**—The container typically maintains an audit trail of detected attempts to breach security. This audit trail is intended for the system administrator to identify security threats.

9.3   Application Provider's View of Security

An EJB application provider has essentially two choices for managing security.

1. The application provider can perform security management in the application code.

2. The application provider can delegate most of the security management to the deployer. The deployer then uses the facilities of the EJB container and the security infrastructure of the target operational environment to secure the application.

We discuss these two options from the perspective of user authentication and authorization.

9.3.1   Client Authentication

We recommend that EJB applications *not* perform user authentication logic in the application code. Instead, developers of EJB applications should rely on the deployer to ensure that the caller of an enterprise bean method has been authenticated prior to invoking the method. At runtime, the EJB container authenticates the client before the container dispatches a business method. The container makes the identity of the method caller available to the invoked enterprise bean method via the `getUserPrincipal` method of the EJBContext interface.

Why is it recommended that EJB applications not perform authentication logic? There are two reasons for this recommendation.

1. Developing bullet-proof authentication logic is not a simple application programming task. Unless the developer is a security expert, he may introduce a security hole in the application.

2. Hard-coding authentication logic makes the EJB application less reusable across multiple operational environments. For example, once authentication logic is embedded in the application code, it is impossible to deploy the enterprise bean in an operational environment that uses a single sign-on framework for all its applications.

9.3.2   Authorization

The guidelines for implementing authorization—the rules that specify which users can perform which business functions—are less straightforward than those for authentication.

Ideally, authorization rules should be decoupled from the application code. This permits the rules to be set based on the operational environment, and lets the container be responsible for their enforcement. When decoupled from the application code, the deployer can modify the authorization rules to meet the unique needs of the particular operational environment. Furthermore, decoupling the authentication logic from the application code enables the container to enforce the authentication rules rather than rely on the application to make the authorization checks itself. Because a vendor with expertise in security typically develops the container, the application overall is more secure when the container enforces the authentication rules.

However, in practice many authorization rules are too fine grained or too application specific (that is, the rules may be a function of data passed by the client and data read from a database) to be decoupled from the application code. An example of such a rule is one that states the following: An expense request larger than $5,000 must be approved by the division's vice president unless the requester is at least a director in the company, or the item to be expensed was purchased from a list of preapproved suppliers.

Consequently, developers must evaluate their own applications and decide whether to delegate an authorization rule to the container to enforce or to handle the rule as part of the application's business logic, and thus code its treatment in the application. We recommend using the following guidelines for this decision:

- Authorization rules that restrict access to the enterprise beans' methods to a group or groups of users should *not* be coded into the application. An example of such a rule is the following: Only users belonging to this department can invoke this method. Instead, use the EJB declarative security mechanism (see Declarative Security Mechanism) to define these authorization rules. When this mechanism is used, the EJB container enforces these authorization rules at runtime.

- Authorization rules that are too fine grained, or rules that use application-specific data, typically do not fit the EJB declarative security mechanism. The application developer should treat these rules as application logic and implement them in the application code. For these cases, however, the application developer should use good programming practices to separate the code implementing the authorization logic from the code implementing the rest of the business logic. This facilitates configuring, modifying, or replacing the authorization logic (if necessary) at application deployment. (Note that this is similar to separating the code implementing data access from the code implementing business logic.)

9.3.3 Declarative Security Mechanism

As mentioned previously, the EJB declarative security mechanism allows decoupling of a certain type of authentication rules from the business logic of the application. Here is how the EJB declarative security mechanism works.

The application provider uses the deployment descriptor to define a set of security roles and their associated method permissions for the enterprise beans. This information represents the client authorization rules intended by the application provider. The deployer uses this information as input when securing the application in a specific operational environment (Figure 9.2).

The definitions of the security roles and their associated method permissions simplify the deployer's task. The definitions of the security roles free the deployer from having to learn each enterprise bean method's function to determine who should be allowed to invoke that method. Instead, the deployer needs to understand a much smaller set of security roles to secure the application.

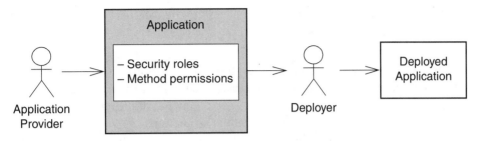

Figure 9.2 Declarative Security Mechanism

9.3.4 Security Roles

The definitions of the security roles advise the deployer on how the application provider envisioned the application will be used from a security perspective. Each security role represents an actor (a type of user) for the application. Each actor performs one or more use cases.

For example, Premium Health, who developed the PremiumHealthPlanEJB enterprise bean, may define two security roles in the `premiumhealth_ejb.jar` file deployment descriptor.

1. The *benefits-app* security role. This security role represents the benefits applications (such as the Wombat application) that invoke PremiumHealthPlanEJB to access the Premium Health plan information.

2. The *plan-admin* security roles. This security role represents the Premium Health plan administration staff that remotely manages the PremiumHealth-Database at the customer site.

9.3.5 Method Permissions

A method permission is a declaration in the deployment descriptor pertaining to security roles. You can think of a method permission as stating that a given security role invokes a given enterprise bean method when running the application. A method permission declaration instructs the tools used by the deployer to ensure that the users with the specified security role be allowed to invoke the method.

For example, Premium Health uses the method permission mechanism in the deployment descriptor to declare the following.

- The security role benefits-app should have access to the following methods: `findByPrimaryKey`, `findMedicalPlans`, `findDentalPlans`, `findByDoctor`, `getPlanId`, `getPlanName`, `getPlanType`, `getCost`, `getAllDoctors`, `getDoctorsByName`, and `getDoctorsBySpecialty`.

- The security role plan-admin needs access to the following methods: `create` and `remove`.

How do security roles and method permissions simplify the deployer's task? When the deployer deploys the `premiumhealth_ejb.jar` file, he is concerned only with the two security roles: benefits-app and plan-admin. He does not have to study each individual enterprise bean method's function.

Typically, the tools used by the deployer display the security roles and prompt him to assign individual users, or user groups, to each security role. The tools and the EJB container automatically ensure that assigned users or user groups have access to the methods specified in the method permissions.

9.3.6   Programmatic Security API

The EJB specification defines two methods in the EJBContext interface that allow an invoked enterprise bean method to obtain security information about the method's caller.

1. **`getCallerPrincipal`**—This method returns the java.security.Principal object representing the current caller. The enterprise bean can use this method to determine the current caller.

2. **`isCallerInRole`**—This method allows the enterprise bean method to test whether the current caller is assigned to a given security role defined in the deployment descriptor.

The application developer or deployer can use these two security methods in the enterprise bean application logic to perform programmatically the authentication checks that are not easily done using the declarative security mechanism.

We illustrate the use of the two methods in an example. Let's assume that the deployer of the PayrollEJB bean wants to allow each employee to access only his salary information (but not the salary of other employees) via the `getSalary` method. In addition, the deployer wants to allow the entire payroll staff to access the salaries of all employees. Note that this authentication rule cannot be expressed using the declarative security mechanism.

One possible way for the deployer to implement this authentication rule is to "subclass" the generic PayrollBean class, which has no security checks, and produce a StarPayrollBean class that includes the desired authentication check (Code Example 9.1).

Code Example 9.1   Adding Authentication Checks to a Bean

```
public class StarPayrollBean extends PayrollBean {
    Session sessionCtx;

    public double getSalary(int emplNumber) {
        Principal callerPrincipal = sessionCtx.getCallerPrincipal();
        int callerEmplNumber =
            Integer.parseInt(callerPrincipal.getName());

        if (sessionCtx.isCallerInRole("employee") &&
                    emplNumber == callerEmplNumber) ||
            sessionCtx.isCallerInRole("payroll-dept")) {
            // Allow access.
            return super.getSalary(emplNumber);
        } else {
            throw new SecurityException("access to salary denied");
        }
    }

    public void setSessionContext(SessionContext sc) {
        sessionCtx = sc;
        super.setSessionContext(sc);
    }
}
```

Notice that StarPayrollBean uses the `getCallerPrincipal` method to obtain the caller's principal, then invokes the `isCallerInRole` method to check the caller's role before allowing access to the salary data. If the caller's role is that of an employee (and the caller's employee number matches the employee number of the salary record) or the caller is part of the payroll department, then it permits access to the salary data; otherwise, it throws a security exception.

In our example, we illustrated how a deployer can use subclassing to add a fine-grained authorization rule to a method. Of course, the PayrollBean bean developer could implement this authorization rule directly in the PayrollBean class, but the PayrollBean would become less reusable.

9.3.7   Example Security Application

The example application from Chapter 7 uses the declarative security mechanism. In this section, we discuss the security views of each of the providers of the application's parts—the developer Wombat, and the two health benefits providers, Providence and Premium Health.

Wombat Developer's View of Security

The security view of the application developer at Wombat differs from that of the health benefits providers. Remember that the Wombat application developer has no knowledge of the security environment at the customer site, in this case Star Enterprise. For example, he does not know the user accounts or user groups defined by the system administrator at Star. Also, the developer has no knowledge of the security roles defined by the developers at Premium Health and Providence.

To handle this situation, an ISV analyzes its application from a security point of view, defining intended use cases of the different application parts and defining security roles for each case. Essentially, the developer details the functions that users of an application will perform, then defines distinct roles permitted to perform particular sets of functions.

Wombat defines three security roles that summarize the intended use cases of the Wombat application's parts from the security point of view.

1. **The employee security role**—This role represents the end user of the application (that is, an employee who uses the benefits self-service application). The employee security role is intended to perform only the benefits enrollment business process. It is not allowed, for example, to modify the benefits plans offered to employees.

2. **The benefits-admin security role**—This role represents the staff of the benefits department. The benefits-admin security role administers the benefits plans offered to employees.

3. **The benefits-app security role**—This is the security role assigned to the benefits application itself. Wombat uses this security role to describe the method permissions needed for the communication among the multiple enterprise beans supplied by Wombat. For example, Wombat uses the benefits-app security role to indicate that the EnrollmentEJB bean needs access to the `getCopy` method of the SelectionEJB bean.

After the Wombat developer identifies the security roles for the enterprise beans, he defines the method permissions that each security role must have to perform its application use cases. The method permissions are depicted in Table 9.1.

Table 9.1 illustrates that the employee security role needs to have access to all the methods of EnrollmentEJB. EnrollmentEJB, in turn, needs to have access to the methods of SelectionEJB, WrapperPlanEJB, and EmployeeEJB, because the implementation of EnrollmentEJB actually calls these methods (that is, these methods are called from the EnrollmentBean class).

Table 9.1   Security Roles for Wombat Methods

Enterprise Bean Name	Method Name	Security Role
Enrollment	`getEmployeeInfo`, `getCoverageOptions`, `setCoverageOption`, `getMedicalOptions`, `setMedicalOption`, `getDentalOptions`, `setDentalOption`, `getSmokerStatus`, `setSmokerStatus`, `getSummary`, `commitSelections`	employee
Selection	`getCopy`, `updateFromCopy`, `remove`	enrollment-app
SelectionHome	`findByPrimaryKey`, `findByEmployee`, `findByPlan`, `remove`, `create`	enrollment-app
WrapperPlan	`getPlanInfo`, `getPlanType`, `getCost`, `getAllDoctors`, `getDoctorsByName`, `getDoctorsBySpecialty`	enrollment-app
	`remove`	benefits-admin
WrapperPlanHome	`findByPlanId`, `findByPrimaryKey`, `findMedicalPlans`, `findDentalPlans`, `findByDoctor`	enrollment-app
	`create`, `remove`	benefits-admin
Employee	`updateFromCopy`, `remove`	
	`getCopy`	enrollment-app
EmployeeHome	`findByPrimaryKey`	enrollment-app
	`remove`	

Note that some enterprise bean methods, such as the `updateFromCopy` method of the EmployeeEJB's remote interface, are not associated with a security role. What does this mean? Wombat designed the interfaces of its enterprise beans to be used by other applications, not just by the enrollment application. The enrollment application does not use some of the methods, and these methods are not associated with a security role.

How should the deployer treat these methods? Unless the deployer wants to enable other applications to access to these methods, the deployer should simply disallow access to these methods.

Premium Health Developer's View of Security

The developer at Premium Health has a somewhat different security view. Similar to the Wombat developer, the Premium Health developer has no direct information about the operational environment at Star Enterprise, nor does he have direct knowledge of the security roles defined in the Wombat application. Therefore, he needs to describe the security view of the parts developed by Premium Health independently of the security views of both the customer site and Wombat. He describes Premium Health's security view in a way that does not depend, for example, on the users and user groups at Star Enterprise or on the security roles or the names of the enterprise beans developed by Wombat. Also, the developer at Premium Health has no knowledge of the security roles defined by the developer at Providence.

Remember that the PremiumHealthPlanEJB enterprise bean will be deployed at a customer site. The Premium Health developer identifies the intended types of clients of the bean, of which there are two.

1. **The benefits applications (that is, the Wombat application) running at the customer site**—These applications perform read-only access to the plan information provided by the PremiumHealthPlanEJB enterprise bean. Therefore, they need access only to the methods that return the plan information.

2. **The Premium Health plan administrators accessing the PremiumHealthPlanEJB enterprise bean remotely**—These plan administrators need full access to all the methods of the PremiumHealthPlanEJB bean.

Once he has identified the types of clients, the developer can define the security roles. The Premium Health developer defines two security roles that describe the two types of users. He names the security roles *benefits-app* and *ph-plan-admin*. The Premium Health developer then defines the method permissions for these roles, as shown in Table 9.2.

Table 9.2 illustrates that the benefits-app security role has access only to the methods that return plan information. It cannot access those methods that modify the plan information.

Table 9.2   Security Roles for Premium Health

Enterprise Bean Name	Method Name	Security Role
PremiumHealthPlan	`getPlanInfo`, `getPlanType`, `getCost`, `getAllDoctors`, `getDoctorsByName`, `getDoctorsBySpecialty`	benefits-app, ph-plan-admin
PremiumHealthPlanHome	`findByPlanId`, `findByPrimaryKey`, `findMedicalPlans`, `findDentalPlans`, `findByDoctor`	benefits-app, ph-plan-admin
	`create`, `remove`	ph-plan-admin

The ph-plan-admin security role has access to all the enterprise beans' methods. This allows the Premium Health plan administration department to modify the plan information at the customer site and to test that the methods used by the security role benefits-app return correct plan data.

Providence Developer's View of Security

At Providence, the developer's view of security is different from both Premium Health and Wombat. Again, keep in mind that the Providence developer has no direct information about Star Enterprise's operational environment nor of the Wombat application. Therefore, his security view must also be independent of the other applications. He needs to describe the security view of the parts developed by Providence in a way that does not depend, for example, on the users and user groups at Star Enterprise or on the security roles or the names of the enterprise beans developed by Wombat. The developer at Providence also has no knowledge of the security roles defined by the developer at Premium Health.

The Providence developer defines a single security role for the Providence-PlanEJB enterprise bean. He names the security role *customer* to signify that a customer's application, such as the Wombat application, that needs access to the Providence plan information should be assigned this security role. The Providence developer defines the method permissions so that the customer security role is granted access to all the methods of the ProvidenceEJB enterprise bean with the exception of the `remove` method. (He does not give the customer role access to the `remove` method because a customer application is not allowed to remove the plans offered by Providence.) Table 9.3 summarizes the method permissions for Providence's security roles.

Table 9.3   Security Roles for Providence

Enterprise Bean Name	Method Name	Security Role
ProvidencePlan	`getPlanInfo, getPlanType, getCost, getAllDoctors, getDoctorsByName, getDoctorsBySpecialty`	customer
	`remove`	
ProvidencePlanHome	`findByPlanId, findByPrimaryKey, findMedicalPlans, findDentalPlans, findByDoctor`	customer
	`remove`	

9.4   Deployer's Responsibility

Security deployment tasks, like all other application deployment tasks, are very specific to the facilities provided by the EJB container and to the overall operational environment. Therefore, we can only describe at a high level how the deployer addresses the security requirements when deploying the benefits application at Star Enterprise.

9.4.1   Deploying Wombat's Enterprise Beans

The deployer assigns the user group *all-employees* (this user group represents all Star employees) to the security role employee defined by the Wombat application. This ensures that all employees can use the application for benefits enrollment.

The deployer assigns the user group *benefits-department* to the benefits-admin security role defined by the Wombat application. This allows the members of Star Enterprise's benefits department to administer the benefits plans.

The deployer ensures that the container allows the enterprise beans of the application to invoke each other, as specified by the method permissions for the enrollment-app security role in Table 9.1 on page 367.

9.4.2   Deploying Premium Health's Enterprise Bean

The deployer needs to ensure that Wombat's benefits application is assigned the security role benefits-app defined by Premium Health. This allows the benefits application to invoke the PremiumHealthPlan bean's method that returns the plan information.

The deployer needs to ensure that Premium Health can remotely administer the information in PremiumHealthDatabase via the methods of the Premium-HealthPlan bean. Most likely, the deployer installs the PremiumHealthAdminWeb Web application on a Web server accessible from Premium Health, and assigns PremiumHealthAdminWeb to the security role ph-plan-admin defined by Premium Health.

9.4.3   Deploying Providence's Enterprise Bean

The deployer needs to ensure that the Wombat's benefits application is assigned the security role customer defined by Providence. This security role allows the benefits application to invoke the methods in the ProvidencePlan bean.

9.5 Conclusion

This chapter explained key security concepts and showed how security is handled within an EJB container. The EJB architecture shifts the responsibility for securing an application out of the hands of the application developer. Instead, it moves these security responsibilities to qualified vendors, such as EJB container and server vendors, who are experts in the security domain.

Configuring an application's security is also done outside the application code, principally by mapping the security roles and method permissions defined in the deployment descriptor to the users and user groups in the target operational environment. These tasks are declarative in nature and typically are carried out by the system administrator and deployer.

This chapter concludes the main portion of the book. It is followed by an API reference appendix for the EJB classes and methods. A second appendix lists some of the supporting code examples that are less central to the example applications.

API Reference

THE EJB architecture defines a set of classes and methods for implementing EJB applications. This appendix provides a reference to these classes and methods, as defined by the EJB 1.1 specification.

Figure A.1 shows a class hierarchy diagram for the EJB classes and interfaces.

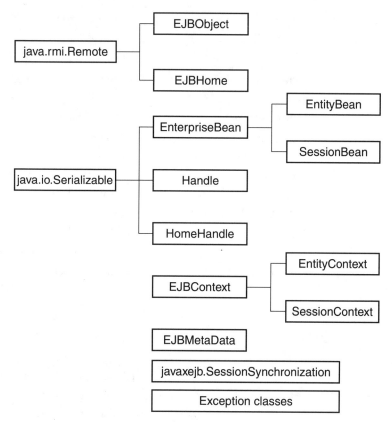

Figure A.1 EJB Class and Interface Hierarchy

Table A.1 lists the methods defined by the EJB interfaces.

Table A.1   EJB Methods

Interface	Method	Description
EJBObject	`getEJBHome`	Obtains the home interface
	`getHandle`	Obtains an object handle
	`getPrimaryKey`	Obtains an object's primary key
	`isIdentical`	Tests if two objects are identical
	`remove`	Removes an enterprise object
EJBHome	`getEJBMetaData`	Obtains the EJBMetaData interface
	`getHomeHandle`	Obtains the home object handle
	`remove`	Removes an enterprise object
EnterpriseBean	None	—
EJBContext	`getCallerIdentity`	Obtains the caller identity
	`getCallerPrincipal`	Obtains principal identifying the caller
	`getEJBHome`	Obtains the home interface
	`getEnvironment`	Obtains the environment properties
	`getRollbackOnly`	Tests if transaction is marked for rollback
	`getUserTransaction`	Obtains transaction demarcation interface
	`isCallerInRole`	Tests caller's security role
	`setRollbackOnly`	Marks transaction for rollback

Table A.1   EJB Methods *(Continued)*

Interface	Method	Description
EJBMetaData	getEJBHome	Obtains the home interface
	getHomeInterfaceClass	Obtains the home interface Class object
	getPrimaryKeyClass	Obtains the bean's primary key Class object
	getRemoteInterfaceClass	Obtains the remote interface Class object
	isSession	Tests if this is a session bean
	isStatelessSession	Tests if this is a stateless session bean
EntityBean	ejbActivate	Removes an instance from the pool of available instances
	ejbLoad	Loads the state of an instance from the database
	ejbPassivate	Ends an instance's association with a specific entity object
	ejbRemove	Removes an entity object
	ejbStore	Stores the state of an instance to the underlying database
	setEntityContext	Sets the associated entity context
	unsetEntityContext	Unsets the associated entity context
EntityContext	getEJBObject	Obtains a reference to the object associated with the instance
	getPrimaryKey	Obtains the primary key of the entity object associated with the instance
Handle	getEJBObject	Obtains the object reference represented by the handle
HomeHandle	getEJBHome	Obtains the home object reference represented by the handle

(continued)

Table A.1   EJB Methods *(Continued)*

Interface	Method	Description
SessionBean	`ejbActivate`	Activates an instance
	`ejbPassivate`	Ends an instance's association with a specific session object
	`ejbRemove`	Removes a session object
	`setSessionContext`	Sets the associated session context
SessionContext	`getEJBObject`	Obtains a reference to the object currently associated with the instance
SessionSynchronization	`afterBegin`	Notifies a session instance that a new transaction has started
	`afterCompletion`	Notifies a session instance that a transaction commit has completed
	`beforeCompletion`	Notifies a session instance that a transaction is about to commit

Table A.2 lists the EJB exception classes and the exceptions they define.

Table A.2   EJB Exception Classes

Exception Name	Description
`CreateException`	Thrown when there is a failure to create an entity bean object
`DuplicateKeyException`	Thrown when an entity object cannot be created because an object with the same key already exists
`EJBException`	Thrown by an instance when a method encounters an unexpected error
`getCausedByException`	Obtains the exception that caused an `EJBException` to be thrown
`FinderException`	Thrown to report a failure to find a requested enterprise bean object
`NoSuchEntityException`	Thrown when the underlying entity is no longer in the database

Table A.2 EJB Exception Classes *(Continued)*

Exception Name	Description
`ObjectNotFoundException`	Thrown by a find method when a specified object does not exist
`RemoveException`	Thrown when an attempt to remove an object does not succeed because the operation is not allowed

A.1   EJBObject Interface Methods

Each enterprise bean has a remote interface, which must extend the javax.ejb.EJBObject interface and define the enterprise bean's specific business methods. An enterprise bean's remote interface provides the client's view of an EJB object. That is, it defines the business methods that can be called by a client. The bean provider defines the remote interface and it is implemented by the EJB container.

The javax.ejb.EJBObject interface extends the java.rmi.Remote interface.

getEJBHome

```
public EJBHome getEJBHome() throws RemoteException;
```

Obtains the enterprise bean's home interface. The home interface defines the enterprise bean's `create`, find, and `remove` operations.

RETURNS:
A reference to the enterprise bean's home interface

EXCEPTIONS:
`RemoteException`	Thrown when the method fails because of a system-level error

getHandle

```
public Handle getHandle() throws RemoteException;
```

Obtains a handle for the enterprise object. The handle can be used later to reobtain a reference to the enterprise bean object, possibly from a different JVM.

RETURNS:
A handle for the enterprise bean object

EXCEPTIONS:

RemoteException   Thrown when the method fails because of a system-level failure

getPrimaryKey

public Object getPrimaryKey() throws RemoteException;

Returns the primary key of the enterprise object. This method can be invoked only on an entity bean. Invoking this method on a session bean results in a RemoteException error.

RETURNS:
The enterprise object's primary key

isIdentical

boolean isIdentical(EJBObject obj) throws RemoteException;

Tests if a specified enterprise object is identical to the invoked enterprise object

PARAMETERS:
obj   The object to test for identity with the invoked object

RETURNS:
True if the specified enterprise object is identical to the invoked object; otherwise, returns false

EXCEPTIONS:
RemoteException   Thrown when the method fails because of a system-level failure

remove

public void remove() throws RemoteException, RemoveException;

Removes the enterprise object

EXCEPTIONS:
RemoteException   Thrown when the method fails because of a system-level failure
RemoveException   Thrown when the enterprise bean or container does not allow the object to be destroyed

A.2   EJBHome Interface Methods

Every enterprise bean must have a home interface, and that home interface must extend the javax.ejb.EJBHome interface. An enterprise bean home interface defines methods that allow a client to create, find, and remove enterprise objects.

The enterprise bean provider defines the home interface, and the EJB container implements this interface.

The javax.ejb.EJBHome interface extends the java.rmi.Remote interface.

getEJBMetaData

```
EJBMetaData getEJBMetaData() throws RemoteException;
```
Obtains the EJBMetaData interface for the enterprise bean. The EJBMetaData interface allows the client to obtain information about the enterprise bean. This information is intended to be used by tools.

RETURNS:
The enterprise bean's EJBMetaData interface

EXCEPTIONS:
RemoteException   Thrown when the method fails because of a system-level failure

getHomeHandle

```
HomeHandle getHomeHandle() throws RemoteException;
```
Obtains a handle for the home object. The handle can be used at later time to reobtain a reference to the home object, possibly in a different JVM.

RETURNS:
A handle for the home object

EXCEPTIONS:
RemoteException   Thrown when the method fails because of a system-level failure

remove

```
void remove(Handle handle) throws RemoteException,
    RemoveException;
void remove(Object primaryKey) throws RemoteException,
    RemoveException;
```

Removes an enterprise object. In the first form, the method removes an enterprise object identified by its handle. In the second form, the method removes an object identified by its primary key.

PARAMETERS:

handle	A handle identifying the enterprise object
primaryKey	An object containing the primary key that identifies the enterprise object

EXCEPTIONS:

RemoteException	Thrown when the method fails because of a system-level failure
RemoveException	Thrown if the enterprise bean or the container does not allow the client to remove the object

A.3   EnterpriseBean Interface

The EnterpriseBean interface must be implemented by every enterprise bean class. It is the common superinterface for the SessionBean and EntityBean interfaces.

The javax.ejb.EnterpriseBean interface extends java.io.Serializable. It defines no methods.

A.4   EJBContext Interface Methods

The javax.ejb.EJBContext interface provides an enterprise bean instance with access to the container-provided runtime context for the instance. The javax.ejb.SessionContext and javax.ejb.EntityContext interfaces both extend EJB-Context, and they provide additional methods specific to their bean types.

getCallerIdentity

```
Identity getCallerIdentity();
```

Obtains the identity of the caller, or returns null. *This method has been deprecated.* The enterprise bean should use the getCallerPrincipal method instead of this method.

RETURNS:

The java.security.Identity object that identifies the caller, or null

getCallerPrincipal

`Principal getCallerPrincipal();`

Obtains the principal that identifies the caller

RETURNS:
The java.security.Principal object that identifies the caller. This method never returns null.

getEJBHome

`EJBHome getEJBHome();`

Obtains and returns the enterprise bean's home interface

RETURNS:
The enterprise bean's home interface

getEnvironment

`Properties getEnvironment();`

Obtains the enterprise bean's environment properties. If the enterprise bean has no environment properties, the method returns an empty java.util.Properties object; it never returns null. *This method has been deprecated.* You should use the JNDI naming context `java:comp/env` to access the enterprise bean's environment rather than this method.

RETURNS:
The environment properties for the enterprise bean as a java.util.Properties object

getRollbackOnly

`boolean getRollbackOnly() throws IllegalStateException;`

Tests if the transaction has been marked for rollback only. After an exception has been caught, an enterprise bean instance can use this operation, for example, to test whether it is worthwhile to continue computation on behalf of the current transaction. Only enterprise beans with container-managed transactions are allowed to use this method.

RETURNS:
True if the current transaction is marked for rollback; otherwise, returns false.

EXCEPTIONS:

IllegalStateException Thrown by the container if an instance is not allowed to use this method. An instance using bean-managed transactions is not allowed to use this method.

getUserTransaction

UserTransaction getUserTransaction() throws IllegalStateException;

Obtains the transaction demarcation interface. Only enterprise beans that use bean-managed transactions are allowed to use the UserTransaction interface, which this method returns. Because entity beans must always use container-managed transactions, only session beans with bean-managed transactions are allowed to invoke this method.

RETURNS:
The UserTransaction interface, which the enterprise bean instance can use for transaction demarcation

EXCEPTIONS:

IllegalStateException Thrown by the container if the enterprise bean instance is not allowed to use the UserTransaction interface. This exception is thrown if this method is called by an instance of a bean using container-managed transactions.

isCallerInRole

boolean isCallerInRole(String roleName);

Tests if the caller has a given security role. Note that the alternative form of this method—boolean isCallerInRole(Identity role);—has been deprecated. Use the form of the method specified here instead.

PARAMETERS:

roleName   The name of the security role. The security role must be a security role defined in the deployment descriptor.

RETURNS:
True if the caller has the specified role; otherwise, returns false

setRollbackOnly

`void setRollbackOnly() throws IllegalStateException;`

Marks the current transaction for rollback. The transaction becomes permanently marked for rollback. A transaction marked for rollback can never commit.

Note that only enterprise beans using container-managed transactions are allowed to use this method.

EXCEPTIONS:

`IllegalStateException` Thrown by the container if an instance that uses bean-managed transactions calls this method (because an instance using bean-managed transactions is not allowed to use this method)

A.5   EJBMetaData Interface Methods

The javax.ejb.EJBMetaData interface lets the client obtain the enterprise bean's metadata.

Metadata is intended for use by development tools building applications that use deployed enterprise beans. Metadata is also intended for clients using a scripting language to access the enterprise bean.

Note that the EJBMetaData interface is not a remote interface. A class implementing this interface is one that is typically generated by container tools. It must be serializable and a valid RMI or Java Interface Definition Language (IDL) value type.

getEJBHome

`EJBHome getEJBHome();`

Obtains the home interface of the enterprise bean

RETURNS:
The EJBHome object for the bean

getHomeInterfaceClass

```
Class getHomeInterfaceClass();
```
Obtains the Class object for the enterprise bean's home interface

RETURNS:
The Class object for the bean's home interface

getPrimaryKeyClass

```
Class getPrimaryKeyClass();
```
Obtains the Class object for the enterprise bean's primary key class

RETURNS:
The Class object for the bean's primary key class

getRemoteInterfaceClass

```
Class getRemoteInterfaceClass();
```
Obtains the Class object for the enterprise bean's remote interface

RETURNS:
The Class object for the bean's remote interface

isSession

```
boolean isSession();
```
Tests if the enterprise bean is a session bean type

RETURNS:
True if the type of the enterprise bean is that of a session bean

isStatelessSession

```
boolean isStatelessSession();
```
Tests if the enterprise bean is a stateless session bean type

RETURNS:
True if the type of the enterprise bean is that of a stateless session bean

A.6   EntityBean Interface Methods

Every entity bean class implements the javax.ejb.EntityBean interface. The container uses the EntityBean methods to notify the entity bean instances of the instance's life cycle events.

The javax.ejb.EntityBean interface extends the javax.ejb.EnterpriseBean interface.

ejbActivate

`public void ejbActivate() throws EJBException, RemoteException;`

Takes the instance out of the pool of available instances. A container invokes this method when the instance is taken out of the pool of available instances to become associated with a specific entity object. This method transitions the instance to the Ready state.

This method executes in an unspecified transaction context.

EXCEPTIONS:

`EJBException`	Thrown by the method to indicate that a system-level error caused the failure
`RemoteException`	Defined in the method signature to provide backward compatibility for enterprise beans written for the EJB 1.0 specification. Enterprise beans written for the EJB 1.1 (and higher) specification should throw `javax.ejb.EJBException` instead.

ejbLoad

`public void ejbLoad() throws EJBException, RemoteException;`

Loads an instance's state from the underlying database. A container invokes this method to instruct the instance to synchronize its state by loading its state from the underlying database. This method always executes in the transaction context determined by the value of the transaction attribute in the deployment descriptor.

EXCEPTIONS:

`EJBException`	Thrown by the method to indicate that a system-level error caused the failure

RemoteException   Defined in the method signature to provide backward compatibility for enterprise beans written for the EJB 1.0 specification. Enterprise beans written for the EJB 1.1 (and higher) specification should throw javax.ejb.EJBException instead.

ejbPassivate

```
public void ejbPassivate() throws EJBException, RemoteException;
```

Ends an instance's association with a specific entity object. The container invokes this method on an instance before the instance becomes disassociated from a specific entity object. After the method completes, the container places the instance in the pool of available instances.

EXCEPTIONS:

EJBException   Thrown by the method to indicate that a system-level error caused the failure

RemoteException   Defined in the method signature to provide backward compatibility for enterprise beans written for the EJB 1.0 specification. Enterprise beans written for the EJB 1.1 (and higher) specification should throw javax.ejb.EJBException instead.

ejbRemove

```
public void ejbRemove() throws RemoveException, EJBException,
    RemoteException;
```

Removes the entity object. A container invokes this method before it removes the entity object currently associated with the instance. This method is invoked when a client invokes a remove operation on the entity bean's home interface or remote interface.

This method transitions the instance from the Ready state to the pool of available instances. This method is called in the transaction context of the remove operation.

EXCEPTIONS:

EJBException   Thrown by the method to indicate that a system-level error caused the failure

RemoteException	Defined in the method signature to provide backward compatibility for enterprise beans written for the EJB 1.0 specification. Enterprise beans written for the EJB 1.1 (and higher) specification should throw `javax.ejb.EJBException` instead.
RemoveException	Thrown when the entity bean does not allow destruction of the object

ejbStore

`public void ejbStore() throws EJBException, RemoteException;`

Stores an instance's state to the underlying database. A container invokes this method to instruct the instance to synchronize its state by storing it in the underlying database. This method always executes in the transaction context determined by the value of the transaction attribute in the deployment descriptor.

EXCEPTIONS:

EJBException	Thrown by the method to indicate that a system-level error caused the failure
RemoteException	Defined in the method signature to provide backward compatibility for enterprise beans written for the EJB 1.0 specification. Enterprise beans written for the EJB 1.1 (and higher) specification should throw `javax.ejb.EJBException` instead.

setEntityContext

`public void setEntityContext(EntityContext ctx) throws EJBException,`
`RemoteException;`

Sets the associated entity context. The container invokes this method on an instance after the instance has been created. This method is called in an unspecified transaction context.

PARAMETERS:

ctx	An EntityContext interface for the instance. The instance should store the reference to the context in an instance variable.

EXCEPTIONS:

EJBException	Thrown by the method to indicate that a system-level error caused the failure
RemoteException	Defined in the method signature to provide backward compatibility for enterprise beans written for the EJB 1.0 specification. Enterprise beans written for the EJB 1.1 (and higher) specification should throw javax.ejb.EJBException instead.

unsetEntityContext

public void unsetEntityContext() throws EJBException, RemoteException;

Unsets the associated entity context. The container calls this method before removing the instance. Note that this is the last method invoked by the container on the instance. Eventually, the Java garbage collector invokes the finalize method on the instance.

This method is called in an unspecified transaction context.

EXCEPTIONS:

EJBException	Thrown by the method to indicate that a system-level error caused the failure
RemoteException	Defined in the method signature to provide backward compatibility for enterprise beans written for the EJB 1.0 specification. Enterprise beans written for the EJB 1.1 (and higher) specification should throw javax.ejb.EJBException instead.

A.7   EntityContext Interface Methods

The EntityContext interface provides an instance with access to the container-provided runtime context of an entity bean instance. The container passes the Entity-Context interface to an entity bean instance after the instance has been created.

The EntityContext interface remains associated with the instance for the lifetime of the instance. Note that the information the instance obtains using the EntityContext interface (such as the result of the getPrimaryKey method) may change as a result of the container assigning the instance to different entity objects during the instance's life cycle.

The javax.ejb.EntityContext interface extends the javax.ejb.EJBContext interface.

getEJBObject

`EJBObject getEJBObject() throws IllegalStateException;`

Obtains a reference to the enterprise object currently associated with the instance. An instance of an entity bean can call this method only when the instance is associated with an entity object identity. The instance is associated with an object identity in the `ejbActivate`, `ejbPassivate`, `ejbPostCreate`, `ejbRemove`, `ejbLoad`, `ejbStore`, and business methods.

An instance can use this method, for example, when it wants to pass a reference to itself in a method argument or result.

RETURNS:
The entity object currently associated with the instance

EXCEPTIONS:
`IllegalStateException` Thrown if the instance invokes this method while in a state that does not allow the invocation of this method

getPrimaryKey

`Object getPrimaryKey() throws IllegalStateException;`

Obtains the primary key of the entity object currently associated with the instance. An instance of an entity bean can call this method only when the instance is associated with an entity object identity, which it is in the `ejbActivate`, `ejbPassivate`, `ejbPostCreate`, `ejbRemove`, `ejbLoad`, `ejbStore`, and business methods.

Note that the result of this method is the same as the result of `getEJBObject.getPrimaryKey`.

RETURNS:
The entity object currently associated with the instance

EXCEPTIONS:
`IllegalStateException` Thrown if the instance invokes this method while in a state that does not allow the invocation of this method

A.8   Handle Interface Methods

All enterprise bean object handles implement the Handle interface. A handle is an abstraction of a network reference to an enterprise bean object. A handle is intended to be used as a "robust" persistent reference to an enterprise bean object.

The javax.ejb.Handle interface extends the java.io.Serializable interface.

getEJBObject

```
public EJBObject getEJBObject() throws RemoteException;
```
Obtains the enterprise bean object reference represented by this handle

RETURNS:
The enterprise bean object reference represented by the handle

EXCEPTIONS:
RemoteException   Thrown when the enterprise bean object cannot be obtained because of a system-level failure

A.9   HomeHandle Interface Methods

All enterprise bean home object handles implement the HomeHandle interface. A handle is an abstraction of a network reference to an enterprise bean home object. A handle is intended to be used as a "robust" persistent reference to an enterprise bean home object.

The javax.ejb.HomeHandle interface extends the java.io.Serializable interface.

getEJBHome

```
public EJBHome getEJBHome() throws RemoteException;
```
Obtains the enterprise bean home object reference represented by this handle

RETURNS:
The enterprise bean home object reference represented by the handle

EXCEPTIONS:
RemoteException   Thrown when the enterprise bean home object cannot be obtained because of a system-level failure

A.10 SessionBean Interface Methods

Every session bean class implements the SessionBean interface. The container uses the SessionBean methods to notify the session bean instances of the instance's life cycle events.

The javax.ejb.SessionBean interface extends the javax.ejb.EnterpriseBean interface.

ejbActivate

`public void ejbActivate() throws EJBException, RemoteException;`

> Activates the instance from its "passive" state and takes it out of the pool of available instances. A container invokes this method when the instance is taken out of the pool of available instances to become associated with a specific session object. The instance should acquire those resources that it had released earlier using the `ejbPassivate` method.
>
> This method is called with no transaction context.

EXCEPTIONS:

`EJBException`	Thrown by the method to indicate that a system-level error caused the failure
`RemoteException`	Defined in the method signature to provide backward compatibility for enterprise beans written for the EJB 1.0 specification. Enterprise beans written for the EJB 1.1 (and higher) specification should throw `javax.ejb.EJBException` instead.

ejbPassivate

`public void ejbPassivate() throws EJBException, RemoteException;`

> Ends an instance's association with a specific session object. The container invokes this method on an instance before the instance enters its "passive" state. The instance should release any resources that it holds; it can re-acquire these resources later using the `ejbActivate` method.
>
> After the method completes, the instance must be in a state that allows the container to use the Java serialization protocol to externalize and store the instance's state.
>
> This method is called with no transaction context.

EXCEPTIONS:

EJBException	Thrown by the method to indicate that a system-level error caused the failure
RemoteException	Defined in the method signature to provide backward compatibility for enterprise beans written for the EJB 1.0 specification. Enterprise beans written for the EJB 1.1 (and higher) specification should throw javax.ejb.EJBException instead.

ejbRemove

```
public void ejbRemove() throws EJBException, RemoteException;
```

Removes the session object. A container invokes this method before it ends the life of the session object. This method is invoked when a client invokes a remove operation or when a container decides to terminate the session object after a time-out.

This method is called with no transaction context.

EXCEPTIONS:

EJBException	Thrown by the method to indicate that a system-level error caused the failure
RemoteException	Defined in the method signature to provide backward compatibility for enterprise beans written for the EJB 1.0 specification. Enterprise beans written for the EJB 1.1 (and higher) specification should throw javax.ejb.EJBException instead.

setSessionContext

```
public void setSessionContext(SessionContext ctx) throws EJBException,
  RemoteException;
```

Sets the associated session context. The container invokes this method on an instance after the instance has been created. The session bean instance should store the reference to the context object in an instance variable.

This method is called with no transaction context.

PARAMETERS:

ctx	A SessionContext interface for the instance. The instance should store the reference to the context in an instance variable.

EXCEPTIONS:

`EJBException`	Thrown by the method to indicate a system-level error caused the failure
`RemoteException`	Defined in the method signature to provide backward compatibility for enterprise beans written for the EJB 1.0 specification. Enterprise beans written for the EJB 1.1 (and higher) specification should throw `javax.ejb.EJBException` instead.

A.11   SessionContext Interface Methods

The SessionContext interface provides access to the runtime session context provided by the container for a session bean instance. The container passes the SessionContext interface to an instance after the instance has been created. The session context remains associated with the instance for the lifetime of the instance.

The javax.ejb.SessionContext interface extends the javax.ejb.EJBContext interface.

getEJBObject

`EJBObject getEJBObject() throws IllegalStateException;`

Obtains a reference to the bean object that is currently associated with the instance. An instance of a session bean can call this method anytime between the execution of the `ejbCreate` and `ejbRemove` methods, including from within these two methods. An instance can use this method, for example, when it wants to pass a reference to itself in a method argument or in a method result.

RETURNS:
The enterprise bean object currently associated with the instance

EXCEPTIONS:

`IllegalStateException`	Thrown if the instance invokes this method while in a state that does not allow the invocation of this method

A.12 SessionSynchronization Interface Methods

The javax.ejb.SessionSynchronization interface allows a session bean instance to be notified by its container of transaction boundaries.

A session bean class is not required to implement this interface. However, it should implement this interface if it intends to synchronize its state with transactions.

afterBegin

```
public void afterBegin() throws EJBException, RemoteException;
```
Notifies a session bean instance that a new transaction has started. Subsequent business methods invoked on the instance will be invoked in the context of the transaction. An instance can use this method, for example, to read data from a database and cache the data in its instance fields.

This method executes in the proper transaction context.

EXCEPTIONS:

EJBException	Thrown by the method to indicate that a system-level error caused the failure
RemoteException	Defined in the method signature to provide backward compatibility for enterprise beans written for the EJB 1.0 specification. Enterprise beans written for the EJB 1.1 (and higher) specification should throw javax.ejb.EJBException instead.

afterCompletion

```
public void afterCompletion(boolean committed) throws EJBException,
    RemoteException;
```
Notifies a session bean instance that a transaction commit protocol has completed. It also informs the instance if the transaction committed or rolled back.

This method executes with no transaction context.

PARAMETERS:

committed	Set to true by the afterCompletion method if the transaction has been committed; otherwise, set to false to indicate that the transaction has been rolled back

EXCEPTIONS:

EJBException — Thrown by the method to indicate that a system-level error caused the failure

RemoteException — Defined in the method signature to provide backward compatibility for enterprise beans written for the EJB 1.0 specification. Enterprise beans written for the EJB 1.1 (and higher) specification should throw javax.ejb.EJBException instead.

beforeCompletion

public void beforeCompletion() throws EJBException, RemoteException;

Notifies a session bean instance that a transaction is about to be committed. An instance can use this method, for example, to write any cached data to a database.

This method executes in the proper transaction context.

Note: The instance may still cause the container to roll back the transaction. It can do so by invoking the setRollbackOnly method on the instance context, or it can throw an exception.

EXCEPTIONS:

EJBException — Thrown by the method to indicate that a system-level error caused the failure

RemoteException — Defined in the method signature to provide backward compatibility for enterprise beans written for the EJB 1.0 specification. Enterprise beans written for the EJB 1.1 (and higher) specification should throw javax.ejb.EJBException instead.

A.13 Exception Classes

This section contains the EJB-specific exception classes.

Figure A.2 shows the class hierarchy for the EJB exception classes.

A.13.1 CreateException Class

The javax.ejb.CreateException class, which extends the java.lang.Exception interface, defines a standard, application-level exception for reporting create failures.

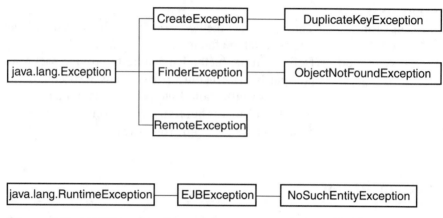

Figure A.2   EJB Exception Class Hierarchy

CreateException

```
public CreateException();
public CreateException(String message);
```

This exception is used as a standard, application-level exception to report a failure to create an entity bean object. All `create` methods defined in an enterprise bean's remote interface must include the `CreateException` exception in their `throws` clauses.

The first form of the constructor constructs `CreateException` with no detailed message. The second form constructs `CreateException` with the specified detailed message.

PARAMETERS:

message   The String object containing the exception message

A.13.2   DuplicateKeyException Class

The javax.ejb.DuplicateKeyException class, which extends `javax.ejb.Create-Exception`, defines the `DuplicateKeyException` exception.

DuplicateKeyException

```
public DuplicateKeyException();
public DuplicateKeyException(String message);
```

The DuplicateKeyException exception is thrown if an entity bean object cannot be created because an object with the same key already exists. The create methods defined in an enterprise bean's home interface may throw this exception.

The first form of the constructor constructs DuplicateKeyException with no detailed message. The second form constructs DuplicateKeyException with the specified detailed message.

PARAMETERS:

message   The String object containing the exception message

A.13.3 EJBException Class

The class javax.ejb.EJBException, which extends java.lang.RuntimeException, defines the EJBException exception.

EJBException

```
public EJBException();
public EJBException(String message);
public EJBException(Exception ex);
```

The EJBException exception is thrown by an enterprise bean instance to its container to report that the invoked business method or callback method could not be completed because of an unexpected error. An example of an unexpected error is when the instance fails to open a database connection.

The first form of the constructor constructs EJBException with no detailed message. The second form constructs EJBException with the specified detailed message. The third form constructs EJBException that has the originally thrown exception embedded within.

PARAMETERS:

message   The String object containing the exception message

ex   The original Exception object

getCausedByException

```
public Exception getCausedByException();
```

Obtains the exception that caused the EJBException to be thrown.

RETURNS:
The Exception object with the original thrown exception

A.13.4 FinderException Class

The javax.ejb.FinderException class, which extends the java.lang.Exception interface, defines a standard, application-level exception for reporting find operation failures.

FinderException

```
public FinderException();
public FinderException(String message);
```

This exception is used as a standard, application-level exception to report a failure to find requested enterprise bean objects. All find methods defined in an enterprise bean's home interface must include the FinderException exception in their throws clauses.

The first form of the constructor constructs FinderException with no detailed message. The second form constructs FinderException with the specified detailed message.

PARAMETERS:
message   The String object containing the exception message

A.13.5 NoSuchEntityException Class

The javax.ejb.NoSuchEntityException class, which extends the javax.ejb.EJBException class, defines the exception NoSuchEntityException.

NoSuchEntityException

```
public NoSuchEntityException();
public NoSuchEntityException(String message);
public NoSuchEntityException(Exception ex);
```

An enterprise bean instance throws the NoSuchEntityException exception to its container to report that the invoked business method or callback method could not be completed because the underlying entity is no longer in the database.

This exception may be thrown by the bean class methods that implement the business methods defined in the bean's remote interface. It may also be thrown by the `ejbLoad` and `ejbStore` methods.

The first form of the constructor constructs `NoSuchEntityException` with no detailed message. The second form constructs `NoSuchEntity-Exception` with the specified detailed message. The third form constructs `NoSuchEntityException` that has the original thrown exception embedded within.

PARAMETERS:

message	The String object containing the exception message
ex	The original thrown Exception object

A.13.6 ObjectNotFoundException Class

The javax.ejb.ObjectNotFoundException class extends the javax.ejb.FinderException class. It defines the exception `ObjectNotFoundException`.

ObjectNotFoundException

```
public ObjectNotFoundException();
public ObjectNotFoundException(String message);
```

This exception is thrown by a find method to indicate that the specified enterprise bean object does not exist.

This exception should be used only by find methods that are declared to return a single enterprise bean object. It should not be thrown by find methods that return a collection of enterprise bean objects. These methods should return a null collection instead of throwing this error.

The first form of the constructor constructs `ObjectNotFoundException` with no detailed message. The second form constructs `ObjectNotFound-Exception` with the specified detailed message.

PARAMETERS:

message	The String object containing the exception message

A.13.7 RemoveException Class

The javax.ejb.RemoveException class, which extends the java.lang.Exception interface, defines the `RemoveException` exception.

RemoveException

```
public RemoveException();
public RemoveException(String message);
```

RemoveException is thrown when there is an attempt to remove an enterprise bean object and the bean or the container does not allow that enterprise bean object to be removed.

The first form of the constructor constructs RemoveException with no detailed message. The second form constructs RemoveException with the specified detailed message.

PARAMETERS:

message   The String object containing the exception message

Code Samples

THIS appendix contains the class implementations for those classes that serve a more peripheral function to the entity example.

B.1 CCI Interface Classes

The following is a brief description of the classes that implement the CCI interface. Tools normally generate these classes from the definition of the mainframe program external interface, such as, for example, from the COBOL Common Area format of a TP program.

The InteractionSpecImpl class implements the InteractionsSpec CCI interface. The InteractionSpecImpl class is used for specifying the name of the target TP program and the direction of argument passing (Code Example B.1).

Code Example B.1 InteractionSpecImpl Class

```
package com.aardvark.payroll.impl;

import javax.resource.cci.InteractionSpec;

public class InteractionSpecImpl implements InteractionSpec {
   private String functionName;
   private int interactionVerb;

   // String with the name of TP program
   public void setFunctionName(String functionName) {
      this.functionName = functionName;
   }
```

```
public String getFunctionName() {
    return this.functionName;
}


// Interaction verb indicates the direction
// of parameter passing. It is one of
// SYNC_SEND, SYNC_SEND_RECEIVE, and SYNC_RECEIVE.
public void setInteractionVerb(int verb) {
    this.interactionVerb = verb;
}
public int getInteractionVerb() {
    return this.interactionVerb;
}
}
```

The RecordImpl class implements the CCI Record interface. Its implementation, shown in Code Example B.2, is used as the superclass for application-specific record classes.

Code Example B.2 RecordImpl Class

```
package com.aardvark.payroll.impl;

import javax.resource.cci.Streamable;
import javax.resource.cci.Record;

import java.io.Serializable;
import java.io.IOException;
import java.io.InputStream;
import java.io.OutputStream;

public class RecordImpl implements Record, Serializable, Streamable
{
    String  name;
    String  desc;

    public RecordImpl() {}

    // Name of the record
    public void setRecordName(String name) {
        this.name = name;
    }
```

```java
    public String getRecordName() {
       return name;
    }

    // Short description string for this record
    public void setRecordShortDescription(String description) {
       this.desc = description;
    }
    public String getRecordShortDescription() {
       return desc;
    }

    // Check if this instance is equal to another record.
    public boolean equals(Object other) {
       // ...
    }

    // Read data from InputStream and initialize fields.
    public void read(InputStream istream) throws IOException {
       //....
    }

    // Write fields of a "streamable" object to OutputStream.
    public void write(OutputStream ostream) throws IOException {
       //...
    }

    public Object clone() throws CloneNotSupportedException {
       return this;
    }
}
```

The EmployeeRecord class defines the interface that a Java application uses to get and set the values of input arguments for communication with the TP programs (Code Example B.3).

Code Example B.3 EmployeeRecord Class

```java
package com.aardvark.payroll.impl;

import javax.resource.cci.Record;
```

```
public interface EmployeeRecord extends Record  {
    void setName(String name);
    void setId(int id);
    void setSalary(double salary);
    void setBenefitsDeduction(double deduction);

    String getName();
    int getId();
    double getSalary();
    double getBenefitsDeduction();
}
```

The EmployeeRecordImpl class implements the EmployeeRecord interface.
This class is responsible for the conversion between the Java representation of the
values of arguments and the representation understood by the mainframe program.
The data in the mainframe representation is passed to a mainframe resource adap-
tor through the InputStream and OutputStream interfaces (Code Example B.4).

Code Example B.4 EmployeeRecordImpl Class

```
package com.aardvark.payroll.impl;

import javax.resource.cci.Streamable;

import java.io.Serializable;
import java.io.IOException;
import java.io.InputStream;
import java.io.OutputStream;

public class EmployeeRecordImpl extends RecordImpl
        implements EmployeeRecord, Serializable, Streamable {

    private String name;
    private int id;
    private double deduction;
    private double salary;

    public EmployeeRecordImpl() {}

    public void setName(String name) {
        this.name = name;
    }
```

```java
   public void setId(int id) {
      this.id = id;
   }
   public void setSalary(double salary) {
      this.salary = salary;
   }
   public void setBenefitsDeduction(double deduction) {
      this.deduction = deduction;
   }

   public String getName() {
      return name;
   }
   public int getId() {
      return id;
   }
   public double getSalary() {
      return this.salary;
   }
   public double getBenefitsDeduction() {
      return this.deduction;
   }

   // Read data from a stream and set the values of fields.
   public void read(InputStream istream) throws IOException {
      super.read(istream);
      //....
   }

   // Write the values of fields to a stream.
   public void write(OutputStream ostream) throws IOException {
      super.write(ostream);
      //...
   }
}
```

B.2   Data Access Command Beans

This section contains the implementations of the data access command beans used by the benefits example in Chapter 7 (Code Examples B.5 through B.18). It also includes the DBQueryBean base class and the DBUpdateBean base class.

Code Example B.5 DBQueryBean Base Class

```
package com.premiumhealth.plan.db;

import java.sql.Connection;
import java.sql.PreparedStatement;
import java.sql.ResultSet;
import java.sql.SQLException;
import javax.sql.DataSource;

public class DBQueryBean {
    protected PreparedStatement pstmt;
    protected ResultSet resultSet = null;
    private Connection con;

    protected DBQueryBean(DataSource ds, String statement)
       throws SQLException
    {
       con = ds.getConnection();
       pstmt = con.prepareStatement(statement);
    }

    public void execute() throws SQLException {
       resultSet = pstmt.executeQuery();
    }

    public boolean next() throws SQLException {
       return resultSet.next();
    }

    public void release() {
       try {
          if (resultSet != null)
             resultSet.close();
          if (pstmt != null)
             pstmt.close();
```

```
            if (con != null)
                con.close();
        } catch (SQLException ex) {
        }
    }
}
```

Code Example B.6 DBUpdateBean Base Class

```java
package com.premiumhealth.plan.db;

import java.sql.PreparedStatement;
import java.sql.Connection;
import java.sql.SQLException;
import javax.sql.DataSource;

public class DBUpdateBean {
    protected PreparedStatement pstmt;
    private Connection con;

    public int execute() throws SQLException {
        int rowCount = pstmt.executeUpdate();
        pstmt.close();
        con.close();
        return rowCount;
    }

    protected DBUpdateBean(DataSource ds, String statement)
        throws SQLException
    {
        con = ds.getConnection();
        pstmt = con.prepareStatement(statement);
    }

    public void release() { }
}
```

Code Example B.7 DBDeleteDoctorByPlanId Command Bean

```java
package com.premiumhealth.plan.db;

import java.sql.SQLException;
```

```java
import javax.sql.DataSource;

public class DBDeleteDoctorByPlanId extends DBUpdateBean {
    static String statement =
        "DELETE FROM Doctors WHERE doc_plan_id = ?";

    public DBDeleteDoctorByPlanId(DataSource ds) throws SQLException
    {
        super(ds, statement);
    }

    public void setPlanId(String planId) throws SQLException {
        pstmt.setString(1, planId);
    }
}
```

Code Example B.8   DBDeletePlan Command Bean

```java
package com.premiumhealth.plan.db;

import java.sql.SQLException;
import javax.sql.DataSource;

public class DBDeletePlan extends DBUpdateBean {
    static String statement =
        "DELETE FROM Plans WHERE plan_id = ?";

    public DBDeletePlan(DataSource ds) throws SQLException {
        super(ds, statement);
    }

    public void setPlanId(String planId) throws SQLException {
        pstmt.setString(1, planId);
    }
}
```

Code Example B.9   DBDeletePremiumByPlanId Command Bean

```java
package com.premiumhealth.plan.db;

import java.sql.SQLException;
import javax.sql.DataSource;
```

```java
public class DBDeletePremiumByPlanId extends DBUpdateBean {
    static String statement =
        "DELETE FROM Premium WHERE prem_plan_id = ?";

    public DBDeletePremiumByPlanId(DataSource ds)
            throws SQLException
    {
        super(ds, statement);
    }

    public void setPlanId(String planId) throws SQLException {
        pstmt.setString(1, planId);
    }
}
```

Code Example B.10 DBInsertPlan Command Bean

```java
package com.premiumhealth.plan.db;

import java.sql.SQLException;
import javax.sql.DataSource;

public class DBInsertPlan extends DBUpdateBean {
    static String statement =
        "INSERT INTO Plans VALUES (?, ?, ?)";

    public DBInsertPlan(DataSource ds) throws SQLException {
        super(ds, statement);
    }

    public void setPlanId(String planId) throws SQLException {
        pstmt.setString(1, planId);
    }
    public void setPlanDescr(String descr) throws SQLException {
        pstmt.setString(2, descr);
    }
    public void setPlanType(int planType) throws SQLException {
        pstmt.setInt(3, planType);
    }
}
```

Code Example B.11 DBQueryAllDoctors Command Bean

```java
package com.premiumhealth.plan.db;

import java.sql.SQLException;
import javax.sql.DataSource;

public class DBQueryAllDoctors extends DBQueryBean {
    static String statement =
        "SELECT doc_first_name, doc_last_name, " +
        " doc_specialty, doc_hospital, doc_practice_since " +
        "FROM Doctors WHERE doc_plan_id = ?";

    public DBQueryAllDoctors(DataSource ds) throws SQLException {
        super(ds, statement);
    }

    public void setPlanId(String planId) throws SQLException {
        pstmt.setString(1, planId);
    }

    public String getFirstName() throws SQLException {
        return resultSet.getString(1);
    }
    public String getLastName() throws SQLException {
        return resultSet.getString(2);
    }
    public String getSpecialty() throws SQLException {
        return resultSet.getString(3);
    }
    public String getHospital() throws SQLException {
        return resultSet.getString(4);
    }
    public int getPracticeSince() throws SQLException {
        return resultSet.getInt(5);
    }
}
```

Code Example B.12 DBQueryDoctorByName Command Bean

```java
package com.premiumhealth.plan.db;

import java.sql.SQLException;
import javax.sql.DataSource;

public class DBQueryDoctorByName extends DBQueryBean {
    static String statement =
        "SELECT doc_first_name, doc_last_name, " +
        "  doc_specialty, doc_hospital, doc_practice_since " +
        "FROM Doctors " +
        "WHERE doc_plan_id = ? " +
        "  AND doc_first_name LIKE ? " +
        "  AND doc_last_name LIKE ?";

    public DBQueryDoctorByName(DataSource ds) throws SQLException {
        super(ds, statement);
    }

    public void setPlanId(String planId) throws SQLException {
        pstmt.setString(1, planId);
    }
    public void setFirstName(String firstName) throws SQLException {
        pstmt.setString(2, firstName);
    }
    public void setLastName(String lastName) throws SQLException {
        pstmt.setString(3, lastName);
    }

    public String getFirstName() throws SQLException {
        return resultSet.getString(1);
    }
    public String getLastName() throws SQLException {
        return resultSet.getString(2);
    }
    public String getSpecialty() throws SQLException {
        return resultSet.getString(3);
    }
    public String getHospital() throws SQLException {
        return resultSet.getString(4);
    }
```

```
      public int getPracticeSince() throws SQLException {
         return resultSet.getInt(5);
      }
   }
```

Code Example B.13   DBQueryDoctorBySpecialty Command Bean

```
package com.premiumhealth.plan.db;

import java.sql.SQLException;
import javax.sql.DataSource;

public class DBQueryDoctorBySpecialty extends DBQueryBean {
   static String statement =
      "SELECT doc_first_name, doc_last_name, " +
      "  doc_specialty, doc_hospital, doc_practice_since " +
      "FROM Doctors " +
      "WHERE doc_plan_id = ? AND doc_specialty = ?";

   public DBQueryDoctorBySpecialty(DataSource ds)
         throws SQLException
   {
      super(ds, statement);
   }

   public void setPlanId(String planId) throws SQLException {
      pstmt.setString(1, planId);
   }
   public void setSpecialty(String specialty) throws SQLException {
      pstmt.setString(2, specialty);
   }

   public String getFirstName() throws SQLException {
      return resultSet.getString(1);
   }
   public String getLastName() throws SQLException {
      return resultSet.getString(2);
   }
   public String getSpecialty() throws SQLException {
      return resultSet.getString(3);
   }
```

```java
    public String getHospital() throws SQLException {
       return resultSet.getString(4);
    }
    public int getPracticeSince() throws SQLException {
       return resultSet.getInt(5);
    }
}
```

Code Example B.14 DBQueryPlan Command Bean

```java
package com.premiumhealth.plan.db;

import java.sql.SQLException;
import javax.sql.DataSource;

public class DBQueryPlan extends DBQueryBean {
    static String statement =
       "SELECT plan_id, plan_descr, plan_type " +
       "FROM Plans WHERE plan_id = ?";

    public DBQueryPlan(DataSource ds) throws SQLException {
       super(ds, statement);
    }
    public void setPlanId(String planId) throws SQLException {
       pstmt.setString(1, planId);
    }

    public String getPlanId() throws SQLException {
       return resultSet.getString(1);
    }
    public String getPlanDescr() throws SQLException {
       return resultSet.getString(2);
    }
    public int getPlanType() throws SQLException {
       return resultSet.getInt(3);
    }
}
```

Code Example B.15   DBQueryPlanByDoctor Command Bean

```
package com.premiumhealth.plan.db;

import java.sql.SQLException;
import javax.sql.DataSource;

public class DBQueryPlanByDoctor extends DBQueryBean {
   static String statement =
      "SELECT plan_id, plan_descr, plan_type " +
      "FROM Plans " +
      "WHERE EXISTS " +
         "( SELECT * FROM Doctors " +
         "  WHERE doc_plan_id = Plans.plan_id " +
         "     AND doc_first_name LIKE ? " +
         "     AND doc_last_name LIKE ? )";

   public DBQueryPlanByDoctor(DataSource ds) throws SQLException {
      super(ds, statement);
   }

   public void setFirstName(String firstName) throws SQLException {
      pstmt.setString(1, firstName);
   }
   public void setLastName(String lastName) throws SQLException {
      pstmt.setString(2, lastName);
   }

   public String getPlanId() throws SQLException {
      return resultSet.getString(1);
   }
   public String getPlanDescr() throws SQLException {
      return resultSet.getString(2);
   }
   public int getPlanType() throws SQLException {
      return resultSet.getInt(3);
   }
}
```

Code Example B.16 DBQueryPlanByType Command Bean

```java
package com.premiumhealth.plan.db;

import java.sql.SQLException;
import javax.sql.DataSource;

public class DBQueryPlanByType extends DBQueryBean {
    static String statement =
        "SELECT plan_id, plan_descr, plan_type " +
        "FROM Plans " +
        "WHERE plan_type = ?";

    public DBQueryPlanByType(DataSource ds) throws SQLException {
        super(ds, statement);
    }

    public void setPlanType(int planType) throws SQLException {
        pstmt.setInt(1, planType);
    }

    public String getPlanId() throws SQLException {
        return resultSet.getString(1);
    }
    public String getPlanDescr() throws SQLException {
        return resultSet.getString(2);
    }
    public int getPlanType() throws SQLException {
        return resultSet.getInt(3);
    }
}
```

Code Example B.17 DBQueryPremium Command Bean

```java
package com.premiumhealth.plan.db;

import java.sql.SQLException;
import javax.sql.DataSource;
```

```java
public class DBQueryPremium extends DBQueryBean {
    static String statement =
        "SELECT prem_amount FROM Premium " +
        "WHERE prem_plan_id = ? AND prem_age = ? " +
        "AND prem_smoker_status = ? AND prem_coverage = ?";

    public DBQueryPremium(DataSource ds) throws SQLException {
        super(ds, statement);
    }

    public void setPlanId(String planId) throws SQLException {
        pstmt.setString(1, planId);
    }
    public void setAge(int age) throws SQLException {
        pstmt.setInt(2, age);
    }
    public void setSmokerStatus(String smokerStatus)
            throws SQLException
    {
        pstmt.setString(3, smokerStatus);
    }
    public void setCoverage(int coverage) throws SQLException {
        pstmt.setInt(4, coverage);
    }

    public double getAmount() throws SQLException {
        return resultSet.getDouble(1);
    }
}
```

Code Example B.18   DBUpdatePlan Command Bean

```java
package com.premiumhealth.plan.db;

import java.sql.SQLException;
import javax.sql.DataSource;

public class DBUpdatePlan extends DBUpdateBean {
    static String statement =
        "UPDATE Plans " +
        "SET plan_descr = ?, plan_type = ?" +
        "WHERE plan_id = ?";
```

```java
   public DBUpdatePlan(DataSource ds) throws SQLException {
      super(ds, statement);
   }

   public void setPlanDescr(String planName) throws SQLException {
      pstmt.setString(1, planName);
   }
   public void setPlanType(int planType) throws SQLException {
      pstmt.setInt(2, planType);
   }
   public void setPlanId(String planId) throws SQLException {
      pstmt.setString(3, planId);
   }
}
```

Glossary

ACID The acronym for the four properties guaranteed by transactions: atomicity, consistency, isolation, and durability.

Activation The process of associating an enterprise bean object with an instance of an enterprise bean class. For a stateful session bean, activation results in restoring a session object's state from secondary memory.

Actor A user or another program that interacts with an enterprise bean application.

Application assembler An individual who combines enterprise beans, and possible other application components, into larger, deployable application units.

Application client A first-tier client component that executes in its own JVM. Application clients have access to some J2EE platform APIs (JNDI, JDBC, RMI-IIOP, JMS).

Authentication A step that occurs as part of the security process, during which a user proves her identity to the enterprise network security manager.

Authorization A step that occurs as part of the security process, during which the target application or database server verifies whether the user has the authority to access the requested application or data.

Bean developer The programmer who writes the enterprise bean code implementing the business logic and produces enterprise beans.

Bean-managed persistence (BMP) An approach to managing entity object state persistence during which the entity bean itself manages the access to the underlying state in a resource manager.

Bean-managed transaction demarcation   An approach to managing transactions during which the bean developer manages transaction boundaries programmatically from within the application code.

Business process   A business object that typically encapsulates an interaction of a user with business entities.

Business entity   A business object representing some information maintained by an enterprise.

Client-view API   The enterprise bean home interface and enterprise bean remote interface.

Collaborative business process   A business process with multiple actors.

Command bean   A JavaBean used by an application to encapsulate a call to another application or a database call. Enterprise applications frequently use this design pattern.

Commit   The point in a transaction when all updates to any resources involved in the transaction are made permanent.

Common Gateway Interface (CGI)   One of the interfaces for developing dynamic HTML pages and Web applications.

Common Object Request Broker Architecture (CORBA)   A language-independent, distributed object model specified by the Object Management Group (OMG).

Connection factory   An object that produces connections.

Connector   A standard extension mechanism for containers to provide connectivity to enterprise information systems. A connector is specific to an enterprise information system and consists of a resource adapter and application development tools for enterprise information systems.

Connector architecture   An architecture for the integration of J2EE products with enterprise information systems. There are two parts to this architecture: a resource adapter provided by an enterprise information system vendor and the J2EE product that allows this resource adapter to plug in. This architecture defines a set of contracts that a resource adapter has to support to plug in to a J2EE product—for example, transactions, security, and resource management.

Container artifacts   Classes generated by the EJB container vendor-provided deployment tools that bind the enterprise beans with the container at runtime. The container artifacts allow the container to interpose on the client calls to the enterprise beans, and to inject its services into the application.

Container-managed persistence (CMP)   An approach to managing entity object state persistence during which the container manages the transfer of data between the entity bean instance variables and the underlying resource manager.

Container-managed transaction demarcation   An approach to managing transactions during which the EJB container defines the transaction boundaries by using the transaction attributes provided in the deployment descriptor.

Conversational business process   A business process with a single actor. A conversational business process means that a single actor engages in a conversation with the application. An example of a conversational business process is an application that displays a sequence of forms to the user and validates the data input by the user.

Conversational state   State retained in a session object during the conversation between the client of the application and the application itself. The state consists of the session bean instance fields plus the transitive closure of the objects that are reachable from the bean's fields.

create method   A method defined in the home interface and invoked by a client to create an enterprise bean.

Declarative transaction demarcation   Container-managed transaction demarcation. Also referred to as *declarative transactions*.

Dependent object   A business entity that is not directly exposed to a multitude of applications. External clients can access dependent objects only through a specific entity bean that uses the dependent object.

Deployer   An expert in the target operational environment who installs enterprise beans in an EJB container. The deployer may also customize the enterprise beans for the target operational environment.

Deployment descriptor   An XML document that contains the declarative information about the enterprise bean. The deployment descriptor directs a deployment tool to deploy enterprise beans with specific container options and describes configuration requirements that the deployer must resolve.

ear file   An enterprise application archive file that contains a J2EE application.

EJB container   A programming environment for the development, deployment, and runtime management of enterprise beans.

EJB container provider   The vendor who provides the EJB container.

ejb-jar file   A Java ARchive (JAR) file that contains one or more enterprise beans with their deployment descriptor.

EJB server   Software that provides services to an EJB container. For example, an EJB container typically relies on a transaction manager that is part of the EJB server to perform the two-phase commit across all participating resource managers. The J2EE architecture assumes that an EJB container is hosted by an EJB server from the same vendor, so it does not specify the contract between these two entities. An EJB server may host one or more EJB containers.

EJB server provider   A vendor that supplies an EJB server.

Enterprise bean   A component that is part of a distributed enterprise application and that implements a business process or business entity. There are two types of enterprise beans: session beans and entity beans.

Enterprise bean class   A Java class that implements the business methods and the enterprise bean object life cycle methods.

Enterprise bean deployment   The process of installing an enterprise bean in an EJB container.

Enterprise bean home objects   Distributed objects that implement the enterprise bean home interface. The EJB container implements these objects.

Enterprise bean objects   Distributed objects that implement the enterprise bean's remote interface. The EJB container implements these objects.

Entity bean   A type of enterprise bean that can be shared by multiple clients and the state of which is maintained in a resource manager. An entity bean can implement a business entity or a business process.

Entity bean home objects   Distributed objects that implement an entity bean's home interface

Entity object   Distributed objects that implement an entity bean's remote interface. These objects are object-oriented representations of real-life business entities and business processes.

Find method   A method defined in the home interface and invoked by a client to locate an entity bean.

Handle   An object that identifies an enterprise bean. A client may serialize the handle and then later deserialize it to obtain a reference to the enterprise bean.

Home handle   An object that can be used to obtain a reference to the home interface. A home interface can be serialized and written to stable storage and deserialized to obtain the reference.

Home interface   One of two interfaces for an enterprise bean. The home interface defines zero or more methods for creating and removing an enterprise bean. For session beans the home interface defines `create` and `remove` methods, whereas for entity beans the home interface defines `create`, find, and `remove` methods.

HTTP   Hypertext Transfer Protocol. The Internet protocol used to fetch hypertext objects from remote hosts. HTTP messages consist of requests from client to server and responses from server to client.

Hypertext Markup Language (HTML)   A markup language for hypertext documents on the Internet. HTML enables the embedding of images, sounds, video streams, form fields, references to other objects with URLS, and basic text formatting.

ISV   Independent software vendor.

Java™ 2 Platform, Enterprise Edition (J2EE)   An environment for developing and deploying enterprise applications. The J2EE platform consists of a set of services, APIs, and protocols that provide functionality for developing multitiered, Web-based applications.

Java™ 2 Platform, Standard Edition (J2SE)   The core Java technology platform.

JavaServer Pages™ (JSP)   An extensible Web technology that uses template data, custom elements, scripting languages, and server-side Java objects to return dynamic content to a client. Typically, the template data is an HTML or XML element, and in many cases the client is a Web browser.

Method permission   A permission to invoke a specified group of methods of an enterprise bean's home and remote interfaces.

Passivation   The process of disassociating an enterprise bean object from an instance of the enterprise bean class. For a stateful session bean, passivation typically results in moving a session object's state to secondary memory.

Persistence   The protocol for making an object's state durable.

Primary key   An object that uniquely identifies an entity bean within a home.

Remote interface One of two interfaces for an enterprise bean. The enterprise bean remote interface defines the business methods that can be called by a client.

Resource manager A resource manager provides access to a set of shared resources. A resource manager participates in a transaction. An example of a resource manager is a relational database management system (RDBMS).

Resource manager connection An object that represents a session with a resource manager.

Resource manager connection factory An object used for creating a resource manager connection.

Remote method invocation (RMI) A technology that allows an object running in one JVM to invoke methods on an object running in a different JVM.

RMI-IIOP A version of RMI implemented to use the CORBA IIOP protocol. RMI-IIOP provides interoperability with CORBA objects implemented in any language, if all the remote interfaces are originally defined as RMI interfaces.

Rollback The point in a transaction when all updates to any resources involved in the transaction are reversed.

Servlet A Java program that extends the functionality of a Web server. Servlets generate dynamic content and interact with Web clients using a request-response paradigm.

Session bean A type of enterprise bean that implements a conversational business process. The state of a session bean is maintained by the container and is not externalized to a resource manager.

Session bean home objects Distributed objects that implement a session bean's home interface.

Session bean objects Distributed objects that implement a session bean's remote interface.

SSL Secure Socket Layer. A security protocol that provides privacy over the Internet. The protocol allows client/server applications to communicate in a tamper-free way that cannot be eavesdropped. Servers are always authenticated and clients are optionally authenticated.

Stateful session bean A type of a session bean class that retains state on behalf of its client across multiple method invocations by the client.

Stateless session bean   A type of a session bean class that does not retain any client-specific state between client-invoked methods. All instances of a stateless session bean are identical.

System administrator   The system administrator configures and administers the enterprise computing and networking infrastructure, which includes the EJB server and container. The system administrator is also responsible for most security-related administration responsibilities.

Transaction   An atomic unit of work that modifies data. A transaction encloses one or more program statements, all of which either complete or roll back. Transactions enable multiple users to access the same data concurrently.

Transaction attribute   A value specified in an enterprise bean's deployment descriptor that is used by the EJB container to control the transaction scope when the enterprise bean's methods are invoked. A transaction attribute can have the following values: Required, RequiresNew, Supports, NotSupported, Mandatory, and Never.

Transaction manager   Provides the services and management functions required to support transaction demarcation, transactional resource management, synchronization, and transaction context propagation.

Transaction service   The same as the transaction manager.

war file   A Web archive file containing the class files for servlets and JSPs.

Web application   An application built for the Internet with Java technologies, such as JSP and servlets, as well as with non-Java technologies, such as CGI and Perl.

Web component   A component, such as a servlet or JSP, that provides services in response to HTTP requests.

Web container   A programming environment for the development, deployment, and runtime management of servlets and JSP.

XML   eXtensible Markup Language. A markup language that allows you to define the tags, or markup, needed to identify data and text in XML documents. The deployment descriptors are expressed in XML.

Index

The Java™ Series

The Java™ Programming Language
Third Edition

Ken Arnold • James Gosling • David Holmes

ISBN 0-201-70433-1

The Real-Time Specification for Java™

ISBN 0-201-70323-8

The Java™ Tutorial, Third Edition
A Short Course on the Basics

Mary Campione • Kathy Walrath • Alison Huml

ISBN 0-201-70393-9

The Java™ Tutorial Continued
The Rest of the JDK™

ISBN 0-201-48558-3

The Java™ Developers ALMANAC 2000

Patrick Chan

ISBN 0-201-43299-4

ISBN 0-201-43297-8

The Java™ Class Libraries Second Edition, Volume 1
java.io java.lang java.math
java.net java.text java.util

Patrick Chan • Rosanna Lee • Douglas Kramer

ISBN 0-201-31002-3

The Java™ Class Libraries Second Edition, Volume 2
java.applet java.awt java.beans

Patrick Chan • Rosanna Lee

ISBN 0-201-31003-1

The Java™ Class Libraries Second Edition, Volume 1
Supplement for the Java™ 2 Platform Standard Edition, v1.2

Patrick Chan • Rosanna Lee • Douglas Kramer

ISBN 0-201-48552-4

Java Card™ Technology for Smart Cards
Architecture and Programmer's Guide

Zhiqun Chen

ISBN 0-201-70329-7

Inside Java™ 2 Platform Security
Architecture, API Design, and Implementation

Li Gong

ISBN 0-201-31000-7

The Java™ Language Specification, Second Edition

James Gosling • Bill Joy • Guy Steele • Gilad Bracha

ISBN 0-201-31008-2

The Java™ Application Programming Interface, Volume 1
Core Packages

James Gosling • Frank Yellin • The Java Team

ISBN 0-201-63453-8

The Java™ Application Programming Interface, Volume 2
Window Toolkit and Applets

James Gosling • Frank Yellin • The Java Team

ISBN 0-201-63459-7

The Java™ FAQ

Jonni Kanerva

ISBN 0-201-63456-2

Designing Enterprise Applications with the Java™ 2 Platform, Enterprise Edition

Nicholas Kassem • Enterprise Team

ISBN 0-201-70277-0

Concurrent Programming in Java™ Second Edition
Design Principles and Patterns

Doug Lea

ISBN 0-201-31009-0

JNDI API Tutorial and Reference
Building Directory-Enabled Java™ Applications

Rosanna Lee • Scott Seligman

ISBN 0-201-70502-8

The Java™ Native Interface
Programmer's Guide and Specification

Sheng Liang

ISBN 0-201-32577-2

The Java™ Virtual Machine Specification Second Edition

Tim Lindholm • Frank Yellin

ISBN 0-201-43294-3

Applying Enterprise JavaBeans™
Component-Based Development for the J2EE Platform

Vlada Matena • Beth Stearns

ISBN 0-201-702-673

Java™ 2 Platform, Enterprise Edition
Platform and Component Specifications

ISBN 0-201-70456-0

The Java 3D™ API Specification, Second Edition

Henry Sowizral • Kevin Rushforth • Michael Deering

ISBN 0-201-71041-2

The JFC Swing Tutorial
A Guide to Constructing GUIs

Kathy Walrath • Mary Campione

ISBN 0-201-43321-4

JDBC™ API Tutorial and Reference, Second Edition
Universal Data Access for the Java™ 2 Platform

White • Fisher • Cattell • Hamilton • Hapner

ISBN 0-201-43328-1

Java™ Platform Performance
Strategies and Tactics

Steve Wilson • Jeff Kesselman

ISBN 0-201-70969-4

The Jini™ Specifications Second Edition
Edited by Ken Arnold

Waldo • The Jini Technology Team

ISBN 0-201-72617-3

Please see our web site (http://www.awl.com/cseng/javaseries)
for more information on these titles.